# Additional Praise for *Xero: A Comprehensive Guide for Accountants and Bookkeepers, U.S. Edition*

"Yes, Amanda is an expert in Xero, but she is a *generous* expert. If she couldn't do backflips inside the software, she could not as generously share her knowledge. She has offered so much support to countless new bookkeepers it is no wonder that so many follow in her footsteps and build a firm on Xero. The bookkeeping world has been begging for a resource like this and it couldn't have been written by anyone else."

—*Kate Josephine Johnson, Owner of Heritage Business Services and Author of* The Bookkeeping Side Hustle Guidebook

"As I was starting out with Xero, Amanda was super supportive of my journey, always available to answer questions, and always knowledgeable of Xero features. She's still one of my main go-to resources when it comes to all things Xero."

—*Trinity Scott, Owner and Chief Technologist of T3 Bookkeeping*

T0337995

# XERO

# A Comprehensive Guide for Accountants and Bookkeepers

## U.S. Edition

Amanda Aguillard

**WILEY**

# Contents

# Contents

# Foreword

Amanda Aguillard was one of the first partners to reach out when I arrived in the United States nearly four years ago from New Zealand, where cloud adoption is high and Xero is a household name. She was an early adopter of Xero and has been, and continues to be, a huge advocate for our brand among the advisor and small business community. We instantly connected.

Our mission at Xero is simple—to make life easier for small businesses. And how we do that is through our powerful cloud-based accounting software platform that connects small businesses and their advisors with information they need to monitor financial performance. There's a massive opportunity for Xero to grow, together with our partners, by helping small businesses. Our goal isn't to be the biggest in the United States. Instead, we aspire to be the most trusted and insightful.

It takes more than just great technology to serve small businesses. It's a combination of technology excellence and the human element, and that's where Amanda shines. She knows Xero products inside and out and has trained the full range of Xero users, from brand-new sole proprietors all the way to Big Four international firms. Amanda is one of our most vocal champions, but also one of our biggest critics; she isn't afraid to tell us what we need to do better. She has built a successful practice and is at the vanguard of a changing profession, challenging us to deliver excellence to the small businesses we serve.

We're honored and thrilled that Amanda is writing about her success with Xero in the United States. As you read this book, I have no doubt you'll channel Amanda's passion and take away many best practices on how to utilize the Xero platform with your firm and your clients. While it is still the early days for widespread cloud adoption in the accounting industry, the global pandemic has helped to accelerate the shift from physical to virtual. We're at the end of the beginning in the United States and will be debuting new product features throughout 2021. We hope that Amanda's book will inspire you to join us on that journey!

Ben Richmond
Country Manager, United States, for Xero

# Preface

In 2012, I found myself divorced with two small children. As those things go, it was half surprise and half expected. I knew I had a short runway to recrafting some kind of career after not working since the birth of my son seven years earlier. I had experience in public accounting, having done time at Deloitte & Touche, and in my last job before my son was born, had earned the role of controller of a large company in New Orleans at age 26. Given the demands of both of those positions, neither seemed reasonable for a newly single mom to kids aged seven and eight.

Over the next few years, I cobbled together some freelance work, inadvertently building an accounting firm. I had little faith in the longevity of this path, but I was fiercely committed to using cloud-based software for as long as it lasted. Turns out, Aguillard Accounting, LLC is still alive and kicking nine years later.

As I taught myself the ins and outs of browser-based accounting software and addons, I realized that there was a whole population of accountants that did not yet understand the power and freedom of the cloud. Half seriously (and half as a way to write off travel with my best friend,) I co-founded Elefant, LLC, a training company for advisors. Our mission is to help accountants and bookkeepers leverage technology to build their dream practices. I hold this close to my heart because it was technology, and specifically Xero, that allowed me to build an accounting firm from my guest bedroom as a single mom to two children.

Back in 2012, I had no idea what a significant part Xero would play in my life. At that time, Xero was hardly known in the United States, but I was immediately drawn to it. The interface was clean, the logic simple, and the framework cutting edge—build a really good general ledger and allow small businesses and their advisors to craft the perfect ecosystem through application programming interfaces (APIs).

As I have become a writer, trainer, and sometimes counselor on all things accounting tech, I have been pushed to learn more about other, more popular, cloud-based general ledger systems. Inevitably, I get frustrated by functionality stuck anywhere it may fit and often catch myself muttering, "I don't know how people live like this." Time and time again, I come back to the safe space of Xero and let out a sigh, knowing this is how beautiful accounting should be.

# Using This Book

This book covers features available in the Established subscription plan in Xero. If you cannot access features or modules, you may be in a lower subscription plan. Unless otherwise noted, any instructions on accessing functions will begin from the organization's Dashboard.

This is a technical guide to the use of accounting software. Because of the nature of the book, I do my best to use consistent terminology throughout. The word *account* refers to a general ledger line or category, not a bank account. *Bank account* is used to refer to checking, savings, or credit card accounts held at banks or other financial institutions. *Invoice* is used to refer to a document for collecting revenue from customers, and *bill* is used for noting a payment due to vendors.

# Accessing Digital Resources

This book also includes digital resources, which are available by visiting www.wwww.www

# Disclaimers

This book is an effort to provide a comprehensive instructional and reference guide for the U.S. version of Xero. Since Xero is a true cloud-based software application, it is regularly updated. As such, some updates may have taken place since the writing of this book. This book makes an effort to explore the features in Xero in detail, but again, recent improvements may not be reflected.

This book is not meant to teach bookkeeping or accounting theory and assumes a basic level of accounting knowledge. Many features discussed herein are available only at the Advisor level of user access or as a certified Xero Partner.

# Acknowledgments

Although I have created lots of accounting content in the last several years, this book has been one of the toughest projects I have ever taken on. It would not have been possible without the support, guidance, and positive energy of so many people. I am humbled and grateful to many beautiful souls for helping manifest one of my greatest dreams, to become a published author, including:

My two children, Avery and Jack, for their patience during this writing and without whom I never would have stretched and found my wings, and their father, for his graceful support in co-parenting, during the writing of this book and also the past 10 years.

My parents, who are unfailingly supportive of everything I do and who have taught me to work hard, ignore others' opinions, and do the right thing.

Monica Fontenot, my partner in Elefant and best friend of more than 25 years.

Katie L'Heureux, who patiently and tirelessly manages my accounting firm, Aguillard Accounting, and without whose support I would have had to pick either this project or the firm.

David Leary and the Accounting Salon, a community of the brightest and most generous spirits in cloud accounting.

My fellow National Xero Ambassadors, Liz Mason, Tate Henshaw, Allison Hawkins, and especially Jay Kimelman, who has never hesitated to jump on a call with me when I needed a technical guru.

Rod Drury, founder of Xero, change agent of cloud accounting, and dear friend. I will never forget meeting him at the first Xerocon Americas in San Francisco in 2013, when he greeted every attendee at the door in jeans, shook their hand, and said, "Hi. I'm Rod." After many years of stale accounting conventions, I knew I had found my people.

The whole Xero team for being incredibly supportive, especially Ben Richmond for contributing the Foreword to this book, Anthony Staltari for answering every overly specific product question I had, Sarah Bleeker for being unfailingly patient and positive, the Partner Consultant team for being my sounding board, and all of the account managers who work tirelessly as evangelists of the best cloud accounting platform in the world.

My emotional support network in New Orleans, the D List.

## Acknowledgments

Jeff Phillips, who has been a strategic advisor and trusted confidante since we first met.

Andrew Lilly, my attorney, who always listens patiently to my wild ideas.

Rob Couhig, who was my first client and trusted me to work on many of his cases. Without Rob, there would be no Aguillard Accounting, Elefant, or *Xero* book.

Ellen Cook, who as the head of the accounting department at my college, nominated me for a tax competition that changed the trajectory of my whole career.

# About the Author

**A**manda Aguillard decided when she was 16 to become a CPA, and never looked back. She started Aguillard Accounting, LLC in 2012, committed to running a cloud-based practice from anywhere in the world.

She was named one of the Top 50 Women in Accounting in 2018 and 2019 and has been a Hubdoc Top 50 Cloud Accountant in the past. She was the Xero Evangelist of the Year in 2016 and used her experience as an instructor of the Xero Certification course to co-found Elefant, a continuing education company for accountants and bookkeepers. She is also the founder of Accounting Salon, a think tank of cloud accounting experts, and its virtual offshoot, SALONv.

While she holds a Masters of Taxation degree from the University of Denver, her passion is to help advisors leverage technology to build their dream practices. She is a Certified Instructional Systems Designer and regularly speaks at state CPA societies and industry technology conferences like Accountex, AICPA Engage, Clio Cloud Conference, and Xerocon.

She spends any spare time cooking for her two kids and reading historical fiction. She is slightly obsessed with Penzeys Spices and backcountry hiking.

# Introduction to Xero

*The difference between Xero and other accounting solutions is that its functionality and language is designed specifically for business owners and operators. The accounting jargon has been banished and replaced with everyday language, such as "money in" and "money out." But the system has by no means been dumbed down. Xero has the capacity to grow with you from your spare room to the boardroom.*

*—Source: Wayne Richard, Partner and COO of Bean Ninjas.*

Unlike other accounting products, Xero was built as a cloud platform from day one. Founded in 2006 in New Zealand, the company started off by offering cloud-based accounting software, but has evolved to provide a full spectrum of connected tools and services that can help small businesses succeed. As a company, Xero's purpose is to make life better for people in small business, their advisors, and communities around the world. Xero helps small businesses work with their closest ally, their accountant or bookkeeper, whether doing taxes, understanding their finances, or making plans to grow. The platform brings all of the necessary data and information together in one place so small businesses and advisors can collaborate together and succeed.

A truly global company, Xero has more than two million subscribers worldwide as of March 31, 2020.[1]

While Xero's home markets of Australia and New Zealand see small business adoption of the cloud in excess of 50%, other regions, including the United States, show adoption of less than 20%.[2] That means there is tremendous opportunity for U.S.-based accountants and bookkeeping professionals to advise clients on cloud technology.

## Working in the Cloud

If you have only previously used desktop accounting software, you are in for a treat! Xero, like other cloud-based applications, runs in an internet browser. This means that both the software and the data live on Xero's servers. No software is installed on your hard drive.

There are many advantages to using cloud-based software, including:

- **Physical security of data.** My companies are based in New Orleans, which, in 2005, faced one of history's biggest natural disasters with Hurricane Katrina. Most New Orleanians left their offices on Friday afternoon, without any indication that a hurricane would hit the city. (At that point, the hurricane was forecast to go to Florida.) The data that was lost on onsite servers to flood, heat, and humidity was immeasurable. By storing our data in redundant remote servers, it is better protected.
- **Automatic software updates.** In my years in public accounting, I can recall many hours of waiting for software updates to be installed on the server, usually at the most inopportune times, like the middle of busy season. With cloud-based software, updates occur in the background and generally without downtime. Because software is upgraded at the application level, developers can constantly make the product better. Each year, Xero releases dozens, if not hundreds of product improvements. Almost universally, these updates are included in the monthly subscription of cloud applications at no additional cost.
- **Reduced capital costs.** Because servers are not needed on premises to hold software, and large hard drives are not required to store data, businesses can be run with minimal hardware. Cloud software typically does not require long-term licenses either, so the commitment is only month to month.
- **Simultaneous user access.** Multiple users can be in the file at the same time and with Xero, an unlimited number of users are included with every subscription.
- **Flexibility in hiring.** One of the biggest struggles for accounting and bookkeeping practices is finding qualified talent. When the firm's software is accessible anywhere, the firm can source employees from a much larger talent pool, and in some cases, take advantage of wage arbitrage.
- **Easier access with better controls.** True browser-based software can be accessed on any hardware with proper login credentials. Because the data is gated by passwords, rather than being downloaded to a hard drive, the data remains secure on any device, yet user access can be denied immediately by firm administrators if needed.
- **Real-time, single-ledger data.** In my time in public accounting, I often communicated year-end adjustments to clients that never made it into the file. Nearly every year, I would have to start with fixing prior year balances. With cloud-based software, the accountant or bookkeeper can make the adjustments on their own and not depend on the client.
- **Availability of mobile apps.** Many small business owners leverage time out of the office to work on their company bookkeeping. Desktop applications do not offer mobile versions. Having the ability to handle simple tasks on a smartphone or tablet gives owners flexibility.
- **Collaboration.** When all users are looking at one common ledger, discussions can occur more easily. Advisors can communicate with other people on the client's support team, like lenders and investors, and share information.

■ **Ability to customize an ecosystem.** Using a cloud-based general-ledger package means the ability to craft an entire ecosystem of operational software around it. Pick the best solution for any piece of business operations and connect with integrations. If needs change, switch out only one piece of software while keeping the core general ledger.

■ **Access to machine learning.** Aggregation of data creates opportunities for software to aid in automating simple tasks, like bank transaction coding, based not only on the learnings from that client's file but also from the billions of transactions processed in apps.

## Xero's Security Protocol

Xero takes security very seriously. It is certified as compliant with ISO/IEC 27001:2013 by EY CertifyPoint and has produced a Service Organization Control (SOC 2) report. Security reports are available at `https://www.xero.com/us/about/security`.

Xero is committed to protecting sensitive data with multiple layers, including:[3]

■ **User access.** Because Xero offers unlimited users for one subscription price, there is no incentive to share login details. Each user should be granted access through their own Xero account. This means that each user's activity will be tracked in the backend of the system. It also means that user permissions can be tailored to the user needs, without giving too much or too little access.

■ **Two-step authentication.** Xero strongly recommends the use of its two-step authentication for login. This allows users to require a second unique code generated by a smartphone application in order to gain access.

■ **Data encryption.** All data transmitted between Xero and the user is encrypted using TLS (Transport Layer Security). Data is also encrypted in storage centers.

■ **Secure data centers.** Xero holds client data in enterprise-grade hosting facilities with constant monitoring and surveillance, onsite security staff, and regular security audits. Data is held in geographically separate, redundant environments.

## Choosing the Right Subscription

There are two kinds of Xero subscriptions.

**Partner edition** subscriptions are available through verified Xero Partners (accountants, bookkeepers, and advisors) and must be paid under the partner billing account.

■ **Ledger** ($3 per month): This is the perfect subscription for annual bookkeeping or write-up work for tax return preparation. It does not include bank feeds or invoicing. Client users can view reports, but cannot reconcile transactions.

- **Cashbook** ($7 per month): This subscription level is great for managed bookkeeping. It allows bank feeds to be connected, but does not include invoicing. Clients are able to code bank transactions, as well as view data and reports.

**Business edition** subscriptions are available to partners, as well as direct to small business users. They have more functionality than the Partner edition accounts.

- **Early** ($11 per month): This subscription has a fully functional general ledger, with usage limits: 20 invoices, 5 bills, and unlimited bank transactions. It does not include Find & Recode or Cash Coding. This is built for do-it-yourself business owners and is extremely attractive at the price point.
- **Growing** ($32 per month): Known in other countries as Standard, this subscription level is the middle option and the choice of many accountants and bookkeepers for their clients. It is a fully functional general ledger with no limits on invoices, bills, or bank transactions.
- **Established** ($62 per month): This premium level subscription includes everything that Growing does, but also includes multicurrency, Xero Projects, and Xero Expenses. For many clients, Projects and Expenses will alleviate the need to add another application for project management, receipt management, and expense reimbursement.

All business edition subscriptions also include Hubdoc, a document collection, storage, and extraction tool, which was purchased by Xero in 2017.

# Xero's Partner Program

Xero's commitment to its accountant and bookkeeper partners is clear. The majority of the U.S. sales team is charged with supporting advisors and their clients. Xero has a physical presence in 12 communities at the time of writing. Those communities have dedicated account management teams and regularly hold community events.

Accountants, bookkeepers, and other advisors can apply to become a Xero Partner at www.xero.com. There are minimal requirements verified by Xero's partner team, and applicants are expected to complete a free certification course within 30 days. All Xero Partners receive a free subscription to use for their practice, access to Xero HQ, and dedicated learning resources but can earn increased rewards and benefits based on a point system.

# Basic Accounting and Nomenclature

Xero is a full-fledged, double-entry accounting general ledger. Xero calls each company or file an "organization." We will use this term throughout.

Xero was built with ease of use for small businesses at top of mind. As such, the modules, especially on the Dashboard, use common, rather than accounting, language. Accounts receivable are noted as "Invoices owed to you" and accounts payable are noted as "Bills you need to pay."

## Notes

1. Xero Limited, Xero Limited Annual Meeting (August 2020), https://www.xero.com/content/dam/xero/pdf/about-us/annual-meeting-presentation-2020.pdf.
2. Ibid.
3. https://www.xero.com/us/about/security.

# Leveraging Xero within an Ecosystem

*Xero is a very innovative organization and their API allows for many other solutions to integrate. This is evidenced by the many integrations available in their App Marketplace. There are many industry or function-specific options available to meet organizational needs.*

—Paul Johnson, Founder of Atlasphere Consulting

Small businesses depend on technology to manage operations. Even the most traditional businesses could not operate without some kind of software, whether that is a bank with online services or email. Because of the pandemic of 2020, businesses, sometimes forced by their customer base, have adopted technology at a quickened pace. Some sources even indicate that the economy "vaulted five years forward in consumer and business digital adoption in a matter of around eight weeks."[1]

Accountants and bookkeepers play an important role in guiding clients in technology selection and implementation, because the data gathered from these applications eventually ends up in the financial records of the business. Whether the company uses a social media platform to sell products or a banking application to collect payments, they are leveraging technology and in doing so, creating electronic data that tells the company's financial story. This group of software that a client uses is its **ecosystem**.

Even though most accountants and bookkeepers are focused on month-end or year-end financial data, the general ledger does not operate in a vacuum. Advisors who ignore the influence of operational applications will be soon pushed out of the market by modern accountants and bookkeepers who understand that business owners are looking for support for the cloud-based software they depend on to run their companies. The applications may or may not be integrated with the general ledger. Having a fully integrated ecosystem yields tremendous efficiencies; however, not all technology can be connected to the accounting system. In those cases, workarounds should be crafted and documented.

As you continue through this book, it is important to understand that, while this publication is focused on Xero, for many clients, Xero is only one piece of the comprehensive technology ecosystem the client depends on. A client's ecosystem will depend on their needs. The advantage of using strictly cloud-based software is that advisors can build custom ecosystems that meet the specific requirements of the client.

In general, an accounting ecosystem is built around the general ledger package. For some small companies, the general ledger may be the entire business ecosystem. In larger companies, the ecosystem can be complex, with a dozen or more applications. Common software add-ons include:

- Payroll
- Ecommerce
- Industry-specific billing, such as law firm management software
- Bill payment
- Document storage and data capture
- Expense reimbursement
- Customer relationship management
- Inventory
- Job invoicing
- Appointment scheduling
- Receipt management
- Reporting
- Time tracking

Because each of the third-party applications is a stand-alone product, usually on a monthly subscription, if the client needs a change or if other software that would be a better fit enters the market, that one piece of the ecosystem can be modified without upending the whole ecosystem.

# A Primer on APIs

You do not have to be a programmer or computer genius in order to advise clients on technology. You do have to have a basic understanding of how software works together. The use of cloud-based software creates a tremendous amount of data within that application, but true efficiency and automation comes from having that data transferred to another application seamlessly.

The way data is moved is through an **API**. An API (application programming interface) is basically a set of rules in one software program that dictates how it can interact with another application. The API of an application will govern the kind of data that can be transferred and how that transfer occurs.

# Xero as Part of a Cloud Accounting Ecosystem

Any ecosystem discussion should begin with the general ledger. The general ledger will be the record set that is used for compliance work, like regulatory filings and tax return preparation. It will also be the data that projections, budgets, and metrics are based on.

Even though many clients rely on operational software, such as sales systems or staffing platforms, in the day-to-day decision making, the general ledger should be the single source of financial truth.

Xero is a clean general ledger with an open API, which means that the rules for data transfer are publicly available and software developers are unrestricted in writing programs that can connect to Xero. This makes Xero an excellent choice as the hub of a customized ecosystem.

Applications can be connected to Xero in three ways. The most common is a **direct integration**. Many software platforms have invested in building products that directly connect with Xero. A complete list can be found at apps.xero.com/us. These programs can generally be integrated with Xero in a matter of minutes.

If an application that the client uses does not have a direct integration with Xero, sometimes a third-party automation software can be used between them. The most common of these is **Zapier**. Zapier was created to connect cloud-based applications when there is no direct integration. Zapier works with over 2,000 applications, including Xero, so it is likely that if a client is using a cloud platform within their ecosystem, it is available in Zapier.

The last way that applications can work together is with custom developed integrations. This requires hiring a programmer to write software that will connect two or more applications. Custom integrations can be expensive, but for large accounting firms with thousands of clients, a one-time investment in code can still be a cost savings over hours of work.

## Understanding Client Needs

When trying to increase a client's efficiency, many advisors start with the software first and try to make it fit into the workflow. The better way to craft an ecosystem is to diagram the client workflow (without regards to software), analyze for pain points, and select applications based on the client's needs.

A typical data mapping for a retailer with online sales may look like Figure 2.1. The general ledger is at the center with supporting functions surrounding. The arrows between functions indicate the flow of data.

In this example, customer details are first entered into a customer relationship management (CRM) system, upon collection from an in-store or online sale. The CRM sales data will continuously sync so that a record of customer purchases is maintained and can be used for promotions or marketing. Both sales systems send revenue, cost of goods sold, and inventory data to the general ledger. The in-store sales system may also keep track of employee clock-ins, which are transmitted to the timekeeping system. From there, hours are sent to the payroll system for processing and eventually payroll details are transmitted to the general ledger. The bank is sending transactional data to the general ledger for

**FIGURE 2.1**

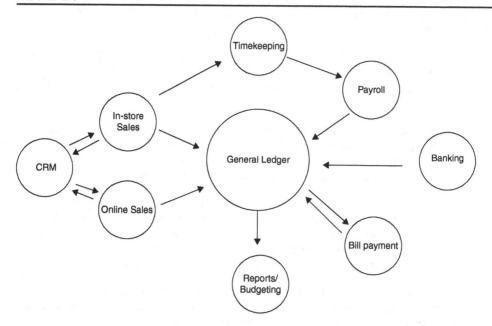

reconciliation. A bill payment processor is receiving unpaid accounts payable information from the general ledger, processing payments, then remitting the payment details back to the general ledger. Lastly, the general ledger data is pulled into a reporting and budgeting tool for analysis.

## Layering Applications

Only after a client's workflow is understood is it appropriate to consider technology solutions. Look at the client's needs; then find software that meets those requirements (Figure 2.2). In our example, we are able to build a comprehensive ecosystem with only five applications: a general ledger (Xero), a payroll system (Rippling), a bank with bill payment capabilities (Relay), a reporting and budgeting tool (Jirav), and a sales platform that manages customer data (Shopify). Without understanding the complete picture, it is easy to get distracted by the next shiny piece of technology.

**FIGURE 2.2**

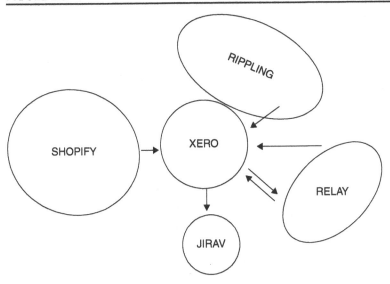

## Samples of Niche Ecosystems

Many advisors are focusing on one or two industry verticals. This enables them to concentrate marketing efforts while building internal efficiencies. The more specialized they become, the more they build a brand of subject matter expertise, commanding higher fees.

One way to decrease internal servicing cost per client, and therefore increase margin per client, is to develop a core ecosystem for each vertical of the practice. A few examples are shown in Figures 2.3, 2.4, and 2.5.

## Professional Services Firm (such as Architects, Engineers, Marketing Agencies)

**FIGURE 2.3**

Needs: Project management and billing, document management, payroll, bill payment, expense reimbursement, dashboarding

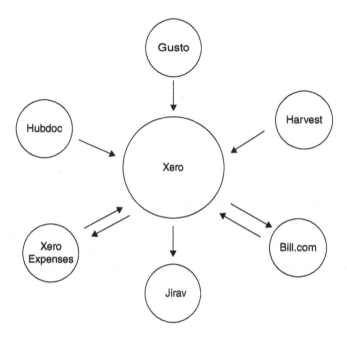

## SaaS Company

**FIGURE 2.4**

Needs: Payment processor, international bill payment, payroll, sophisticated CRM, revenue recognition, subscription analytics

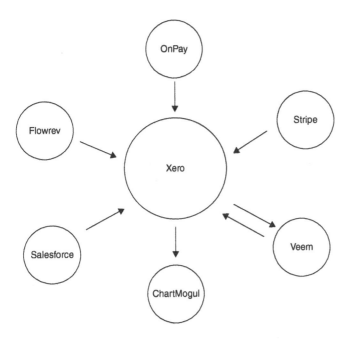

## Law Firm

**FIGURE 2.5**

Needs: Separate IOLTA accounting, time and expense management, payroll

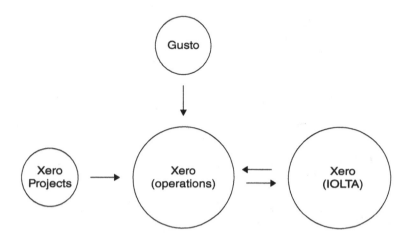

# Note

1. https://www.mckinsey.com/business-functions/mckinsey-digital/our-insights/the-covid-19-recovery-will-be-digital-a-plan-for-the-first-90-days

# Xero HQ

*Report Templates allow my team to standardize the reporting coming out of our clients without extreme effort to individually customize reports. The time savings this feature allows us is notable and appreciated. We have gotten great feedback from banks and other financial statement users that the consistency, the attractiveness, and the comprehensiveness of our Report Template reporting packages are awesome.*

*—Liz Mason, CEO and Founder of High Rock Accounting*

> Author's note: At the time of writing, Xero HQ is undergoing significant improvements, so screenshots and specific navigation instructions may differ between this book and the product. Features in Xero HQ may be somewhat improved or located in different menus than stated, but the functionality should be mostly consistent with the content presented here.

## Overview of Xero HQ

Xero HQ is Xero's client management software. It is available to all Xero Partners. Conceptually, it sits above the accounting software and should be the control center of your practice. Xero HQ is branded by a black header.

Xero HQ has several important modules:

- An **Activity** feed
- A **Clients** listing
- **Explorer**, which aggregates client insights at a practice level
- **Reports**, for managing practice-level report templates
- **Xero Ask**, a built-in query system
- A **Staff** management portal
- Practice-level settings

Xero HQ does not have a Dashboard in the way that Xero does. Each of the modules is a separate tab at the top of the screen (Figure 3.1). Two other important functions available from this screen are User Profile and Account Settings, which are accessed by clicking on the last icon on the top right, usually the user's initials.

**FIGURE 3.1**

Description: Xero HQ does not have a Dashboard in the way that Xero does. Each of the modules is a separate tab at the top of the screen.

Summers & Howell ▾    Activity    Clients    Explorer    Reports    Ask    Staff    Practice

*Source:* Xero Limited

# Accessing Xero HQ

When working in Xero, Xero HQ can be accessed by using the pull-down for the organization name in the top left and navigating to **Xero HQ**, near the bottom.

# Editing User Profile

To edit your profile, select the icon at the top right of the header and select **Edit profile**. At the top of the screen, select whether you would like your profile to be public on the Xero website (Figure 3.2). Below, you can enter or edit Basic Information, Contact Details, and Public Profile Settings. Basic Information is automatically shared if your profile is public, but you can choose whether to show Contact Details by checking the box to the right of each piece of information.

**FIGURE 3.2**

Description: Below, you can enter or edit Basic Information, Contact Details, and Public Profile Settings.

**Join the Xero community and share your knowledge with others**

Turn on your public profile to become listed in our user directory and become part of our growing community where you can ask and give advice to like-minded Xero users. You can also help improve Xero by suggesting and voting on new features for Xero. Find out more about public profiles.

Public profile ○ On ⊙ Off

*Source:* Xero Limited

# Account Settings

Also under the icon at the far right is account settings, labeled **Account.** This is where you can change your login email and password and enable two-step authentication. It is also where you can change your login preference. Choose to be directed to **The organization I was last in, Xero HQ Activity,** or **Xero HQ Clients** when you log into Xero (Figure 3.3).

**FIGURE 3.3**

Description: It is also where you can change your login preference. Choose to be directed to The organization I was last in, Xero HQ Activity or Xero HQ Clients when you log into Xero

**Preferences**

Log in to

| Xero HQ Clients | ▾ |
| --- | --- |

The organisation I was last in

Xero HQ Activity

Xero HQ Clients

*Source:* Xero Limited

# Activity

The Activity tab in Xero HQ acts as a notification feed at the practice level but is customized to the user. Alerts can be filtered using the tabs on the left of the listing. You can also use the search bar to filter for specific clients.

There are two types of alerts in the feed: custom and system.

## Custom Alerts

Custom alerts are alerts set by the user and are specific to the login. At this time, the only custom alerts available are for bank reconciliation. The threshold for bank reconciliation alerts is based on exceeding either a number of line items to reconcile or the number of days since there were zero lines to reconcile. This alert can be set for all clients or specific clients.

To create an alert for all clients:

1. From the **Activity** tab, select **Settings**.
2. Select **Custom** alerts on the left.
3. Use the toggle next to **All-clients bank reconciliation** alert to turn on custom notifications.
4. Enter either a **Number of Transactions** to code or **Days since fully reconciled** (Figure 3.4).
5. Click **Save**.

**FIGURE 3.4**

Description: Enter either a Number of Transactions to code or Days since fully reconciled

Custom alerts

System alerts

**All-clients bank reconciliation alert**
Create an alert rule for all clients that don't have a client-specific rule set up. If any clients exceed the limits, you'll get alerts in your activity feed.

Transactions to code

25

OR

Days since fully reconciled

Save

*Client-specific rules override all-clients rules*

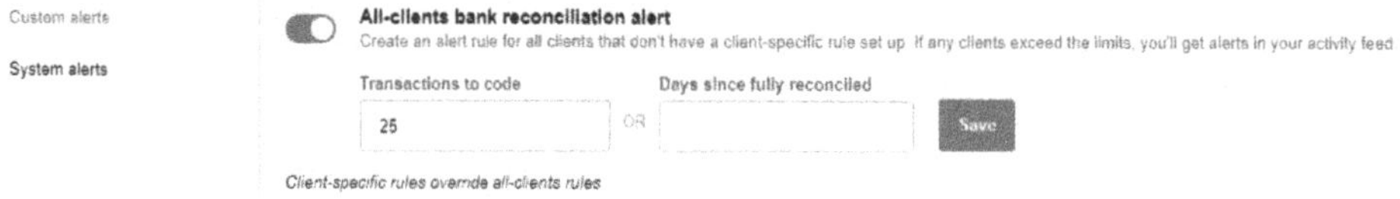

*Source:* Xero Limited

Notice that the custom alert is populated below for each client; however, the all-clients alert can be overridden with a client-specific rule.

To add a client-specific alert rule:

1. Navigate to the **Activity** tab.
2. Select the **Settings** tab on the left.
3. Choose **Custom** alerts on the left.
4. Use the overflow menu on the right of the client name to navigate to **Edit rule**.
5. Enter the new parameters for the alert. Note that even if the all-clients alert rule is based on one threshold, for example, transactions to code, the overriding client-specific rule can be on the other criteria. Simply delete the value in one field and enter a value in the other.
6. Click **Save**.

## System Alerts

System alerts are preset alerts that Xero includes in the Activity feed. These cannot be customized. System alerts include:

- Xero Ask alerts: When a client responds to a Xero Ask query, Xero will show an alert.
- Bank alerts: If a client has a direct bank feed that includes statement balance and the balance does not tie to Xero's calculated statement balance, Xero will show an alert.
- Connected app alerts: Certain applications that are connected to client organizations will create alerts based on their parameters.

## Managing Alerts

Alerts of both types will appear in the same Activity feed. To take an action on the alert, use the button to the right of the client name. Each type of alert will show a button that is customized for the appropriate action. For example, bank reconciliation alerts will show a **Reconcile** button (Figure 3.5).

**FIGURE 3.5**

Description: Alerts of both types will appear in the same Activity feed. To take an action on the alert, use the button to the right of the client name. Each type of alert will show a button that is customized for the appropriate action. For example, bank reconciliation alerts will show a Reconcile button.

**Island Escape Pool Service**  111 transactions to reconcile
Bank | Last reconciled 632 days ago                                        Reconcile ⋮

*Source:* Xero Limited

You can use the overflow menu to the right to manage or delete alerts. Making changes here will only affect the logged in user's view, not the view of anyone else in the practice.

To modify or delete the alerts for a client:

1. Navigate to the **Activity** tab.
2. Click the overflow menu, indicated by three dots, to the right of the client.
3. Choose one of the options: **Turn off (this type) of alerts for this client**, **Turn off all (this type) of alerts**, **Turn off all alerts for this client**, or **Delete this alert**.

When a system alert has been turned off, you can restore it by navigating to the **Settings** menu and selecting **System** alerts. Click the **X** to the right of the alert modification to restore it.

# Client

The Clients tab in Xero HQ shows all clients in a single list. The format of the listing can be customized, allowing it to be used as a home base for client data. Many advisors choose to customize their login to arrive at the Clients tab, because it provides a comprehensive listing of all clients for the practice. It is important to note that Xero HQ was built to manage the entire client load of a practice, whether or not they use Xero.

## Navigating the Clients Tab

The Clients tab is where your client listing is managed. On the upper left is a pull-down showing the total number of practice clients. By clicking the arrow, you can change the listing view to show Archived clients (Figure 3.6).

The **Export** button on the top right will allow you to export a .csv file of your client listing, their contact information and other data.

Next to the Export button is a pull-down to **Manage client groups**. Groups can be used to organize clients and is discussed later in this chapter.

Clients can be added by using the **Add client** pull-down in the top right. If the client already has a Xero organization, select **Existing Xero organization**. To add a client without a Xero file, use **New client**.

**FIGURE 3.6**

Description: The Clients tab is where your client listing is managed. On the upper left is a pulldown showing the total number of practice clients. By clicking the arrow, you can change the listing view to show Archived clients.

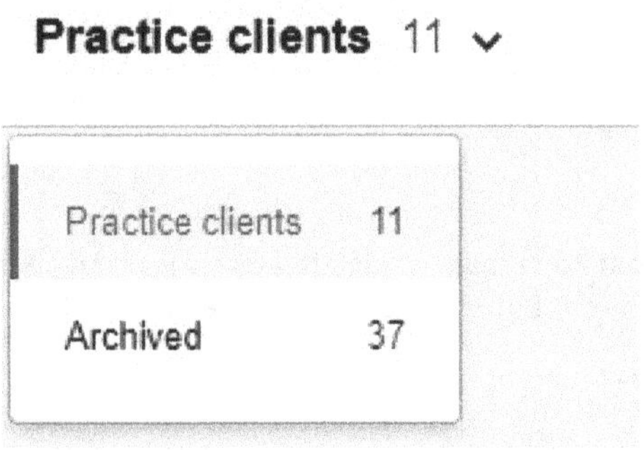

**Practice clients**  11  ⌄

| Practice clients | 11 |
|---|---|
| Archived | 37 |

*Source:* Xero Limited

The default view for the client listing is in alphabetical order. Use the search field to find clients by name.

Clients can also be organized with preset filters. Use the **Filter** link to narrow the listing. They are three filters: type of Xero subscription, Business structure, and Industry. These filters cannot be changed.

The **Customise columns** link allows the user to change the data that is viewable on this screen. Use the checkboxes to include or exclude information on the client line (Figure 3.7).

On each client line there is a quick link to **Go to Xero**, if the client has a Xero organization. Using this link will open the client's Xero file in the current browser tab.

At the end of the line is an overflow menu indicated by three dots. It includes an **Edit details** option, where client information can be added. Note that information entered here does not transfer to the details in the Xero organization, nor does it affect your listing in the Xero Advisor Directory. For purposes of the Advisor Directory, client addresses must be entered in each organization's Organizational Settings. To learn more, see Chapter 3.

There is a link to view **Staff access** on the client. To remove the client from the current listing, use **Archive**. The client will not be visible on the Practice clients listing but will be accessible in Archived clients.

## Viewing and Managing Client Details

The Clients tab in Xero HQ can function as simple customer relationship management (CRM) software. By clicking on the client name, you are taken to the client record.

At the top of the client screen are headers representing functions within Xero HQ. There is a **Notes** section where notes can be added, and even tagged. You may want to add notes about communications with the client or important details, like birthdays or the name of

**FIGURE 3.7**

Description: The Customise columns link allows the user to change the data that is viewable on this screen. Use the checkboxes to include or exclude information on the client line.

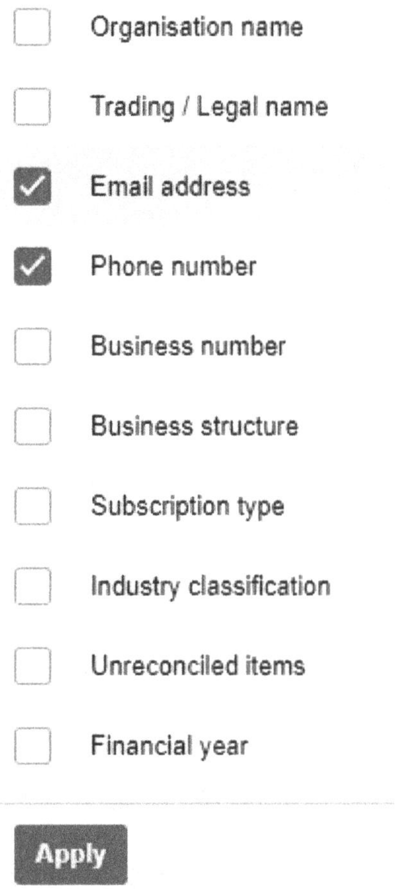

- ☐ Organisation name

- ☐ Trading / Legal name

- ☑ Email address

- ☑ Phone number

- ☐ Business number

- ☐ Business structure

- ☐ Subscription type

- ☐ Industry classification

- ☐ Unreconciled items

- ☐ Financial year

**Apply**

*Source:* Xero Limited

their tax preparer (Figure 3.8). To add a note, use the **Add a note** link at the top of the screen and type within the field. Add one or more tags by using the **Add tags** pull-down and checking the box to the left of the desired tag. Use the **New tag** and **Manage tags** options at the bottom of the listing to add or delete tags.

The **Activity** section of the client record shows alerts from the Xero HQ Activity, specific to the chosen client (Figure 3.9).

The **Information** section shows the Business structure and Industry classification of the chosen client.

**FIGURE 3.8**

Description: To add a note, use the Add a note link at the top of the screen and type within the field. Add one or more tags by using the Add tags pulldown and checking the box to the left of the desired tag. Use the New tag and Manage tags options at the bottom of the listing to add or delete tags.

| Notes | Activity | Information | Staff | Relationships |

Add a note                                                                Show: All notes ▼

AA   **Amanda Aguillard**                                                        ⋮

The tax prep firm is C&K.

Tax

*Source:* Xero Limited

**FIGURE 3.9**

Description: The Activity section of the client record shows alerts from the Xero HQ Activity, specific to the chosen client.

| Activity | Information | Staff | Relationships |

IEP   **111 transactions to reconcile**                                     Reconcile ⋮
Bank  Last reconciled 632 days ago

*Source:* Xero Limited

The **Staff** section shows which practice staff have access to the organization and what level that access is.

A client can be associated with more than one contact, such as employees, advisors, or tax preparers. This is managed in the **Relationships** section of Clients. Use the **Add a contact** button to search for existing contacts to associate with the client. If a new contact needs to be created, use the **+Create new contact** link.

## Client Groups

There is no limit to the number of groups a practice can have, and a client can be in multiple groups. Some examples of groups are:

- Annual write-up
- 1099

- Corporate tax prep
- Quarterly accounting

To create a custom client group:

1. Navigate to the **Clients** tab in Xero HQ.
2. Click the **Client groups** link.
3. Select **+New group**.
4. Enter a name for the group.
5. Click **Create**.

To add a client to a group:

1. Navigate to the **Clients** tab in Xero HQ.
2. Click the box to the left of one or more clients to add to the group.
3. Use the **Add to group** pull-down that appears at the bottom of the screen.
4. Choose the group (Figure 3.10).
5. Click **Apply**.

Once clients are added, the view can be changed to show only that group.

To view a client group:

1. Navigate to the **Clients** tab in Xero HQ.
2. Click the **Client groups** link.
3. Select a group name. The view will filter to show only clients assigned to that group.

**FIGURE 3.10**

Description: Choose the group.

*Source:* Xero Limited

To remove a client from a group:

1. Navigate to the **Clients** tab in Xero HQ.
2. Click the **Client groups** link.
3. Select a group name.
4. Click the box to the left of one or more clients to remove from the group.
5. Click the **Remove from group** button at the bottom of the screen.

If a group becomes obsolete, it can be deleted. To delete a group:

1. Navigate to the **Clients** tab in Xero HQ.
2. Use the **Manage client groups** pull-down at the top of the screen to select **Manage groups**.
3. Click the **Remove** link to the right of the group name.

# Explorer

The Explorer tab gives you practice level insights into client data, including the applications tied to client files, the banks they use, and industries they work in.

## Navigating the Explorer Tab

At the time of writing, the leftmost tab within Explorer is COVID-19 support. This screen has tiles of resources for advisors and clients in light of the pandemic. The other tabs are permanent functions of Xero HQ: **Apps**, **Industry**, and **Banks**.

## Apps

The **Apps** screen shows a graphical representation of the third-party applications that your clients are using (Figure 3.11). Note that this screen only accounts for software that is connected to the Xero API, so it will not include applications being used that are standalone or are tied to other platforms. Use the dots at the bottom of the graph to scroll. Below the graph is a summary of how many clients have apps attached to the Xero organization. Clicking on a bar in the graph will show a listing of the clients using that application. This is useful for determining which clients might be affected by software updates or outages.

## Industry

The **Industry** screen shows a graph of client industries (Figure 3.12). As in the Apps screen, each bar on the graph can be selected to view the clients that make up the group. Below the graph is a summary of how many clients are assigned an industry. There is also a link to a listing of clients that do not have an industry assigned.

**FIGURE 3.11**

Description: The Apps screen shows a graphical representation of the third party applications that your clients are using.

*Source:* Xero Limited

**FIGURE 3.12**

The Industry screen shows a graph of client industries. (Figure 3.12) As in the Apps screen, each bar on the graph can be selected to view the clients that make up the group.

*Source:* Xero Limited

Industry assignments are important, not just for internal understanding but for the Xero Advisor Directory. One component of the Advisor Directory is industries served. Unlike apps connected or Xero status, which are automatically figured, the firm enters clients' industries manually. By leaving clients untagged, you are missing opportunities to attract more clients in the verticals you serve.

To add an industry for a client:

1. Locate the client in the listing and click the **+Add an industry** link.
2. In the **What does this organization do?** field, type an industry in plain language. Xero will filter and you can choose the appropriate category.
3. Xero will assign an industry based on the Australian and New Zealand Standard Industrial Classification (ANZSIC) industry divisions.

To change the client's industry, use the overflow menu at the right to **Edit details**.

## Banks

The **Banks** screen shows a graph of client banks (Figure 3.13). As in the other screens, each bar on the graph can be selected to view the clients that make up the group. Below the graph is a summary of how many clients have a connected bank. There is also a link to a listing of clients that do not have a connected bank. This is a helpful screen when there are bank feed problems because it makes it simple to identify which clients are affected.

**FIGURE 3.13**

The Banks screen shows a graph of client banks.

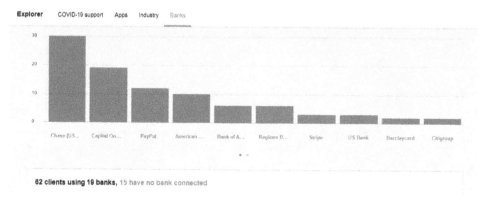

*Source: Xero Limited*

# Reports

One of the most useful features in Xero HQ is the ability to format reports at a practice level to be used throughout client organizations. Since creating repeatable reports based on charts of accounts would be impossible since nearly every client's chart is different, **report templates** are structured on report codes. Report templates can be used to standardize the view of reports so staff can create them for the client.

## Understanding Report Codes

Report codes essentially provide a mapping from a chart of account line to an account type. The codes are sets of three letter keys that start at the most general level of account types and continue in levels of specificity. Each account in the chart of accounts has a code assigned to it. Because the report codes are consistent across clients, a single report framework can be used (Figure 3.14).

In addition to report templates, Xero has indicated that they will be leveraging report codes for intelligence tools in the future.

**FIGURE 3.14**

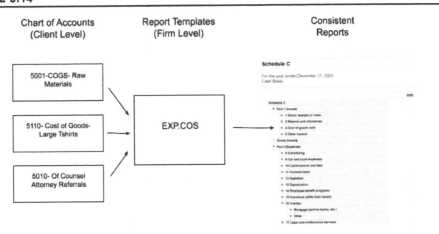

## Commonly Used Report Codes

| Report code | Name |
| --- | --- |
| ASS | Assets |
| ASS.CUR | Current assets |
| ASS.CUR.CAS | Cash and cash equivalents |
| ASS.CUR.CAS.BAN | Bank accounts/(overdraft) |
| ASS.CUR.CAS.CAS | Cash on hand |
| ASS.CUR.CAS.CEQ | Cash equivalents |
| ASS.CUR.INY | Inventories |
| ASS.CUR.INY.FIN | Finished goods |
| ASS.CUR.INY.RAW | Raw materials |
| ASS.CUR.INY.WIP | Work in progress |
| ASS.CUR.REC | Other receivables (current) |
| ASS.CUR.REC.ACR | Accounts receivable |
| ASS.CUR.REC.ACR.ADA | Allowance for doubtful accounts receivable |
| ASS.CUR.REC.EMP | Employee advances/receivables |
| ASS.CUR.REC.PRE | Prepayments (current) |
| ASS.CUR.REL | Related party receivables (current) |
| ASS.CUR.STI | Short-term investments |
| ASS.NCA | Noncurrent assets |
| ASS.NCA.DIR | Loans to directors (noncurrent) |
| ASS.NCA.FIX | Fixed assets |
| ASS.NCA.FIX.BUC | Building and improvements |
| ASS.NCA.FIX.BUC.ACC | Accumulated depreciation of buildings |
| ASS.NCA.FIX.CAP | Capital lease asset |
| ASS.NCA.FIX.CAP.ACC | Accumulated depreciation of capital lease asset |
| ASS.NCA.FIX.FNF | Furniture and fixtures |
| ASS.NCA.FIX.FNF.ACC | Accumulated depreciation of furniture and fixtures |
| ASS.NCA.FIX.LAC | Land and land improvements |
| ASS.NCA.FIX.LAC.REV | Land revaluation |
| ASS.NCA.FIX.LEA | Leasehold improvements |
| ASS.NCA.FIX.LEA.ACC | Accumulated amortization of leasehold improvements |
| ASS.NCA.FIX.PLA | Plant and equipment |
| ASS.NCA.FIX.PLA.ACC | Accumulated depreciation of plant and equipment |

| Report code | Name |
| --- | --- |
| ASS.NCA.FIX.VEH | Vehicles |
| ASS.NCA.FIX.VEH.ACC | Accumulated depreciation of vehicles |
| ASS.NCA.INT | Intangible assets |
| ASS.NCA.INT.AMO | Accumulated amortization of intangibles |
| ASS.NCA.LTI | Long-term investments |
| ASS.NCA.PRE | Prepayments (noncurrent) |
| EQU | Equity/Owners' capital |
| EQU.ADV | Owners/Partners capital contribution |
| EQU.DRA | Owners/Partners draw |
| EQU.PFT | Owners/Partners profit distribution |
| EQU.RET | Retained earnings/Accumulated funds |
| EQU.RET.CUR | Current year earnings |
| EQU.RET.DIS | Beneficiary/Partner distributions |
| EQU.RET.DIV | Dividends paid equity |
| EQU.SHA.ORD | Common stock |
| EXP | Expense |
| EXP.ADV | Advertising |
| EXP.AMO | Amortization of intangibles |
| EXP.AUD | Audit and assurance fees |
| EXP.BAD | Bad debts |
| EXP.CHA | Charitable contributions |
| EXP.COS | Cost of goods sold |
| EXP.COS.CLO | Closing inventory |
| EXP.COS.LAB | Direct labor |
| EXP.COS.OPE | Opening inventory |
| EXP.COS.PUR | Purchases |
| EXP.COS.WPC | Closing WIP |
| EXP.COS.WPO | Opening WIP |
| EXP.DEP | Depreciation |
| EXP.DIR | Directors salary |
| EXP.DIS | Distribution to beneficiary/partner |
| EXP.DIV | Dividends paid expense |
| EXP.EMP | Employment costs |
| EXP.EMP.CON | Contract labor expense |

3

| Report code | Name |
| --- | --- |
| EXP.EMP.HEA | Health insurance |
| EXP.EMP.PPP | Pension and profit-sharing plans |
| EXP.EMP.SHA | Shareholder salaries |
| EXP.EMP.SUP | Employee benefit programs |
| EXP.EMP.WAG | Wages and salaries |
| EXP.ENT | Entertainment |
| EXP.ENT.NON | Nondeductible entertainment |
| EXP.FBT | Fringe benefits tax |
| EXP.FOR | Foreign currency gains/losses |
| EXP.GEX | General and administrative expenses |
| EXP.GPP | Guaranteed payments to partners |
| EXP.INC | Income tax expense |
| EXP.INS | Insurance expense |
| EXP.INT | Interest and finance charges |
| EXP.LIC | Licenses |
| EXP.LOS | Loss on disposal of fixed assets |
| EXP.NON | Other nondeductible items |
| EXP.OFF | Office expenses |
| EXP.OFR | Officer salaries |
| EXP.OTH | Other expenses |
| EXP.PRO | Professional fees |
| EXP.REA | Research and development expense |
| EXP.REN | Rental and lease payments |
| EXP.REN.OPE | Operating lease payments |
| EXP.REP | Repairs and maintenance |
| EXP.SEL | Selling expenses |
| EXP.TAX | Taxes |
| EXP.TAX.EMP | Payroll taxes |
| EXP.TAX.OTH | Other taxes |
| EXP.TAX.PRP | Property taxes |
| EXP.TRA | Travel and accommodation |
| EXP.UTI | Utilities |
| EXP.VEH | Vehicle expenses |
| LIA | Liabilities |

| Report code | Name |
| --- | --- |
| LIA.CUR | Current liabilities |
| LIA.CUR.ACC | Accrued liabilities |
| LIA.CUR.DEF | Deferred income |
| LIA.CUR.DEP | Deposits |
| LIA.CUR.INT | Interest payable (current) |
| LIA.CUR.LOA | Loans (current) |
| LIA.CUR.LOA.CAP | Capital lease (current) |
| LIA.CUR.LOA.DIR | Loans from directors (current) |
| LIA.CUR.PAY | Trade and other payables |
| LIA.CUR.PAY.CRC | Credit cards |
| LIA.CUR.PAY.DIV | Dividends payable |
| LIA.CUR.PAY.EMP | Employee-related liabilities (wages, vacation leave, etc.) |
| LIA.CUR.PAY.OTH | Other payables |
| LIA.CUR.PAY.TRA | Accounts payable |
| LIA.CUR.REL | Related party payables (current) |
| LIA.CUR.TAX | Taxes payable |
| LIA.CUR.TAX.SAL | Sales and excise tax payable |
| LIA.NCL | Non-current liabilities |
| LIA.NCL.LOA | Loans (noncurrent) |
| LIA.NCL.LOA.CAP | Capital lease (noncurrent) |
| LIA.NCL.LOA.DIR | Loans from directors (noncurrent) |
| LIA.NCL.NCT | Noncash liability |
| LIA.NCL.PFT | Beneficiary/Shareholder profit distribution |
| LIA.NCL.REL | Related party payables (noncurrent) |
| LIA.NCL.TAX | Tax liabilities (noncurrent) |
| REV | Revenue |
| REV.GRA | Grants |
| REV.INV | Investment revenue |
| REV.INV.DIV | Dividends |
| REV.INV.INT | Interest |
| REV.INV.REN | Rents |
| REV.INV.ROY | Royalties |
| REV.NON | Nontaxable income |
| REV.OCI | Other comprehensive income |

3

| Report code | Name |
|---|---|
| REV.OTH | Other revenue |
| REV.OTH.CAP | Capital gain on disposal of fixed assets |
| REV.RET | Returns and allowances |
| REV.SAL | Sales |
| REV.SAL.GOO | Sale of goods |
| REV.SAL.SER | Services revenue |

## Mapping Accounts to Report Codes

Ideally, the charts of accounts used when the organization is created will include report codes. If not, the codes will need to be added in the client organization.

To update report codes in bulk:

1. Open the client organization.
2. Navigate to **Accounting**, then **Advanced** and select **Report Codes**.
3. Select the **Export** button (Figure 3.15). Xero will download a .csv file.
4. Make report code changes and save the file.
5. Click the **Import** button.
6. Click the **Browse** button and select the revised file.
7. Click **Import**.

**FIGURE 3.15**

Select the Export button. (Figure 3.15) Xero will download a .csv file.

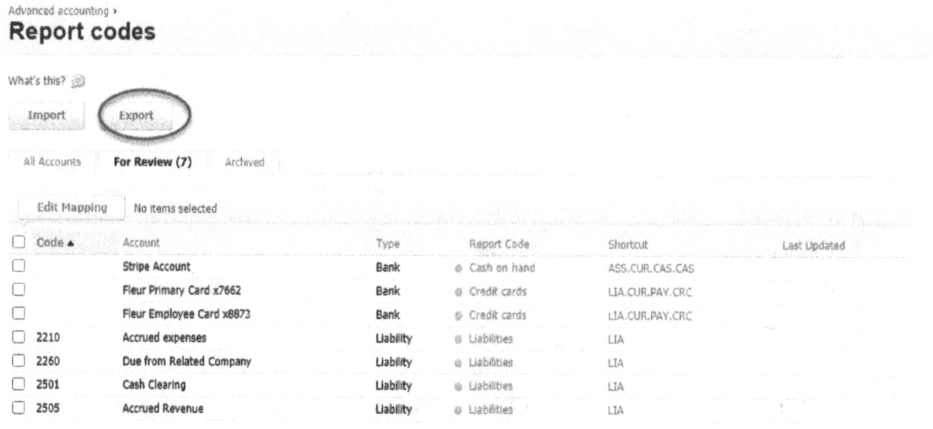

*Source:* Xero Limited

When new general ledger accounts are added to an organization, Xero adds a report code based on the account type; however, the account type is a very high level report code. Xero will list accounts in the For Review tab of Report codes to alert the user that attention should be given to the coding.

To add edit the mapping:

1. Open the client organization.

2. Navigate to the **Accounting**, then **Advanced** and select **Report Codes.**

3. Check the box to the left of the account you want to map.

4. Click the **Edit Mapping** button at the top.

5. Select the code you wish to associate with the account, using the arrows to open codes beneath (Figure 3.16).

6. Click **OK.**

**FIGURE 3.16**

Select the code you wish to associate with the account, using the arrows to open codes beneath.

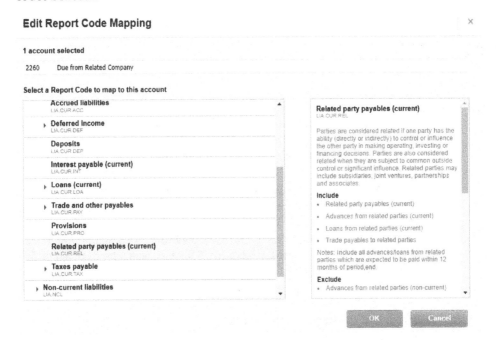

*Source:* Xero Limited

## Setting Up Template Details

Before using report templates for the first time, you may wish to customize a few of the features available. These features will help tailor reports for clients.

### Report Publishing Styles

To brand reports on behalf of your firm, use Report Publishing Styles. You can add the firm logo and select a report border color.

To set up Report Publishing Styles:

1. Navigate to the **Reports** tab in Xero HQ.
2. Click the **Report Publishing Styles** button.
3. In the Practice Logo section, use the **Browse** button to select the firm's logo, then click **Upload** (Figure 3.17).
4. Under Border Color, either select a color from the box pull-down or enter a hex value.
5. Add any optional footer text in the space provided.
6. Click **Save**.

### Report Fields

Xero allows advisors to further customize reports by using Report Fields. These are custom fields of text that will automatically populate in reports generated by templates. They can be short text strings that are embedded in paragraphs and automatically update, such as date references, or long lists of things like shareholders or board members.

There are three kinds of report fields:

- **Preset:** These are fields set by Xero that meet common needs. They are Current Date, Current Year, Depreciation Rates, Display Name, EIN, Legal or Trading Name, Physical Address, Postal Address, Report End Date, Report End Year, and Tax TD Number.
- **Client:** This is for including client-specific information on reports. The field is defined at the Xero HQ level, but the underlying text is established in each client organization. An example would be the board of directors listing.
- **Practice:** This is for static text that may need to be used across reports. The text is set when the field is created in Xero HQ. Examples would be a listing of firm management or firm disclaimers.

To create client or practice report fields:

1. Navigate to the **Reports** tab in Xero HQ.
2. Click the **Report Fields** button.

**FIGURE 3.17**

In the Practice Logo section, use the Browse button to select the firm's logo, then click Upload.

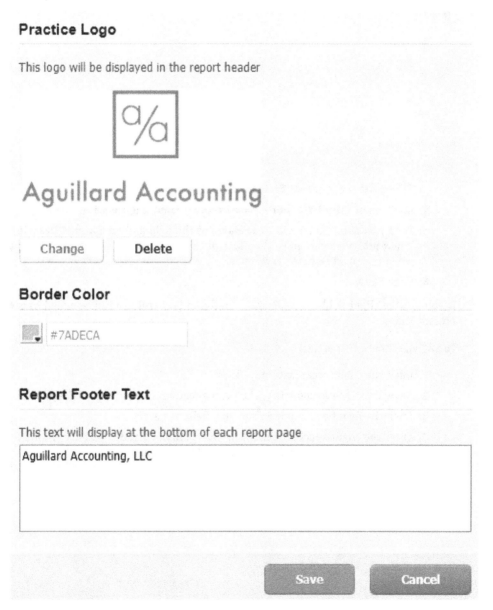

### Practice Logo

This logo will be displayed in the report header

Aguillard Accounting

| Change | **Delete** |

### Border Color

#7ADECA

### Report Footer Text

This text will display at the bottom of each report page

Aguillard Accounting, LLC

Save    Cancel

*Source:* Xero Limited

**FIGURE 3.18**

Click +New Client Field or + New Practice Field.

Report Templates ›
**Report Fields**                                        Summers & Howell

**Client Field (1)**    Practice Fields (0)

( + New Client Field )

Name                        Description                    Last Edited ▾

Mission Statement                                          Just now by Amanda Aguillard

*Source:* Xero Limited

3. Select either the **Client Fields** or **Practice Fields** tab.

4. Click **+New Client Field** or **+ New Practice Field** (Figure 3.18).

5. For a new client field, enter the **Name** of the field and an optional **Description**. For a new practice field, enter the name of the field and the text that will be populated when that field is added to a report.

6. Click **Save.**

If you created client fields, the specific underlying text will need to be added in each client organization.

To add client details to fields:

1. Open the client organization.

2. Navigate to the **Accounting**, then **Advanced** and select **Report Fields.**

3. Open the field by clicking on the blue field name.

4. Enter the client-specific text in the space provided and click **Save & Edit Next** (if there are other fields to edit) or **Save & Close** (Figure 3.19).

**FIGURE 3.19**

Enter the client-specific text in the space provided and click Save & Edit Next (if there are other fields to edit) or Save & Close.

## Edit Report Field                                           ×

### Mission Statement

**B**    *I*    <u>U</u>    ≔        ≔        ⊞

> Island Escape provides superior swimming pool maintenance that exceeds expectations so families can enjoy time together.

[ Save ]    [ Cancel ]

*Source:* Xero Limited

## Understanding the Structure of Report Templates

Report templates refer to sets of report skeletons that are standardized at the firm level, but used at the client level. They provide a framework so that reports generated at the client level are consistent across the practice. They also save the work of formatting reports in separate organizations. A report template can be a customization of a single report, such as an income statement with expense groupings, or it can be a pack of many reports, including lots of text narratives.

## Navigating the Report Templates Screen

The Templates screen has three tabs for various states of templates: Ready to Use, Draft, and Archive. Only the Ready to Use templates are available to the client organization. Draft templates are in progress, and Archived reports are no longer used.

By hovering over the template line, an options menu, indicated by a blue arrow, will appear. This menu will allow you to manage the template, including copying, renaming, archiving, and deleting.

## Creating Report Templates

Report templates can be created a number of ways. They can be created from scratch or edited from templates provided by Xero. The provided templates include:

- Law Firm
- Professional Services
- Retail
- Sample Compilation Report
- Prepared Financial Statements
- Schedule C

You can view the contents of a template by opening it, then using the Contents pull-down at the top of the report. If there is a report template that is similar to what you would like to create, it will save time to copy, then edit an existing template.

To copy a report template:

1. Navigate to the **Reports** tab in Xero HQ.
2. Use the **New Template** pull-down to select **Copy from** (Figure 3.20).
3. Choose the template to copy.
4. Enter a **Name** for the new template.
5. Add an optional **Description**.
6. Click **Copy**.

The new copy will now be listed in the **Draft** tab of Report Templates where it can be edited for use in client files.

**FIGURE 3.20**

Use the New Template pulldown to select Copy from.

*Source:* Xero Limited

Alternatively, a new, blank report can be created.

To create a new, blank report template:

1. Navigate to the **Reports** tab in Xero HQ.
2. Use the **New Template** pull-down to select **New Template**.
3. Use the **+Add report link** to access a list of reports that can be added to the template. Most common reports can be added to the template. You can also add reports that are included in other report templates (Figure 3.21).
4. Click **Add.**

**FIGURE 3.21**

Use the +Add report link to access a list of reports that can be added to the template. Most common reports can be added to the template. You can also add reports that are included in other report templates.

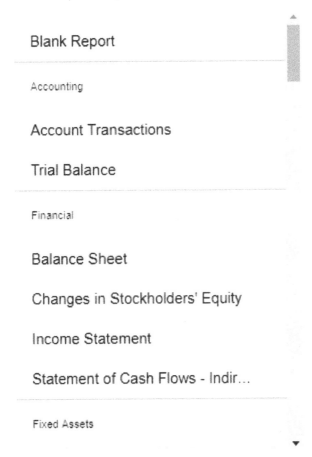

Blank Report

Accounting

Account Transactions

Trial Balance

Financial

Balance Sheet

Changes in Stockholders' Equity

Income Statement

Statement of Cash Flows - Indir...

Fixed Assets

*Source:* Xero Limited

## Editing Report Templates

Report templates can be customized to standardize sets of reports for clients.

At the top of the report template is a pull-down listing the contents included in the template (Figure 3.22). Use the left and right arrows to scroll through the contents. Click the blue **Edit** link to modify which reports are included in and the order of the reports. Add a report by using the **+Add a Report** link at the bottom of the list. To remove a report from the template, use the **X** that appears on the right of the report (Figure 3.23). To reorder the contents, drag and drop the report with your cursor.

The **Report Settings** button at the top of the screen manages settings for the whole template. Use this screen to add comparative balances, choose between accrual and cash basis, and show decimals.

To include a Contents or Cover page with the template, use the **Options** pull-down on the right to select **Publishing**. Set the Publishing defaults to include the pages desired.

When the report template is final, click **Ready to use**. This will make it available to the firm's client organizations.

**FIGURE 3.22**

At the top of the report template is a pulldown listing the contents included in the template.

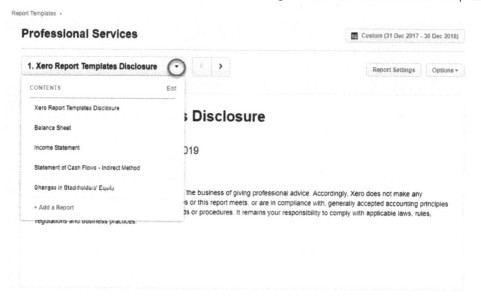

*Source:* Xero Limited

**FIGURE 3.23**

To remove a report from the template, use the X that appears on the right of the report.

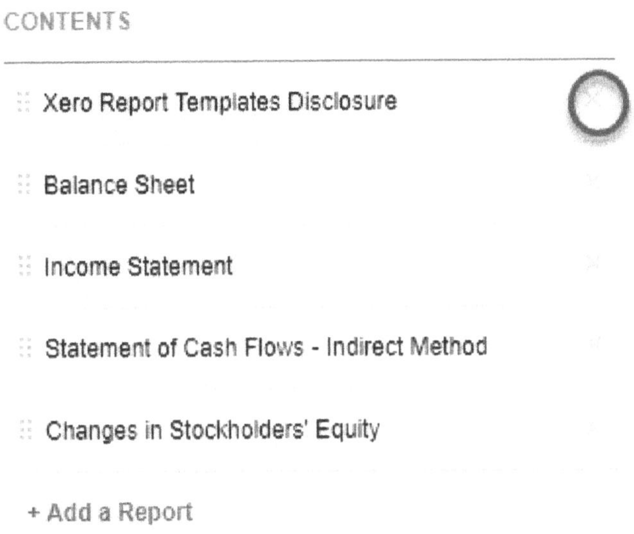

CONTENTS

⠿ Xero Report Templates Disclosure

⠿ Balance Sheet

⠿ Income Statement

⠿ Statement of Cash Flows - Indirect Method

⠿ Changes in Stockholders' Equity

+ Add a Report

*Source:* Xero Limited

## Editing Reports within Templates

Editing a report within a template in Xero HQ is fundamentally identical to editing those same reports in a client organization. See Chapter 16 for more about the report layout editor. One difference is the availability of report fields in text boxes. Reports in Xero HQ have more scalable, narrative power when report fields are used.

To add a field to a text box in a report:

1. Place your cursor where you would like to insert a field.
2. Use the **Insert Field** pull-down on the right to select the field to insert (Figure 3.24).

**FIGURE 3.24**

Use the Insert Field pulldown on the right to select the field to insert.

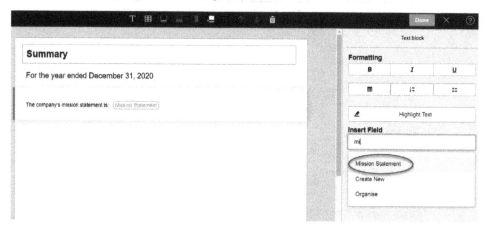

*Source:* Xero Limited

## Using Report Templates in a Client Organization

Because report templates are only the framework for reports and do not hold financial data, you must run reports from a client organization. In the organization, navigate to **Accounting**, then **Reports**. Choose the **Advisor** tab at the top of the screen to view available report templates. Click the desired report set, and it will open in the browser populated with client data.

# Ask

Xero Ask is a secure portal for the exchange of information from clients to advisors. Queries are sent to clients and clients return the requested information, all within Xero.

## Creating a Query

A query is a group of questions or information requests that will be sent to a client. There are six question types that can be added to a query:

- **Checkbox:** select one or more choices
- **File attachment:** submit a file, limited to 25MB
- **Multiple choice:** select only one choice
- **Multiple text entry:** submit more than one text answer
- **Text entry:** submit one text answer
- **Yes/No:** choose yes or no

**FIGURE 3.25**

Click the green New query button at the top right.

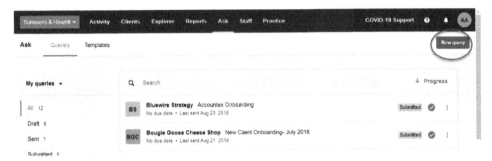

*Source:* Xero Limited

Creating a client query is similar to creating a form in a form app. To create a new query:

1. Navigate to the **Ask** menu at the top of the Xero HQ screen.
2. Click the green **New query** button at the top right (Figure 3.25).
3. You can elect to use a query template.
4. Enter a name for the request in **Query name**. It could be related to a specific process, like Onboarding, or a time of the year, like Year-End Tax Planning.
5. Enter an optional **Financial period**.
6. Enter an optional **Due date**.
7. Click **Save and continue** (Figure 3.26).
8. Select the recipients who will receive the query or click the **Save** button at the top right to move on without selecting recipients.
9. Add questions to the query, organized by section, if desired.

## Creating a Query Template

If you will be requesting the same information for multiple clients, such as for client onboarding, you may want to create a query template. Query templates are listed in the Templates tab in Ask. They are filtered by Published and Draft on the left.

To create a query template:

1. Navigate to the **Ask** menu at the top of the Xero HQ screen.
2. Select **Templates** at the top left (Figure 3.27).
3. Click the green **New template** button at the top right.
4. Enter a **Template name** and **Template description**.

**FIGURE 3.26**

Click Save and continue.

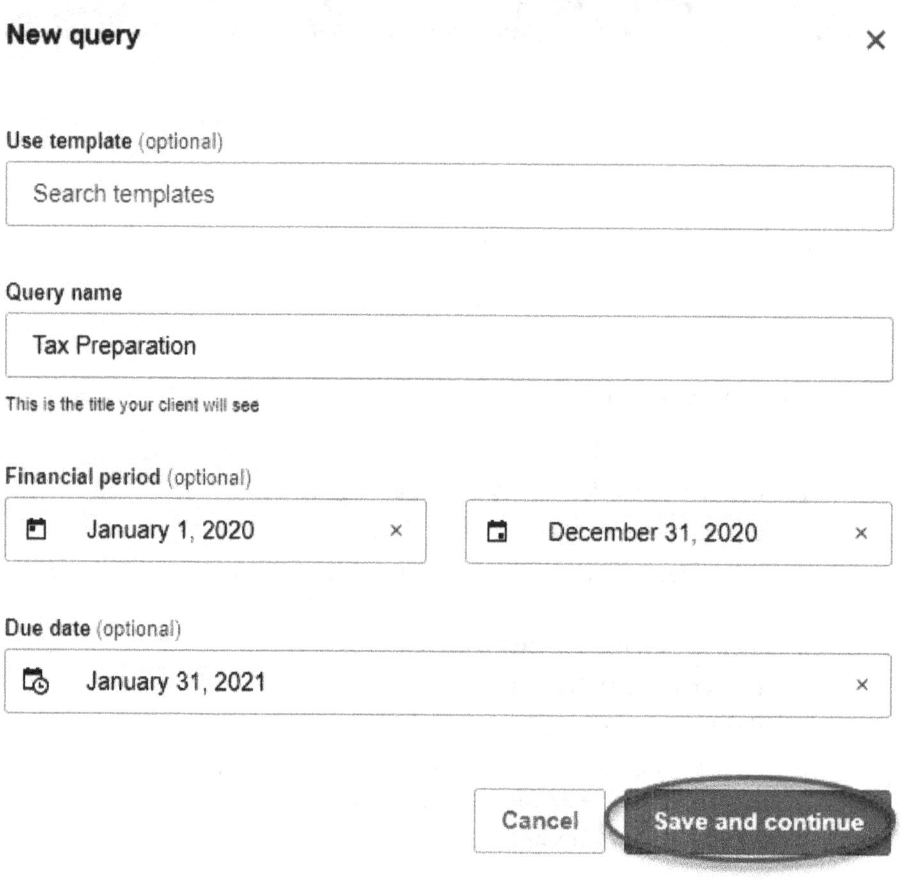

**New query**                                                                    ✕

Use template (optional)

Search templates

Query name

Tax Preparation

This is the title your client will see

Financial period (optional)

📅   January 1, 2020                      ✕        📅   December 31, 2020              ✕

Due date (optional)

📅   January 31, 2021                                                               ✕

Cancel          **Save and continue**

*Source:* Xero Limited

5. Click **Create**.
6. Add questions to the query, organized by section, if desired.
7. Click **Publish**.

## Sending a Query

Once a query has been created, it can be sent to one or more recipients. Recipients will receive an email that a request has been sent. The email will contain a link to the Ask query. In order to view and respond, users must have a Xero account. If the recipient does not, Xero will prompt them to create one.

**FIGURE 3.27**

Select Templates at the top left.

*Source:* Xero Limited

To send a query:

1. Navigate to the **Ask** menu at the top of the Xero HQ screen.
2. Select **Queries** at the top left.
3. Choose the query to send and click **Send query**.
4. Make any changes to the email copy and click **Send**.

## Reviewing Query Submissions

When the client responds to the query, you will receive an email and receive an alert in the Activity feed. The query does not have to be completed. Even one answered question will trigger the email and alert. View the client responses by opening the query.

# Staff

User permissions are covered in Chapter 6; however, it is a best practice to use Settings for nonstaff users and manage firm staff through Xero HQ.

To add staff to Xero HQ:

1. Navigate to the **Staff** menu at the top of the Xero HQ screen.
2. Click the **Invite** staff button at the top right.
3. Enter the staff member's name and email.
4. Click **Next**.
5. Choose the appropriate HQ permission: Standard or Administrator.
6. To allow the staff to edit report templates, check the box under **Extra permissions**.
7. Click **Invite to Xero HQ**.

8. The next screen will allow you to select which clients the staff has access to. Select each by checking the box to the left and click **Next**.

9. Choose specific permissions for the staff.

10. Click **Save**.

Staff members are managed on the main Staff screen. Use the overflow menu at the right to change permissions or to remove from the practice.

# Practice

## Practice Overview in Xero HQ

To see a dashboard of your practice, navigate to the **Practice** tab, then **Overview**. Each section of the Practice tab is a stand-alone tile (Figure 3.28). Tiles will show an overview of your firm, including your status and advisor directory statistics. It also displays your Xero account manager with contact details and lists partner resources available. The options

**FIGURE 3.28**

To see a dashboard of your practice, navigate to the Practice tab, then Overview. Each section of the Practice tab is a standalone tile.

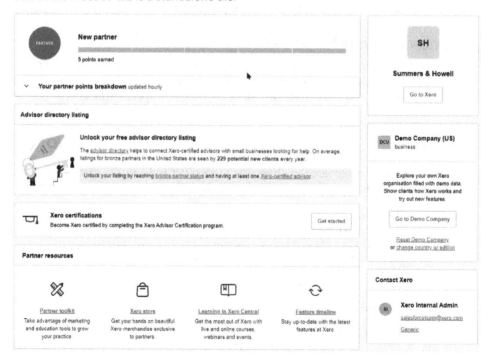

*Source:* Xero Limited

available to you will depend on your status with Xero. Tiles that may be available to you are described later.

### Import Clients from Xero Practice Manager

Xero Practice Manager (XPM) is a platform for firm workflow, time management, and productivity metrics. It is available to Xero partners, either for a fee or comped, depending on the level of the advisor.

One of the tiles in the Practice tab is an option to import clients from XPM into Xero HQ.

### Redirect to Practice's Xero Org

In the top right corner is a tile that displays a link to the firm's Xero organization.

### Partner Status

Xero recognizes its accountant and bookkeeper partners by bestowing status levels based on points. Points are awarded based on subscriptions paid by the practice, organizations invited into by the client, and the use of Xero-owned software and modules, like Hubdoc, WorkflowMax, Expenses, and Projects.

Levels of status range from Bronze to Group Platinum. Benefits scale with status and include free access to Xero Practice Manager, funds for co-branded marketing, conversion support and discounts on subscriptions. The Partner Status tile on the Practice tab lets you know what level your firm is and the number of points needed to reach the next tier. It also includes a pull-down that shows the specific breakdown of points earned (Figure 3.29).

### Demo Company Access

Xero offers a demo company prepopulated with fictitious data so users can try features without worry. The Demo Company operates like a real company using Xero and allows access to all of the modules and features of Xero. The Demo Company is specific to the user, and as such, no additional users can be added. It can, however, be connected to third-party applications, which makes it a wonderful testing ground. Changes made in the Demo Company will remain even if the user logs out; however, Xero typically resets the company every 28 days.

To access the Demo Company from Xero HQ:

1. Navigate to the **Practice** menu at the top of the screen and choose **Overview**.
2. Click the link **Go to Demo Company** on the right side.

3

**FIGURE 3.29**

The Partner Status tile on the Practice tab lets you know what level your firm is and the number of points needed to reach the next tier. It also includes a pulldown that shows the specific breakdown of points earned.

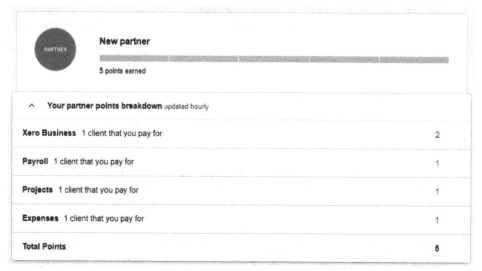

| | | |
|---|---|---|
| **PARTNER** | **New partner** | |
| | 5 points earned | |
| ∧ **Your partner points breakdown** updated hourly | | |
| **Xero Business** 1 client that you pay for | | 2 |
| **Payroll** 1 client that you pay for | | 1 |
| **Projects** 1 client that you pay for | | 1 |
| **Expenses** 1 client that you pay for | | 1 |
| **Total Points** | | 6 |

*Source:* Xero Limited

There is a link to **Reset Demo Company,** which will clear all user changes in the organization and return the file to the original data set. There is also a link to **Change country or edition**. To practice, be sure that you are using the United States edition of Xero (Figure 3.30).

### Advisor Directory Listing

One of the most impactful benefits of achieving bronze status is a listing on the Xero Advisor Directory. The Advisor Directory is available to small businesses looking for assistance with Xero. The Advisor directory listing tile shows your listing's performance in the previous month, including search appearances, listing views, and referrals. Xero also calculates a conversion percentage, which represents the ratio of referrals to search appearances (Figure 3.31).

The tile also contains redirect links to your listing on the Advisor Directory, as potential clients would see it, as well as a **Manage listing** button. Advisor listings are discussed more fully later in this chapter.

### Contact Xero

The Contact Xero tile on the right shows your assigned account manager and his or her contact details.

**FIGURE 3.30**

There is also a link to Change country or edition. To practice, be sure that you are using the United States edition of Xero.

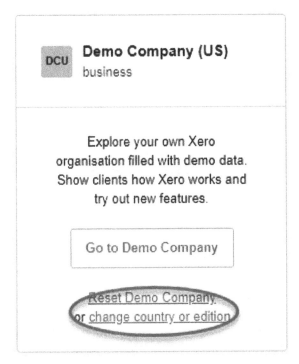

*Source:* Xero Limited

### Xero Certifications

The Xero certification tile shows how many staff members of the practice hold Xero certifications.

### Partner Resources

The Partner resources tile is a collection of Xero websites that contain important information for partners, including the Partner toolkit, the Xero store, education available in Xero Central, and the Xero feature timeline.

## Advisory Directory

For full access to your Advisor Directory listing, navigate to **Practice** then **Advisor directory.** On the left of the screen are tabs: About, Practice details, Contact information, and Your staff.

FIGURE 3.31

Xero also calculates a conversion percentage which represents the ratio of referrals to search appearances.

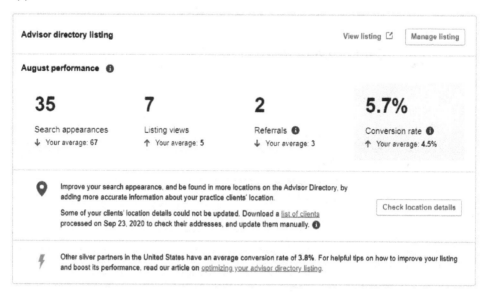

*Source:* Xero Limited

The **About** tab contains the date that your listing was published, with a link to the view of the listing that small businesses will see. It also has a link to tips for optimizing your listing.

Some keys for getting more views in the advisory directory:

- Be sure clients are geotagged for location. Location is one of the main filters in the directory search.
- Add industries for your clients. This also influences results.
- If you have more than one office, make sure all are listed.
- Increase your status—the higher the status, the higher the listing.

The **Practice details** tab shows an input screen for entering or updating your listing details. When details are entered, use the **Publish** button at the bottom to submit.

The **Contact information** allows you to manage how potential clients who find you in the directory can contact you. This is also where you will enter your office locations.

For virtual only offices, check the box next to **We're an online practice without a public office location.** Selecting this option will use your client's locations to help leads find you.

For physical locations, enter the address in the Full street address field. Xero will search for identifiable locations. You can add up to nine additional locations using the **+Add another office** link at the bottom.

The **Your staff** tab shows a listing of your staff and allows you to select to have their profiles included on your practice directory listing. The profile narratives are shown on the screen. To update a staff member's profile, he or she should update their profile in their own settings. To include a staff member profile on the advisor directory, check the box to the left and click the **Publish** button at the bottom.

## Chart of Accounts

One of the most requested features of Xero is chart of accounts templates that can be applied across organizations within the practice. Xero has started to build out that functionality by creating a Chart of accounts library in the Practice tab.

At the time of writing, there are ten preset charts of accounts that can be customized. Each chart of accounts can be viewed by selecting it from the listing (Figure 3.32). Each account has a four-digit code, an account type, tax rate, and report code. As discussed earlier in this chapter, report codes are becoming increasingly important as Xero builds out more practice-level functionality.

To customize a chart of accounts:

1. Navigate to the **Practice** menu at the top of the screen and choose **Chart of Accounts**.
2. Choose a template to begin with and use the **Copy template** button on the right to create a duplicate to be edited. This will keep the original template unchanged.
3. Rename the template and click **Copy**.
4. Add additional general ledger accounts to the Chart of Accounts by using the **New account** button at the top right. Enter the details for the new account in the fields provided.
5. Click **Save**.
6. Remove accounts from the template by selecting the account to be removed and using the **Delete account** link in the top right of the screen.

Practice level charts of accounts, including customized, will be listed in the **What chart of accounts would you like to use?** pull-down in the first setup screen for new organizations.

3

**FIGURE 3.32**

At the time of writing, there are ten preset charts of accounts, but none are customizable. Each chart of accounts can be viewed by selecting it from the listing.

Chart of accounts library
**Non Profit**

| Code | Name | Type | Tax Rate | Report Code |
|------|------|------|----------|-------------|
| 1100 | Short Term Investments | Current Asset | Tax Exempt | ASS.CUR.STI |
| 1210 | Allowance for Doubtful Accounts | Current Asset | Tax Exempt | ASS.CUR.REC.ACR.ADA |
| 1220 | Membership Dues Receivable | Current Asset | Tax Exempt | ASS.CUR.REC.ACR |
| 1230 | Grants Receivable | Current Asset | Tax Exempt | ASS.CUR.REC.ACR |
| 1250 | Employee Advances | Current Asset | Tax Exempt | ASS.CUR.REC.EMP |
| 1260 | Other Receivables | Current Asset | Tax Exempt | ASS.CUR.REC |
| 1300 | Prepaid Expenses | Current Asset | Tax Exempt | ASS.CUR.REC.PRE |
| 1350 | Deferred Tax Asset | Current Asset | Tax Exempt | ASS.CUR.TAX.DEF |
| 1400 | Inventory | Current Asset | Tax Exempt | ASS.CUR.INY |
| 1410 | Raw Materials | Current Asset | Tax Exempt | ASS.CUR.INY.RAW |
| 1420 | Work in Progress | Current Asset | Tax Exempt | ASS.CUR.INY.WIP |
| 1430 | Finished Goods | Current Asset | Tax Exempt | ASS.CUR.INY.FIN |
| 1500 | Office Equipment | Fixed Asset | Tax Exempt | ASS.NCA.FIX.PLA |
| 1505 | Accumulated Depreciation: Office Equipment | Fixed Asset | Tax Exempt | ASS.NCA.FIX.PLA.ACC |
| 1510 | Computer Equipment | Fixed Asset | Tax Exempt | ASS.NCA.FIX.PLA |

*Source:* Xero Limited

## Connected Apps

Some applications are connected not only to client organizations but also to Xero HQ. This allows alerts to populate in the Activity feed. Apps that are connected to HQ are shown on the Connected apps screen under Practice. For a list of apps that can connect to HQ, visit the Xero App Marketplace at www.apps.xero.com.

# Navigating through Xero

*Xero's user interface is intuitive to use with clean design, no accounting lingo, and clear menu items. It makes for a very efficient workflow. It allows any user (accountant or not) to fully leverage each tool. And my clients love running their businesses on the go with the slick mobile app!*

—*Marie Phillips, Founder and CEO of Connected Accounting*

Xero is presented with a clean user interface, more intuitive than other small business platforms. Where other accounting software feels like functions are added where there is space, Xero is deliberate about its design, yielding a product that is streamlined and linear.

## Accessing the Xero Organization

There are several ways to access a Xero organization. You may be invited into a specific client file and emailed a link directly to that organization. Someone at your firm may add you to many organizations at once. If you are a user on multiple accounts, you may be logging into Xero HQ, which is an advisor platform discussed in Chapter 3.

This chapter will focus on navigating within the client file or organization.

## General Tips

Throughout Xero, any blue text or shapes indicate links and can be clicked. The blue link may be constant or may appear by hovering the mouse over black text. In some newer screens, header tabs are not in blue and may be less obvious, but are functional.

To open a new screen in a Xero organization without losing your place, hold down the **Control** key while clicking on a link. This will open the link in another browser tab. Refresh often while working between the two tabs to be sure you are working in a current view. To work in more than one organization at one time, use different browsers (i.e., Chrome and Safari) or open incognito windows.

# Dashboard

When you log into a client file or organization, you will land on the Xero Dashboard (Figure 4.1). The header of the client Dashboard is blue. If instead you see a black header, you are in Xero HQ, rather than a client file.

Most of the navigation from this screen will occur from the header menus: **Dashboard**, **Business**, **Accounting**, **Projects** (only visible if the Xero subscription includes Projects), and **Contacts**. Clicking the **Dashboard** menu item from anywhere in the system will return you to this screen.

On the Dashboard are several tiles for quick access to the most used functions of Xero. The default tile layout is Bank (including credit card) Accounts on the left and Business Performance, Account Watchlist, Invoices, Bills, and Expense Claims on the right. The layout of the tiles can be edited by scrolling to the bottom of the page and clicking **Edit dashboard**. This allows you to hide any tiles from the Dashboard by clicking the **Hide** link in the top right of the tile. You can also move the tiles by dragging and dropping in a new position. To save the edited layout, click **Save Changes** at the bottom of the screen.

**FIGURE 4.1**

When you log into a client file or organization, you will land on the Xero Dashboard.

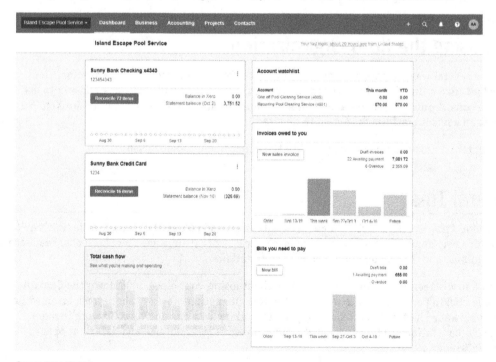

*Source:* Xero Limited

**FIGURE 4.2**

The bank and credit card account tiles provide a snapshot of the current status of the account. If there are bank lines to be reconciled, that number of lines is indicated in a blue button within the tile.

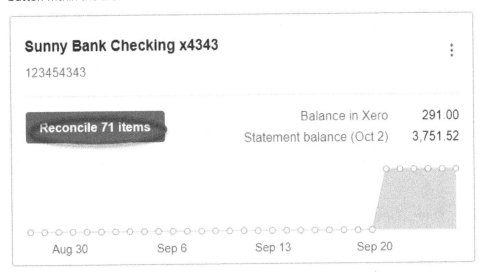

*Source:* Xero Limited

The bank and credit card account tiles provide a snapshot of the current status of the account. If there are bank lines to be reconciled, that number of lines is indicated in a blue button within the tile (Figure 4.2).

Clicking on the button will redirect you to the bank reconciliation screen for that bank account. The tile shows two balance values: balance in Xero and statement balance. **Balance in Xero** is the general ledger balance for the bank account. Unreconciled bank lines have not been coded or posted; therefore, they are not included in this balance. **Statement balance** shows a calculated running balance of the account through the date in parentheses, which is the latest date of any bank transactions in Xero. The statement balance will include unreconciled bank transactions. Below the balances is a graphical representation of the balance in the account.

In the top right corner of the tile are three dots, referred to as an overflow menu. This menu shows all options for working with the bank account (Figure 4.3). The same menu is found in several places in Xero and will be explained more in Chapter 9.

The **Business performance tile** shows standardized metrics as selected by the user. Ratios are chosen by navigating to **Accounting**, then **Reports,** and selecting **Business Performance.** See Chapter 18 for more details on the available metrics.

The **Account watchlist** is a marquis of general ledger account balances of your choosing (Figure 4.4). Typical uses for this include clearing accounts or due to or from related entities. Some advisors also include key revenue or expense accounts.

**FIGURE 4.3**

The same menu is found in several places in Xero and will be explained more in the Banking chapter.

| Find | New | Reconcile |
|------|-----|-----------|
| Account Transactions | Spend Money | Reconcile Account |
| Bank Statements | Receive Money | Bank Rules |
| | Transfer Money | Reconciliation Report |
| | | Import a Statement |

Sunny Bank Checking x4343 123454343

**FIGURE 4.4**

Typical uses for this include clearing accounts or due to or from related entities. Some advisors also include key revenue or expense accounts.

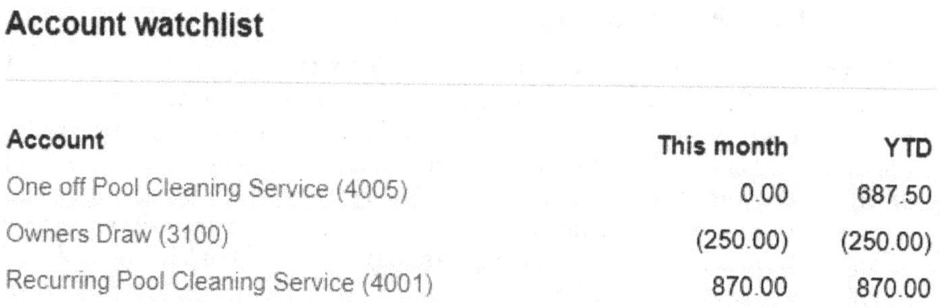

## Account watchlist

| Account | This month | YTD |
|---------|-----------|-----|
| One off Pool Cleaning Service (4005) | 0.00 | 687.50 |
| Owners Draw (3100) | (250.00) | (250.00) |
| Recurring Pool Cleaning Service (4001) | 870.00 | 870.00 |

To add an account to the Watchlist:

1. Navigate to **Accounting**, then **Advanced**.
2. Select **Chart of Accounts**.
3. Select the account to be listed by clicking on the account name.
4. Check the box to the left of **Show on Dashboard Watchlist**.
5. Click **Save**.

**FIGURE 4.5**

There is also a graphical representation of invoices or bills by week.

**FIGURE 4.6**

There is also a graphical representation of invoices or bills by week.

## Expense claims

| New claim | 1 draft | 0.00 |
| --- | --- | --- |
| | 1 to review | 243.92 |
| | 1 to pay | 457.89 |

| Recent submissions | # | Total |
| --- | --- | --- |
| Amanda Aguillard, CPA | 1 | 243.92 |

The **Invoices owed to you** and **Bills you need to pay** tiles show summaries of accounts receivable and accounts payable, respectively (Figure 4.5). On these tiles there is a button to create a **New sales invoice** or **New bill**. There is a summary of balances, including draft, awaiting payment, and overdue. There is also a graphical representation of invoices or bills by week.

The final tile in the default layout is the **Expense Claims** tile. The tile shows a summary of claims to be reviewed and paid (Figure 4.6).

# Business Tab

The Business tab on the Dashboard is where most of the work items related to running a business are found.

**FIGURE 4.7**

A relatively new feature in Xero, Short-term cash flow gives an overview of the expected cash movement in bank and credit card accounts based on invoices and bills.

*Source:* Xero Limited

## Short-Term Cash Flow

A relatively new feature in Xero, **Short-term cash flow** gives an overview of the expected cash movement in bank and credit card accounts based on invoices and bills (Figure 4.7). For more information on Short-term cash flow, see Chapter 18.

## Business Snapshot

**Business snapshot** is a limited dashboard of preset metrics embedded in Xero (Figure 4.8). For more information on Business snapshot, see Chapter 18.

## Sales Overview, Quotes, and Invoices

The next three menu items are all related to managing and levying sales invoices. **Sales overview** will redirect the user to the main sales module, whereas **Quotes** and **Invoices** are quick links for creating those two items.

## Purchase Overview, Bills to Pay, and Purchase Orders

Like the sales options earlier, **Purchase overview** will bring the user to the main Purchases screen. **Bills to pay** and **Purchase orders** are redirects to those specific functions.

**FIGURE 4.8**

Business snapshot is a limited dashboard of preset metrics embedded in Xero.

*Source:* Xero Limited

## Expense Claims

This is a link to **Xero Expenses**, an expense reimbursement feature included with an Established Xero subscription. For more information on Expenses, see Chapter 19.

## Products and Services

Previously known in Xero as Inventory items, **Products and services** is where tracked and untracked inventory items are managed. To learn more, see Chapter 8.

## Checks

This link is for the management of paper checks issued by the company.

# Accounting Tab

The **Accounting** tab on the Dashboard includes features that would be done periodically or by an accountant or bookkeeper. It also includes features only available to Advisor level users.

## Bank Accounts

The **Bank accounts** screen will show all the bank and credit card accounts in the organization, including those that have been hidden from the main Dashboard (Figure 4.9). It also includes functions affecting bank and credit card accounts.

## Reports

The **Reports** screen is where standard, custom, and published reports can be found.

## Advanced

The **Advanced** menu contains items around financial settings and advisor features, like journal entries, bulk recoding, and fixed asset management.

## Reports (Starred) and Advanced (Starred)

These are selected favorited items from the Reports and Advanced screens for quick access. Favorited items are specific to the user that is logged in. To edit the features listed in this shortcut, navigate to the Report or Advanced screen, and toggle on or off the blue star to the left of the feature (Figure 4.10).

**FIGURE 4.9**

The Bank accounts screen will show all of the bank and credit cards accounts in the organization, including those that have been hidden from the main Dashboard.

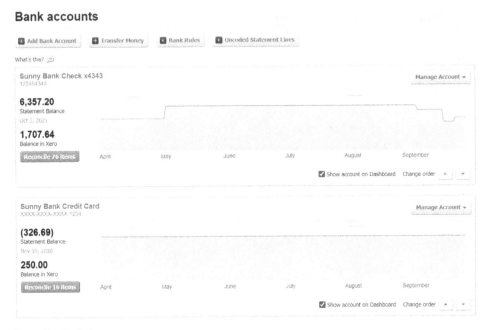

*Source:* Xero Limited

# Projects

Xero **Projects** is a job costing and management system that is available in the Established subscription plan. See Chapter 20 for more details.

# Contacts

The **Contacts** tab is where all contacts are managed. Under this tab, Xero also differentiates between **Customer** and **Suppliers** and gives quick links to any contact groups that are created. Learn more about Contacts in Chapter 7.

# Quick Add (+)

In the upper right of the screen, you will see a + icon. This menu allows users to create new transactions quickly and easily from anywhere in Xero, rather than navigating to a particular module (Figure 4.11).

**FIGURE 4.10**

To edit the features listed in this shortcut, navigate to the Report or Advanced screen, and toggle on or off the blue star to the left of the feature.

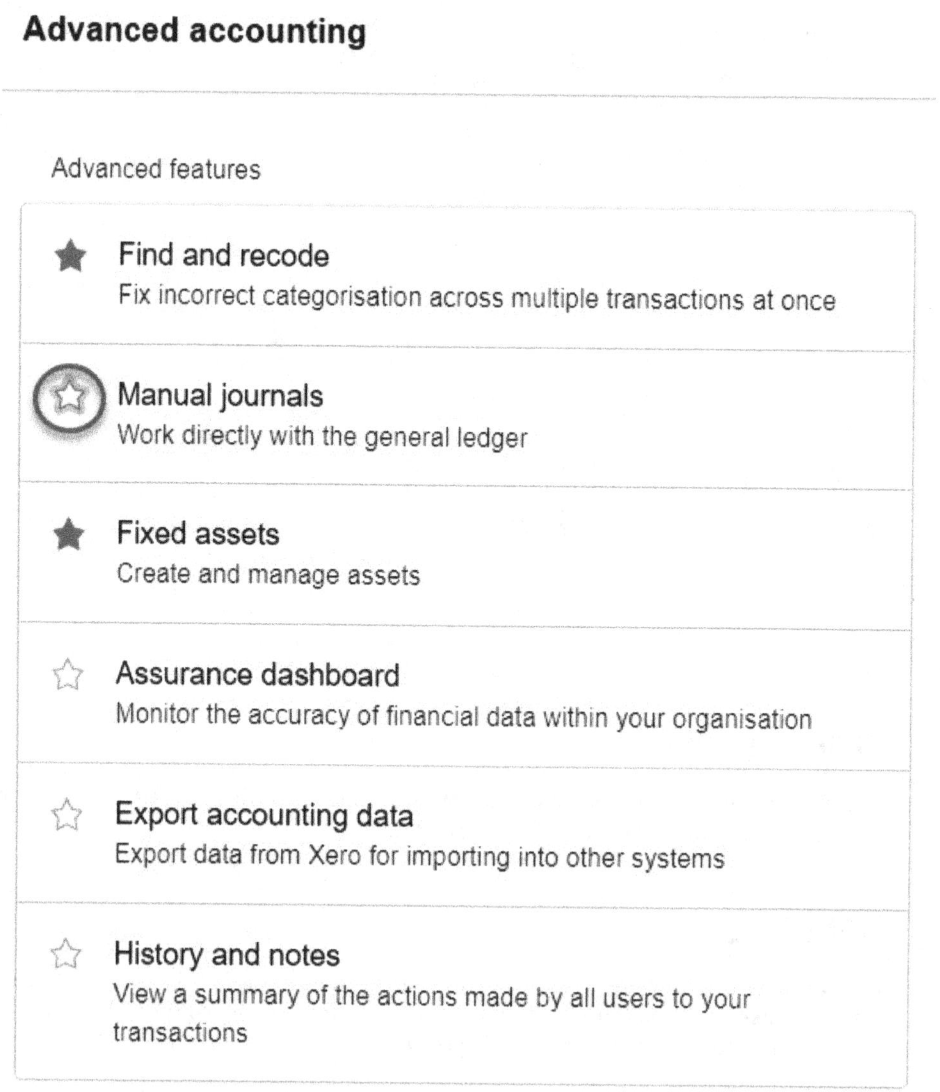

## Advanced accounting

Advanced features

 **Find and recode**
Fix incorrect categorisation across multiple transactions at once

 **Manual journals**
Work directly with the general ledger

 **Fixed assets**
Create and manage assets

 **Assurance dashboard**
Monitor the accuracy of financial data within your organisation

 **Export accounting data**
Export data from Xero for importing into other systems

 **History and notes**
View a summary of the actions made by all users to your transactions

*Source: Xero Limited*

**FIGURE 4.11**

In the upper right of the screen, you will see a + icon. This menu allows users to create new transactions quickly and easily from anywhere in Xero, rather than navigating to a particular module.

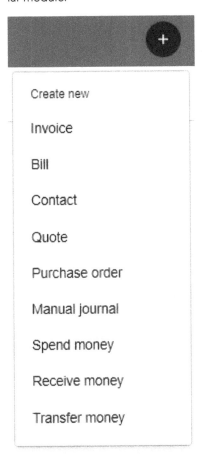

Create new

Invoice

Bill

Contact

Quote

Purchase order

Manual journal

Spend money

Receive money

Transfer money

*Source:* Xero Limited

# Search

**Global search**, represented by a looking glass, allows users to search for contacts and transactions throughout Xero without first navigating to other screens. By typing a name or other information in the search bar, Xero will filter relevant results (Figure 4.12).

**FIGURE 4.12**

Global search, represented by a looking glass, allows users to search for contacts and transactions throughout Xero without first navigating to other screens. By typing a name or other information in the search bar, Xero will filter relevant results.

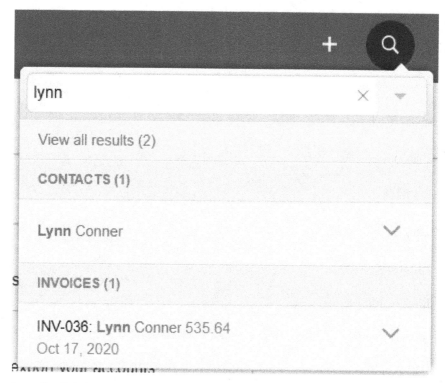

*Source:* Xero Limited

# Notifications

The bell icon at the upper right is a notifications feed. Alerts regarding bank feeds, file uploads, and other system issues will appear here. Note that the alert feed is specific to the user, not the Xero organization, so the feed will include alerts for all Xero organizations that the user has access to. To manage notifications, use the **Settings** link at the bottom of the feed (Figure 4.13).

**FIGURE 4.13**

To manage notifications, use the Settings link at the bottom of the feed.

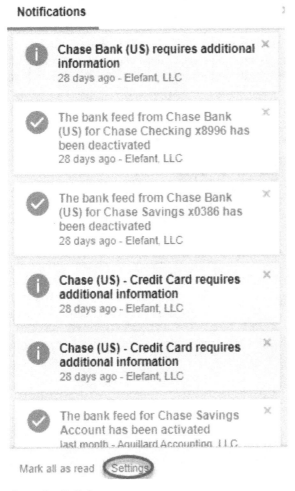

# Help

The question mark icon at the top right of the screen links to a dynamic help menu (Figure 4.14). The first few lines of the menu will be topics relevant to the current screen. Below is a redirect link to Xero's online support database called **Xero Central.** Xero Central is an excellent resource for questions about product features. The last link on the Help menu is a redirect to send a ticket to Xero's customer support department. Xero does not have a telephone number for customer support; however, response times to email support are generally quick, and a customer support team member will call you back if you request that in your ticket submission.

## User Profile

The last link on the top right of the screen, usually indicated by your initials, is your account profile. You can edit your details and elect to have your profile shared on Xero's advisor database. This is the same profile edit screen that can be reached from Xero HQ, discussed in Chapter 3.

**FIGURE 4.14**

The question mark icon at the top right of the screen links to a dynamic help menu.

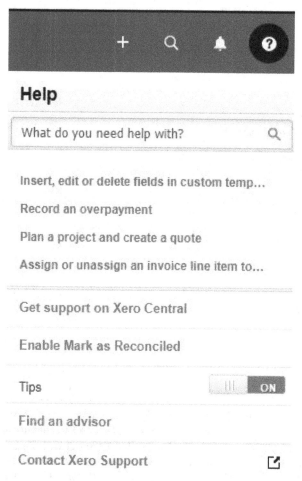

*Source:* Xero Limited

**FIGURE 4.15**

Xero has a simple file box embedded in the software. (Figure 4.15) This allows users to upload or email static (non-moving) files to the Xero organization, where they can be stored or attached to transactions

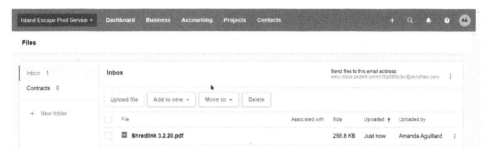

*Source:* Xero Limited

In the same pull-down are settings, accessible by selecting **Account**. This is where you can update login details and password, and set up two-step authentication. Two-step authentication requires the use of an authenticator application on your smartphone. More advisors are requiring employees, and even clients, to use two-step authentication.

# Other Features and Apps under the Organization Name

There are other features and applications accessible under the organization's name in the top left corner.

## Files

Xero has a simple file box embedded in the software (Figure 4.15). This allows users to upload or email static (nonmoving) files to the Xero organization, where they can be stored or attached to transactions. Xero will accept .doc and .xls files, but .pdf files are best. Folders can be created to organize files.

## Settings

Users will find basic account settings, like organization details and default copy for out-going emails, here. You will learn more about settings in Chapter 6.

## Subscription and Billing

This screen will display the holder of the subscription and the current subscription level. It is also where a user may change or cancel the subscription.

## Additional Applications

The remaining options are redirect links to other Xero modules (like Projects or Xero HQ), applications owned by Xero (like Hubdoc or WorkflowMax) or third-party applications with which Xero has a partnership (like Gusto).

# Creating a Xero Organization

*I used to think the absence of sub-accounts was a drawback. Now I'm a raving fan. Being able to design different sets of financials for the accountant at year end vs the managers doing all the things every day has been such a godsend. I don't have to try and choose which point of view I will prioritize in my company set-up. I can have both. And I can have both without a lot of fuss.*

—*Kristen Nies Ciraldo, Owner and Field Guide of The Friday Guide*

## Creating a Xero Organization from Xero HQ

Xero HQ is Xero's partner dashboard. It has a black header and includes firm level functionality. Learn more about Xero HQ in Chapter 3.

The Client screen in Xero allows you to manage all firm clients, not just those who have a Xero file. A Client listing in Xero HQ is separate from the actual working general ledger file; thus, there are two steps to creating a company organization from Xero HQ.

The first is to create a Client in Xero HQ.

1. From Xero HQ, select **Clients** from the header menu.
2. Use the **Add client** pull-down at the top right to access **New client** (Figure 5.1).
3. Select a **Business structure** and enter **Name**, **Email**, and **Phone**.
4. Select **Create**.

Next, you will be directed to a client page in Xero HQ, where you will create the working Xero file.

1. On the right, click the **Connect to Xero** button (Figure 5.2).
2. Complete the form, including selecting a chart of accounts.
3. Select **Start Trial** to get 30 days free access or **Buy Now** to add to your partner billing account.

**FIGURE 5.1**

Use the Add client pulldown at the top right to access New client.

*Source:* Xero Limited

**FIGURE 5.2**

On the right, click the Connect to Xero button.

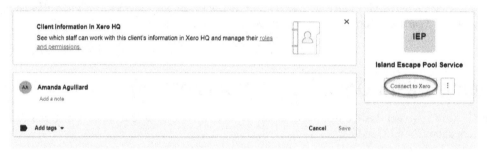

*Source:* Xero Limited

# Converting from Other Systems

Xero offers resources to help advisors migrate client historical data from other systems into Xero. For more information about outsourced conversions, contact your account manager.

# Chart of Accounts

The basis of a chart of accounts is to provide a structure for financial reporting, both now and into the future. It is the responsibility of the advisor to be able to predict which categories of revenues and expenses will need to be segregated years from now without being cumbersome in operations and reports. Thus, there is a balance between detail and simplicity. It is much easier to get it right from the start than to need to go backward and reclassify historical transactions.

Although a chart of accounts can be modified at any time, it is best to start with a custom set of accounts from the beginning. In practice, many Xero advisors will take time to develop a custom chart of accounts for each type of industry they work with, and use them over and over. This creates consistency between clients and allows for systemizing of reports and scaling of processes.

## Structure of the Chart of Accounts

Xero's general ledger is based on a simple chart of accounts framework. Every account is equal in value, and there are no subaccounts, unlike other systems. Advisors used to operating with subaccounts will see later that they are unnecessary and similar reporting can be gained by editing report layouts.

Xero has features such as Tracking Categories and Projects that will allow you to dissect data further than a general ledger account. Before creating new accounts to provide detailed financial information, consider whether one of these may allow for the granularity needed without cluttering the chart of accounts.

When creating the chart of accounts, there are four required fields and a number of optional fields.

The required fields are:

| | |
|---|---|
| **Code** | Xero will allow the account code to be up to ten alphanumeric characters or symbols. In practice, many advisors use a four-digit coding system that follows the account type, and generally within each balance sheet account from most liquid to least liquid: |

| | |
|---|---|
| 1000–1999 | Assets (with Current Assets having lower numbers) |
| 2000–2999 | Liabilities (with Current Liabilities having lower numbers) |
| 3000–3999 | Equity |
| 4000–4999 | Revenues |
| 5000–5999 | Cost of Goods Sold |
| 6000–7999 | Expenses except Cost of Goods Sold |
| 8000–9999 | Other income and expenses, typically nonoperational, such as depreciation and accruals for income tax |

| | |
|---|---|
| **Name** | Xero will allow up to 150 alphanumeric characters or symbols. |
| **Type** | Accounts must be one of these types: |

Bank Account
Current Asset
Fixed Asset
Inventory
Noncurrent Asset
Prepayment
Current Liability
Liability
Noncurrent Liability
Equity
Other Income
Revenue
Sales
Depreciation
Direct Costs
Expense
Overhead

5

| Tax Rate | The tax rate affects how sales tax is calculated. If you are unsure about the sales tax effect on a general ledger account, use Tax Exempt (0%). You can always edit the account or any transactions using the account. See Chapter 6 for more on tax rates. |
|---|---|

Optional fields are:

| Reporting Name | A reporting name appears on Reports marked (New) and Report Templates. It is only an option for nonbank accounts. |
|---|---|
| Description | A description will appear only in the Chart of Accounts screen or download. It is useful for guiding clients in knowing when an account should be used. |
| Dashboard | This must be Yes or No and will indicate whether the account is shown on the Account Watchlist on the Dashboard. |
| Expense claims | This must be Yes or No and will indicate whether the account is available to users under expense claims. |
| Enable payments | This must be Yes or No and will indicate whether the account will be an option when recording a payment on an invoice, bill, or expense claim. For bank accounts, this field should be No (which would eliminate it from payment options) or blank (which will allow payments to be posted to or from the bank account). |
| Balance | You can use this field to import conversion balances. The value must be positive for debit balances and negative for credit balances. |
| Report Code | Report codes are only available for use by Xero partners. Using report codes will allow advisors to build report templates at the practice level to be used in each client organization. Learn more about report codes in Chapter 3. |

## Importing a Chart of Accounts

In general, charts of accounts are imported during the set up of a Xero organization. However, a chart of accounts can be imported at any time, but accounts and balances existing prior to the import may be overwritten or archived.

As throughout Xero, the import file type for a chart of accounts is .csv. To import a chart of accounts from the Dashboard:

1. Select **Accounting ⮞ Advanced ⮞ Chart of accounts**.
2. Click **Import** (Figure 5.3).
3. Leave the selection of Xero for **What system are you importing from?**
4. Select **Yes** or **No** for Does the file you are importing contain account balances?
5. Browse to the .csv file prepared for import.
6. Click **Import**.

**FIGURE 5.3**

Click Import.

*Source:* Xero Limited

7. Xero will show a summary of the changes, including new, updated, deleted, and archived accounts (Figure 5.4).

A Chart of Accounts import file including a column for Report Code can be found in the digital resources link.

## Working with Accounts

General ledger accounts in Xero can be added, edited, deleted, or archived from the Chart of accounts screen found under **Accounting > Advanced**.

While the most efficient way to add accounts to the Xero organization is to import via a file, there are instances where a single account must be created.

**FIGURE 5.4**

Xero will show a summary of the changes, including new, updated, deleted and archived accounts.

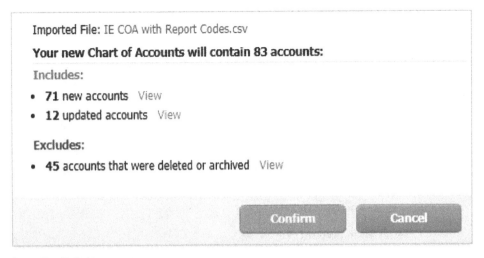

*Source:* Xero Limited

**FIGURE 5.5**

Select +Add account.

Advanced accounting ›
## Chart of accounts

*Source:* Xero Limited

**FIGURE 5.6**

The Add New Account screen will list the required and optional fields related to the account.

### Add New Account                                                    ✕

**Account Type**

Current Asset          ▾

**Code**

A unique code/number for this account (limited to 10 characters)

1250

'1250' is available

**Name**

A short title for this account (limited to 150 characters)

Deposits in transit

+ add Reporting Name

**Description** (optional)

A description of how this account should be used

**Tax**

The default tax setting for this account

Tax Exempt (0%)          ▾

☐ Show on Dashboard Watchlist

☐ Show in Expense Claims

☐ Enable payments to this account

Save        Cancel

**How account types affect your reports**

| Income Statement | Balance Sheet |
|---|---|
| Income | Current Assets |
| Revenue | Current Assets |
| Sales | Inventory |
| Less Cost of Sales | Prepayments |
| Direct Costs | Plus Bank |
| GROSS PROFIT | Bank Accounts |
| Plus Other Income | Plus Fixed Assets |
| Other Income | Fixed Assets |
| Less Expenses | Plus Non-current Assets |
| Expenses | Non-current Assets |
| Depreciation | TOTAL ASSETS |
| Overheads | Less Current Liabilities |
| NET PROFIT | Current Liabilities |
| | Less Non-current Liabilities |
| | Liabilities |
| | Non-current Liabilities |
| | NET ASSETS |
| | Equity |
| | Equity |
| | Plus Net Profit |
| | TOTAL EQUITY |

You can also modify where accounts appear in your reports using Customized Report Layouts

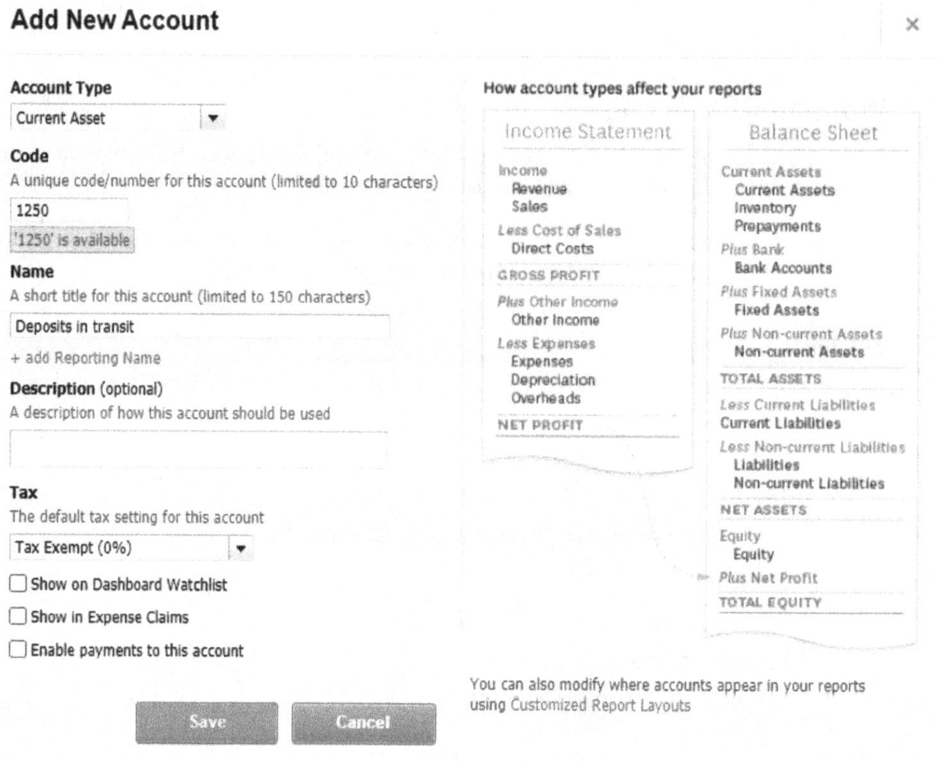

*Source:* Xero Limited

To add a nonbank account in Xero:

1. Select **+Add account** (Figure 5.5).
2. The **Add New Account** screen will list the required and optional fields related to the account (Figure 5.6).

3. Use the **Account Type** pull-down to select the type of account to be added. Note that Xero does not make any distinction among the account types Expense and Overhead, Liability and Noncurrent Liability, and Revenue and Sales.

4. Enter a unique account **Code**. If you enter a code that has previously been used, Xero will give you a warning that the code cannot be used.

5. Give the account a **Name** (and a **Reporting Name**, if desired).

6. Add an optional **Description** to help clients understand the use of the account.

7. Select the default **Tax Setting** for the account.

8. If you wish to see the account on the Account Watchlist tile on the Dashboard, select **Show on Dashboard Watchlist.**

9. If you wish for the account to be an option in Expense Claims, select **Show in Expense Claims**. (Note that some software integrations require this to be selected to work properly.)

10. If you wish for the account to be an option in applying payments for Invoices and Bills, such as a clearing account, select **Enable payments to this account**.

11. Click **Save.**

To add a bank account in Xero:

1. Select **+Add Bank Account**.

2. Use the search field to search for the bank or credit card issuer.

3. If a direct or third-party bank feed exists, Xero will filter results. Select the appropriate bank.

4. If a bank feed does not exist, you will see a message that Xero could not find the bank along with a link to **Add it anyway.** Click this link (Figure 5.7).

For banks with a bank feed, enter these details:

1. Account name: This will be the name of the bank account on the chart of accounts and will be listed on reports and within bank reconciliation. Many advisors choose to use a naming convention of the issuing bank + type of account + last four digits of the account number (i.e., Sunny Bank Credit Card x8765). A naming convention like this will make reconciliation of transfers between accounts easier and will make creating company paid expense claims seamless.

2. Account code: This is an alphanumeric code within the chart of accounts. Normally, this will be a 100 or 1,000 value.

3. Account number: The account or credit card number.

5

**FIGURE 5.7**

If a bank feed does not exist, you will see a message that Xero could not find the bank along with a link to Add it anyway. Click this link.

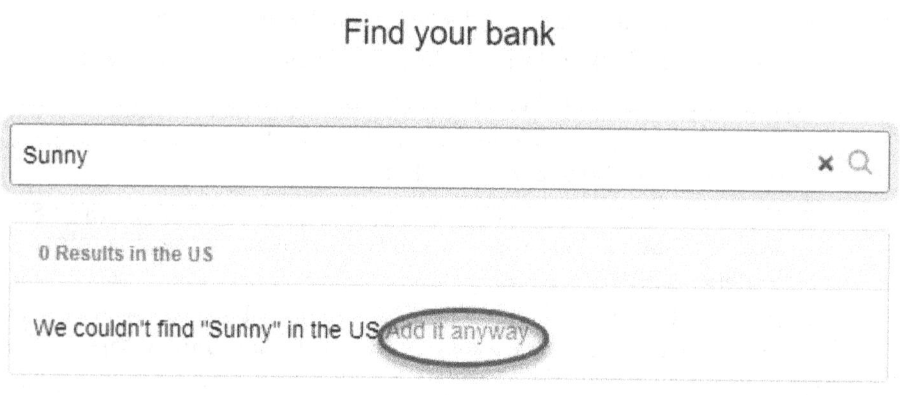

Find your bank

Sunny                                                                    × Q

0 Results in the US

We couldn't find "Sunny" in the US Add it anyway

*Source:* Xero Limited

For banks without a bank feed, enter these additional details:

1. Bank: List the banking institution.
2. Account type: If the account being set up is a credit card, indicate it here. Otherwise, select Other for all types of deposit accounts.

If you need to make changes to the name, code, or other details of an account, navigate to the chart of accounts page.

To edit an account:

1. Select the account by clicking the name of the account in blue.
2. Edit the relevant fields in the Account Details screen.
3. Click **Save.**

In some cases, accounts are no longer useful and you may wish to remove them from the chart of accounts. You can delete or archive accounts. Deleted accounts are removed forever, as if they never existed. Archived accounts are only removed from the current listing of accounts and will not be an option for transactions going forward. The history of archived accounts is retained and they can be restored.

**FIGURE 5.8**

Click the Delete or Archive button above the list of accounts.

| | Code ▲ | Name | Type | YTD |
|---|---|---|---|---|
| 🔒 | 1200 | Accounts Receivable<br>Outstanding invoices the company has issued out to the client but has not yet received in cash at balance date. | Current Asset | 0.00 |
| ☑ | 1250 | Deposits in transit | Current Asset | 0.00 |
| ☐ | 1300 | Prepayments<br>An expenditure that has been paid for in advance. | Current Asset | 0.00 |

*Source:* Xero Limited

To delete or archive an account:

1. Check the box to the left of the account that you wish to delete.
2. Click the **Delete** or **Archive** button above the list of accounts (Figure 5.8).
3. Xero will confirm that you wish to delete or archive the account. Note that if any transactions have ever been posted to an account, you cannot delete it. You will be given an option here to archive instead of deleting.
4. Click **OK** to confirm your choice.

Some special types of accounts in Xero are restricted in editing or deleting. These are locked or system accounts and are shown in the chart of accounts screen with a padlock icon left of the account code, rather than a checkbox (Figure 5.9).

**Locked accounts** include accounts where the editing or deleting could cause errors based on scheduled or anticipated transactions. Examples include accounts used for repeating invoices or bills, accounts used in bank rules, and tracked inventory accounts. Accounts that are locked are able to be edited, deleted, or archived once the bank rules or related transactions have been deleted.

**System accounts** are accounts set by Xero for specific accounting purposes. Examples are Accounts Payable, Accounts Receivable, and Current Earnings. These accounts are

**FIGURE 5.9**

Some special types of accounts in Xero are restricted in editing or deleting. These are locked or system accounts, and are shown in the chart of accounts screen with a padlock icon left of the account code, rather than a checkbox.

| | | | | |
|---|---|---|---|---|
| 🔒 | 2000 | Accounts Payable<br>Outstanding invoices the company has received from suppliers but has not yet paid at balance date | Current Liability | 0.00 |
| ☐ | 2060 | Gift Card Liability | Current Liability | 0.00 |
| 🔒 | 2100 | Unpaid Expense Claims<br>Expense claims typically made by employees/shareholder employees still outstanding. | Current Liability | 0.00 |

*Source:* Xero Limited

5

calculated by underlying transactions and, therefore, cannot be deleted, nor are journal entries allowed to be posted. Other system accounts that cannot be deleted but do allow for journal entries are Retained Earnings, Rounding, and Sales Tax. In any case, System accounts cannot be unlocked, deleted, or archived.

Even though you cannot post adjustments to system accounts directly, it is possible to create the appearance of an adjustment through report layout customization. To change the apparent balance of a system account:

1. Create a new account with a similar name, such as Accounts Receivable ADJ, giving the account a type similar to the system account (i.e., Current Asset).
2. Post the adjustment to the new account using a Manual Journal.
3. Customize the Balance Sheet by creating a row group that is named the same as the system account (i.e., Accounts Receivable).
4. Drag both the original system account and the new adjusted account under the account group, and click Done.

To learn more about Report Layout editing, see Chapter 16.

## Manually Entering Conversion Balances

In lieu of a conversion of a historical accounting system file, many advisors elect to archive the prior system backup file and start fresh in Xero. Reasons can include:

- The prior system is a mess and includes errors that the advisor does not want to migrate to Xero.
- The prior system is overly complicated and unnecessarily detailed.
- The new system will include a restructured chart of accounts that does not match in detail to the prior system.

Xero allows advisors to enter beginning or **conversion balances,** as well as selected information, rather than a full conversion of the prior data. Xero may be used without entering conversion balances, or by entering some, but not all balances. However, current account balances will not be accurate until all conversion balances are entered correctly.

To access the conversion balances screen from the organization dashboard:

1. Select **Accounting** from the top menu, then **Advanced**.
2. Select **Conversion balances**.

To enter conversion balances, you must first select the date of the conversion.

1. Enter the conversion date by selecting the **Conversion Date** button (Figure 5.10).
2. Select the month that you will begin using Xero. Note that the conversion date will be the first day of the month you select. Midmonth conversions are not accepted.

**FIGURE 5.10**

Enter the conversion date by selecting the Conversion Date button.

Advanced accounting  ›

# Conversion balances

➕ Add Comparative Balances   ▣ Conversion Date

*Source:* Xero Limited

> Xero shows the conversion date that will correspond with the beginning of the selected month, which is the day prior (Figure 5.11).

3. Click **Save**.

> The balance screen will reappear with a header including the conversion date. This screen will allow you to enter beginning balances for the client on the day you will begin to use Xero.

**FIGURE 5.11**

Xero shows the conversion date that will correspond with the beginning of the selected month, which is the day prior.

Conversion Date

Enter the date that you began processing all your transactions in Xero. It's easiest when you set your conversion date to be the start of a Sales Tax period. Tips for Choosing a Conversion Date.

Month
January ▼

Year
2021 ▼

For this conversion date you need to enter conversion balances (also known as opening balances) as at: **31 Dec 2020.**

Save    Cancel

5

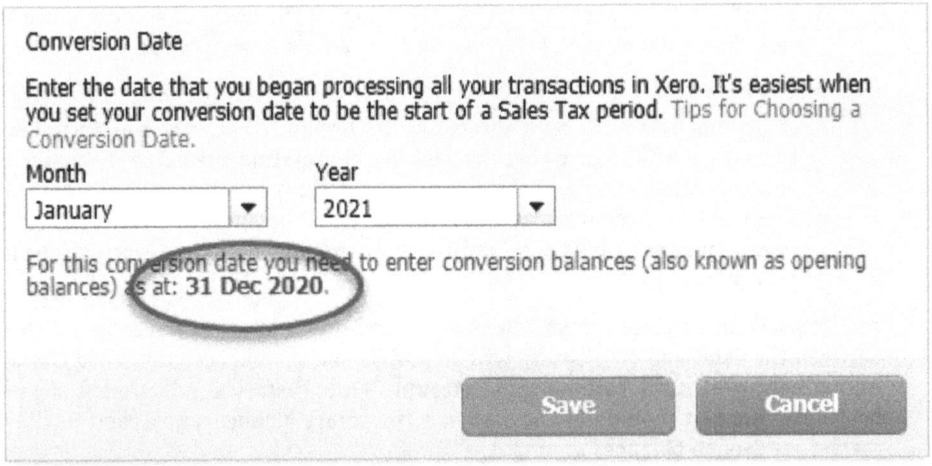

*Source:* Xero Limited

In general, conversion balances will equal the final trial balance from the end of the month prior. There are two exceptions:

1. Bank account balances
2. Credit card balances

These two types of accounts will either be connected to bank feeds or have transactions imported into Xero starting on the conversion date; therefore, the balance in the conversion screen needs to be the bank or credit card statement balance, not the general ledger balance.

For example, if the ending trial balance shows a balance of $4,130.98 for the checking account, but that includes a $100 deposit in transit on the date of conversion, you must use the bank statement balance of $4,030.98. After the beginning of the month, that deposit in transit will show in the bank feed or statement import, so having it in the conversion balance would effectively double-count the deposit. The same would be true for uncleared checks.

Any uncleared deposits or checks should be shown in the conversion balance screen as a clearing account, such as Deposits in Transit or Uncleared Checks, that will not be connected to a bank feed or statement import. When the deposits or checks clear the bank after the Xero file has been set up, the transaction coding will be to the appropriate clearing account.

To enter balances into the Conversion balances screen:

1. Click the **Show all accounts** link to show every general ledger account on the screen (Figure 5.12).
2. Enter the balance amounts on the conversion dates using the debit and credit columns.
3. To add a new account, not already existing on the chart of accounts, use the **Add a new line button**, then the pull-down to **+Add a new account**.
4. Click **Save**.
5. If any amounts have been entered in the Accounts Receivable or Accounts Payable lines, Xero will require that invoices or bills totaling the balance amount be entered. Alternatively, if there are many invoices or bills, leave the Accounts Receivable or Accounts Payable lines without a balance, and import a .csv listing of the invoices or bills outstanding at the conversion date. (Instructions later in this chapter.)

You may save incomplete conversion balances and revise later. However, any difference between the debit and credit sums will be posted to a system account called **Historical Adjustment**, which is a balance sheet account. While Historical Adjustment is a useful holding account, it should only be used as a temporary balance adjustment until the final correct conversion balances are input.

**FIGURE 5.12**

Click the Show all accounts link to show every general ledger account on the screen.

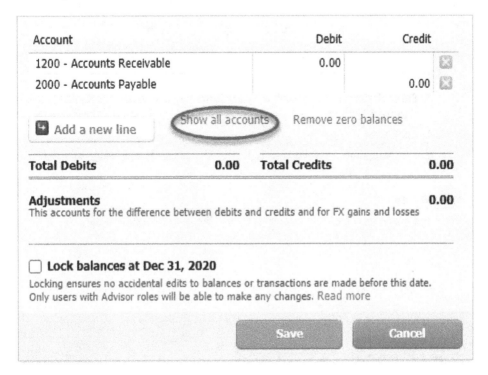

## Enter your account balances as at Dec 31, 2020

| Account | Debit | Credit | |
|---|---|---|---|
| 1200 - Accounts Receivable | 0.00 | | ☒ |
| 2000 - Accounts Payable | | 0.00 | ☒ |

⊞ Add a new line    Show all accounts    Remove zero balances

| **Total Debits** | **0.00** | **Total Credits** | **0.00** |
|---|---|---|---|

**Adjustments**                                                                              **0.00**
This accounts for the difference between debits and credits and for FX gains and losses

☐ **Lock balances at Dec 31, 2020**
Locking ensures no accidental edits to balances or transactions are made before this date.
Only users with Advisor roles will be able to make any changes. Read more

Save    Cancel

*Source:* Xero Limited

When conversion balances are finalized, check the box at the bottom of the screen to **Lock balances at** the conversion date. This will prevent any changes to the conversion data (Figure 5.13).

**FIGURE 5.13**

When conversion balances are finalized, check the box at the bottom of the screen to Lock balances at the conversion date. This will prevent any changes to the conversion data.

☑ **Lock balances at Dec 31, 2020**
Locking ensures no accidental edits to balances or transactions are made before this date.
Only users with Advisor roles will be able to make any changes. Read more

*Source:* Xero Limited

5

# Adding Invoices and Bills

Accounts receivable and accounts payable are system balances in Xero. This means that Xero will require that the sum of underlying invoices and bills equal the conversion balances. Invoices and bills can be added manually in the conversion balance screen or imported in bulk.

To add an invoice or bill manually in the conversion screen:

1. Navigate to **Accounting**, then **Advanced**.
2. Select **Conversion Balances**.
3. Enter the accounts receivable or accounts payable general ledger balances (Figure 5.14).
4. Click **Save**.
5. Xero will show a screen that indicates the accounts receivable or accounts payable is out of balance.

**FIGURE 5.14**

Enter the accounts receivable or accounts payable general ledger balances.

| Account | Debit | Credit | |
|---|---|---|---|
| 1200 - Accounts Receivable | 1,525.00 | | |
| 2000 - Accounts Payable | | 258.10 | |

Add a new line    Show all accounts    Remove zero balances

| **Total Debits** | **1,525.00** | **Total Credits** | **258.10** |
|---|---|---|---|

**Adjustments**                                                         **1,266.90**
This accounts for the difference between debits and credits and for FX gains and losses

☐ **Lock balances at Dec 31, 2020**
Locking ensures no accidental edits to balances or transactions are made before this date. Only users with Advisor roles will be able to make any changes. Read more

Save    Cancel

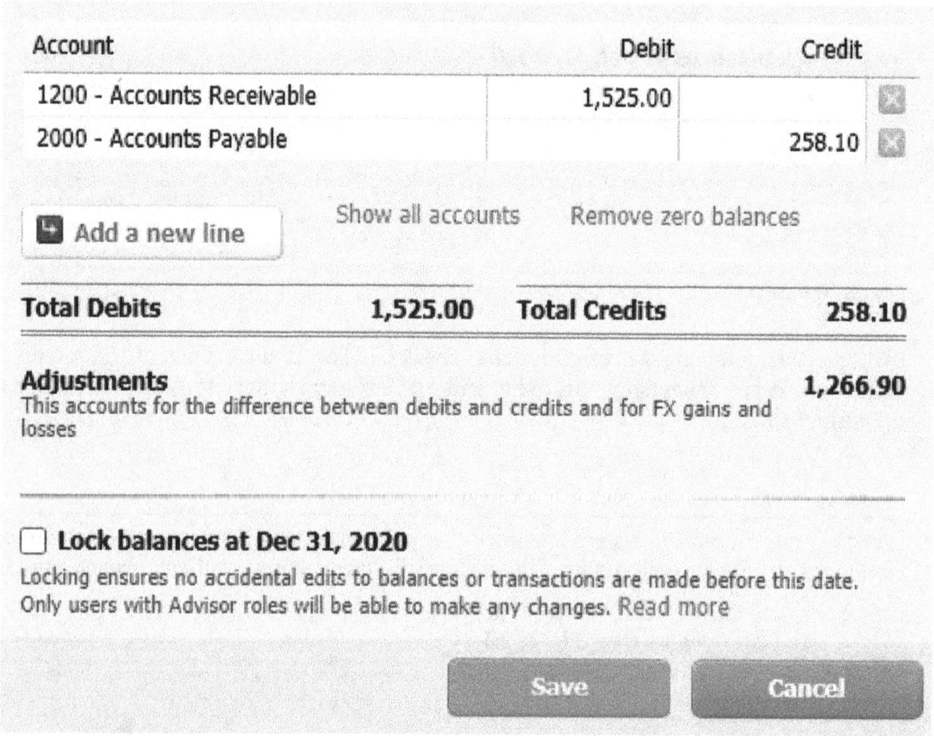

*Source: Xero Limited*

**FIGURE 5.15**

Use the +Add Bill or +Add Invoice button to enter one or more invoices or bills.

*Source:* Xero Limited

6. Use the **+Add Bill** or **+Add Invoice** button to enter one or more invoices or bills (Figure 5.15).

7. Click **Save**.

8. On the Conversion Balances screen, click **Save**. Xero will indicate that the balances have been saved.

If you choose to import invoices or bills, you will need to prepare an import file. Be sure that the invoice or bill dates are prior to the conversion date.

To import invoices or bills:

1. Navigate to **Business**, then **Invoices** or **Bills**.

2. Click the **Import** button at the top of the screen.

3. Use the **Browse** button to find the import file.

4. Click **Import**.

The invoices or bills will be imported as drafts. You must approve them to add to the receivables or payables balance. See Chapters 11 and 12 for details.

# Adding Fixed Assets

Fixed assets is also a subledger of Xero; however, it is not tied to the general ledger in the way that receivables and payables are. You will need to add existing assets in the Fixed Assets module if you will be using it for depreciation. If you do not plan to use the Fixed Assets module and will be making manual entries for depreciation, you do not need to add the assets in Xero. See Chapter 13 for information on adding assets.

5

# Importing Conversion Balances on Chart of Accounts

If you have a long chart of accounts, importing conversion balances will be much more efficient than entering each on the conversion balances screen. The file used for importing conversion balances is the chart of accounts, with an extra column. The balance of each account on the day prior to the conversion date (for example, December 31 for a January 1 conversion date) is entered in the **Balance** column on the chart of accounts import file. The balance must be a positive value for debit balances and a negative value for credit balances. There is a sample import file in the digital resources.

When importing conversion balances, the conversion date must be set before the chart of accounts is imported. The balances are imported in the chart of accounts screen, rather than the conversion balances screen.

To import a chart of accounts with conversion balances:

1. Navigate to **Accounting**, then **Advanced**.
2. Select **Conversion balances**.
3. Click the **Conversion Date** button and enter the conversion date.
4. Click **Save**.
5. Navigate to **Accounting**, then **Advanced**.
6. Select **Chart of accounts**.
7. Click the **Import** button at the top of the screen (Figure 5.16).
8. Select **Yes** for **Does the file you are importing contain account balances?** (Figure 5.17).
9. Confirm the conversion date.
10. Use the **Browse** button to select the import file.
11. Click **Import.**
12. Return to the conversion balances screen to confirm that balances were imported. Click **Save**.

**FIGURE 5.16**

Click the Import button at the top of the screen.

Advanced accounting ›
## Chart of accounts

Add Account  Add Bank Account  Map Accounts to Tax Lines  Print PDF  Import  Export

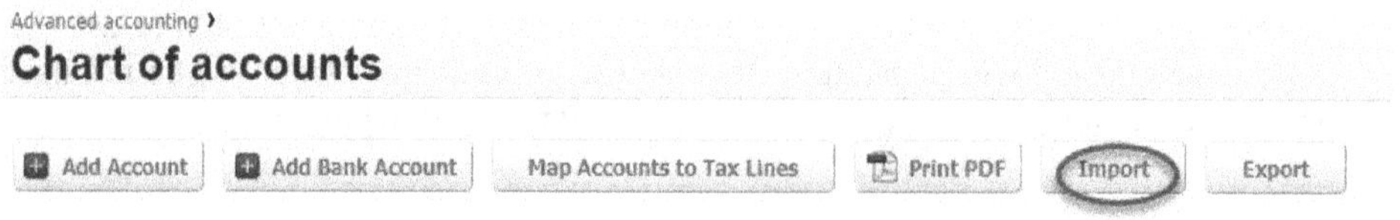

*Source:* Xero Limited

**FIGURE 5.17**

Select Yes for Does the file you are importing contain account balances?

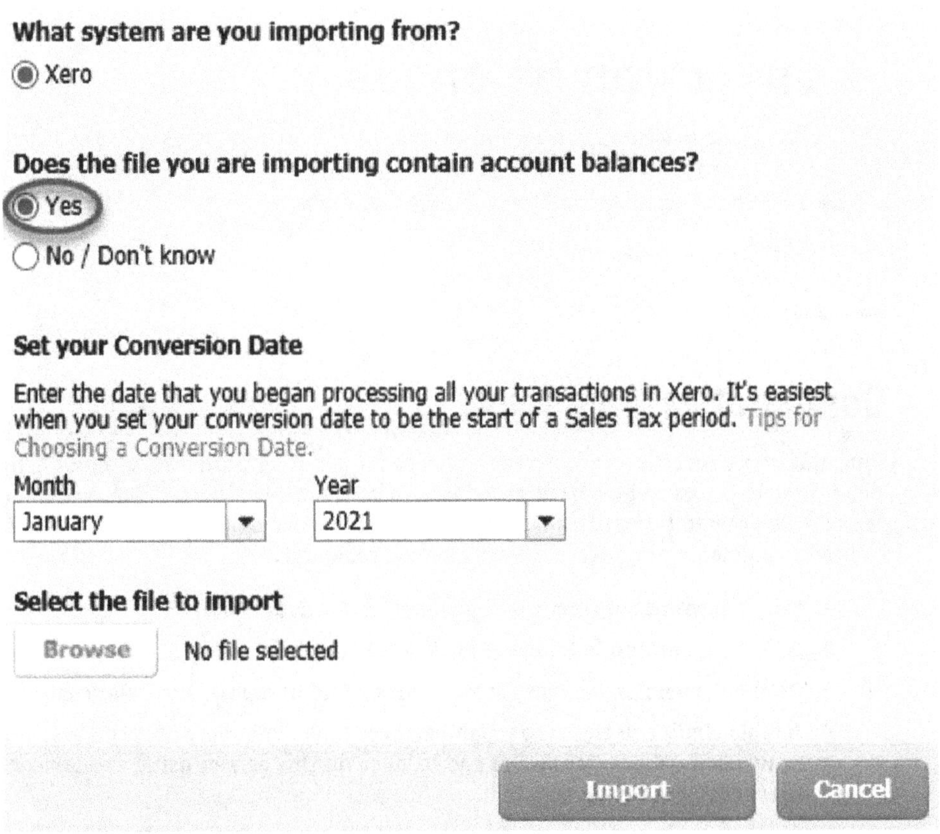

**What system are you importing from?**

◉ Xero

**Does the file you are importing contain account balances?**

◉ Yes

◯ No / Don't know

**Set your Conversion Date**

Enter the date that you began processing all your transactions in Xero. It's easiest when you set your conversion date to be the start of a Sales Tax period. Tips for Choosing a Conversion Date.

Month

| January ▼ |

Year

| 2021 ▼ |

**Select the file to import**

| Browse |  No file selected

| Import |   | Cancel |

*Source:* Xero Limited

**FIGURE 5.18**

Select Conversion balances.

*Source:* Xero Limited

## Comparative Balances

Comparative balances are end-of-year balances for periods prior to using Xero. Xero will allow these balances to be posted to be used in comparative reports. Comparative balances can only be entered for each 12-month period prior to the conversion year end and cannot be used to add more granular, such as monthly, comparatives.

1. Select **Accounting** from the top menu, then **Advanced**.
2. Select **Conversion balances** (Figure 5.18).
3. On the Conversion balances screen, click **+Add Comparative Balances.**
4. A table similar to the conversion balances table will appear for the year prior to the conversion date. Enter period end balance on this screen using the same methods for conversion balances.
5. For more comparative periods, click **+Add Comparative Balances.**

# Settings

*Xero tracking categories and reporting together allows me to provide NFP clients a full-service solution that allows them to run grant reports, prepare donation receipts and simulate fund reporting from a single source of truth—their general ledger without the cost and complexity of other systems.*

*—Allison Hawkins, Co-Founder, Hawkins & Co. Accounting*

Whether you set up a Xero organization from scratch or inherit a file from someone else, you may need to refine its settings. Settings in Xero are split into two categories: Organization and Advanced.

## Organization Settings

Organization settings deal with general features like basic demographic information and invoice defaults. To access these settings, use the pull-down arrow to the right of the company name, then navigate to **Settings**.

### Organization Details

At the top of the screen, you may see a banner (Figure 6.1) regarding including information in online invoices. Selecting the **On** radio button will activate **Include** checkboxes to the right of the company detail fields that can be checked to be included in online invoices.

In **Organization details** you will find basic demographic information for the company. A few tips:

- **Display name** will be the name of the company you see as you use Xero, whereas the **Legal/Trading name** will appear on reports.
- Use the **Quick find** field for address information, rather than typing in each of the address fields. Xero will search the internet for a verifiable address, then populate the correct fields. This is also important for validating the location of your clients. The Xero Advisor Directory tags advisors by locations of their clients based on the address entered here.
- Several other fields, including social media accounts, are accessible from the **+Add contact field** link at the bottom of the screen.

**FIGURE 6.1**

At the top of the screen, you may see a banner (Figure 6.1) regarding including information in online invoices. Selecting the On radio button will activate Include checkboxes to the right of the company detail fields that can be checked to be included in online invoices.

*Source:* Xero Limited

## Users

The **Users** screen will show all users with access to the organization. To quickly change a user's permissions within the file, use the overflow menu (three dots) and navigate to Change permissions. Note that user permissions discussed here are different from user permissions at the practice level in Xero HQ. Those permissions are discussed in Chapter 3.

To add a user:

1. Use the pull-down next to the organization name and navigate to **Settings**.
2. Select **Users**.
3. Click the **Invite a user** button at the top right of the screen.
4. Enter the user's details. The user will login with their email address.
5. Select **Projects**, **Expenses** and/or **Business and accounting**. Projects or Expenses access would be appropriate for users entering time or expense claims, but not needing access to the accounting system. Business and accounting is for access to the accounting system.
6. Select the level of access the user requires. (See Figure 6.2a–d for details.)

The **Invoice only** role allows the user to create quotes or invoices and bills but does not allow access to the bank accounts or any general ledger transactions. Within Invoice only permissions, the level of approval of invoices and bills can be set to draft only or to allow approval. Additional access can be granted by checking the appropriate boxes. These include banking and reporting functions.

The **Standard** role allows the user to work in the bank accounts, settings, fixed assets, and inventory in addition to invoices and bills. This is the appropriate access level for most employees of the client, as well as owners who do not need to spend much time in the details of the accounting system.

The **Advisor** role gives the user full access to all of the functionality of Xero. This would be an appropriate level of permission for accountants and bookkeepers, and owners who are skilled in finances.

**FIGURE 6.2A**

Select the level of access the user requires

| Settings | Advisor | Standard + View Reports |
|---|:---:|:---:|
| Can be allowed to add and remove users and change permissions | ✓ | ✓ |
| Edit organisation and financial settings | ✓ | ✓ |
| Set lock dates | ✓ | - |
| Turn on sales tax lookup | ✓ | ✓ |
| Edit invoice settings, add or edit invoice branding | ✓ | ✓ |
| Add or edit payment services | ✓ | ✓ |
| Set up or disconnect connected apps | ✓ | ✓ |
| Use tracking | ✓ | ✓ |
| Set and update conversion balances | ✓ | ✓ |
| Access, import and export chart of accounts | ✓ | ✓ |
| Send Xero network key | ✓ | ✓ |

The **Read-only** role allows the user full access to view transactions and reports but no ability to make changes. This access was created for bankers, auditors, directors, and trustees.

1. Within each user role, you will be able to calibrate further permissions with regard to banking details, reports, and other settings options.

2. Click **Invite user**.

## Currencies

Xero handles multiple currencies within the general ledger with an Established subscription plan. Currency movement is updated hourly based on exchange rates from XE.com.

The base currency of the company is established during setup. Any additional currencies will need to be added under Settings.

To add a currency:

1. Use the pull-down next to the organization name and navigate to **Settings**.

2. Select **Currencies**.

3. Select **+Add Currency.**

**FIGURE 6.2B**

Select the level of access the user requires

| Reporting | Advisor | Standard + View Reports | Invoice Only | Read Only |
|---|---|---|---|---|
| View published reports | ✓ | ✓ | - | ✓ |
| View, print and export reports (excluding 1099) | ✓ | ✓ | - | ✓ |
| Save a report as a draft | ✓ | - | - | - |
| Access custom reports | ✓ | ✓ | - | ✓ |
| Save a report as a custom report | ✓ | ✓ | - | - |
| Set a custom report as the default or remove a default | ✓ | ✓ | - | - |
| Set up and run 1099 report* | ✓ | - | - | - |
| File sales tax returns online | ✓ | - | - | - |
| Publish sales tax reports and Bank Reconciliation Summary | ✓ | ✓ | - | - |
| Publish all reports | ✓ | - | - | - |
| Copy and edit published reports | ✓ | - | - | - |
| Add or edit budgets (Budget Manager) | ✓ | ✓ | - | - |
| View and run reports on the Reports screen | ✓ | ✓ | - | ✓ |
| View Expense Claim Summary | ✓ | ✓ | ✓ | ✓ |
| Access the Advisor reports on the Reports screen | ✓ | - | - | - |
| Delete reports | ✓ | - | - | - |
| View History and Notes Activity | ✓ | - | - | - |
| View and favourite Business Performance graphs | ✓ | ✓ | - | ✓ |

4. Use the pulldown menu to **Select a currency**.

5. Confirm by clicking the green **Add Currency** button.

Learn more about multicurrency use of Xero in Chapter 14.

You can add as many currencies as you need, but they cannot be deleted after you add them.

## Connected Apps

This option is less of a setting than a control panel for all applications connected to Xero. Here you will find all of the applications connected to Xero through its API, along with a button to **Disconnect** (Figure 6.3).

## Invoice Settings

Defaults and layouts for invoices, statements, quotes, credit notes, remittances, and purchase orders are managed in Invoice Settings.

**FIGURE 6.2C**

Select the level of access the user requires

| | Advisor | Standard | Invoice Only + Draft | Invoice Only + Sales | Invoice Only + Purchases | Invoice Only + Approve and pay | Read Only |
|---|---|---|---|---|---|---|---|
| **Sales** | | | | | | | |
| Draft sales invoices | ✓ | ✓ | ✓ | ✓ | - | ✓ | - |
| View and edit sales invoices you created | ✓ | ✓ | ✓ | ✓ | - | ✓ | - |
| View sales invoices created by others | ✓ | ✓ | - | ✓ | - | ✓ | ✓ |
| Edit sales invoices created by others | ✓ | ✓ | - | ✓ | - | ✓ | - |
| Copy or delete sales invoices you created | ✓ | ✓ | ✓ | ✓ | - | ✓ | - |
| Copy, delete or void sales invoices created by others | ✓ | ✓ | - | ✓ | - | ✓ | - |
| Approve invoices | ✓ | ✓ | - | ✓ | - | ✓ | - |
| Record payment on invoices | ✓ | ✓ | - | ✓ | - | ✓ | - |
| Recode invoices | ✓ | - | - | - | - | - | - |
| Email invoices | ✓ | ✓ | - | ✓ | - | ✓ | - |
| Print invoices | ✓ | ✓ | - | ✓ | - | ✓ | ✓ |
| View online invoices | ✓ | ✓ | - | ✓ | - | ✓ | - |
| Send statements | ✓ | ✓ | - | ✓ | - | ✓ | - |
| Create a batch deposit | ✓ | ✓ | - | ✓ | - | ✓ | - |
| Edit a batch deposit | ✓ | ✓ | - | ✓ | - | - | - |
| View debtors list/pie chart | ✓ | ✓ | - | ✓ | - | ✓ | ✓ |
| Draft and revise quotes you created | ✓ | ✓ | ✓ | ✓ | - | ✓ | - |
| Revise quotes created by others | ✓ | ✓ | - | ✓ | - | ✓ | - |
| View quotes you created | ✓ | ✓ | ✓ | ✓ | - | ✓ | - |
| View quotes created by others | ✓ | ✓ | - | ✓ | - | ✓ | ✓ |
| Email quotes | ✓ | ✓ | - | ✓ | - | ✓ | - |
| Print quotes PDFs | ✓ | ✓ | - | ✓ | - | ✓ | ✓ |
| Mark quotes as accepted | ✓ | ✓ | - | ✓ | - | ✓ | - |
| Copy quotes to invoices or new quotes you created | ✓ | ✓ | ✓ | ✓ | - | ✓ | - |
| Copy quotes to invoices or new quotes created by others | ✓ | ✓ | - | ✓ | - | ✓ | - |
| Create invoices from quotes you created | ✓ | ✓ | ✓ | ✓ | - | ✓ | - |
| Create invoices from quotes created by others | ✓ | ✓ | - | ✓ | - | ✓ | - |
| Delete quotes you created | ✓ | ✓ | ✓ | ✓ | - | ✓ | - |
| Delete quotes created by others | ✓ | ✓ | - | ✓ | - | ✓ | - |
| Create and approve customer credit notes | ✓ | ✓ | - | ✓ | - | ✓ | - |
| View customer credit notes created by others | ✓ | ✓ | - | ✓ | - | ✓ | ✓ |
| Edit, delete or void customer credit notes | ✓ | ✓ | - | ✓ | - | ✓ | - |
| Allocate credit to invoices and refund customer credit notes | ✓ | ✓ | - | ✓ | - | ✓ | - |
| Recode customer credit notes | ✓ | - | - | - | - | - | - |
| Email customer credit notes | ✓ | ✓ | - | ✓ | - | ✓ | - |
| Print customer credit notes | ✓ | ✓ | - | ✓ | - | ✓ | ✓ |
| View debtors list or pie chart | ✓ | ✓ | - | ✓ | - | ✓ | ✓ |
| **Purchases** | | | | | | | |
| Draft and edit bills you created | ✓ | ✓ | ✓ | - | ✓ | ✓ | - |
| Approve and pay bills | ✓ | ✓ | - | - | ✓ | ✓ | - |
| View bills you created | ✓ | ✓ | ✓ | - | ✓ | ✓ | - |
| View bills created by others | ✓ | ✓ | - | - | ✓ | ✓ | ✓ |
| Edit bills created by others | ✓ | ✓ | - | - | ✓ | ✓ | - |
| Copy or delete own bills | ✓ | ✓ | ✓ | - | ✓ | ✓ | - |
| Copy or delete others' bills | ✓ | ✓ | - | - | ✓ | ✓ | - |
| Record payment of bills | ✓ | ✓ | - | - | ✓ | ✓ | - |
| Recode bills | ✓ | - | - | - | - | - | - |
| Send bill from Xero to Xero | ✓ | ✓ | - | - | ✓ | ✓ | - |
| Print bill PDF | ✓ | ✓ | - | - | ✓ | ✓ | ✓ |
| Create or edit a batch payment | ✓ | ✓ | - | - | ✓ | ✓ | - |
| Send a remittance advice | ✓ | ✓ | - | - | ✓ | ✓ | - |
| Draft and edit purchase orders you created | ✓ | ✓ | ✓ | - | ✓ | ✓ | - |
| Approve purchase orders | ✓ | ✓ | - | - | ✓ | ✓ | - |
| View purchase orders you created | ✓ | ✓ | ✓ | - | ✓ | ✓ | - |
| View purchase orders created by others | ✓ | ✓ | - | - | ✓ | ✓ | ✓ |
| Edit purchase orders created by others | ✓ | ✓ | - | - | ✓ | ✓ | - |
| Copy purchase orders to bills or new purchase orders you created | ✓ | ✓ | ✓ | - | ✓ | ✓ | - |
| Copy purchase orders to bills or new purchase orders created by others | - | - | - | - | ✓ | ✓ | - |
| Copy purchase orders to sales invoices you created | ✓ | ✓ | ✓ | - | - | ✓ | - |
| Copy purchase orders to sales invoices created by others | - | - | - | - | - | ✓ | - |
| Mark purchase orders as billed | ✓ | ✓ | - | - | ✓ | ✓ | - |
| Delete own purchase orders | ✓ | ✓ | ✓ | - | ✓ | ✓ | - |
| Delete others' purchase orders | ✓ | ✓ | - | - | ✓ | ✓ | - |
| Recode purchase orders | ✓ | - | - | - | - | - | - |
| Email purchase orders | ✓ | ✓ | - | - | ✓ | ✓ | - |
| Print purchase order PDFs | ✓ | ✓ | - | - | ✓ | ✓ | ✓ |
| Add new delivery address | ✓ | ✓ | - | - | ✓ | ✓ | - |
| Create and approve supplier credit notes | ✓ | ✓ | - | - | ✓ | ✓ | - |
| View supplier credit notes created by others | ✓ | ✓ | - | - | ✓ | ✓ | ✓ |
| Edit, delete or void supplier credit notes (own or others') | ✓ | ✓ | - | - | ✓ | ✓ | - |
| Allocate credit to bills and refund supplier credit notes | ✓ | ✓ | - | - | ✓ | ✓ | - |
| Recode supplier credit notes | ✓ | - | - | - | ✓ | ✓ | - |
| Print supplier credit notes | ✓ | ✓ | - | - | ✓ | ✓ | ✓ |

## FIGURE 6.2D

| Banking | Advisor | Standard + Cash Coding | Standard without Cash Coding | Invoice Only + Draft | Invoice Only + Sales | Invoice Only + Purchases | Invoice Only + Approve and pay | Read Only |
|---|---|---|---|---|---|---|---|---|
| View bank balance and balance in Xero | ✓ | ✓ | ✓ | - | - | - | - | ✓ |
| View account transactions in Xero | ✓ | ✓ | ✓ | - | - | - | - | ✓ |
| View imported bank statements | ✓ | ✓ | ✓ | - | - | - | - | - |
| Add comments to unreconciled bank statement lines | ✓ | ✓ | ✓ | - | - | - | - | - |
| Add, edit, archive or delete bank accounts | ✓ | ✓ | ✓ | - | - | - | - | - |
| Import manual statements, delete statements | ✓ | ✓ | ✓ | - | - | - | - | - |
| Add a spend money or receive money | ✓ | ✓ | ✓ | - | - | - | - | - |
| Add a prepayment or overpayment | ✓ | ✓ | ✓ | - | - | - | - | - |
| Activate a direct feed | ✓ | ✓ | ✓ | - | - | - | - | - |
| Set up, refresh, or stop a Yodlee feed | ✓ | ✓ | ✓ | - | - | - | - | - |
| Reconcile and unreconcile bank transactions | ✓ | ✓ | ✓ | - | - | - | - | - |
| Cash code transactions during bank reconciliation* | ✓ | ✓ | - | - | - | - | - | - |
| Recode bank transactions | ✓ | - | - | - | - | - | - | - |
| Export uncoded bank statement lines | ✓ | - | - | - | - | - | - | - |
| Add bank rules | ✓ | ✓ | ✓ | - | - | - | - | - |
| View 'Invoices owed to you' graph | ✓ | ✓ | ✓ | ✓ | ✓ | - | ✓ | ✓ |
| View 'Bills you need to pay' graph | ✓ | ✓ | ✓ | ✓ | - | ✓ | ✓ | ✓ |

## FIGURE 6.3

Use the pulldown menu to Select a currency.

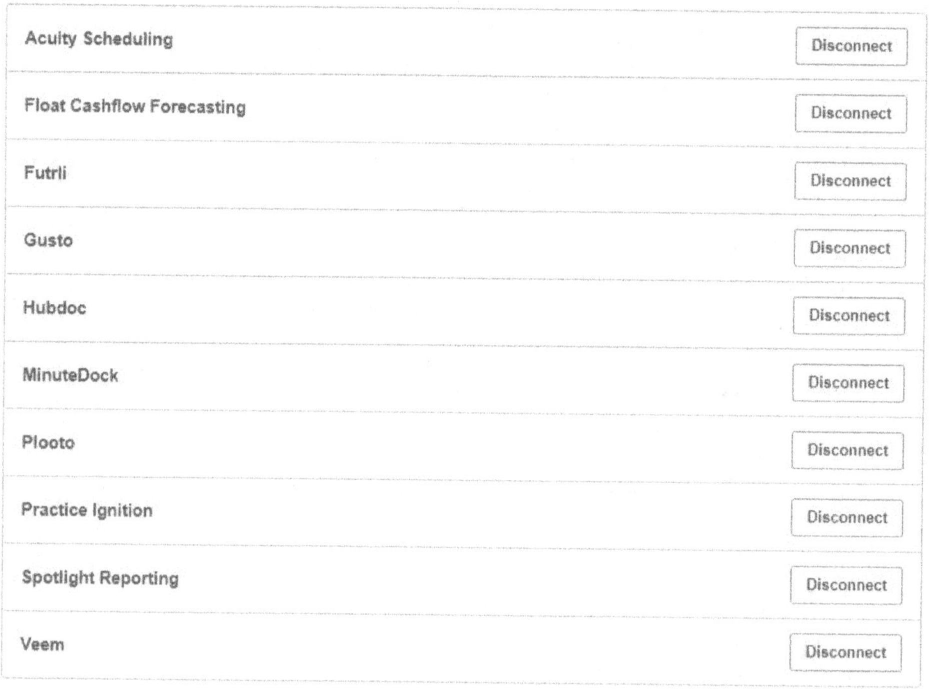

| Acuity Scheduling | Disconnect |
|---|---|
| Float Cashflow Forecasting | Disconnect |
| Futrli | Disconnect |
| Gusto | Disconnect |
| Hubdoc | Disconnect |
| MinuteDock | Disconnect |
| Plooto | Disconnect |
| Practice Ignition | Disconnect |
| Spotlight Reporting | Disconnect |
| Veem | Disconnect |

*Source:* Xero Limited

**FIGURE 6.4**

Xero organizations have one standard theme template by default. Existing templates are listed on the Invoice Settings page as individual tiles with a summary of the invoice. (Figure 6.4)

*Source:* Xero Limited

## Invoice Branding Themes

Xero has two kinds of templates or layouts for invoices, which it calls **branding themes**. The first is a **Standard** theme, which allows for only limited customization. The second is a **Custom** theme, which is built from fields within a Word document.

Themes can be created within Settings and selected at the time of document creation. A company may have multiple layouts for use in different divisions, locations, or service lines. For example, a client may want to use different logos or location addresses for different projects, all within one company. In any Xero organization, there can be only 15 custom templates, but there may be unlimited standard templates.

Xero organizations have one standard theme template by default. Existing templates are listed on the Invoice Settings page as individual tiles with a summary of the invoice (Figure 6.4). To edit an existing template, use the **Options** pull-down in the upper right corner of the tile and navigate to **Edit**. Make needed changes and click **Save**.

If a new Standard template is needed, it can be easily created. To create a new Standard template:

1. Use the pull-down next to the organization name and navigate to **Settings** (Figure 6.5).
2. Select **Invoice settings.**
3. Use the pull-down arrow next to **+New Branding Theme** to select **Standard.**
4. Assign a name to the template in the Name field. This is how the template will be identified when an invoice is created.
5. Confirm or edit the default layout dimensions and margins.
6. Confirm or edit the font and font size.

**FIGURE 6.5**

Use the pulldown next to the organization name and navigate to Settings.

Organization settings ›
## Invoice settings

What's this?

| New Branding Theme ▲ | Default Settings | Payment Services | Invoice Reminders |

Standard
Custom .docx

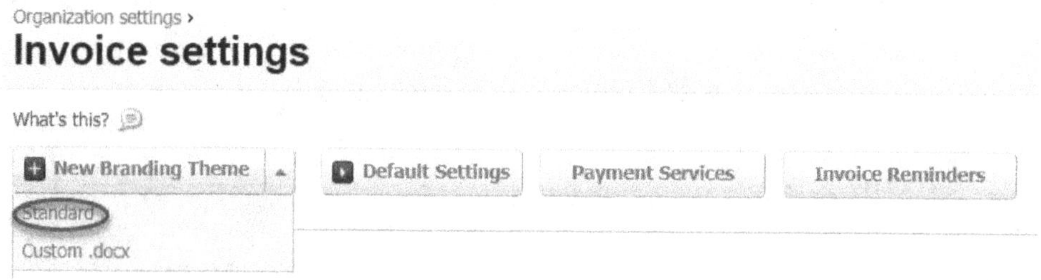

*Source:* Xero Limited

7. Confirm or edit the titles to be used for each of the document types.

8. Check or uncheck the fields to be included on the document.

9. Choose a left or right logo alignment.

10. Choose for sales taxes to be shown exclusive or inclusive of the sales price.

11. Confirm or edit the contact details to be shown on the document.

12. Choose how tax components should be displayed.

13. Choose an electronic payment service for each credit card, PayPal, and ACH payments. (Note that this must be set up in order for options to populate.)

14. Add language to be included as terms and payment instructions for invoices and statements, and terms for quotes.

15. Click **Save.**

While functional, Xero's Standard themes are not much to look at. To get fully customized and designed invoices, you must create a Custom branding theme. This can be a laborious process, but it is worth investing the time and effort.

Custom invoice themes are built from Microsoft Word files, which include static text, images, and fields. Fields are dynamic and will change for each document. Xero provides custom .doc templates to get you started. A few things to note:

- Template documents must use TableStart and TableEnd fields to indicate the beginning and end of invoice fields.
- Fields must be inserted, moved, or deleted using the instructions.
- The template document cannot be larger than 1MB.

To create a new Custom template, start by downloading a template for the sales document you wish to customize:

1. Use the pull-down next to the organization name and navigate to **Settings.**

2. Select **Invoice settings.**

3. Use the pull-down arrow next to **+New Branding Theme** to select **Custom .docx.**

4. Assign a name to the template. This is how the template will be identified when an invoice is created.

5. Scroll down to the tile that has been created for this branding theme.

6. Note that there are five different templates, one for each type of sales document: invoice, credit note, statement, purchase order, and quote.

7. Click the **Download** button to download a .zip file with Word templates for each of the five sales documents (Figure 6.6).

Next, customize the downloaded .doc file (Figure 6.7).

To add fields to the template:

1. Open the downloaded file in Microsoft Word.

2. The .doc file can be stylized by changing the font, inserting logos or other design elements, and changing text color, without affecting the merge fields needed to populate the document.

3. To insert a merge field, put your cursor where the field should be inserted. (To see a list of available fields, visit Xero Central.)

4. Select **Insert** at the top of the Microsoft Word screen.

5. Use the **QuickParts** pull-down to navigate to **Field**.

6. Select **MergeField** from the Field names list.

7. In the Field name box, type the field you wish to insert.

8. Click **OK**.

To edit fields within the template:

1. Highlight the field.

2. Right-click and select **Edit Field**.

---

**FIGURE 6.6**

Click the Download button to download a .zip file with Word templates for each of the five sales documents. (Figure 6.6)

*Source:* Xero Limited

**FIGURE 6.7**

Next, customize the downloaded .doc file

# «INVOICETITLE»

«ContactName»
«ContactPostalAddress»
«ContactTaxDisplayName» «ContactTaxNumber»

**«ORGANISATIONNAME» - ISLAND DIVISION**
«OrganisationPostalAddress»

| Invoice Date «InvoiceDate» | Invoice Number «InvoiceNumber» | Reference «Reference» | «OrganisationTaxDisplayName» «OrganisationTaxNumber» |
|---|---|---|---|
| **Description** | **Quantity** | **Unit Price** | **Amount «InvoiceCurrency»** |
| «TableStart:LineItem»«Code», «Description» | «Quantity» | «UnitAmount» | «LineAmount»«TableEnd:LineItem» |
| | | Subtotal | «InvoiceSubTotal» |
| | | «TableStart:TaxSubTotal»Total «TaxCode» | «TaxTotal»«TableEnd:TaxSubTotal» |
| | | Invoice Total «InvoiceCurrency» | «InvoiceTotal» |
| | | Total Net Payments «InvoiceCurrency» | «InvoiceTotalNetPayments» |
| | | Amount Due «InvoiceCurrency» | «InvoiceAmountDue» |

Due Date: «InvoiceDueDate»

PAYMENT ADVICE

«OrganisationName»
«OrganisationPostalAddress»

*Online payment preferred – pay directly to our account 123456789 or use the 'Pay online now' link to pay via PayPal with your credit card.*

«PayPalImage»
«PayPalMessageAndUrl»

«DefaultCurrencyTaxMessage»
«CurrencyConversionMessage»

| | |
|---|---|
| Customer | «ContactName» |
| Invoice Number | «InvoiceNumber» |
| Amount Due | «InvoiceAmountDue» |
| Due Date | «InvoiceDueDate» |
| Amount Enclosed | |

Enter the amount you are paying above.

*Source:* Xero Limited

3. In the Field name box, type the field you wish to insert.

4. Click **OK.**

To delete a field:

1. Highlight the field.

2. Press **Delete.**

When the template is updated, be sure to save it where it can be accessed for upload into Xero.

To upload the template into Xero:

1. Use the pull-down next to the organization name and navigate to **Settings.**

2. Select **Invoice settings.**

3. Navigate to the newly created branding theme.

4. Select **Upload** and use the **Browse** button to upload the template for each of the document types.

5. Click **Upload.**

### Default Settings

**Default settings** is where payment terms and document numbering are managed (Figure 6.8).

Setting bill and invoice **default due dates** will auto-populate due dates when those documents are created. The options for default due dates are:

- A certain number date of the following month
- A number of days after the bill or invoice date
- A number of days after the end of the invoice month
- A certain number date of the current month

Note that even though this will add a due date as each bill or invoice is created, the due date can easily be overwritten.

Unless you specify a numbering system and starting number for sales and purchases documents under **Automatic Sequencing**, Xero will use preset prefixes and the number "0001."

The prefixes are:

- INV for invoices
- CN for credit notes
- PO for purchase orders
- QU for quotes

**FIGURE 6.8**

Default settings is where payment terms and document numbering are managed

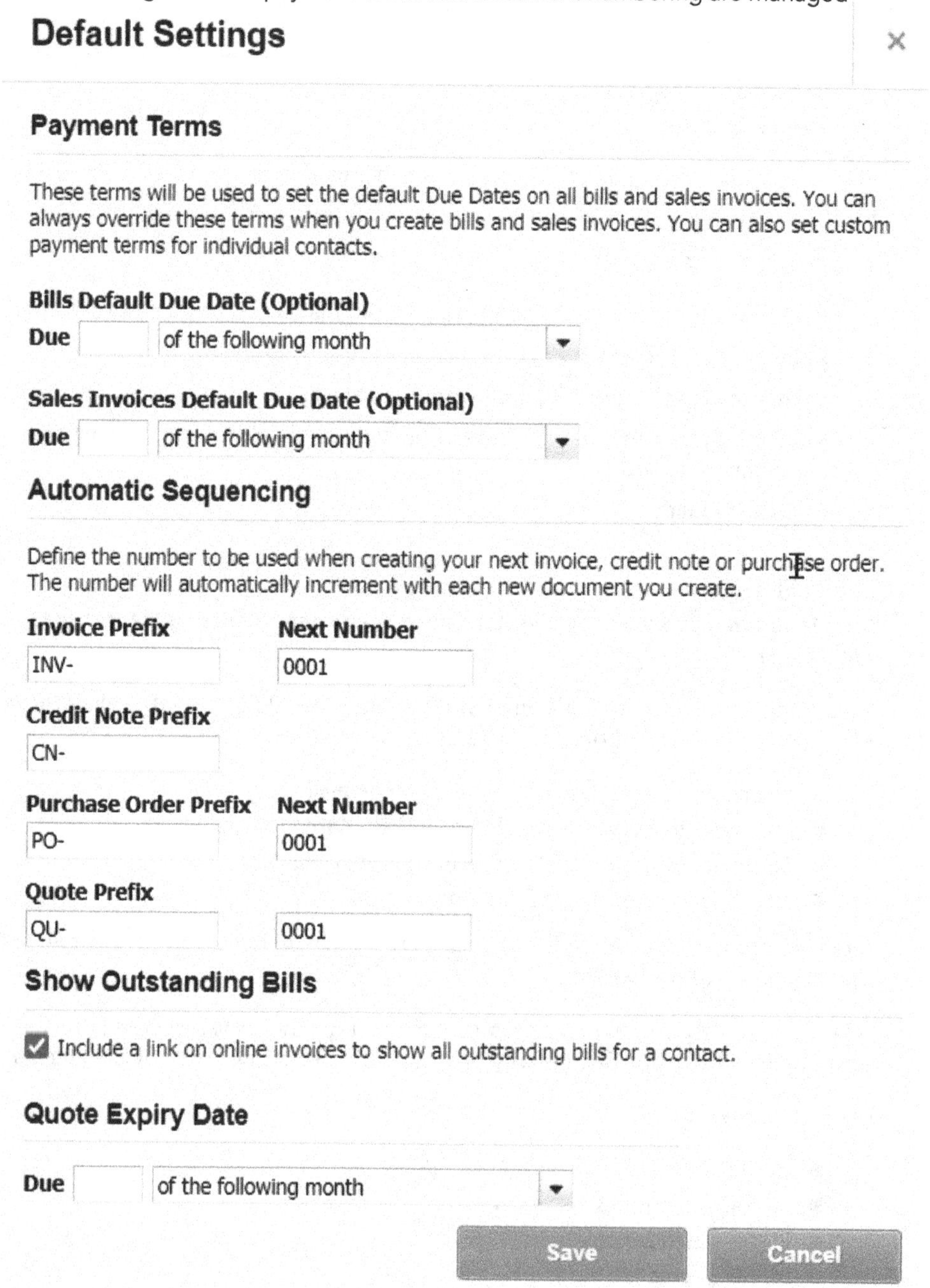

## Default Settings                                              ✕

### Payment Terms

These terms will be used to set the default Due Dates on all bills and sales invoices. You can always override these terms when you create bills and sales invoices. You can also set custom payment terms for individual contacts.

**Bills Default Due Date (Optional)**

Due [     ] | of the following month ▼ |

**Sales Invoices Default Due Date (Optional)**

Due [     ] | of the following month ▼ |

### Automatic Sequencing

Define the number to be used when creating your next invoice, credit note or purchase order. The number will automatically increment with each new document you create.

| **Invoice Prefix** | **Next Number** |
| INV- | 0001 |

**Credit Note Prefix**

CN-

| **Purchase Order Prefix** | **Next Number** |
| PO- | 0001 |

| **Quote Prefix** | |
| QU- | 0001 |

### Show Outstanding Bills

☑ Include a link on online invoices to show all outstanding bills for a contact.

### Quote Expiry Date

Due [     ] | of the following month ▼ |

[ Save ]   [ Cancel ]

*Source:* Xero Limited

To change the naming convention for these documents, simply replace the prefixes and starting numbers.

Xero's default on electronic invoices is to include a link that shows all outstanding invoices for a contact. To omit this link, uncheck the box under **Show Outstanding Bills**.

The last option on this screen is to specify a **Quote Expiry Date**. The options for an expiration date are the same as bill and invoice due dates mentioned earlier.

### Connecting Payment Services to Electronic Invoices

A Xero client will be most efficient when using electronic payment services along with online invoicing. By using the link at the top of the Invoice Settings screen you can connect to **Payment services**. Unlike other accounting software platforms that have their own payment services, Xero partners with industry leaders like Stripe, PayPal, and GoCardless to process invoice payments.

The first step in connecting a payment service is to create an account with the third-party processor. This can be done outside of Xero, directly with the processor, or can be initiated by clicking the **Get Started** button next to the app. Once the processor is connected to Xero, the user can assign payment services to each invoice template, called a branding theme. See below for more details on branding themes.

### Invoice Reminders

**Invoice reminders** are automatic emails to customers about amounts due, and one of the biggest time-savers in the system for companies that use online invoicing.

It is important to understand how invoice reminders work. The default in any Xero organization is that reminders are turned off. There is a hierarchy of activation:

1. Reminders are turned on globally for the entire organization.
2. Reminders can be turned off for a contact, eliminating reminders for all of that contact's invoices.
3. Reminders can be turned off for a specific invoice, eliminating reminders for that invoice, but retaining them for all other invoices.

To turn on invoice reminders:

1. Use the pull-down next to the organization name and navigate to **Settings**.
2. Select **Invoice settings.**
3. Click the **Invoice Reminders** button at the top of the screen.
4. Check the box next to **Email customers when an invoice is. . . .**
5. Edit the cadence of email reminders by clicking the **Edit** link in each tile.

    a. Choose whether to send a reminder email if the invoice is **overdue by** a number of days, or even before it is due by using **due in** a number of days. Using **due in 0 days** is an easy way to send reminders on the due date of any invoice.

    b. Edit the body of the email reminder template. Dynamic fields, shown in brackets, can be added or edited by using the **Insert placeholder pull-down** in the top right of the screen.

    c. Click **Save**.

    d. Repeat for the remainder of reminders, adding additional reminders by clicking the **+Add reminder link**, if desired.

6. The reminders settings default to including a quick link to online invoice and detail summary and including a link to the invoice .pdf. Uncheck these boxes if you do not want these defaults. (There is more information about invoice .pdfs in Chapter 11, including why you may not want to send a .pdf invoice to a customer.)

7. If you do not wish for reminders to be sent for small invoice balances, check the box next to **Don't send reminders for amounts owing on an invoice under** and add a threshold amount.

8. Click **Save**.

A company may have sensitive customers or those with irregular cash flow, and invoice reminders should be turned off for all invoices for that contact. To turn off all invoice reminders for a contact:

1. Navigate to **Contacts** at the top of the screen.

2. Select **All contacts**, then select the contact for which you wish to turn off reminders.

3. Use the **Options** pull-down at the top right of the screen and select **Turn off invoice reminders** (Figure 6.9).

4. If you wish to turn reminders on again, use the **Options** pull-down and select **Turn on invoice reminders**.

**FIGURE 6.9**

Check the box next to Email customers when an invoice is

*Source:* Xero Limited

**FIGURE 6.10**

Choose whether to send a reminder email if the invoice is overdue by a number of days, or even before it is due by using due in a number of days. Using due in 0 days is an easy way to send reminders on the due date of any invoice

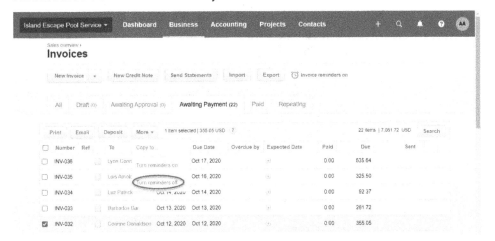

*Source:* Xero Limited

In the case of a disputed invoice, the company may want to discontinue reminders for that specific invoice but retain them for all other invoices for that contact. To turn off invoice reminders for an invoice:

1. Navigate to **Business** at the top of the screen, then **Invoices**.
2. Select the **Awaiting Payment** tab.
3. Locate the invoice or invoices for which you wish to turn off reminders.
4. Select the invoices by using the checkbox to the left of the listing.
5. Use the **More** pull-down to select **Turn reminders off** (Figure 6.10).
6. If you wish to turn reminders on again, use the **More** pull-down and select **Turn reminders on**.

## Email Settings

Xero will send emails created in the system for several purposes, including sending electronic invoices, issuing credit notes, sending remittances, and sending receipts. In **Email settings** you can change the outgoing email address and modify the default email copy for each type of email.

The default address from which emails originate is the user's login, but it can be changed. Many companies use department-specific emails like billing@client.com.

To change the outgoing email address:

1. Use the pull-down next to the organization name and navigate to **Settings**.
2. Select **Email settings.**
3. Click **Edit** on the right in the Email address tile.
4. Click **+Add email address** to add the address of another person or a system inbox for the company, like billing@client.com (Figure 6.11).
5. The new email will be verified by a test to that address.
6. Once verified, select the email by using the radio button to the left, and click **Save.**

Xero provides eight standard email templates:

- Credit Note
- Purchase Order

**FIGURE 6.11**

Click +Add email address to add the address of another person or a system inbox for the company, like billing@client.com.

## Add a new reply email address                    ✕

**'Reply to' Email address**

| billing@client.com | ▼ |

**Email name**

| Accounting Department |

Emails sent from this organization will use this name and email address.

For more information view help.

| Add email | Cancel |

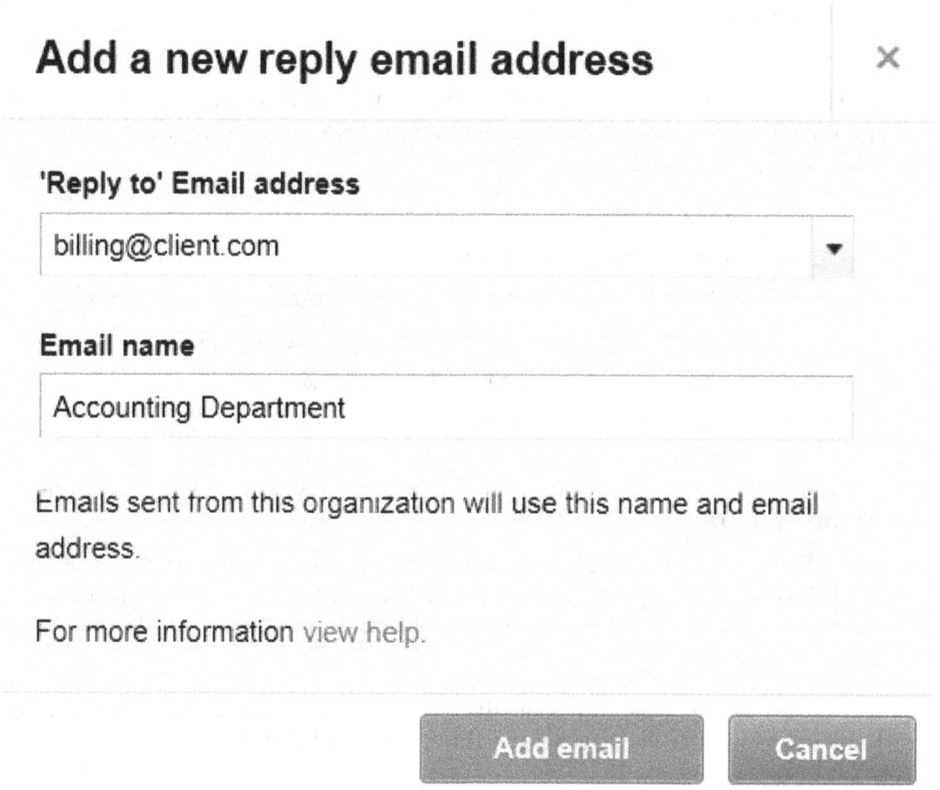

*Source:* Xero Limited

- Quote
- Receipt
- Remittance
- Repeating Invoice
- Sales Invoice
- Statement

The Xero provided templates are labeled **Basic** and are the default for each type of communication, but can be edited.

To edit an email template:

1. Click an email template to open it. Notice that the subject line and the body contain text and dynamic fields, noted in brackets.
2. Edit the copy by deleting and typing.
3. Add additional fields by using the **Insert placeholder** pull-down (Figure 6.12).
4. Click **Save**.

In certain situations, a company may wish to have more than one template for the same type of email template. One example is for an invoice that is set to be paid automatically using a payment platform. The company may want the invoice email template to indicate that funds should not be remitted because they will automatically be drafted.

To create additional email templates:

1. Click **+Add email template** at the bottom of the screen.
2. Select the type of template.
3. Give the template a name that can be easily identified in the template list, like "Do not pay."
4. If you want the new email template to be the default for this type of email, check the box to the left of **Default**.
5. Edit the copy in the message fields, using the **Insert placeholders** pull-down for adding fields.
6. Click **Save**.

You will see the new template in the listing. You will be able to select the new template in the screen where the document is sent.

## Check Styles

In the United States, many companies still use paper checks. The **Check styles** setting is where the print layout of checks can be modified.

**FIGURE 6.12**

Add additional fields by using the Insert placeholder pulldown

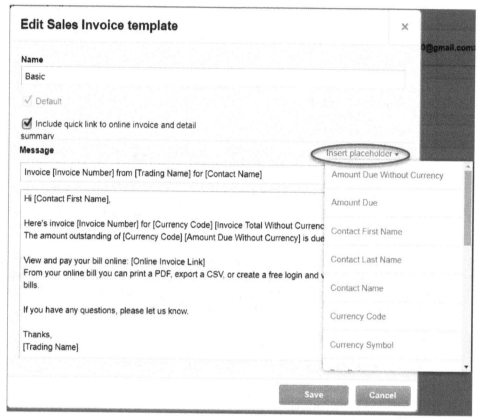

*Source:* Xero Limited

New files will be created with a standard check style or layout that will likely need to be modified to work with the company's check stock. To determine if the layout needs adjustment, print a check on regular paper and hold it up next to the check stock. You will be able to tell what adjustments need to be made. You can learn more about making check payments in Chapter 12.

To open the check layout editor:

1. Use the pull-down next to the organization name and navigate to **Settings**.
2. Select **Check styles**.
3. In the tile for the style, use the **Options** pull-down and select **Edit**.

To add additional check styles, use the **+New Style** button at the top of the screen.

This screen contains all of the options to edit the check layout. A few important notes:

- Most check stock in the United States is preprinted, so **Paper type** should be **Preprinted stock**.
- In general, preprinted check stock already shows the company logo, company name and address, check number, cut line, and bank name and address, so those fields should be unchecked on the left (Figure 6.13).
- To properly align the remaining fields, use your cursor to drag and drop the field boxes against the gridlines on the check layout.
- Below the check layout is the voucher. Use the boxes on the left to select what information should be printed on the voucher.

## Xero to Xero

Xero maintains an internal network between organizations. By connecting organizations directly, invoices and bills are automatically sent to the recipient's Xero organization, bypassing email. The connection is made by adding a company's unique Xero network key to the contact record in the sender's Xero file.

To access a company's network key:

1. Access the recipient's Xero organization. This is the company that will be receiving invoices or bills.
2. Use the pull-down next to the organization name and navigate to **Settings**.

**FIGURE 6.13**

In general, preprinted check stock already shows the company logo, company name & address, check number, cut line and bank name & address, so those fields should be unchecked on the left

*Source:* Xero Limited

**FIGURE 6.14**

Click the Edit button and paste the key in the Xero Network Key field.

Xero Network Key   H9B9YJPQUZKR1MFYRT6GMQJWLIXV

*Source: Xero Limited*

3. Select **Xero to Xero**.
4. Copy the network key on the right.
5. Return to the sending company's Xero organization.
6. Navigate to the recipient in **Contacts**.
7. Click the **Edit** button and paste the key in the **Xero Network Key** field (Figure 6.14).
8. Click **Save**.

# Advanced Settings

Advanced settings deal with accounting details like year-end, sales tax, and reporting management. In most cases, only someone who understands business finances, such as an accountant or bookkeeper, should manage these settings. To access these settings, navigate to the **Accounting** tab, then **Advanced**.

## Financial Settings

This screen is for configuring sales tax and managing year-end and lock dates. Normally, the fiscal year-end will be established when the Xero organization is created. If it is not, or if the fiscal year of the company changes, the date must be set here.

To establish or change the company's fiscal year-end:

1. Navigate to the **Accounting** tab, then **Advanced**.
2. Select **Financial settings**.
3. Click the **Change** link under Financial Year End.
4. Select the month and day that represents the fiscal year-end.
5. Click **Save**.

If the company needs to collect and remit sales tax, you must verify a few settings in Xero.

1. Navigate to the **Accounting** tab, then **Advanced**.
2. Select **Financial settings**.
3. Under Sales Tax, choose if sales tax will be remitted on a **Cash** or **Accrual** basis.
4. Provide the **Tax ID Number** and **Tax ID Display Name**. Note that Xero does not remit sales tax directly, but this information will show on sales tax reports (Figure 6.15).

**FIGURE 6.15**

Provide the Tax ID Number and Tax ID Display Name. Note that Xero does not remit sales tax directly, but this information will show on sales tax reports.

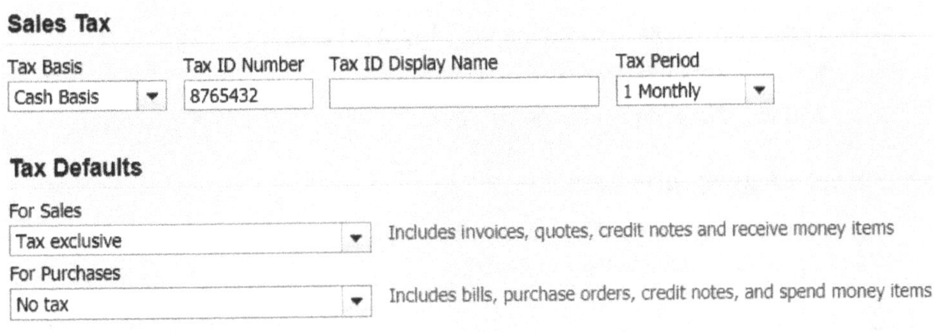

**Sales Tax**

| Tax Basis | Tax ID Number | Tax ID Display Name | Tax Period |
|---|---|---|---|
| Cash Basis ▼ | 8765432 | | 1 Monthly ▼ |

**Tax Defaults**

For Sales

| Tax exclusive ▼ | Includes invoices, quotes, credit notes and receive money items |
|---|---|

For Purchases

| No tax ▼ | Includes bills, purchase orders, credit notes, and spend money items |
|---|---|

*Source:* Xero Limited

5. Choose the sales tax period. The most common options are **1 Monthly** (monthly), **3 Monthly** (quarterly), and **Annually.**

6. Under Tax Defaults, choose how sales tax is calculated. In the United States, sales tax is calculated and collected on sales but not purchases.

    a. Under **For Sales**, select **Tax exclusive.** This means that tax will be calculated on top of the sales price and added to the purchase for a total. (In other regions of the world, tax is included as part of the purchase price and must be accounted for.)

    b. Under **For Purchases**, select **No tax.** This means that no portion of a purchase price will be accrued to a tax payable. (Again, in other regions, a portion of a purchase may be a tax and has to be accounted for.) Note that an indication that this setting is incorrect would be many small debits to the Sales Tax Payable account.

7. Click **Save.**

It is important to **lock dates** in the system so that transactions cannot be changed once the books are closed for the year.

To lock dates:

1. Navigate to the **Accounting** tab, then **Advanced.**

2. Select **Financial settings.**

3. Under **Lock Dates**, select a date to **stop all users (except advisors)** from changing any data. It is a good idea to set this date as soon as possible after the beginning of a new fiscal year, so invoices and bills are not inadvertently levied in a prior year.

4. Once the tax return is filed, set the year-end date in the **stop all users from making changes** field.

5. Click **Save.**

Xero maintains a detailed history of activity in the system. It is important to make sure the time zone is accurate for the company.

To set the time zone:

1. Navigate to the **Accounting** tab, then **Advanced**.
2. Select **Financial settings**.
3. Under **Time zone**, use the pull-down to select the correct time zone.

## Chart of Accounts

The chart of accounts for the organization is an Advanced setting. A full discussion of the chart of accounts is included in Chapter 5.

## Tax Rates

If a company collects and remits sales tax, the rates must be set within Xero. Xero offers a connection to Avalara, a third-party provider, to look up sales tax rates automatically. This could be helpful for companies with nexus in many sales tax jurisdictions. For more information on this partnership, click the Learn more link in the **Sales Tax Lookup** tile.

For companies with limited nexus, using Xero's tax rates functionality works fine. It is important to understand the structure of tax rates. Each tax rate is made of as many as six components. Each component represents a taxing authority to which tax must be remitted. By breaking a total tax rate into underlying components, Xero is able to create reports of tax liabilities for each taxing authority. For example, Orleans Parish total sales tax is 9.45%, of which 4.45% is remitted to the State of Louisiana and 5% is remitted to the City of New Orleans. The tax rate is Orleans Parish and the components are the State of Louisiana and the City of New Orleans.

Xero has a few default tax rates: Tax Exempt (0%), Tax on Purchases (0%), and Tax on Sales (0%). While every transaction in Xero must have an associated tax rate, these 0% rates eliminate the calculation of any tax liability. If the company is not in an industry that requires the collection of sales tax, these rates will be sufficient.

For companies who do need to collect sales tax, the tax rate for each jurisdiction must be created in Xero. To create a tax rate:

1. Navigate to the **Accounting** tab, then **Advanced**.
2. Select **Tax rates**.
3. Click the **Edit** link on the right of Tax Rates.
4. Click **+New Tax Rate**.
5. In the **Tax Rate Display Name** field, type a name for the rate (i.e., New Orleans).

6. Under **Tax Components** list the name of the first component of the rate and its rate. Note that in order for Xero to aggregate sales tax accrued to the same taxing authority, the component name must be identical. For example, State of Louisiana and Louisiana would not be aggregated on reports (Figure 6.16).

7. To add additional components for the rate, use the **Add a Component** button.

8. Click **Save**.

## Fixed Asset Settings

Fixed assets settings work in conjunction with the fixed assets module. Fixed assets are covered in Chapter 13.

## Tracking Categories

Tracking categories in Xero are a way to add a custom field array to any transaction in the system. Tracking categories can be used to filter transactions for reporting or used to compare data between different categories. They are most commonly used for location, department, and class but are flexible enough to be used for many other reasons.

Tracking categories do have two important limitations. A Xero organization can only have two different categories and each of those can only have 100 options or labels. This means

**FIGURE 6.16**

Under Tax Components list the name of the first component of the rate and its rate. Note that in order for Xero to aggregate sales tax accrued to the same taxing authority, the component name must be identical. For example, State of Louisiana and Louisiana would not be aggregated on reports.

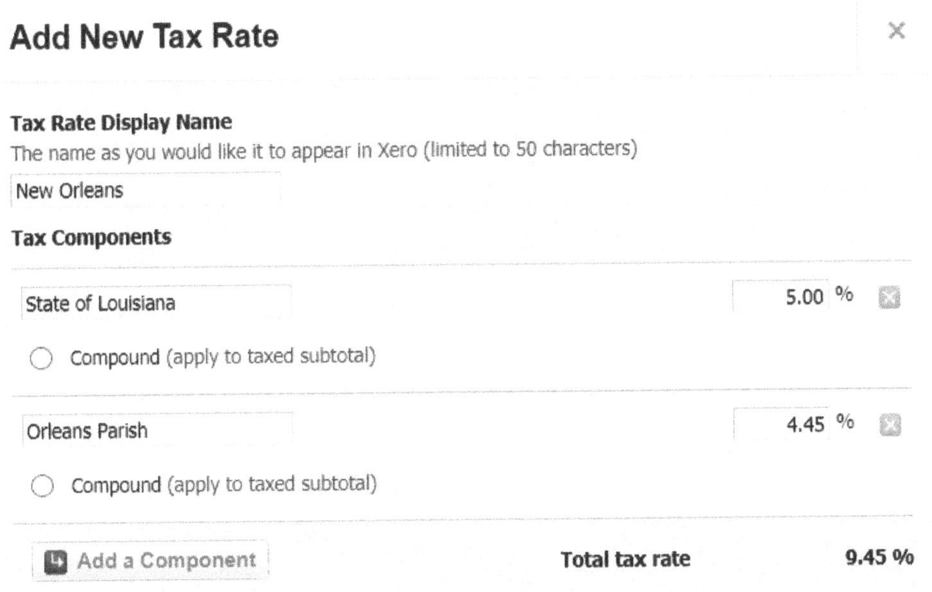

### Add New Tax Rate                                                    ✕

**Tax Rate Display Name**
The name as you would like it to appear in Xero (limited to 50 characters)

New Orleans

**Tax Components**

| State of Louisiana | 5.00 % |
|---|---|

○ Compound (apply to taxed subtotal)

| Orleans Parish | 4.45 % |
|---|---|

○ Compound (apply to taxed subtotal)

| 🔾 Add a Component | **Total tax rate** | **9.45 %** |
|---|---|---|

that tracking categories are not really appropriate for jobs or cases, where it is feasible that the company will need more than 100 labels.

Some third-party apps will include tracking categories in their integrations, which give additional flexibility in data dicing and makes them really powerful.

These are some examples of tracking categories use:

- Attorney in a law firm
- Funding source in a nonprofit organization
- Different real estate properties held in the same entity
- Sales channels in ecommerce companies

**FIGURE 6.17**

Under Category options, list the labels or options you need for the category, using the Add another item button if you need additional options.

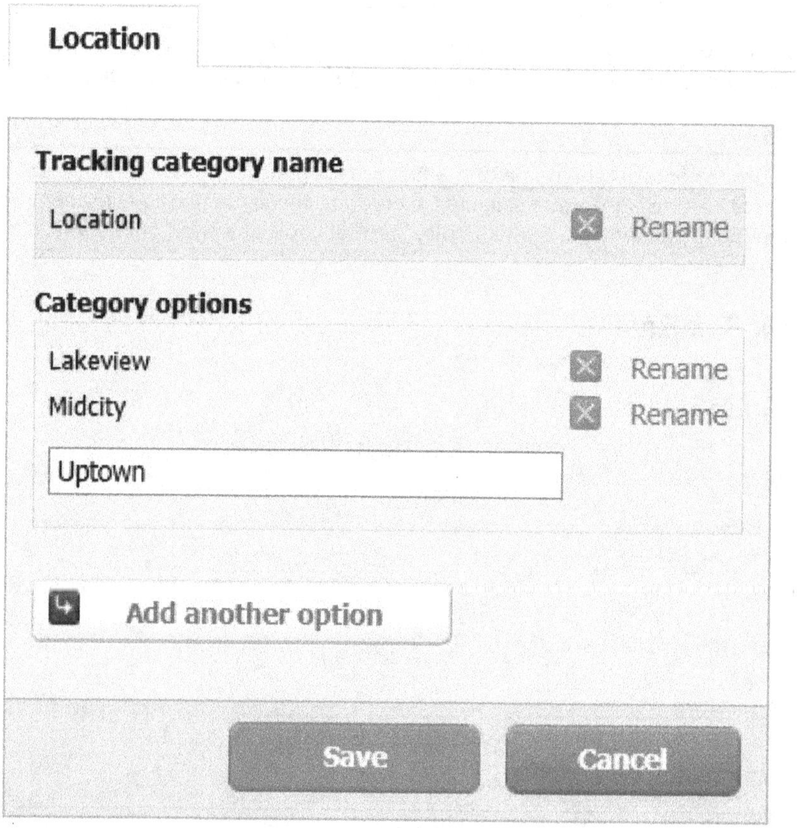

Source: Xero Limited

To create tracking categories:

1. Navigate to the **Accounting** tab, then **Advanced**.
2. Select **Tracking categories**.
3. Click **+Add Tracking Category**.
4. Type a name for the category under **Tracking category name**.
5. Under **Category options**, list the labels or options you need for the category, using the **Add another item button** if you need additional options (Figure 6.17).
6. Click **Save**.

When tracking categories are activated, Xero will insert a new column (or two new columns if both categories are used) in each transaction detail in the system. You will see this pull-down in bank reconciliation, invoicing, and bills, although it will always be optional.

## Report Codes and Report Fields

Report templates, based on report codes and report fields, are a feature only available to Xero Partners. Report codes and fields are covered in Chapter 2 as part of Xero HQ.

## Conversion Balances

**Conversion balances are the starting balances for companies in Xero. They are generally set when a new organization is created, and they are covered in Chapter 5.**

# Contacts

*The ability to easily manage contacts is amazing. I can quickly merge multiple contacts, place them in groups, and save time by mass invoicing. As an accountant user, this makes sorting out my 1099 clients at year-end a breeze.*

—*Katie L'Heureux, Principal of KSL Accounting*

In Xero, **Contacts** refers to customers and suppliers either input into the system deliberately or created by Xero from transactions.

## Navigating the Contacts Screen

The Contacts screen is accessed by navigating to **Contacts**, then **All contacts** (Figure 7.1). This view shows an alphabetical list of all contacts within Xero. This main view of contacts also includes minimal data about the contact, including city, email, and current payable and receivable balances. To view additional contact details, click the blue contact name.

On the left are filters, groups, and Smart Lists. In a new Xero organization, the default filters will be **Customers**, **Suppliers**, and **Archived** (Figure 7.2).

Xero categorizes whether a contact is a customer, supplier, or both based on invoices, bills, and spend or receive money transactions. Contacts cannot be moved into either category manually.

**Groups** are custom lists of selected contacts set up by a user (Figure 7.3). Groups can be used for bulk invoicing, so contact groups may be created specifically for that purpose. Groups are also useful for gathering 1099 vendors for easy preparation of year-end forms.

Xero also provides selected default **Smart Lists** within Contacts. These are queried lists based on conditions existing within the system, like contacts who have purchased certain items or are located in a certain city. Creating custom Smart Lists is discussed further, later.

**FIGURE 7.1**

The Contacts screen is accessed by navigating to Contacts, then All contacts.

*Source:* Xero Limited

**FIGURE 7.2**

On the left are filters, groups and Smart Lists. In a new Xero organization, the default filters will be Customers, Suppliers and Archived

*Source:* Xero Limited

**FIGURE 7.3**

Groups are custom lists of selected contacts set up by a user

*Source:* Xero Limited

# Contact Fields

The details of a contact are held in fields. The population or editing of those fields have different effects in Xero. The following are a few important notes about contact fields.

The **Contact Name** field is one of the primary fields (along with email) that Xero uses to match contacts, especially for integrated applications. Changing a contact name will not change the contact on existing bills, invoices, or transactions, nor will changing a contact name update a repeating invoice template. The template must be updated separately.

The **Account Number** field can be used for any identifying information using a combination of letters and numbers. It is a field that can be searched in the Contacts screen, although not in Global Search (the magnifying glass) in the product header. Note that the same Account Number cannot be used for more than one contact.

A contact's **Email** will be the default used for sending invoices. If there is no email associated with the contact, Xero will prompt you for the email address when the invoice is sent. The email entered in the invoice screen will be saved as the contact's email.

The **Postal Address** of a contact is the address shown on sales documents, like invoices and credit notes. To show the contact's **Street Address** on sales documents, you must create custom templates that include those fields. See Chapter 6 for more information on custom invoice templates.

# Adding Contacts

Contacts are added in Xero in three ways: manually, imported, or created by Xero from transactions.

## Manually Adding Contacts

Contacts are manually added to Xero when a new vendor or customer is established. Setting up the record manually before creating any transactions for the contact will allow the contact details to be fully entered at once.

To add a contact in Xero:

1. Navigate to the **Contacts** tab, then **All contacts**.
2. Click the green **Add contact** button.
3. Use the contact form to enter details about the contact and click **Save** (Figure 7.4).

**FIGURE 7.4**

Use the contact form to enter details about the contact and click Save

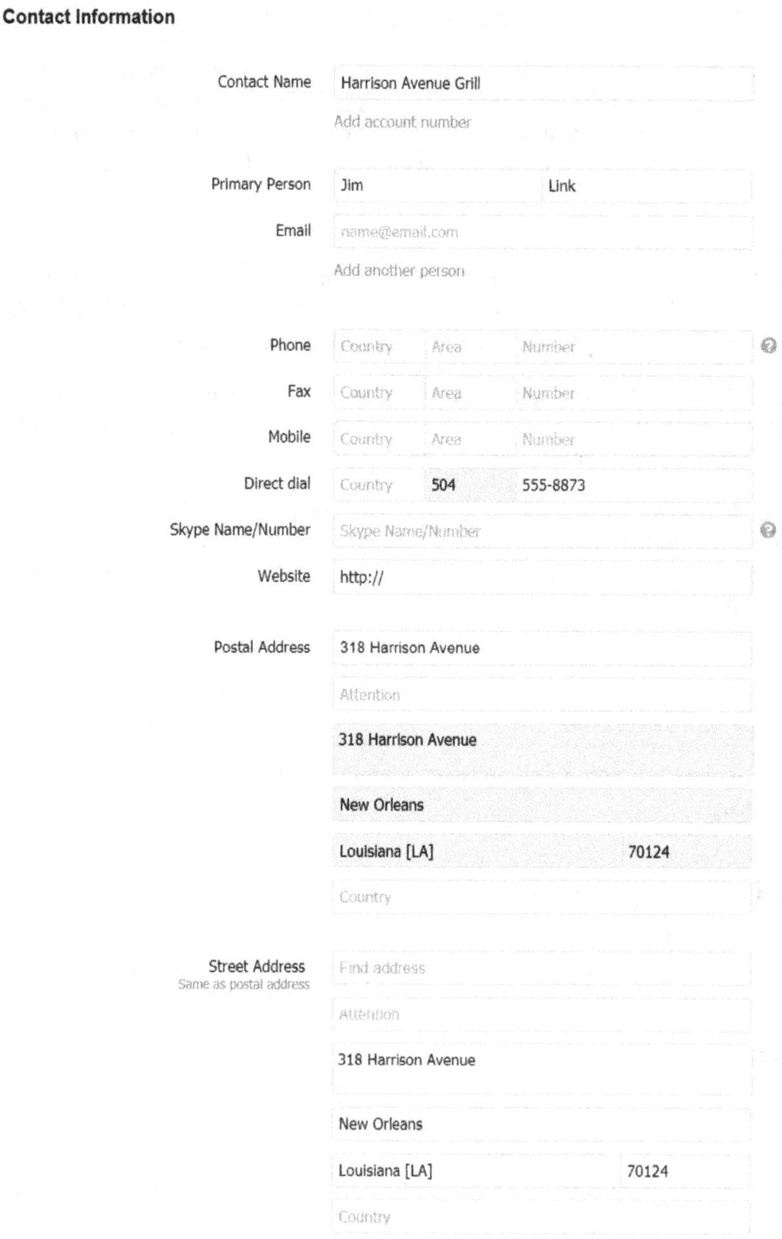

**Contact Information**

| | |
|---|---|
| Contact Name | Harrison Avenue Grill |
| | Add account number |
| Primary Person | Jim                    Link |
| Email | name@email.com |
| | Add another person |
| Phone | Country  Area  Number |
| Fax | Country  Area  Number |
| Mobile | Country  Area  Number |
| Direct dial | Country  **504**  555-8873 |
| Skype Name/Number | Skype Name/Number |
| Website | http:// |
| Postal Address | 318 Harrison Avenue |
| | Attention |
| | **318 Harrison Avenue** |
| | **New Orleans** |
| | **Louisiana [LA]**          70124 |
| | Country |
| Street Address<br>Same as postal address | Find address |
| | Attention |
| | 318 Harrison Avenue |
| | New Orleans |
| | Louisiana [LA]          70124 |
| | Country |

*Source:* Xero Limited

## Importing Contacts

Importing contacts into Xero will save time when there are more than a few new contacts to be entered. This is most commonly done when the file is created.

To import contacts:

1. Navigate to the **Contacts** tab, then **All contacts.**
2. Click the **Import** button at the top of the screen (Figure 7.5).
3. The Contacts import screen is similar to the other import screens you will find throughout Xero, including a download of the import template .csv file. Download and open the template file (Figure 7.6).
4. Enter the contact information in the file. Each row will be a new contact. The only required field is Contact Name, indicated by an asterisk in the header.
5. Save the file.
6. Click the **Browse** button and navigate to the location of the saved file.
7. Choose how you wish for Xero to handle empty fields in the template file. **Ignore empty fields** is the more common choice.
8. Click **Import.**

## Contacts Created by Xero

Xero will automatically create contacts from the coding of bank transactions and the creation of invoices and bills.

For bank transactions, the contact created will be one of the following:

- The name entered in the **Who** field of the **Create** tab in bank reconciliation
- The contact set in the **Contact** field of an applied bank rule
- The payee data from the bank if cash coding is used
- "Unknown" if cash coding was used and there was no payee data from the bank

For invoices and bills, the contact will be the name entered in the **To** field when the invoice or bill is created. If the invoice or bill is emailed to the contact, the email address entered will be added to the contact record as well.

**FIGURE 7.5**

Click the Import button at the top of the screen

**Contacts**

*Source:* Xero Limited

**FIGURE 7.6**

The Contacts import screen is similar to the other import screens you will find throughout Xero, including a download of the import template .csv file. Download and open the template file.

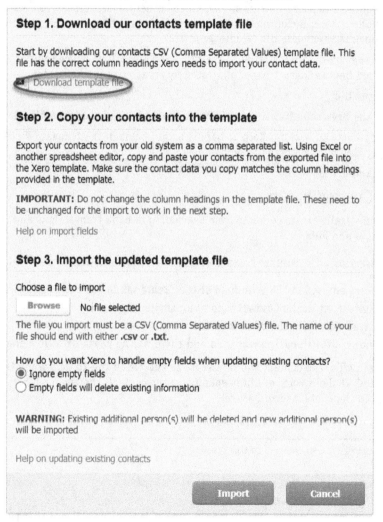

Contacts ›

# Import Contacts

To import contacts from another system please follow the steps below...

## Step 1. Download our contacts template file

Start by downloading our contacts CSV (Comma Separated Values) template file. This file has the correct column headings Xero needs to import your contact data.

    Download template file

## Step 2. Copy your contacts into the template

Export your contacts from your old system as a comma separated list. Using Excel or another spreadsheet editor, copy and paste your contacts from the exported file into the Xero template. Make sure the contact data you copy matches the column headings provided in the template.

**IMPORTANT:** Do not change the column headings in the template file. These need to be unchanged for the import to work in the next step.

Help on import fields

## Step 3. Import the updated template file

Choose a file to import

    Browse    No file selected

The file you import must be a CSV (Comma Separated Values) file. The name of your file should end with either **.csv** or **.txt**.

How do you want Xero to handle empty fields when updating existing contacts?
- ● Ignore empty fields
- ○ Empty fields will delete existing information

**WARNING:** Existing additional person(s) will be deleted and new additional person(s) will be imported

Help on updating existing contacts

    Import        Cancel

*Source:* Xero Limited

# Editing Contact Details

Contact details are easily edited in Xero. You can view a contact's information by clicking the contact name, which opens the record (Figure 7.7).

On the left side of the contact screen, you will see a listing of open transactions, including invoices, bills, and purchase orders. Further down, Xero provides three tabs that can be used to manage a contact's activity:

1. **Activity** is a transaction history by date. The details can be viewed by clicking on the transaction.
2. **Notes** is a place to add notes to the contact.

**FIGURE 7.7**

Contact details are easily edited in Xero. You can view a contact's information by clicking the contact name, which opens the record

Contacts •

## Caleb Vincent

| New ▾ | | | | Options ▾ | Edit |

**1 invoice awaiting payment**                    THEY OWE **440.43**
View recent invoices report                                OVERDUE 440.43

| ITEM | ACTIVITY DATE ▼ | TOTAL |
|------|-----------------|-------|
| Invoice awaiting payment - INV-017<br>Sep 23, 2020 | Due 5 days ago | **440.43** |

Money in over last 12 months

| Oct | Nov | Dec | Jan | Feb | Mar | Apr | May | Jun | Jul | Aug | Sep |

**Activity**  Notes  Email                         Add a note

| ITEM | ACTIVITY DATE ▼ | TOTAL |
|------|-----------------|-------|
| Created<br>By Amanda Aguillard<br>Caleb Vincent has been created. | Sep 25, 2020 | |
| Invoice awaiting payment - INV-017<br>Sep 23, 2020 | Due Sep 23, 2020 | **440.43** |

2 total items

**Contact Details**

🕐 Invoice reminders on

📍 Postal Address
3344 Hwy 98
Key West
FL 33115
View Map

**Groups** 2

[ 1099 ] [ Monthly accounting ]

Remove from group

**Financial Details**

Click 'Edit' to store the contact's default financial settings, such as accounts, tax rates, and due dates

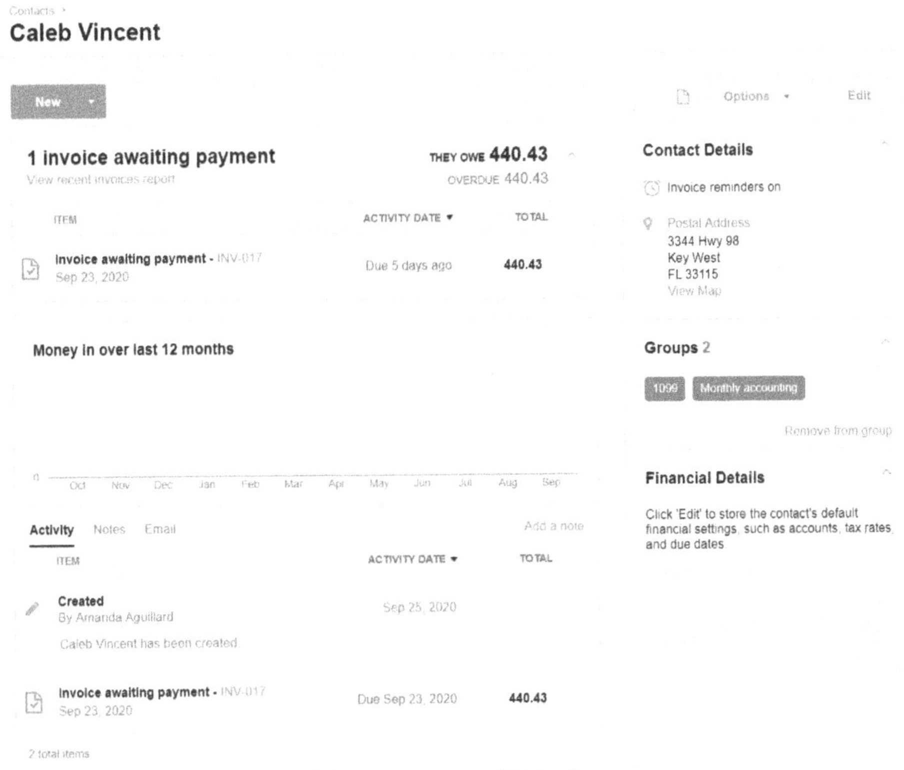

*Source:* Xero Limited

3. **Email** allows the organization to be integrated with Google or Office365 so that relevant emails will be duplicated here, eliminating the need for another program to be searched. Emails where the contact's email address are included in the To, From, or CC fields are also displayed in Xero.

On the right side of the contact screen is an abbreviated version of the contact's information.

To edit the contact information:

1. Navigate to the **Contacts** tab, then **All contacts**.
2. Open the contact you wish to edit by clicking the blue contact name. To quickly find a contact, use the **Search** field at the top of the screen (Figure 7.8).
3. Click the **Edit** button at the top right.
4. Add information or make changes in the fields on this screen.
5. Click **Save**.

# Merging Contacts

You may find that after some use, there are contacts in Xero that are actually duplicates. This could happen because contacts are mistakenly entered with slightly different names. Sometimes third-party add-ons may send contact information to Xero that varies from the existing Xero contact, thereby creating a duplicate. It also happens when cash

**FIGURE 7.8**

Open the contact you wish to edit by clicking the blue contact name. To quickly find a contact, use the Search field at the top of the screen.

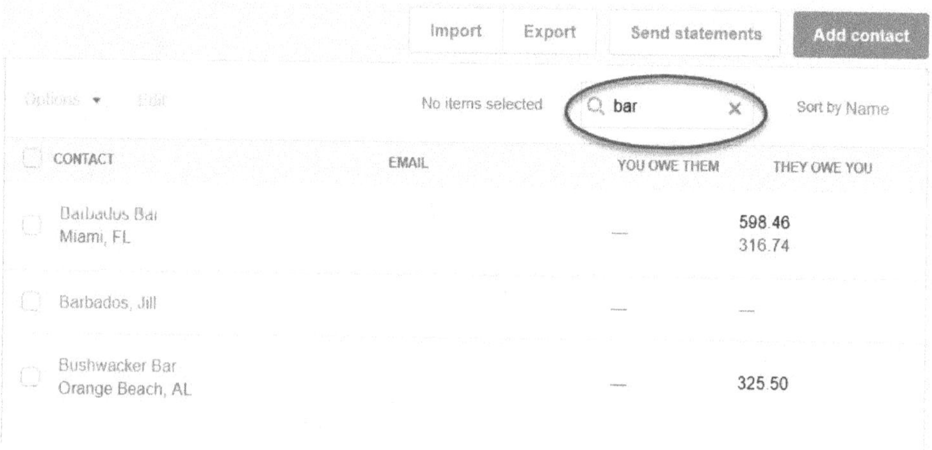

*Source:* Xero Limited

coding is used in bank reconciliation and the payee field from the bank includes specific transactional identifiers, which end up in the contact name.

When merging contacts, it is important to decide which of the duplicates will be the contact that is kept. Because Xero merges transaction history, but not contact details like address, you may want to keep the duplicate with more complete contact details even if it is the misspelled duplicate. The misspelled name can be corrected after the merge.

To merge duplicate contacts:

1. Navigate to the **Contacts** tab, then **All contacts**.
2. Locate the contact you wish to archive by merging into another contact.
3. Click the box to the left of the duplicate contact listing.
4. Use the **Options** pull-down to select **Merge**.
5. Type the contact you wish to merge with in the **Find a contact to merge into** field (Figure 7.9).

**FIGURE 7.9**

Type the contact you wish to merge with in the Find a contact to merge into field

## Merge contacts

You're about to merge the transaction history of **Barbados, Jill** into the contact selected below.

**ⓘ Barbados, Jill** will be archived.

Barbados Bar

☑ I understand the transaction histories for **all selected contacts** will be stored together in **Barbados Bar**.

Cancel          Merge

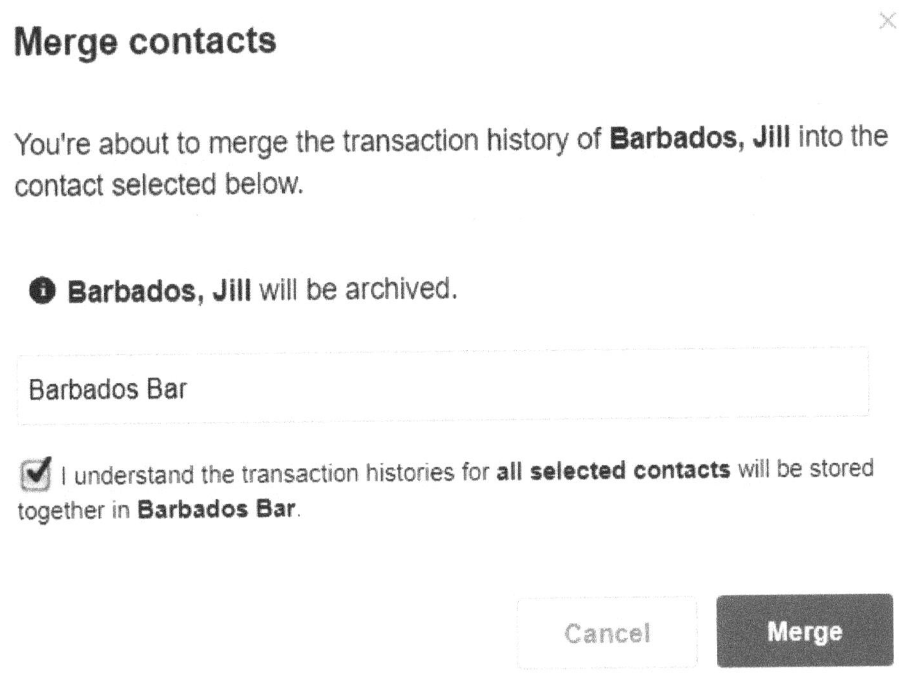

*Source:* Xero Limited

6. Verify the merge by clicking the box to the left of the statement.

7. Click **Merge**.

# Archiving Contacts

If a contact is no longer being used, it can be archived. Arching a contact will remove the contact from the **All** contacts group, as well as the **Customer** and **Suppliers** filters. It will also prevent Xero from populating the contact information on newly created invoices and bills. Once created, contacts can only be archived, not deleted.

To archive a contact:

1. Navigate to the **Contacts** tab, then **All contacts**.

2. Locate the contact you wish to archive.

3. Check the box to the left of the contact.

4. Use the **Options** pull-down to select **Archive** (Figure 7.10).

5. Confirm by selecting **Archive**.

Archived contacts will be visible under the **Archived** group of **All** contacts. A contact can be restored in order to make it an active option for transactions.

To restore an archived contact:

1. Navigate to the **Contacts** tab, then **All contacts**.

2. Select the filter on the left labeled **Archived**.

3. Locate the contact you wish to restore.

4. Open the contact by clicking on the contact name.

**FIGURE 7.10**

Use the Options pulldown to select Archive

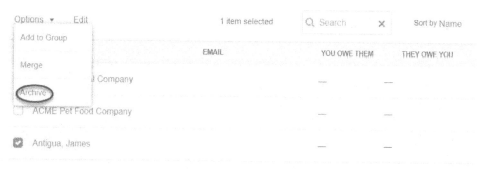

Source: Xero Limited

**FIGURE 7.11**

Click the Restore button in the top right

Contacts ›
### Antigua, James

**No invoices awaiting payment**
View recent invoices report

THEY OWE **0.00**

**Contact Details**

⏱ Invoice reminders on

*Source:* Xero Limited

5. Click the **Restore** button in the top right (Figure 7.11).

6. Confirm you wish to restore the contact by selecting **Restore**.

# Contact Groups

Xero allows contacts to be arranged in custom groups. This can help keep massive numbers of contacts organized and will also allow a user to perform bulk actions, including sending invoices and statements. Contact groups are listed on the left bar of the Contacts screen.

There are two steps to categorizing contacts into groups. You must first create the group, then assign contacts to the group.

To create a new group:

1. Navigate to the **Contacts** tab, then **All contacts**.

2. On the left, click the blue **New** link next to the **Groups** header (Figure 7.12).

3. Enter the name of the new group.

4. Click **Save**.

**FIGURE 7.12**

On the left, click the blue New link next to the Groups header.

# Groups

1099 42

## Monthly accounting 11

*Source:* Xero Limited

**FIGURE 7.13**

Use Options pulldown to select Add to Group

| Options ▼   Edit | 1 item selected | Q b | ✕ | Sort by Name |
|---|---|---|---|---|
| Add to Group | EMAIL | | YOU OWE THEM | THEY OWE YOU |
| Merge | | | — | |
| Archive | | | | |
| ☐ Barbados Bar<br>Miami, FL | | | — | 598.46<br>316.74 |
| ☐ Barbados, Jill | | | — | — |
| ☐ Bayside Part Payment | | | — | — |
| ☑ Beach, Tony | | | — | — |

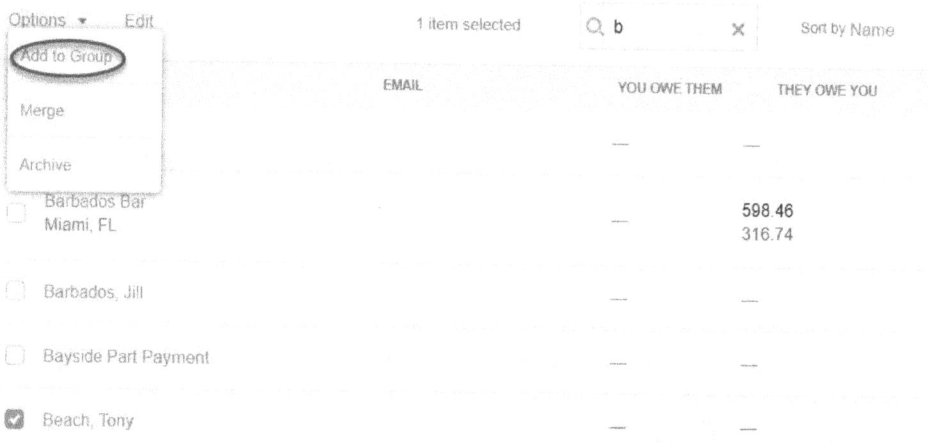

*Source:* Xero Limited

To add contacts to the group:

1. Navigate to the **Contacts** tab, then **All contacts**.
2. Locate the contact to be added to the group and check the box to the left.
3. Use **Options** pull-down to select **Add to Group** (Figure 7.13).
4. Select the group you wish to add the contact into.
5. Click **Add**.

Note that assigning a contact to a group does not remove the contact from any other groups, including Xero's predefined groups Customers and Suppliers.

# Smart Lists

**Smart Lists** in Xero are preset or custom queries that are based on financial qualifiers in the system. Where group contacts are set by the user, Smart List contacts are selected based on financial transactions or history, and due to the nature of the query, are dynamic. One use of these lists is to find contacts meeting criteria for targeted marketing purposes. Smart Lists are shown on the left bar of the Contacts screen.

Xero provides four preset Smart List searches:

- Have purchased an item
- Outstanding > 30 days
- Overdue > 7 days
- Paid us (in the last year).

You can also create a new Smart List query, either by modifying an existing list or creating an original list. Examples of useful queries include:

- Contacts who have purchased a specific item so a product review can be requested.
- Contacts who have not purchased a specific item so a marketing campaign can be created around that item.
- Contacts who have invoices over a certain amount that are overdue by more than a week so an employee can make a phone call to the contact.
- Contacts located in a particular city so that meetings can be scheduled in clusters.

To run a Smart List query :

1. Navigate to the **Contacts** tab, then **All contacts**.
2. Either select one of the preset searches or use the **New** link to the right of the Smart Lists header.
3. Create the Query by modifying the existing conditions or adding additional conditions (Figure 7.14).

**FIGURE 7.14**

Create the Query by modifying the existing conditions or adding additional conditions

**New Smart List**

Find customers matching   All   of the following conditions:

| Invoice | Any | More than | 100 Ever | × |

+ Add a condition

Run Search    Save Search

No items selected   ☐ Select all 13 customers   Sort by Name

| CONTACT | EMAIL | YOU OWE THEM | THEY OWE YOU |
| --- | --- | --- | --- |
| Barbados Bar
Miami, FL | | — | 598.46
316.74 |
| Bushwacker Bar
Orange Beach, AL | | — | 325.50 |
| Caleb Vincent
Key West, FL | | — | 440.43
440.43 |

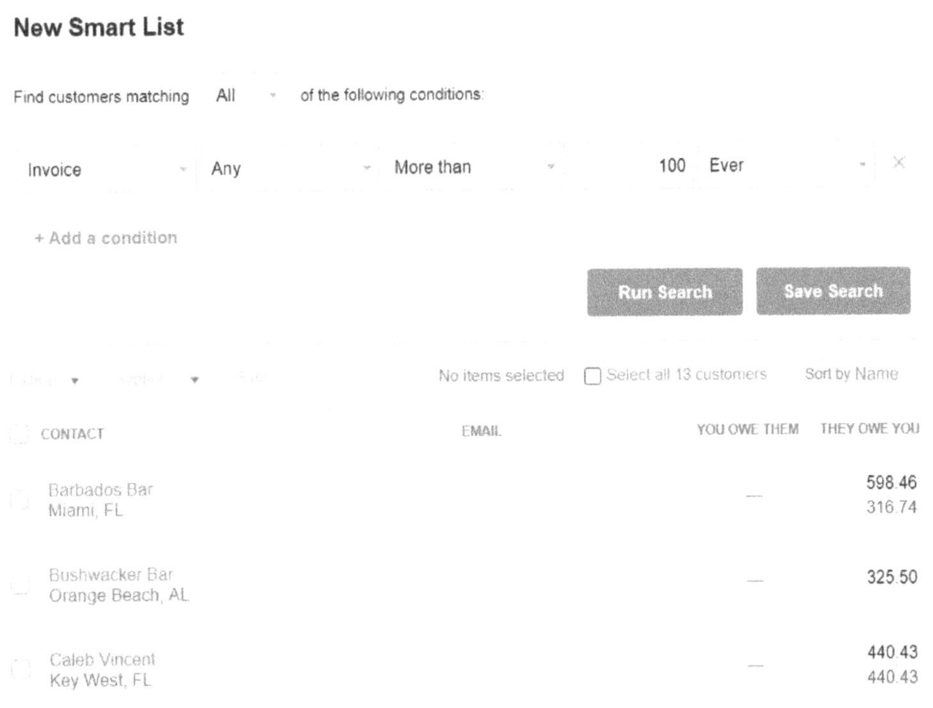

*Source:* Xero Limited

4. If you wish to use these conditions again, click **Save Search** and give the query a name.

5. Use **Run Search** to find contacts who match the conditions. Matching contacts will show below.

6. You can export this list by using the **Export** pull-down.

# Inventory

*I absolutely love the inventory feature of Xero for creating proposals in my own practice. I have inventory items for each of the services and packages that I offer, with full descriptions and prices. It has been a huge weight off my shoulders. I just use my item codes and proposals are automatically built!*

—*Kat Bussey, Founder of Geek Girl Financial Services*

Xero has a very basic inventory module included in its subscription. For companies with limited stock types, it provides an in-product solution to managing stock levels. However, for companies with sophisticated inventory requirements, a third-party inventory application is recommended. Learn more about integrated applications in Chapter 2.

There are two types of inventory in Xero, although they are managed in the same way. **Untracked inventory** refers to inventory items for which a running balance is not tracked. These items are basically a listing of keystroke shortcuts for populating invoices and bills quickly. **Tracked inventory** items allow Xero to keep a stock balance and inventory value for each product based on sales and purchases.

Inventory is accessed by navigating to **Business**, then **Products and services.** This view shows a listing of all inventory items, both tracked and untracked.

## Adding Inventory Items

Before using inventory in Xero, items must be added either manually or by importing. Manually adding items individually will be used when a user must add an item or two to an existing Xero organization. When an organization is being set up, inventory is being added for use for the first time or there are many changes to the current inventory listing, importing will be much faster.

## Manually Adding Untracked Inventory Items

To add an untracked inventory item in Xero:

1. Navigate to the **Business** tab, then **Products and services**.

2. Click the **+New Item** button.

3. Enter a unique **Item Code** (Figure 8.1). This can be an abbreviated name or standard reference code, like SKU or ISBN, but is limited to 30 characters. The item code is generally not visible on invoices or bills.

**FIGURE 8.1**

Enter a unique Item Code. This can be an abbreviated name or standard reference code, like SKU or ISBN, but is limited to thirty characters. The item code is generally not visible on invoices or bills.

**New Item**                                                                    ✕

| Item Code | Item Name |
|-----------|-----------|
| CLEAN | Pool cleaning |

☑ **I purchase this item**

Unit Price    Purchases Account    Tax Rate

**Purchases Description** (for my suppliers)
Pool cleaning

☑ **I sell this item**

Unit Price    Sales Account    Tax Rate

**Sales Description** (for my customers)
Pool cleaning

☐ **I track this item**

This treats your item as a tracked inventory asset. Xero will record the quantity on hand and prevent you selling below a quantity of zero.
**Note:** this option can not be changed once you have recorded transactions against the item.

Find out if tracked inventory is right for you.

Save ▾    Cancel

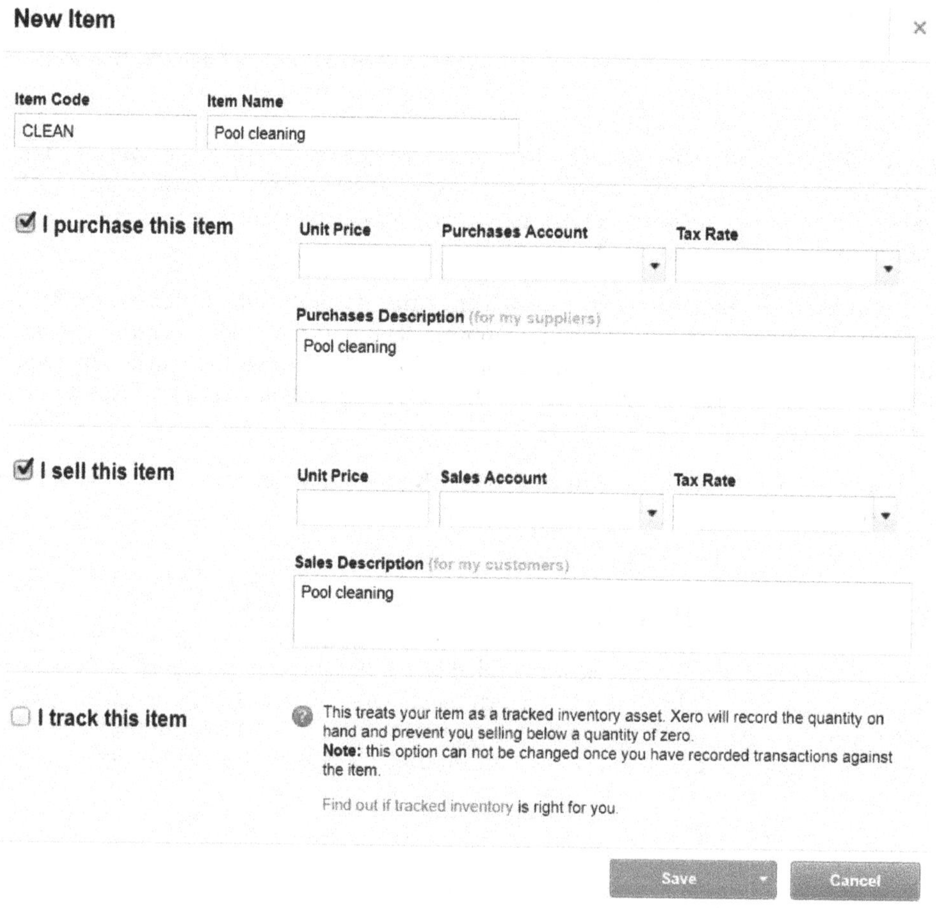

*Source:* Xero Limited

4. Enter the **Item Name**. The item name is limited to 50 characters. The name is generally not visible on invoices, but can be added on custom branded invoices.

5. Decide if this is an item that will be used in purchases, sales, or both, and check the box next to the appropriate statements.

6. Enter the **Unit Price**.

7. Under Purchases Account or Sales Account, select the general ledger account that will be the default when this item is purchased or sold.

8. Select the default **Tax Rate** for purchases and sales.

9. Enter a description for the item. The description will appear on invoices and bills.

10. Do not check the **I track this item** checkbox.

11. Click **Save**.

## Manually Adding Tracked Inventory Items

To add a tracked inventory item in Xero:

1. Navigate to the **Business** tab, then **Products and services**.

2. Click the **+New Item** button.

3. Check the **I track this item** checkbox near the bottom.

4. Enter a unique **Item Code** (Figure 8.2). This can be an abbreviated name or standard reference code, like SKU or ISBN, but is limited to 30 characters. The item code is generally not visible on invoices or bills.

5. Enter the **Item Name**. The item name is limited to 50 characters. The name is generally not visible on invoices but can be added on custom branded invoices.

6. Decide if this is an item that will be used in purchases, sales, or both, and check the box next to the appropriate statements.

7. Enter the **Unit Price**.

8. Under **Cost of Goods Sold Account** or **Sales Account**, select the general ledger account that will be the default when this item is purchased or sold.

9. Select the default **Tax Rate** for purchases and sales.

10. Enter a description for the item. The description will appear on invoices and bills.

11. Select the **Inventory Asset Account** to use for this item.

12. Click **Save**.

## Adding Description-Only Items

Inventory items can also be used as data-entry shortcuts to add language to invoices, rather than as an actual item to be sold. Advisors often use this timesaver to add return policies or holiday greetings to client invoices.

**FIGURE 8.2**

**FIGURE 8.2**

Enter a unique Item Code. This can be an abbreviated name or standard reference code, like SKU or ISBN, but is limited to thirty characters. The item code is generally not visible on invoices or bills

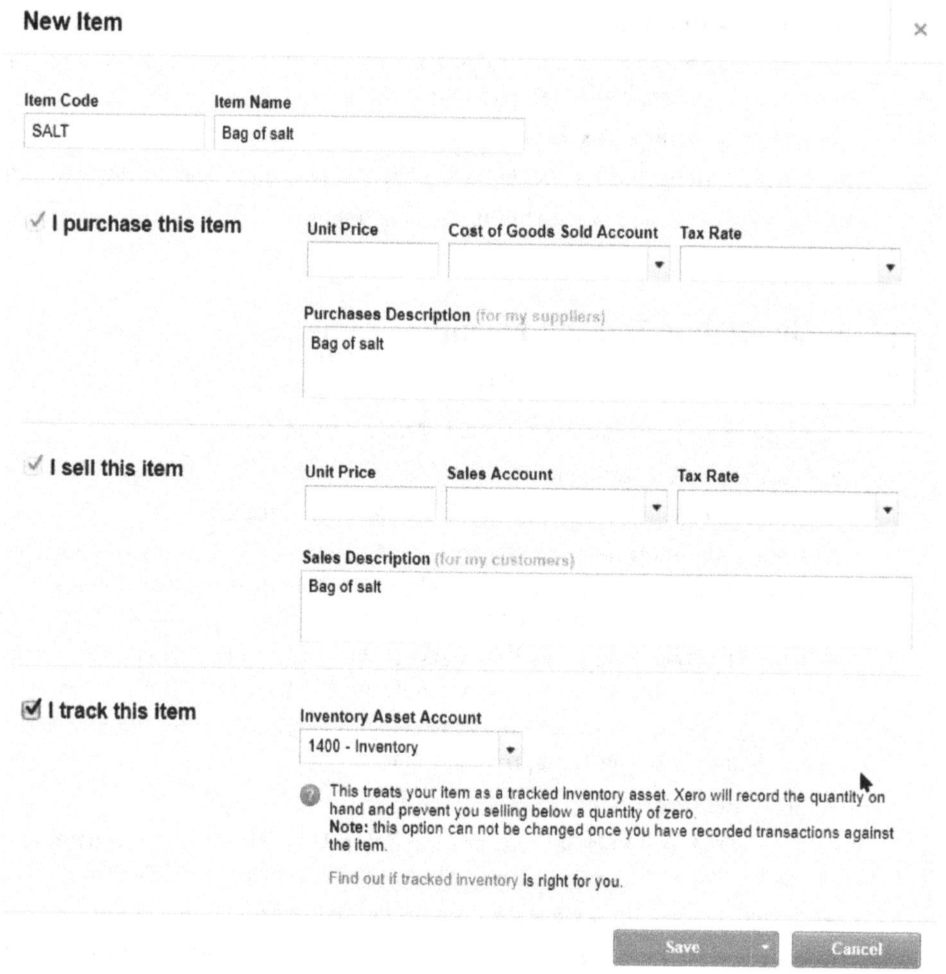

**New Item**                                                                          ✕

| Item Code | Item Name |
|---|---|
| SALT | Bag of salt |

✓ **I purchase this item**     Unit Price     Cost of Goods Sold Account     Tax Rate

Purchases Description (for my suppliers)

Bag of salt

✓ **I sell this item**     Unit Price     Sales Account     Tax Rate

Sales Description (for my customers)

Bag of salt

☑ **I track this item**     Inventory Asset Account

1400 - Inventory

ⓘ This treats your item as a tracked inventory asset. Xero will record the quantity on hand and prevent you selling below a quantity of zero.
**Note:** this option can not be changed once you have recorded transactions against the item.

Find out if tracked inventory is right for you.

Save ▾     Cancel

*Source: Xero Limited*

To create a description-only item:

1. Navigate to the **Business** tab, then **Products and services**.
2. Click the **+New Item** button.
3. Enter a unique **Item Code** (Figure 8.3).
4. Skip the **I purchase this item** section.

**FIGURE 8.3**

Enter a unique Item Code

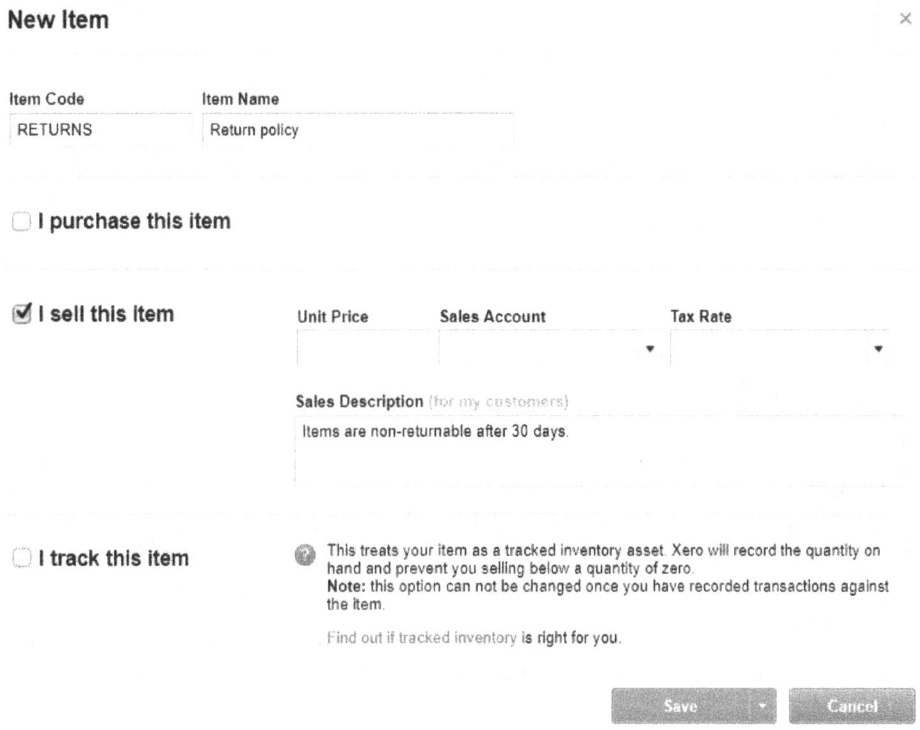

**New Item**                                                                                          ×

| Item Code | Item Name |
|-----------|-----------|
| RETURNS   | Return policy |

☐ **I purchase this item**

☑ **I sell this item**     Unit Price        Sales Account                    Tax Rate
                                                              ▼                              ▼

                           **Sales Description** (for my customers)

                           Items are non-returnable after 30 days.

☐ **I track this item**    ⓘ  This treats your item as a tracked inventory asset. Xero will record the quantity on
                              hand and prevent you selling below a quantity of zero.
                              **Note:** this option can not be changed once you have recorded transactions against
                              the item.

                              Find out if tracked inventory is right for you.

                                                              Save   ▾      Cancel

*Source:* Xero Limited

5. In the **Sales Description** field, enter the language you wish to include when the item code is entered.

6. Click **Save**.

## Importing Inventory Items

The process for importing inventory items into Xero consists of two steps: preparing an import file and importing the file into Xero. Note that only 1,000 items may be imported at a time.

To prepare the import file:

1. Navigate to the **Business** tab, then **Products and services**.

2. Use the **Import** pull-down at the top right to select **Items**.

3. Click **Download template file** to access a .csv template.

4. Prepare the file by entering one inventory item per line. The only required field is ItemCode, which is indicated by an asterisk. If a column is not needed, leave it blank. Do not delete it. The InventoryAssetAccount and CostOfGoodsSoldAccount fields are only used for tracked inventory items.

5. Save the template file where it can be easily located.

To import the inventory file:

1. Use the **Browse** button to select the file for import.

2. Click **Continue**.

3. Xero will show an orange confirmation of how many items will be created and updated. If this is correct, click **Complete Import**.

# Editing Inventory Item Details

Inventory item details are easily edited in Xero. You can view an item's details by clicking the item name, which opens the item record. The item record will show the defaults or settings for the purchase or sale of the item. It will also list all recent transactions that use the item and a history of all activity related to the creation or editing of the item.

**FIGURE 8.4**

Use the Edit item button at the top right to access the item's editable fields.

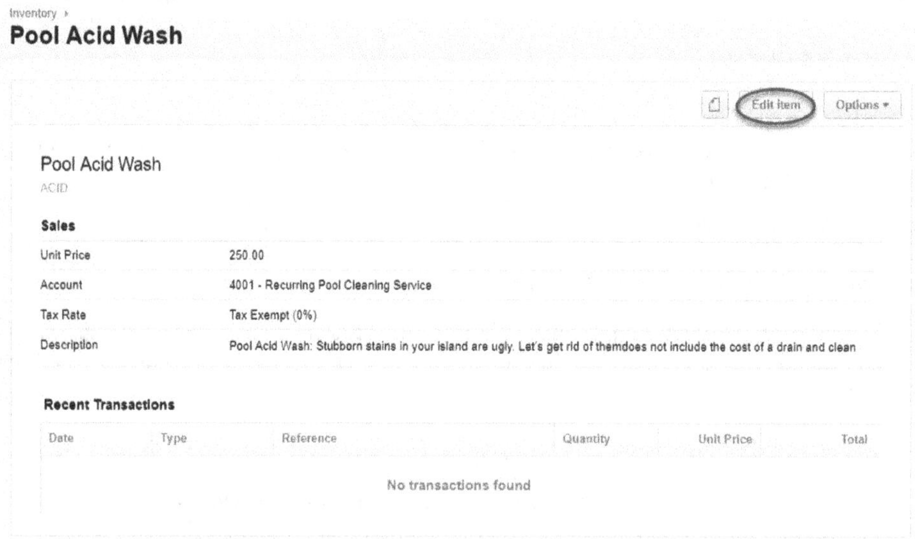

Inventory ›
**Pool Acid Wash**

| | Edit item | Options ▾ |

Pool Acid Wash
ACID

**Sales**

| | |
|---|---|
| Unit Price | 250.00 |
| Account | 4001 - Recurring Pool Cleaning Service |
| Tax Rate | Tax Exempt (0%) |
| Description | Pool Acid Wash: Stubborn stains in your island are ugly. Let's get rid of themdoes not include the cost of a drain and clean |

**Recent Transactions**

| Date | Type | Reference | Quantity | Unit Price | Total |
|---|---|---|---|---|---|
| | | No transactions found | | | |

*Source:* Xero Limited

To edit the item settings:

1. Navigate to the **Business** tab, then **Products and services**.
2. Open the item record by clicking the blue item name.
3. Use the **Edit item** button at the top right to access the item's editable fields (Figure 8.4).
4. Make changes to the item settings.
5. Click **Save**.

# Importing Beginning Balances

If you need to establish beginning balances for inventory, you will want to import the balances. The process for importing inventory balances consists of two steps: preparing an import file and importing the file into Xero.

To prepare the import file:

1. Navigate to the **Business** tab, then **Products and services**.
2. Use the **Import** pull-down at the top right to select **Opening Balances** (Figure 8.5).
3. Select the date of the opening balances. If you are converting data from another system, this will be the conversion date.
4. Click **Download template file** to access a .csv template.
5. Prepare the file by adding amounts in Quantity on Hand, Total Value on Hand, and Adjustment Account.
6. Save the template file where it can be easily located.

To import the inventory file:

1. Use the **Browse** button to select the file for import.
2. Click **Continue**.
3. Xero will show a confirmation of how many items will be updated and a draft of the adjustment entry that will be posted. If this is correct, click **Complete Import**.

**FIGURE 8.5**

Use the Import pulldown at the top right to select Opening Balances

### Products and services

*Source:* Xero Limited

# Managing Inventory Balances

Xero will keep a running balance stock quantity for tracked inventory items based on purchases and sales, but if there are changes that are not related to purchases or sales, such as damages or theft losses, you will need to adjust inventory levels.

To make an inventory adjustment to an inventory item:

1. Navigate to the **Business** tab, then **Products and services**.
2. Open the item record by clicking the blue item name.
3. Use the **Options** pull-down to access **New adjustment** (Figure 8.6).
4. Under **Adjustment type** select **Decrease quantity**, **Increase quantity**, or **Revaluation**. Decreasing or increasing the quantity will change the number of items in stock. Revaluation will not change the number of items but will only change the value of items on hand.
5. Enter the **Date** for the adjustment.
6. Enter the quantity of the adjustment or the cost of the adjustment, depending on the adjustment type.

**FIGURE 8.6**

Use the Options pulldown to access New adjustment

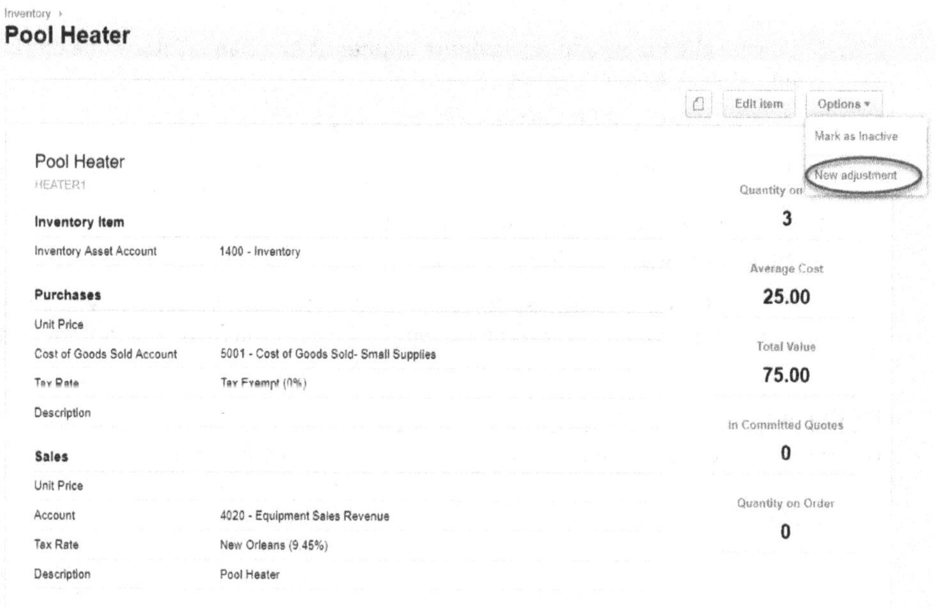

*Source:* Xero Limited

7. Select the **Adjustment Account**, which is the general ledger account that should be posted against. In general, this is an income or expense account. You may also enter a tracking category for the adjustment.

8. Enter a reason for the adjustment under Notes.

9. Click **Review Adjustment.**

10. Xero will provide a draft of the adjustment, including a journal entry, for your review.

11. Click **Post Adjustment.**

# Deleting or Inactivating Items

There may be a case with a company where inventory items that have been added are not needed. If an item has never been used on an invoice, bill, spend money or receive money, and no adjustments have been made to its balance, it can be deleted. If any transactions have been posted using the item, it cannot be deleted but can be marked as inactive. Inactive items cannot be selected on new transactions, but historical transactions using the item will still be accessible.

**FIGURE 8.7**

Select Mark as Inactive or Delete

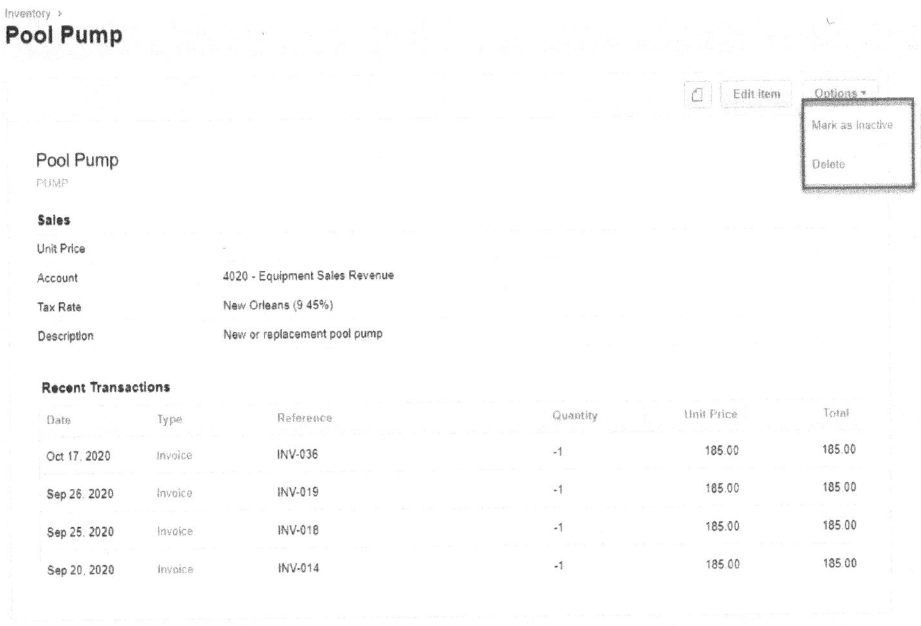

Source: Xero Limited

To delete or inactivate an inventory item:

1. Navigate to the **Business** tab, then **Products and services.**
2. Open the item record by clicking the blue item name.
3. Use the **Options** pull-down at the top right.
4. Select **Mark as Inactive** or **Delete** (Figure 8.7).

# Banking and Bank Feeds

*The tight Stripe integration with Xero makes reconciling a client's books (or your own) quick and easy. Having all the Stripe items come into Xero as a bank feed, including the processing fees, keeps the process super simple. The auto reconciliation that occurs when a Xero invoice is paid is super slick.*

*—Trinity Scott, Owner and Chief Technologist of T3 Bookkeeping*

In small business accounting, a majority of the company's financial data, perhaps 85% or more, is gathered from transactions that exist in bank or credit card accounts. By efficiently and accurately assembling bank data at the transaction level and automating the coding and assignment of those transactions, advisors can free up time to provide more high value services.

## Overview of the Bank Accounts Screen

In Xero, while the Dashboard shows a selection of bank and credit card accounts and is often the starting point for reconciliation, bank accounts have their own dedicated screen. The Bank accounts screen is accessed by navigating to **Accounting,** then **Bank accounts.** This screen is where all bank checking, savings, and credit card accounts are managed. The Dashboard may only show selected bank accounts, where the Bank accounts screen will show all. The Bank accounts screen has a series of buttons across the top, as well as a tile for each bank or credit card account (Figure 9.1).

The **Add Bank Account** button is a quick link to add a new bank or credit card to the Xero file.

The **Transfer Money** button is a shortcut to move funds between bank or credit card accounts and is discussed in the following chapter.

The **Bank Rules** button is a quick access link to a list of all current bank rules in effect for the company. Bank rules are discussed at length in the next chapter.

One of the most useful reports for communicating with clients is the **Uncoded Statement Lines** report (Figure 9.2). This report will show all uncoded bank transactions within all or certain bank

**FIGURE 9.1**

The Bank accounts screen has a series of buttons across the top, as well as a tile for each bank or credit card account.

# Bank accounts

| ➕ Add Bank Account | ➕ Transfer Money | ▶ Bank Rules | ▶ Uncoded Statement Lines |

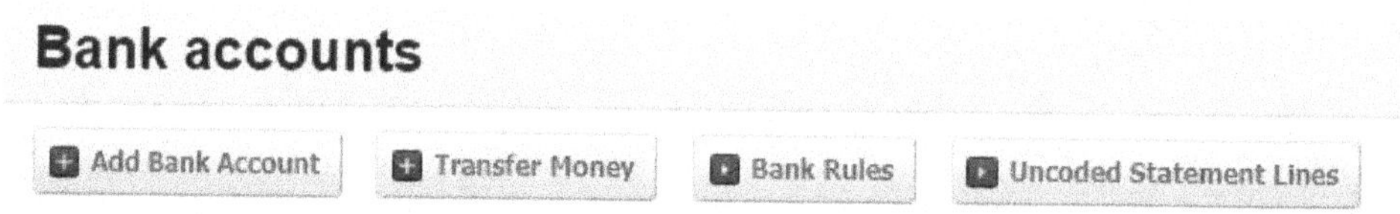

*Source:* Xero Limited

**FIGURE 9.2**

One of the most useful reports for communicating with clients is the Uncoded Statement Lines report.

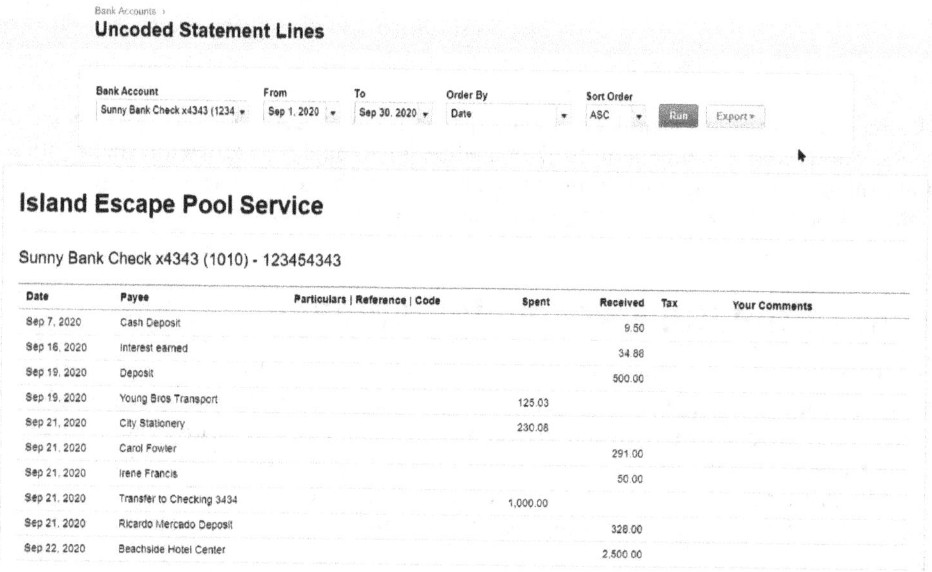

Bank Accounts ›
### Uncoded Statement Lines

| Bank Account | From | To | Order By | Sort Order | | |
|---|---|---|---|---|---|---|
| Sunny Bank Check x4343 (1234 ▾ | Sep 1, 2020 ▾ | Sep 30, 2020 ▾ | Date ▾ | ASC ▾ | Run | Export ▾ |

## Island Escape Pool Service

Sunny Bank Check x4343 (1010) - 123454343

| Date | Payee | Particulars \| Reference \| Code | Spent | Received | Tax | Your Comments |
|---|---|---|---|---|---|---|
| Sep 7, 2020 | Cash Deposit | | | 9.50 | | |
| Sep 16, 2020 | Interest earned | | | 34.88 | | |
| Sep 19, 2020 | Deposit | | | 500.00 | | |
| Sep 19, 2020 | Young Bros Transport | | 125.03 | | | |
| Sep 21, 2020 | City Stationery | | 230.08 | | | |
| Sep 21, 2020 | Carol Fowler | | | 291.00 | | |
| Sep 21, 2020 | Irene Francis | | | 50.00 | | |
| Sep 21, 2020 | Transfer to Checking 3434 | | 1,000.00 | | | |
| Sep 21, 2020 | Ricardo Mercado Deposit | | | 328.00 | | |
| Sep 22, 2020 | Beachside Hotel Center | | | 2,500.00 | | |

*Source:* Xero Limited

or credit card accounts for a period. The report will show the date of the transaction, the payee from the bank (if that is a field populated in bank data), additional data pulled from the bank line, the transaction amount, comments saved in the Discuss tab in bank reconciliation, and room for additional explanatory comments. The report can be exported as a .pdf or .csv for distribution. Many advisors use this report to communicate any remaining coding questions for clients after a first effort at the end of the month or year.

Below the buttons in the Bank accounts screen are tiles for each of the bank or credit card accounts of the company, unless the account has been archived from the chart of accounts. The key components of the bank account tiles are discussed below.

**FIGURE 9.3**

Xero shows two balances on the bank account tile: Statement Balance and Balance in Xero.

**Sunny Bank Check x4343**
123454343

**6,196.23**
Statement Balance

Oct 2, 2021

**1,609.01**
Balance in Xero

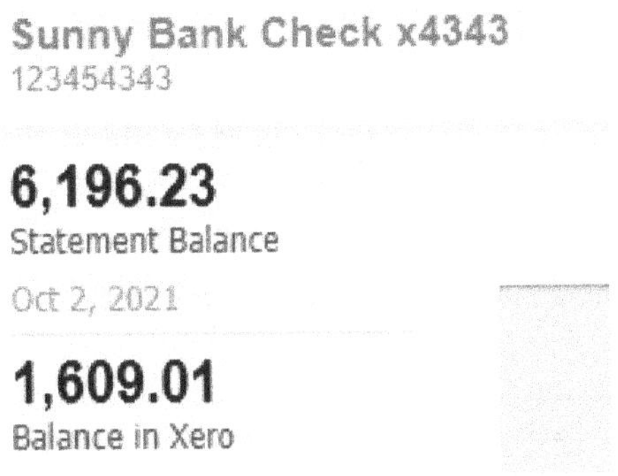

*Source:* Xero Limited

Xero shows two balances on the bank account tile: Statement Balance and Balance in Xero (Figure 9.3). The **Statement Balance** is the account balance calculated by using the current general ledger balance and adjusting for any unreconciled bank transactions through the last date of transactions imported. The **Balance in Xero** is the general ledger balance without any adjustments for unreconciled transactions.

The **Reconcile # items** button shows how many bank lines are uncoded on the account (Figure 9.4). Clicking this button will redirect you to the reconciliation screen for the account.

**FIGURE 9.4**

The Reconcile # items button shows how many bank lines are uncoded on the account.

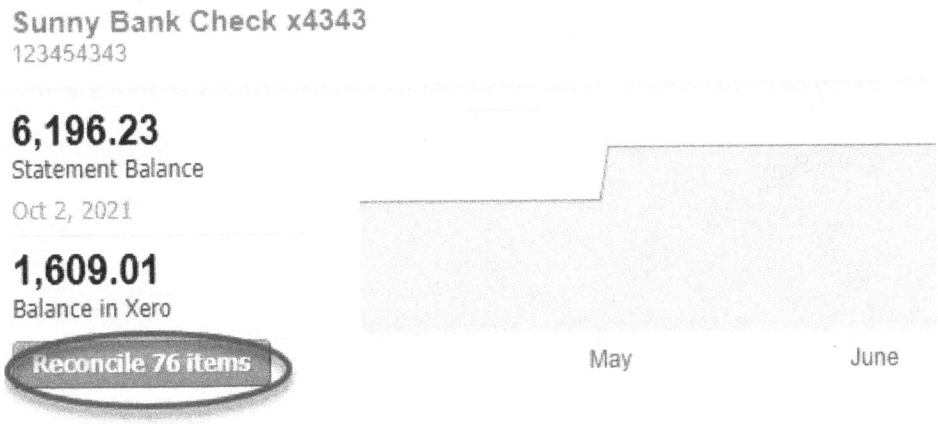

**Sunny Bank Check x4343**
123454343

**6,196.23**
Statement Balance

Oct 2, 2021

**1,609.01**
Balance in Xero

Reconcile 76 items

May          June

*Source:* Xero Limited

The **Manage Account** pull-down is the main list of maintenance and settings for the bank account (Figure 9.5). It includes creating new transactions, accessing bank rules, and importing statements. Note that although this button is duplicated on the Dashboard with an overflow symbol, any problem solving on the bank account should be done here in the Bank Accounts screen.

Checking the box to the left of **Show account on Dashboard** will add a tile on the Dashboard for the bank account (Figure 9.6). If you wish to remove an account from the Dashboard, in the case of a closed account, for example, uncheck this box.

To move the account tile up or down in the order, use the **Change order** arrows.

### FIGURE 9.5

The Manage Account pulldown is the main list of maintenance and settings for the bank account.

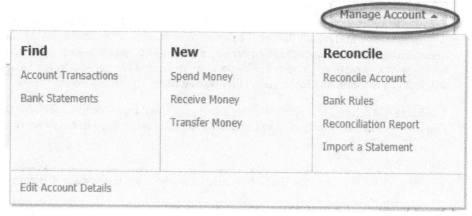

*Source:* Xero Limited

### FIGURE 9.6

Checking the box to the left of Show account on Dashboard will add a tile on the Dashboard for the bank account.

*Source:* Xero Limited

# Bank Accounts

Bank accounts (and credit card accounts) in Xero are very important. It is through bank accounts and bank feeds that most of the transactions of the business will be entered into the system. While adding business bank accounts seems clear-cut, that is not always the case. Bank accounts that hold strictly business transactions are obvious, but what about accounts that have both personal and business expenses?

## Which Bank Accounts to Add

The key to determining which bank or credit card accounts should be added to Xero is to compare the amount of business data gathered by including a particular bank feed versus the amount of nonbusiness "junk" that will need to be excluded. In general, it is easier to capture more transactions and eliminate non-business than to seek out business transactions separately and add manually.

Here are some suggestions:

| | |
|---|---|
| Bank or credit card account (100% business transactions) | Include account and feed in Xero |
| Bank or credit card account (50% business transactions, 50% personal) | Include account and feed in Xero; code non-business transactions to Owner's Draw or Distributions, using Bank Rules where possible to automate |
| Bank or credit card account (10% business, 90% personal) | Do not include account or feed in Xero; book a journal entry to record business expenses with an offsetting Due to Owner liability |

Another complex situation with bank feeds is with employee or **subordinate credit cards.** Some banks set up company credit cards with one master primary card and underlying subordinate cards. Often, the subordinate card feeds will include the charges to the credit card account, but not payments on the account. The primary card feed will show the entire payment on the account (and possibly charges made directly on that account). The problem occurs at month-end reconciliation, where multiple card feeds make up the ending statement balance. This complexity confuses some users to the point of frustration, and they elect not to include the subordinate cards in Xero, instead making manual entries.

The appropriate treatment is to create an account for each card that has a separate feed. This will allow the company to gather all charges on the cards automatically. Reconciliation can be managed with a series of transfers to the master level card. (See Chapter 10 for an explanation.)

9

Another case that causes advisors grief is the management of payment service feeds, like Stripe. **Stripe** is a payment processor and, in the United States, is the preferred credit card payment processor for Xero invoices. Stripe is also used by many other ecommerce platforms, so it is very common to see Stripe deposits in a business bank account. Stripe will process payments on behalf of the company, then deposit an amount, net of fees, to the business checking account within a few days. The payments may come from Xero-generated invoices or may come from other platforms. The decision to be made by the advisor is whether to code the net deposits that arrive in the checking account or create a separate bank feed for the Stripe account.

The answer likely depends on the volume processed by Stripe and who is doing the monthly reconciliation. Adding the Stripe direct feed makes coding the gross sales payment, along with the processing fee, much easier, but if not reconciled properly can lead to problems. Generally, the higher the volume of Stripe transactions, the more sense it makes to add a Stripe bank feed to Xero. The mechanics behind the reconciliation are covered in Chapter 10.

## Adding a New Bank Account

When you have decided which bank, credit card, or processor accounts should be included in the Xero organization, you will need to add them. Adding a bank account in Xero means to create a new account in the chart of accounts with the type of bank account. You will then need to connect a bank feed, if available, or import bank data.

To add a new bank or credit card account to Xero that was not previously created during conversion:

1. Navigate to the **Accounting** tab, then **Bank accounts.**
2. Click the **+Add Bank Account** button.
3. Enter the name of the bank, credit card issuer, or payment processor in the **Search for your bank** field.
4. If Xero locates the bank, that means there is a direct or third-party bank feed available. Choose the bank or credit card issuer, taking care to select a credit card feed, if available and appropriate. Depending on your bank, you may be prompted to enter login credentials to activate the bank feed.
5. If your bank does not appear on the list, there is no bank feed available at this time and you will have to import transactions. You should enter the full name of the bank or credit card issuer and click **Add it anyway** (Figure 9.7).
6. Enter the details for the new bank account. For more information on account details, see Chapter 5.
7. Click **Save.**
8. The new bank account will appear on the Bank accounts screen.

**FIGURE 9.7**

If your bank does not appear on the list, there is no bank feed available at this time and you will have to import transactions. You should enter the full name of the bank or credit card issuer and click Add it anyway.

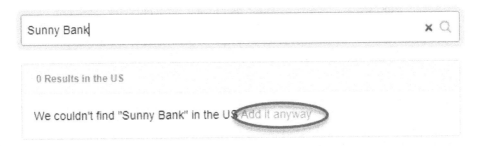

Find your bank

Sunny Bank

0 Results in the US

We couldn't find "Sunny Bank" in the US Add it anyway

*Source:* Xero Limited

# Bank Feeds

## Types of Bank Feeds

High-fidelity bank feeds are the backbone of Xero bookkeeping. Bank feeds refer to the electronic transmission of bank transactional data into the general ledger. The transaction data must contain a date and amount, but may also include payee, reference, and description fields. Some direct feeds will also include account balances. Effective management of all of the data in bank transactions will keep the general ledger organized and clear.

There are three types of bank feeds in Xero:

1. Direct bank feeds
2. Third-party
3. Payment processor

**Direct bank feeds** are direct integrations with a banking institution. There is a direct API connection between the bank and Xero, and new transactions appear in Xero overnight. Direct feeds provide the most consistent and accurate bank data because there is no chance of misinterpretation by a third-party application. At the time of writing, the following U.S. banks have direct feeds with Xero: BBVA USA, Brex, Capital One, City National Bank, CurrencyFair, Emburse, Farm Credit Services of America (FCSA), Mercury, NorthOne, Novo, Relay Financial, Silicon Valley Bank (SVB), TransferWise, and Wells Fargo.

**Third-party bank feeds** are feeds where an external application is used to connect the bank to Xero where a direct integration does not exist. In the United States, at the time of writing, Yodlee is the current provider of this service. There are thousands of banks that

9

can be connected to Xero via Yodlee. Yodlee stores the bank credentials in a secure system for use in accessing transactional data only. Each night Yodlee will scrape bank transactions, parse the data, and send to Xero. Third-party feeds are slightly less reliable than direct feeds, especially when a bank changes its user interface. Since Yodlee is scraping the visual data, a change in the way the transactions are presented on the screen can affect the accuracy of the transaction data.

**Payment processor feeds** are feeds not from banking institutions but from electronic payment processors, like Stripe. These feeds show payments processed and cash transferred out, and generally include gross deposits and merchant fee amounts. Payment processor feeds can be tricky with regards to workflow to be sure deposits are matched correctly to sales or invoice transactions. For more details, see Chapter 10 about managing the reconciliation of these accounts.

## Activating Bank Feeds

Generally, a bank account feed is activated during setup of the Xero organization. However, there could be reasons that the feed is not established at the same time that the account is created. The user adding the bank account may not have login credentials or it may be firm policy that a specific login other than the creator connect the bank feed so it can be managed by the firm. A bank feed can only be managed by the login of the user who originally connected it. Some advisors create a specific "bank feed user" that multiple staff members have access to, so that in the event a client bank feed needs to be reset, anyone in the firm can handle it.

If an account is created for a bank with a feed, there will usually be a green **Get bank feeds** button on the account tile (Figure 9.8). Alternatively, use the **Manage Account** button at the top right of the account tile (or the overflow menu of three dots if on the Dashboard) to navigate to **Get bank feeds**. Xero will prompt for bank credentials and may require security questions.

If the bank login allows access to more than one bank account, the user will have to select the matching bank feed from a pull-down of all accounts. The user must also select the start date of transactions to import. Either a specific date can be selected or the user can import all available transactions. Note that for many banks, only 90 days of transactions

**FIGURE 9.8**

If an account is created for a bank with a feed, there will usually be a green Get bank feeds button on the account tile.

*Source:* Xero Limited

**FIGURE 9.9**

On occasion, a bank feed will break. This could be from a lapse in service by the bank, a reformat of the online interface or a bug with the third-party software. Generally, Xero will give a warning in red that "There is a problem with this bank feed." Often the problem will be solved by updating the connection, refreshing the feed or deactivating and reconnecting.

| Find | New | Reconcile | Bank Feeds |
|------|-----|-----------|------------|
| Account Transactions | Spend Money | Reconcile Account | Update bank connection |
| Bank Statements | Receive Money | Bank Rules | Refresh Bank Feed |
| | Transfer Money | Reconciliation Report | Update Feed Login |
| | | Import a Statement | Deactivate Feed |
| | | | View Status Updates |

Edit Account Details

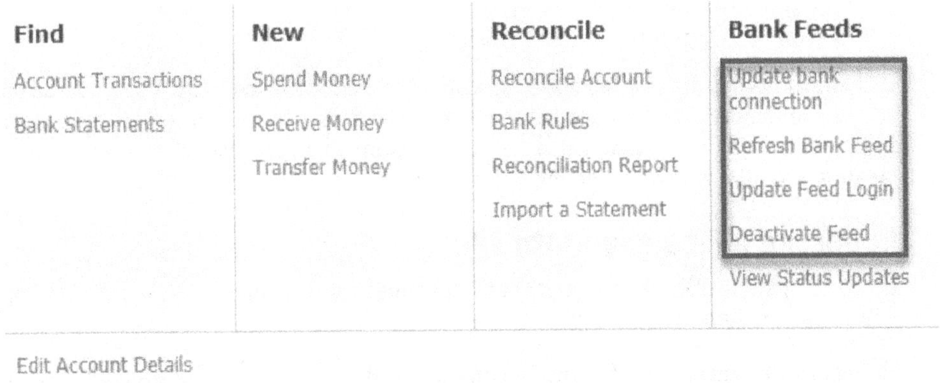

*Source:* Xero Limited

will be available. In the case that older transactions are needed, you will need to import a bank statement for the missing dates. More information on importing statements is found later in this chapter.

## Refreshing and Deactivating Bank Feeds

On occasion, a bank feed will break. This could be from a lapse in service by the bank, a reformat of the online interface, or a bug with the third-party software. Generally, Xero will give a warning in red that "There is a problem with this bank feed." By updating the connection, refreshing the feed, or deactivating and reconnecting, the problem will often be solved (Figure 9.9). Both options are listed under the **Manage Account** button at the top right of the account tile (or the overflow menu of three dots, if on the Dashboard).

# Importing Bank Statements

Importing bank statements refers to importing a file with bank data to add bank transactions to an account in Xero. There are several reasons you may import bank transactions:

- A direct or third-party feed does not exist for the company bank.
- A feed does exist but does not go back in history as far as needed.
- The user may want to precode the statement lines on a .csv import file to expedite bank reconciliation, such as for year-end write-up.

The process for importing a bank statement into Xero involves two steps: downloading or preparing an import file and importing the file into Xero. Note that import files are limited to 1,000 transactions. If you need to import more transactions, you will need to split the data into more than one file.

There are several file types that Xero will accept directly without formatting or mapping of the data. These are:

- .ofx (preferred): Open Financial Exchange
- .qbo: a Quickbooks Online variant of an OFX file
- .qfx: a Quicken variant of an OFX file
- .qif: Quicken Interchange Format

If these file types are available as a download format from the bank, they will be the fastest way to import data because Xero will read the financial data automatically. If these file types are not available, a download of transactions in a spreadsheet format can be used to create a .csv file, which can be imported.

## Importing a Financial Data File

If the company bank offers an option to download an .ofx, .qbo, .qfx, or .qif file type, this will be faster than using a .csv.

To import a financial data file into a bank account:

1. Navigate to the **Accounting** tab, then **Bank Accounts**.
2. Use the Manage Account pull-down in the top right of the bank account tile and select **Import a Statement** (Figure 9.10).
3. Click the **Browse** button and select the financial data file (Figure 9.11).
4. Click **Import**.

The data will be imported and you will be redirected to the reconciliation screen for the account.

## Importing a .csv File

There are situations when a .csv file will be the best option for importing bank data. Some examples are:

- A financial data file type is not offered by the bank, but a spreadsheet format is.

**FIGURE 9.10**

Use the Manage Account pulldown in the top right of the bank account tile and select Import a Statement.

*Source:* Xero Limited

**FIGURE 9.11**

Click the Browse button and select the financial data file.

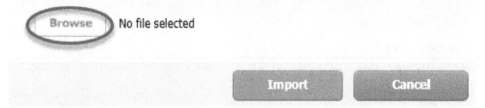

1. **In a new window, go to your credit card web site.**

2. **Download your bank statement.** File type must be OFX, QFX, QBO, QIF or CSV
   The most recent transaction imported was:

|  | Spent | Received |
|---|---|---|
| Nov 10, 2020<br>Bow Wow Babies Wholesale<br>Orange County 042695 03/21 | 25.17 |  |

3. **Upload the bank statement file here...**

   Browse    No file selected

   Import        Cancel

*Source:* Xero Limited

- The client may be trying to recreate very old records, and electronic access to the bank is no longer available. Transactions can be transposed from paper bank statements to a spreadsheet, either using software or manually.
- A bank feed becomes disconnected, leaving a small gap in transactions. Dropping missing lines in a spreadsheet will be faster than creating separate spend and receive money transactions.
- There are many months of transactions to code, such as year-end write-up, and importing a precoded bank statement will be most efficient.

Xero offers a bank statement template in the import screen, but the file should be prepared correctly.

- Date and amount are the only required columns, but additional data will be useful reconciliation.
- If there are any blank rows in the data, the file will not import.
- Dates must be in date format.

9

- All transaction amounts must be in one column, in number format. Many banks export draws in a debit column and deposits in a credit column. These will need to be consolidated in a single column with deposits as positive amounts and draws as negative amounts.
- Xero will create a contact for every unique entry in the Payee column, so if the bank export includes extraneous details in the Payee field, it makes sense to clean up the data before importing.

To import a .csv file into a bank account:

1. Navigate to the **Accounting** tab, then **Bank Accounts.**
2. Use the Manage Account pull-down in the top right of the bank account tile and select **Import a Statement.**
3. On the right, download the template file (Figure 9.12).
4. Copy the downloaded bank data into the template. Depending on the format of the downloaded transactions, you may need to manipulate the data to conform with the template.
5. Save the file where it can be easily located.
6. Click the **Browse** button and select the saved import file.
7. Click **Import.**

**FIGURE 9.12**

On the right, download the template file.

## File formats you can import

| Format | Find out more |
| --- | --- |
| OFX (recommended) | OFX help |
| QFX | QFX help |
| QBO | QBO help |
| QIF | QIF help |
| CSV | CSV help |

Download our CSV template to create your own bank statement file.

Import a maximum of 1000 bank statement lines at a time.

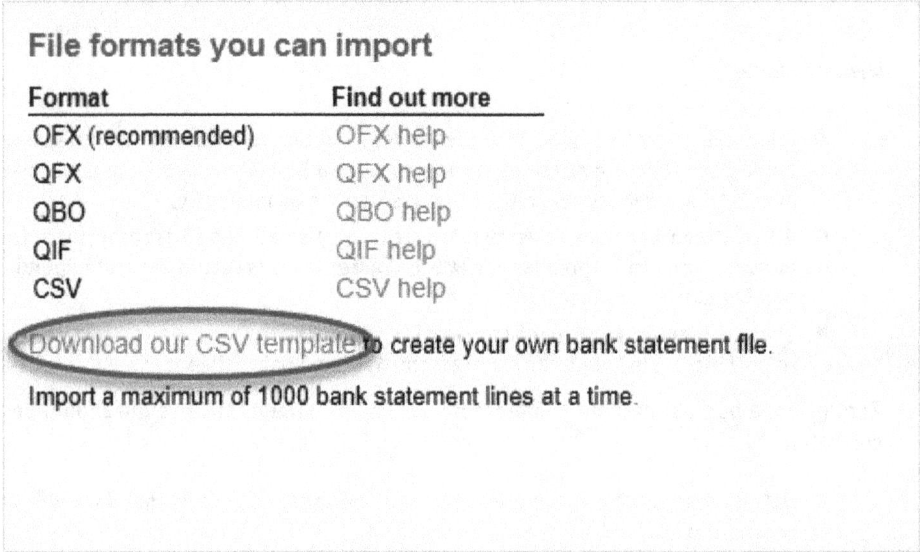

*Source:* Xero Limited

8. Xero will attempt to map the statement columns to the appropriate field in Xero. This mapping can be updated by using the pull-downs under **Assign to**. A summary of the mapping with sample bank data will show on the right (Figure 9.13).

9. Confirm the import by clicking **Save**.

If the import fails, you will receive a warning. Check that the **Date** and **Amount** columns are in the correct format types and that there are no blank rows in the data. Also, try moving the columns around and reimporting them. Moving the columns forces Xero to remap the fields and sometimes clears problems.

## Importing Precoded Bank Statements

Advisors may prepare the bookkeeping for some companies only once per year in advance of tax return preparation. One strategy to reconcile a year's worth of bank lines quickly and efficiently is to upload a **precoded bank statement**.

A precoded bank statement is a .csv import file with all of the bank lines over a given period that includes two additional columns: account code and tax type. For each line, enter an account code that matches the code from the chart of accounts and the relevant tax rate. The entered fields must match exactly (Figure 9.14).

The statement is imported using the same method just described. Be sure that the columns are mapped to the correct fields, including Account Code and Tax Type (Figure 9.15).

**FIGURE 9.13**

Xero will attempt to map the statement columns to the appropriate field in Xero. This mapping can be updated by using the pulldowns under Assign to. A summary of the mapping with sample bank data will show on the right.

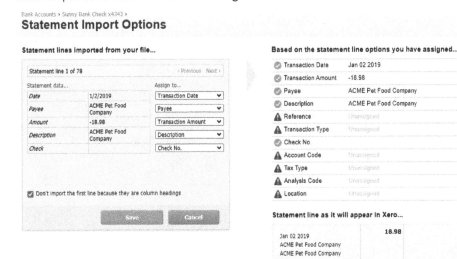

*Source:* Xero Limited

## FIGURE 9.14

A precoded bank statement is a .csv import file with all of the bank lines over a given period that includes two additional columns: account code and tax type. For each line, enter an account code that matches the code from the chart of accounts and the relevant tax rate. The entered fields must match exactly.

| | A | B | C | D | E |
|---|---|---|---|---|---|
| 1 | Posting Date | Amount | Description | AccountCode | TaxRate |
| 2 | 10/20/2020 | -32.83 | Chlorine Warehouse 45645 St. Charles | 5000 | Tax Exempt (0%) |
| 3 | 10/27/2020 | -22.5 | Chlorine Warehouse 45645 St. Charles | 5000 | Tax Exempt (0%) |
| 4 | 10/27/2020 | -17.61 | Chlorine Warehouse 45645 St. Charles | 5000 | Tax Exempt (0%) |
| 5 | 11/1/2020 | -17.07 | Office Depot #1149 SPRINGVILLE     682601 06/29 | 6510 | Tax Exempt (0%) |
| 6 | 11/6/2020 | -39.91 | BIG DADDY'S PIZZA (S 8-01--7467499 UT     06/30 | 6840 | Tax Exempt (0%) |
| 7 | 11/14/2020 | -19.78 | The Real Pool Superstore 033788 | 5000 | Tax Exempt (0%) |
| 8 | 11/18/2020 | -19.27 | The Real Pool Superstore 034534 | 5000 | Tax Exempt (0%) |
| 9 | 11/19/2020 | -85.98 | The Real Pool Superstore 052920 | 5000 | Tax Exempt (0%) |
| 10 | 11/22/2020 | -263.41 | The Real Pool Superstore 05244 | 5000 | Tax Exempt (0%) |
| 11 | 11/23/2020 | -11 | Xero, Inc. | 6540 | Tax Exempt (0%) |
| 12 | 11/23/2020 | -99 | Sunny Bank Annual Membership | 6040 | Tax Exempt (0%) |
| 13 | 11/29/2020 | -170.44 | Chlorine Warehouse 45645 St. Charles | 5000 | Tax Exempt (0%) |
| 14 | | | | | |

*Source:* Xero Limited

## FIGURE 9.15

The statement is imported using the same method as above. Be sure that the columns are mapped to the correct fields, including Account Code and Tax Type.

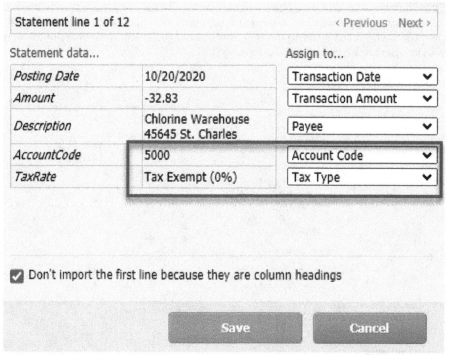

*Source:* Xero Limited

## FIGURE 9.16

When these lines are imported, you will see a notification that the lines are imported directly as reconciled transactions.

# Import Results

12 statement lines were imported. 0 were duplicates. 12 were imported directly as reconciled transactions.

*Source:* Xero Limited

## FIGURE 9.17

They will appear in the Account Transactions tab as reconciled transactions.

| | Date ▲ | Description | Reference | Payment Ref | Spent | Received | Balance | Bank Transaction Source | Status |
|---|---|---|---|---|---|---|---|---|---|
| ☐ | Oct 20, 2020 | Chlorine Warehouse 45645 St. Charles | | | 32.83 | | (32.83) | Imported | Reconciled |
| ☐ | Oct 27, 2020 | Chlorine Warehouse 45645 St. Charles | | | 22.50 | | (55.33) | Imported | Reconciled |
| ☐ | Oct 27, 2020 | Chlorine Warehouse 45645 St. Charles | | | 17.61 | | (72.94) | Imported | Reconciled |
| ☐ | Nov 1, 2020 | Office Depot #1149 SPRINGVILLE 682601 06/29 | | | 17.07 | | (90.01) | Imported | Reconciled |
| ☐ | Nov 6, 2020 | BIG DADDY'S PIZZA (3-8-81-7467499 UT 06/30 | | | 39.91 | | (129.92) | Imported | Reconciled |
| ☐ | Nov 14, 2020 | The Real Pool Superstore 033788 | | | 19.78 | | (149.70) | Imported | Reconciled |

*Source:* Xero Limited

When these lines are imported, you will see a notification that the lines are imported directly as reconciled transactions (Figure 9.16). They will not appear in the **Reconcile** tab. They will automatically be reconciled against a spend-or-receive money and removed from the Reconcile queue. They will appear in the **Account Transactions** tab as reconciled transactions (Figure 9.17).

Precoded statement imports should be used for strictly cash-based companies only. This method should not be used where bank lines must be matched to invoices or bills, and it cannot be used to precode transfers between bank accounts. You can find a template for a precoded statement in digital resources.

## Common Statement Import Errors

Errors while importing bank statements are frustrating, but there is often an easy fix. Here are some common errors and the solutions:

| | |
|---|---|
| The import fails because the date column is not in date format. | Select the column and format as Short Date. |

| | |
|---|---|
| The import fails because the amount column is not in amount format. | Select the column and format as Amount. |
| The import fails because there is a blank row in the data set. | Find and delete the blank row. |
| The import fails because one or more fields exceed the maximum characters allowed. | Reduce the characters in the field. **Reference** is limited to 255 characters and **Check** is limited to 20 characters. |
| The statement is imported to the wrong bank account. | Go to the Bank statements tab, delete the statement, and reimport. |
| The date format selected was a non-U.S. format creating wrong dates in the imported statement. | Delete the statement, reorder the columns in the .csv import file, and remap the columns, using U.S. date formats. |
| The statement is imported into the bank account without Xero giving a mapping screen, and the mapping assumptions are incorrect. Columns are linked to incorrect fields in Xero. | Delete the statement from Xero. Open the import file and change the order of the columns. Save and reimport. |

# Managing Bank Statements and Statement Lines

## Reviewing Bank Statements in Xero

Whether bank transactions arrived in Xero from a bank feed or a statement import, it is important to understand where to find them and how to manage them. Each individual transaction is referred to as a **statement line**, and a group of transactions entered into Xero at the same time make up a **bank statement**.

All statement lines are shown in the **Bank statements** tab within the bank account (Figure 9.18). To access the Bank statements tab, navigate to **Accounting**, then **Bank accounts**. Select the bank or credit card account you wish to review and open the **Bank statements** tab.

This tab shows every transaction line that is presumed to affect the bank account, whether it has been reconciled or not. The default view is to show each statement line and is identified by the **Statement lines** pull-down on the top left of the data. This link is a toggle between **Statement lines** and **Statements**. Changing the view to Statements aggregates the lines based on the import or bank feed date. Each view is discussed further next.

## FIGURE 9.18

All statement lines are shown in the Bank statements tab within the bank account.

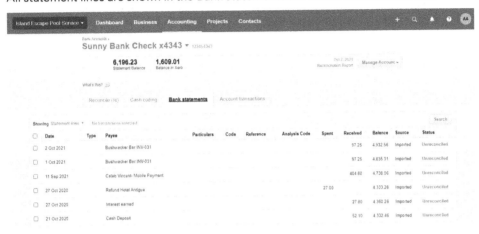

*Source:* Xero Limited

In the **Statement lines** screen, the columns represent fields of the bank transaction. To view the details of a transaction, click the blue date link. If the statement line has been reconciled, you will be able to see the general ledger transaction that the statement line was reconciled with (Figure 9.19). Transactions are listed in date order, but there is a **Search** button and transactions can be searched by keyword, amount, date, or status.

To delete one statement line, such as in the case of a duplicate or other error, select the checkbox to the left of the line you wish to delete and click the Delete button that appears above. Confirm by selecting **Delete** (Figure 9.20).

## FIGURE 9.19

In the Statement lines screen, the columns represent fields of the bank transaction. To view the details of a transaction, click the blue date link. If the statement line has been reconciled, you will be able to see the general ledger transaction that the statement line was reconciled with.

*Source:* Xero Limited

**FIGURE 9.20**

To delete one statement line, such as in the case of a duplicate or other error, select the checkbox to the left of the line you wish to delete and click the Delete button that appears above. Confirm by selecting Delete.

*Source:* Xero Limited

**FIGURE 9.21**

If a statement line was deleted in error, it can be restored by selecting the checkbox to the left and clicking the Restore button.

*Source:* Xero Limited

**FIGURE 9.22**

In the Statements screen, the Imported date will be the date that a group of statement lines was imported into Xero via a statement file or a bank feed. Each line will show the earliest and latest dated transactions within that import or feed.

*Source:* Xero Limited

If a statement line was deleted in error, it can be restored by selecting the checkbox to the left and clicking the **Restore** button (Figure 9.21).

In the **Statements** screen, the Imported date will be the date that a group of statement lines was imported into Xero via a statement file or a bank feed. Each line will show the earliest and latest dated transactions within that import or feed (Figure 9.22). To view the underlying statement lines, click the blue Imported Date link.

To delete an entire statement, such as in the case of a statement being imported into the wrong bank account accidentally, open the statement to be deleted by clicking the blue date link. Scroll to the bottom of the screen and click the red **Delete Entire Statement** link (Figure 9.23). Confirm by selecting **Delete**.

**FIGURE 9.23**

To delete an entire statement, such as in the case of a statement being imported into the wrong bank account accidentally, open the statement to be deleted by clicking the blue date link. Scroll to the bottom of the screen and click the red Delete Entire Statement link.

### Transactions from Oct 20, 2020 to Nov 23, 2020

| | Date | Type | Payee | Particulars | Code | Reference | Analysis Code | Spent | Received | Balance | Status |
|---|---|---|---|---|---|---|---|---|---|---|---|
| | Oct 20, 2020 | Opening Balance | | | | | | | | (170.44) | |
| ☐ | Oct 20, 2020 | | Chlorine Warehouse 45645 St. Charles | | | | | 32.83 | | (203.27) | Reconciled |
| ☐ | Oct 27, 2020 | | Chlorine Warehouse 45645 St. Charles | | | | | 22.50 | | (225.77) | Reconciled |
| ☐ | Oct 27, 2020 | | Chlorine Warehouse 45645 St. Charles | | | | | 17.61 | | (243.38) | Reconciled |
| ☐ | Nov 1, 2020 | | Office Depot #1149 SPRINGVILLE 682601 06/29 | | | | | 17.07 | | (260.45) | Reconciled |
| ☐ | Nov 6, 2020 | | BIG DADDY'S PIZZA (S 8-01- -7467499 UT 06/30 | | | | | 39.91 | | (300.36) | Reconciled |
| ☐ | Nov 14, 2020 | | The Real Pool Superstore 033788 | | | | | 19.78 | | (320.14) | Reconciled |
| ☐ | Nov 18, 2020 | | The Real Pool Superstore 034534 | | | | | 19.27 | | (339.41) | Reconciled |
| ☐ | Nov 19, 2020 | | The Real Pool Superstore 052920 | | | | | 85.98 | | (425.39) | Reconciled |
| ☐ | Nov 22, 2020 | | The Real Pool Superstore 05244 | | | | | 263.41 | | (688.80) | Reconciled |
| ☐ | Nov 23, 2020 | | Xero, Inc | | | | | 11.00 | | (699.80) | Reconciled |
| ☐ | Nov 23, 2020 | | Sunny Bank Annual Membership | | | | | 99.00 | | (798.80) | Reconciled |
| ☐ | Nov 29, 2020 | | Chlorine Warehouse 45645 St. Charles | | | | | 170.44 | | (969.24) | Deleted |
| | Nov 23, 2020 | Closing Balance | | | | | | | | 0.00 | |

Restore  Delete   No transactions selected

Delete Entire Statement    Cancel

*Source:* Xero Limited

# Bank Reconciliation

*Cash coding has saved me and my team hours of time that we would have wasted reconciling or correcting transactions one by one. We can now spend more time advising our clients, and less time on the minutiae.*

—*Cristina Garza, Chief Number Cruncher of Accountingprose*

Bank reconciliation is commonly understood in the United States to be the matching of bank statement transactions to general ledger transactions and the identification of any differences. In other accounting platforms, a bank reconciliation is a stand-alone process that occurs at the end of the period. In Xero, however, the reconciling of transactions to the general ledger happens simultaneously with transaction coding.

Because Xero was built in the cloud as an effort to reduce data-entry to "zero," the approach to the reconciliation is different from other general ledgers. The assumption is that data that enters into Xero is accurate, and the advisor need only cull out any discrepancies. In other general ledgers, every transaction must be accepted or entered into the system.

When items are "reconciled" in the **Bank reconciliation** tab of Xero, two things are happening: a posting or entry is being made to the general ledger (the right side of the bank reconciliation screen), and the bank statement line (the left side of the screen) is being reconciled with that posting. Where other systems would have you mark lines as accepted or reconciled at month-end, Xero rolls the process together with coding.

By understanding the underlying mechanics of the right side of the bank reconciliation screen, you will be able to create transactions as needed and solve problems as they arise.

There are basically five ways that entries can be made to the books of any organization:

1. Spend and receive money transactions
2. Transfers
3. Bill and invoices (and related credit notes)
4. Payments on bills or invoices
5. Manual journal entries.

Three of these can be created in bank reconciliation and are explored next.

**Spend and receive money transactions** are postings in which the debit or credit, depending on the direction of funds, is a bank account. A spend-or-receive money transaction can be created without a bank line and will remain unreconciled until matched with a bank transaction. Alternatively, Xero will create it when using the **Create** tab in bank reconciliation. The transaction will be both created and reconciled when the **OK** button is clicked.

**Transfers** are similar to spend and receive money transactions, except that both sides of the posting are bank accounts.

**Payments on bills or invoices** are entries made to clear specific accounts receivable or payable. In most cases payments will be related to bank accounts, indicating that an account receivable has been collected in cash or an account payable has been satisfied with cash; however, other accounts, such as clearing accounts, can be used to clear bills and invoices. It is important to note that when a bank line is matched directly to an invoice or bill, Xero is actually creating a payment and reconciling it to the bank line.

# Overview of Bank Reconciliation Screen

When you navigate to a bank account in Xero, you are directed to a screen with two balances and four tabs, all dealing with the coding and reconciliation of bank transaction lines. Most of the work of bank reconciliation is handled here (Figure 10.1).

At the top, the bank account name is shown in blue with a pull-down arrow. Using the arrow will allow you to navigate to any other bank account without going back to the Dashboard (Figure 10.2).

**FIGURE 10.1**

When you navigate to a bank account in Xero, you are directed to a screen with two balances and four tabs, all dealing with the coding and reconciliation of bank transaction lines. Most of the work of bank reconciliation is handled here.

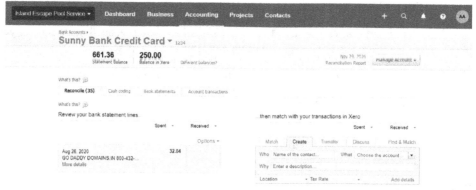

*Source:* Xero Limited

**FIGURE 10.2**

At the top, the bank account name is shown in blue with a pulldown arrow. Using the arrow will allow you to navigate to any other bank account without going back to the Dashboard.

*Source:* Xero Limited

Two bank balances are shown, **Statement Balance** and **Balance in Xero**, the difference between which is generally unreconciled bank transactions (Figure 10.3). The Balance in Xero is the posted general ledger balance. It includes all transactions posted to the bank account but not any bank feed lines that have not been reconciled. The Statement Balance is a running balance that Xero calculates by starting with the general ledger balance and adding or subtracting unreconciled bank lines.

The **Manage Account** button on the top right will allow you to easily navigate to functions dealing with the bank account (Figure 10.4).

**FIGURE 10.3**

Two bank balances are shown, Statement Balance and Balance in Xero, the difference between which is generally unreconciled bank transactions.

Bank Accounts ›

# Sunny Bank Check x4343 ▼ 123454343

**6,196.23**
Statement Balance

**1,609.01**
Balance in Xero

Different balances?

*Source:* Xero Limited

**FIGURE 10.4**

The Manage Account button on the top right will allow you to easily navigate to functions dealing with the bank account.

Bank Accounts ›
**Sunny Bank Credit Card** ▼ 1234

**661.36**
Statement Balance

**250.00**
Balance in Xero

Different balances?

Nov 29, 2020
Reconciliation Report

Manage Account ▼

*Source:* Xero Limited

10

Each of the four tabs below has a specific purpose:

**Reconcile:** The Reconcile tab (Figure 10.5) is for coding and reconciling bank transactions one at a time. The left side of the screen shows a tile for every statement line from the bank feed or import. The right side shows tiles for either creating new general ledger entries or for matching with transactions that already exist on the general ledger.

- **Cash coding:** The Cash coding tab (Figure 10.6) reformats unreconciled transactions, except those that Xero perceives could match existing general ledger entries, into a table. This allows the user to see much more data in one screen and code in bulk.

**FIGURE 10.5**

Reconcile- The Reconcile tab (Figure 10.5) is for coding and reconciling bank transactions one at a time.

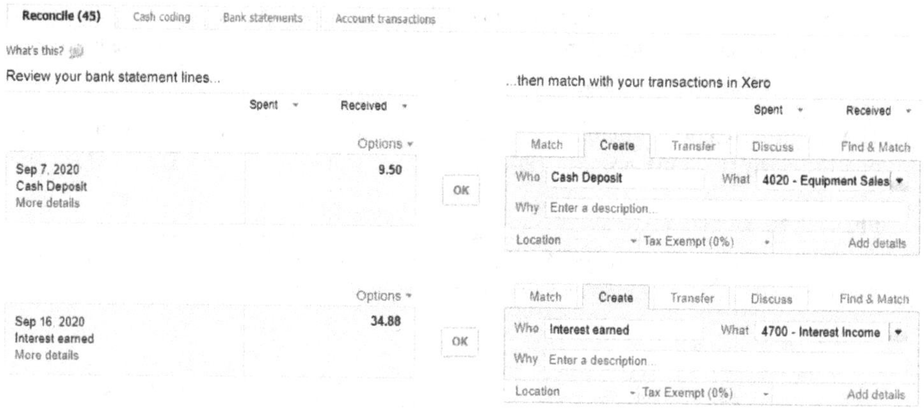

*Source:* Xero Limited

**FIGURE 10.6**

Cash coding- The Cash coding tab (Figure 10.6) reformats unreconciled transactions, except those that Xero perceives could match existing general ledger entries, into a table.

*Source:* Xero Limited

- **Bank statements:** The Bank statement tab (Figure 10.7) shows all bank transactions that have been imported or fed into Xero. It includes both reconciled and unreconciled bank lines. It also shows a summary of transactions by statement.
- **Account transactions:** The Account transactions tab (Figure 10.8) lists all transactions that have been posted on the general ledger against the bank account, whether they are reconciled or not. Examples of unreconciled, but posted, transactions are payments on invoices and bills and spend or receive money transitions that have not been matched with a bank line.

**FIGURE 10.7**

Bank statements- The Bank statement tab (Figure 10.7) shows all bank transactions that have been imported or fed into Xero.

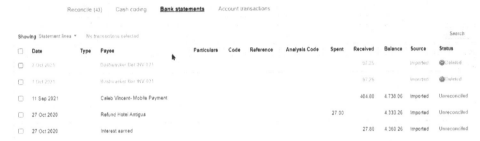

| Date | Type | Payee | Particulars | Code | Reference | Analysis Code | Spent | Received | Balance | Source | Status |
|---|---|---|---|---|---|---|---|---|---|---|---|
| 2 Oct 2021 | | Bushwacker Bar INV-031 | | | | | | 97.25 | | Imported | Deleted |
| 1 Oct 2021 | | Bushwacker Bar INV-031 | | | | | | 97.25 | | Imported | Deleted |
| 11 Sep 2021 | | Caleb Vincent- Mobile Payment | | | | | | 404.80 | 4.738.06 | Imported | Unreconciled |
| 27 Oct 2020 | | Refund Hotel Antigua | | | | | 27.00 | | 4.333.26 | Imported | Unreconciled |
| 27 Oct 2020 | | Interest earned | | | | | | 27.80 | 4.360.26 | Imported | Unreconciled |

***Source:*** **Xero Limited**

**FIGURE 10.8**

Account transactions- The Account transactions tab (Figure 10.8) lists all transactions that have been posted on the general ledger against the bank account, whether they are reconciled or not.

| Date | Description | Reference | Payment Ref | Spent | Received | Bank Transaction Source | Status |
|---|---|---|---|---|---|---|---|
| Sep 19, 2020 | ACME Chemical Company | | | 16.50 | | Imported | Reconciled |
| Sep 21, 2020 | ACME Chemical Company | | | 45.60 | | Imported | Reconciled |
| Sep 28, 2020 | ACME Chemical Company | | | 87.65 | | Imported | Reconciled |
| Oct 1, 2020 | ACME Chemical Company | | | 77.80 | | Imported | Reconciled |
| Oct 1, 2020 | ACME Chemical Company | | | 176.00 | | Imported | Reconciled |

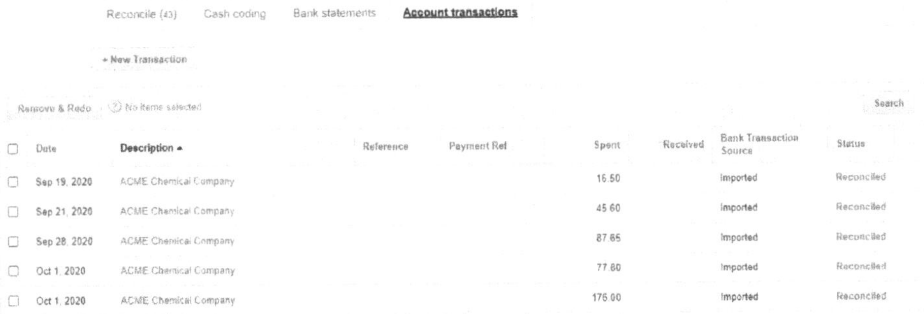

***Source:*** **Xero Limited**

10

# Posting Transactions to the Bank Account

As described earlier, the reconciliation process that takes place in the bank reconciliation screen matches a bank line to a general ledger transaction, where the bank account is either debited or credited. There are three types of transactions in Xero that are made against a bank or credit card account and can therefore be matched to a bank line.

## Spend or Receive Money Transactions

The first is the spend (or receive money) transaction. A **spend money** transaction credits the bank or credit card account and debits another general ledger account. A **receive money** transaction debits the bank or credit card account and credits another general ledger account. Note that spend and receive money transactions are often used to book revenue and expenses but also for any other account on the general ledger.

It is a common objection to Xero that journal entries cannot be made to bank accounts (or certain types of accounts, for that matter). That is an untrue statement. Manual entries can be made to bank accounts in Xero, but they are not created in the normal manual journal screen. They are made with spend or receive money transactions.

A spend or receive money transaction can be created in two ways. The more common way, especially with cash-basis clients, is to use the **Create** tab in bank reconciliation to simultaneously create a ledger entry and match it to a bank line (Figure 10.9).

A spend or receive money can also be generated without a bank line by using either the + icon (Figure 10.10) at the top of the screen or under the **Manage Account** button in Bank accounts. This method will post the entry immediately, rather than waiting for a bank statement line to be imported to Xero, which can take a few days.

Assume the company sells $150 of pool chemicals and receives a check payment that is immediately deposited in the business checking account. Posting a receive money transaction will increase the checking account balance on the general ledger and recognize the appropriate revenue account.

**FIGURE 10.9**

A spend or receive money transaction can be created in two ways. The more common way, especially with cash-basis clients, is to use the Create tab in bank reconciliation to simultaneously create a ledger entry and match it to a bank line.

*Source: Xero Limited*

**FIGURE 10.10**

A spend or receive money can also be generated without a bank line by using either the + icon (Figure 10.10) at the top of the screen or under the Manage Account button in Bank accounts.

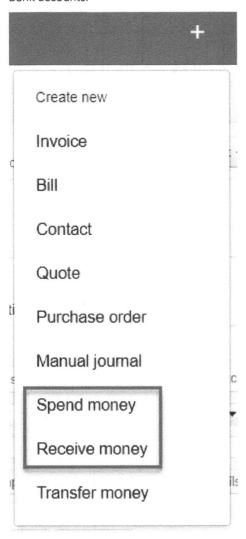

To create a receive money transaction for the deposit:

1. Use the + icon to navigate to **Receive money**.
2. Choose the bank account the deposit will be made to (Figure 10.11).

10

3. Click **Next**.
4. Enter the details of the deposit (Figure 10.12).
5. Click **Save**.

**FIGURE 10.11**

Choose the bank account the deposit will be made to.

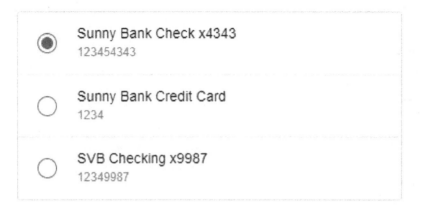

## Select a bank account to make payment to

- ● Sunny Bank Check x4343
  123454343

- ○ Sunny Bank Credit Card
  1234

- ○ SVB Checking x9987
  12349987

*Source:* Xero Limited

**FIGURE 10.12**

Enter the details of the deposit.

*Source:* Xero Limited

**FIGURE 10.13**

Spend and receive money transactions will remain unreconciled until they are matched to a bank statement line. To view all unreconciled transactions posted to the bank, use the Account Transactions tab and sort by the Status header.

| | Date | Description | | Reference | Payment Ref | Spent | Received | Bank Transaction Source | Status ▲ |
|---|---|---|---|---|---|---|---|---|---|
| ☐ | Sep 15, 2020 | Payment Entergy | | Batch Payment | | 655.00 | | | Unreconciled |
| ☐ | Oct 1, 2020 | Deposit | | Onsite sales | | | 150.00 | | Unreconciled |

*Source:* Xero Limited

Spend and receive money transactions will remain unreconciled until they are matched to a bank statement line. To view all unreconciled transactions posted to the bank, use the **Account Transactions** tab and sort by the **Status** header (Figure 10.13).

## Transfer Transactions

The second type of transaction that can be posted to a bank account is **Transfers**. Transfers are the movement of funds between two bank or credit card accounts in Xero. A transfer is a journal entry where both sides of the entry are bank or credit card accounts. The use of transfers in Xero may overlap with electronic bank transfers, but they should not be confused. When money is moved between bank accounts at the same bank, it would be clear that this is a transfer in Xero. However, the payment of a business credit card balance with a check from the checking account would also be a transfer, because funds are moving between two general ledger accounts in Xero with the type of bank account.

Assume the company mails a check to the credit card company for $455. Posting a transfer will reduce both the checking account and credit card balances.

To create a transfer for the payment:

1. Use the + icon to navigate to **Transfer money**.
2. Enter the **From** and **To** accounts, along with Date, Amount, and Reference (Figure 10.14).
3. Click **Transfer**.

## Bill or Invoice Payments

The final type of transaction that is posted to a bank account is an invoice or bill **payment**. This is similar to a spend or receive money transaction in that it debits or credits the bank account, but the other half of the transaction is the satisfaction of a bill or invoice, and the reduction of the accounts receivable or accounts payable balance. When an invoice or bill is selected in bank reconciliation and matched, Xero is actually creating a payment to resolve the invoice or bill and matching the payment.

10

**FIGURE 10.14**

Enter the From and To accounts, along with Date, Amount and Reference.

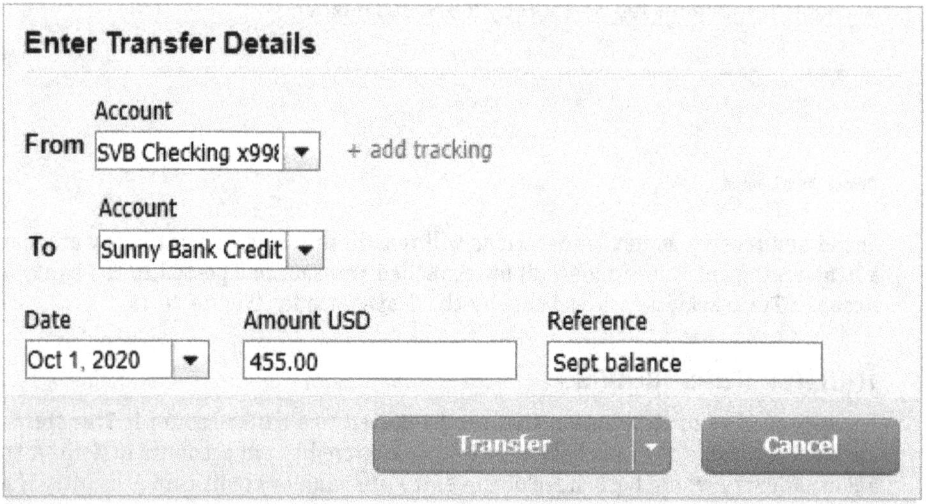

**Enter Transfer Details**

Account

From  SVB Checking x99{ ▼  + add tracking

Account

To  Sunny Bank Credit ▼

| Date | Amount USD | Reference |
|------|-----------|-----------|
| Oct 1, 2020 ▼ | 455.00 | Sept balance |

Transfer ▼   Cancel

*Source:* Xero Limited

**FIGURE 10.15**

Scroll to the bottom of the screen and enter details in Receive a payment.

Receive a payment

| Amount Paid | Date Paid | Paid To | Reference | |
|-------------|-----------|---------|-----------|---|
| 92.37 | Oct 1, 2020 ▼ | 1010 - Sunny Bank Checl ▼ | Check #474 | Add Payment |

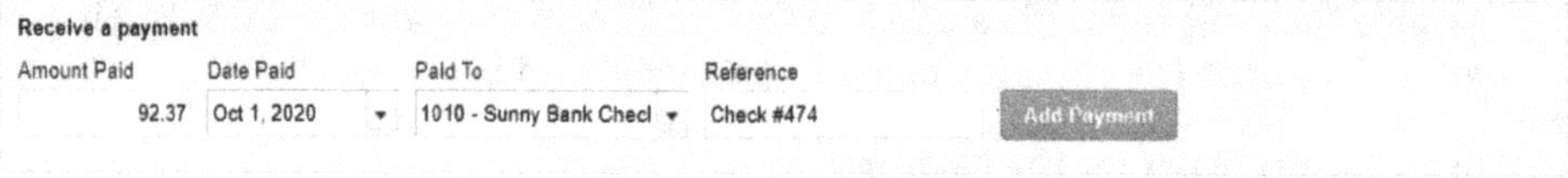

*Source:* Xero Limited

If a company receives a check payment for $92.37 for an outstanding invoice to a customer, the company should immediately apply a payment in Xero to that invoice. Any delay in applying the payment in Xero will mean that the accounts receivable detail is incorrect, and could lead to customer relation problems if notices are sent for an overdue invoice when payment has already been made. Applying the payment will increase the general ledger balance of the bank account and reduce the amount due from the customer.

To quickly post a payment on an invoice:

1. Navigate to the **Business**, then **Invoices**.
2. Open the invoice that is paid.
3. Scroll to the bottom of the screen and enter details in **Receive a payment** (Figure 10.15).
4. Click **Add Payment**.

**FIGURE 10.16**

On the Dashboard, Xero makes it clear how many unreconciled items are in the queue in each bank account. Click on the blue Reconcile XX items button to access the bank reconciliation screen.

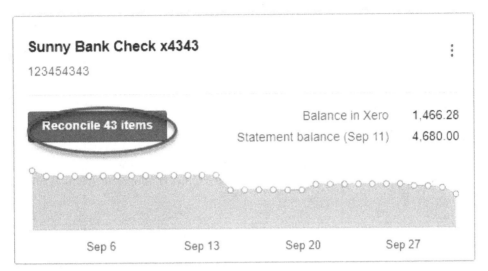

Source: Xero Limited

When posting bank transactions, it is very important to choose the correct bank account. Xero will not allow you to match pending payments or spend and receive money transactions in any accounts other than the one selected when created.

# Reconciling Bank Transactions

On the Dashboard, Xero makes it clear how many unreconciled items are in the queue in each bank account. Click on the blue **Reconcile XX items** button to access the bank reconciliation screen (Figure 10.16). The unreconciled lines will be listed as separate tiles on the left side of the screen. From here, there are several ways to code and reconcile bank lines in Xero.

## Accepting Matched Suggestions

One of the most efficient methods of bank reconciliation in Xero is automatch. When Xero recognizes that a bank statement line in Xero is the same amount as a general ledger transaction that already exists, the tile on the right will turn green and an **OK** button will appear between the tiles (Figure 10.17). The matched line on the right can be a spend money, a receive money, a payment to a bill or invoice, or an outstanding bill or invoice.

10

**FIGURE 10.17**

One of the most efficient methods of bank reconciliation in Xero is auto-match. When Xero recognizes that a bank statement line in Xero is the same amount as a general ledger transaction that already exists, the tile on the right will turn green and an OK button will appear between the tiles.

| | Options ▾ | | | Match | Create | Transfer | Discuss | Find & Match |
|---|---|---|---|---|---|---|---|---|
| Sep 19, 2020<br>Deposit<br>More details | 500.00 | OK | | ↖ 10 Sep 2020<br>Payment: Phil Santos | | | | 500.00 |

*Source:* Xero Limited

**FIGURE 10.18**

If Xero recognizes that more than one general ledger line is the same amount as the bank line, it will propose a match of one of the transactions, but will also show a link to the other possibilities. To see the other matches, click the Other Possible Match Found link.

| | Options ▾ | | | Match | Create | Transfer | Discuss | Find & Match |
|---|---|---|---|---|---|---|---|---|
| Sep 21, 2020<br>Ricardo Mercado Deposit<br>More details | 328.00 | OK | | ↦ 01 Sep 2020<br>Ricardo Mercado<br>Ref INV-105<br>Other Possible Match Found | | | | 328.00 |

*Source:* Xero Limited

Xero matches on the exact amount and direction of the bank line. Xero will not offer the match unless the amount is exactly the same and in the same direction (deposit or draw). If the correct transaction is suggested as the match to the bank line, click **OK.** This will reconcile the bank line to the general ledger line and remove the bank line from the reconciliation queue.

If Xero recognizes that more than one general ledger line is the same amount as the bank line, it will propose a match of one of the transactions but will also show a link to the other possibilities. To see the other matches, click the **Other Possible Match Found** link (Figure 10.18). Highlight the correct transaction and click **OK.** It is very important that the correct transactions be matched.

When a bank line is reconciled to an existing invoice or bill, not only is the bank account adjusted on the general ledger, but the invoice or bill will be moved from **Awaiting Payment** to **Paid**, and the underlying Accounts Receivable or Accounts Payable detail will be adjusted.

## Autosuggest Previous Coding

You may notice that Xero will populate the **Create** tab of bank transactions when a similar transaction has previously been coded. This is **autosuggest.** Xero memorizes the coding

**FIGURE 10.19**

This feature is turned on by default in Xero organizations. To turn it off, uncheck the box at the bottom of the Reconcile tab next to Suggest previous entries.

*Source:* Xero Limited

details of previously reconciled transactions and applies them to new lines with similar payees and references. To accept the suggestion, click **OK** between the tiles. To make any changes to the suggestion, edit the fields in the corresponding tile.

This feature is turned on by default in Xero organizations. To turn it off, uncheck the box at the bottom of the Reconcile tab next to **Suggest previous entries** (Figure 10.19).

## Creating a New Transaction

Many small businesses operate on a strictly cash basis and only classify transactions when the bank line appears in the Xero feed. In these cases, there may not be any automatched transactions. Each bank line will need to be coded and reconciled.

To create a general ledger line and link it to the bank transaction, use the **Create** tab. Using the Create tab will generate a Spend Money or Receive Money transaction on the general ledger. Enter the details for the bank line as described here:

- **Who:** This is the payee or contact for the transaction. This field will be used to create a Contact record and added to the Customer or Supplier group, depending on the direction of the flow of funds. Who is a required field.
- **What:** This is the general ledger account that will be debited or credited, depending on the direction of the bank transaction. Some system accounts, like inventory, accounts receivable, and accounts payable, cannot be selected. What is a required field.
- **Why:** Why is a description field and is optional.
- **Tracking category:** If tracking categories are set up, they can be selected using the pull-downs at the bottom of the tile.
- **Tax rate:** The tax rate will default to the rate assigned to the general ledger account selected. It can be changed using the pull-down menu at the bottom of the tile.

To create a transaction that is more complex, use the **Add details** link (Figure 10.20). Selecting this link will expand the input tile and allow you to create transactions such as:

- Allocating a bank line between more than one general ledger account
- Adding a Reference to the transaction
- Using inventory items in the transaction
- Assigning a cost to a customer using billable expenses
- Recording a receipt as an Overpayment or Prepayment

10

**FIGURE 10.20**

To create a transaction that is more complex, use the Add details link.

*Source:* Xero Limited

## Billable Expenses

When a company spends money in Xero, either in a spend money transaction or using a bill, those costs can be associated with a customer or project to be recovered later on an invoice. This is a **billable expense.** Unlike coding or tracking categories, billable expenses are not a general ledger entry. There is no general ledger account for billable expenses. They are akin to a queue or a reminder list. When created, the transactions are posted to the general ledger account for the cost. The related invoice is a separate transaction entirely on the general ledger, but the creation will remove the billable expense from the queue.

To track a transaction as a billable expense from bank reconciliation:

1. Navigate to the **Reconcile** tab in the bank account.
2. Locate the bank transaction and select **Add details** to enlarge the input screen.
3. Complete the fields needed to code the transaction, such as Account and Tax Rate.
4. Click the **Assign expenses to a customer** (or Assign expenses to a customer or project, if Xero Projects is enabled) button. This button will not appear for bank transactions where funds are being deposited, only for draws (Figure 10.21).
5. Find the customer or project in the **Search for a customer or project** field.
6. Select the transaction lines to apply to the customer. Note that for split transactions where there is more than one bank line, each line can be assigned to a customer or project separately.
7. Click **Assign** next to the customer or project name.
8. Confirm that the correct customer or project is shown to the right of the transaction (Figure 10.22).
9. Click **OK** to save.
10. The assignment of the expense will be noted in the **Description** field.
11. Save the transaction.

**FIGURE 10.21**

Click the Assign expenses to a customer (or Assign expenses to a customer or project, if Xero Projects is enabled) button. This button will not appear for bank transactions where funds are being deposited, only for draws.

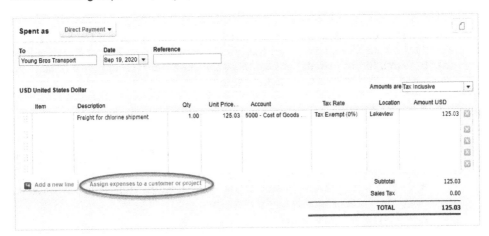

*Source:* Xero Limited

**FIGURE 10.22**

Confirm that the correct customer or project is shown to the right of the transaction.

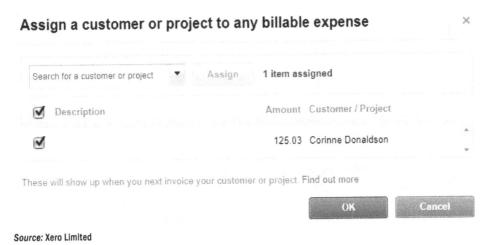

*Source:* Xero Limited

Creating an invoice with a billable expense is discussed in Chapter 11, and assigning billable expenses from a bill is discussed in Chapter 12.

## Using Find & Match to Deal with Customer Payments

There are circumstances where a bank line needs to be linked to an existing general ledger line in Xero, but automatch is not triggered because the amount of the bank line is not exactly the same as a single ledger line. In those cases, using **Find & Match** will allow the user to search for uncleared items, connect the bank transaction to one or more existing items, and make any necessary adjustments.

Use Find & Match to:

- Match one bank line to more than one existing general ledger transaction
- Reconcile a bank line to only a partial amount of an existing general ledger transaction
- Reconcile a bank line to an existing general ledger transaction and simultaneously create a new general ledger transaction
- Overview of Find & Match

Find & Match is a link above the coding tile in bank reconciliation that will expand the normal reconciliation tile to offer many more options. This screen will show unreconciled general ledger transactions, including invoices, bills, spend or receive monies, and payments.

The default listing will include only unreconciled transactions posted in the direction of the highlighted bank line. For instance, if the screen is opened from a bank deposit, only outstanding invoices, payments on invoices, and receive money transactions will be shown. To show general ledger transactions in the opposite direction of the bank line, select the checkbox next to **Show Spent Items** at the top of the tile (Figure 10.23). (If the bank line is a draw, you would select the checkbox next to **Show Received Items.**)

Note that the headers in the listing are sorting links. Click the header to sort by that column. Transactions can also be located by using one of two search options—name or reference and amount.

### Matching to Two or More Invoices

If a customer has more than one invoice outstanding, it would be common to send one payment for all of the outstanding invoices. In this case, a deposit amount that satisfies more than one invoice will not be matched by Xero because the sum does not match any single general ledger line.

To match one bank line to more than one general ledger transaction:

1. Navigate to the **Reconcile** tab in the bank account.
2. Locate the bank transaction and select **Find & Match** to open the screen.

## FIGURE 10.23

To show general ledger transactions in the opposite direction of the bank line, select the checkbox next to Show Spent Items at the top of the tile. (If the bank line is a draw, you would select the checkbox next to Show Received Items.)

*Source:* Xero Limited

> 3. Find the invoices that have been paid and select by checking the box to the left. The tile will turn green when the selected invoices total the amount of the bank deposit (Figure 10.24).
>
> 4. Click **Reconcile**.

## FIGURE 10.24

Find the invoices that have been paid and select by checking the box to the left. The tile will turn green when the selected invoices total the amount of the bank deposit.

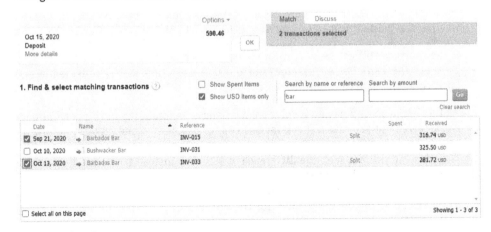

*Source:* Xero Limited

When the bank line is matched to the outstanding invoices, the bank account ledger is adjusted and the invoices are marked as **Paid** in the Accounts Receivable or Accounts Payable subledger.

The process would be the same if the company issues a single check by hand for more than one bill. However, if Xero is used for the generation of the check or electronic payment, Xero will clear the bills by posting a batch payment for the total amount. When the bank line clears, Xero will recognize it as an automatch for the total payment amount.

### Reconciling Deposits Net of Bank Fees

When a payment processing company is used to collect funds from customers, the related merchant fee is often deducted from the deposit, yielding a net deposit that does not match the gross sales amount. In this case, the bank deposit must be reconciled to the outstanding invoice or payment and an adjustment for the fee must be made.

To match a bank deposit that has been reduced by a merchant fee to an outstanding invoice or payment:

1. Navigate to the **Reconcile** tab in the bank account.
2. Locate the bank transaction and select **Find & Match**.
3. Select the outstanding invoice or payment that applies to the bank deposit.
4. Use the **Adjustments** pull-down to access **Bank Fee**.
5. Complete the fields to create a new transaction for the merchant fee (Figure 10.25).
6. Click **Reconcile**.

### Reconciling Minor Differences

In business, there are sometimes small differences between an amount that is expected for a transaction and the actual amount deposited in a bank account. The difference could be the customer's mistake, like a transposition error on a check that results in accidentally paying an amount less than the amount due. The key determination in how to handle the difference is whether the shortage is material and should be tracked for later collection from the customer.

If the shortage will not be sought for collection, the most efficient way to handle it would be to use the **Bank Fee Adjustment** button. If the shortage will be collected later, use the **Split** function, explained later in this chapter.

Assume the company has an invoice for a customer outstanding in the amount of $256.86 but receives and deposits a check for $256.68 for payment of the invoice. Xero will not match the deposit to the awaiting payment invoice because the amounts are different. The company will not seek the difference of $.14, but instead post the adjustment against Sales Revenue, which was the general ledger account used on the invoice. You will need to manually match the deposit to the invoice, since the payment will satisfy the amount due, and make an offsetting adjustment for the difference.

**FIGURE 10.25**

Complete the fields to create a new transaction for the merchant fee.

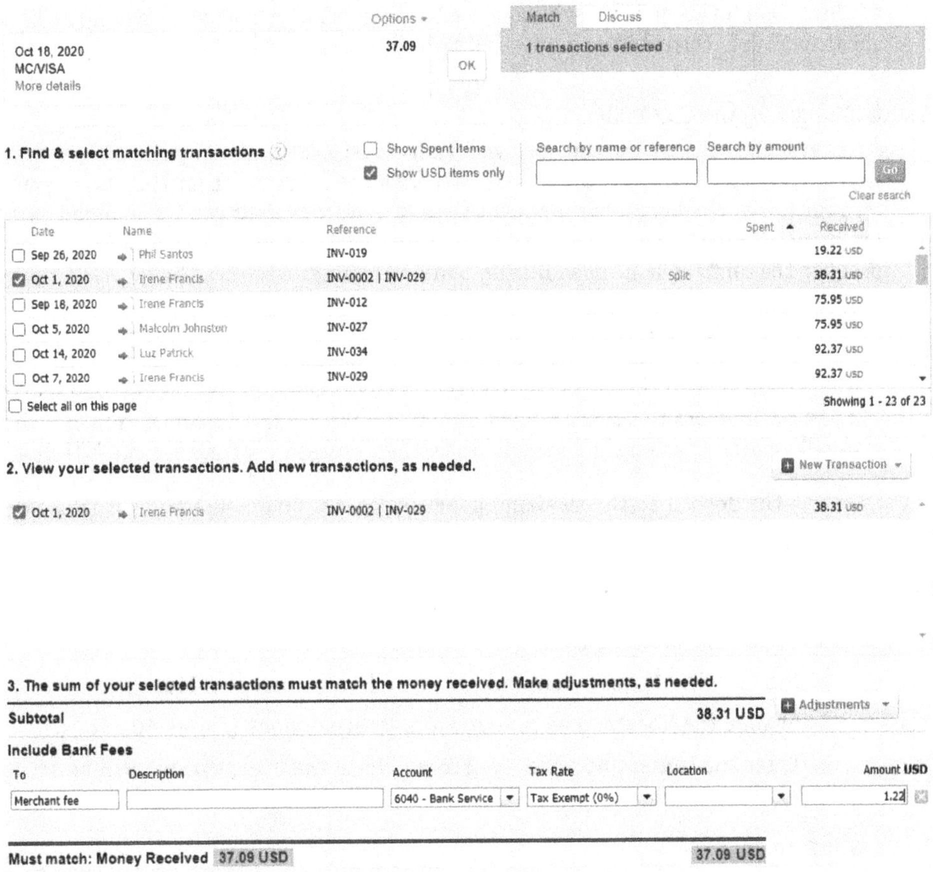

| | | Options ▾ | | | Match | Discuss | | |
|---|---|---|---|---|---|---|---|---|

Oct 18, 2020
MC/VISA
More details

37.09  OK

1 transactions selected

**1. Find & select matching transactions** ⑦

☐ Show Spent Items
☑ Show USD items only

Search by name or reference    Search by amount

Go

Clear search

| | Date | Name | Reference | | Spent ▲ | Received |
|---|---|---|---|---|---|---|
| ☐ | Sep 26, 2020 | ➦ Phil Santos | INV-019 | | | 19.22 USD |
| ☑ | Oct 1, 2020 | ➦ Irene Francis | INV-0002 \| INV-029 | Split | | 38.31 USD |
| ☐ | Sep 18, 2020 | ➦ Irene Francis | INV-012 | | | 75.95 USD |
| ☐ | Oct 5, 2020 | ➦ Malcolm Johnston | INV-027 | | | 75.95 USD |
| ☐ | Oct 14, 2020 | ➦ Luz Patrick | INV-034 | | | 92.37 USD |
| ☐ | Oct 7, 2020 | ➦ Irene Francis | INV-029 | | | 92.37 USD |

☐ Select all on this page

Showing 1 - 23 of 23

**2. View your selected transactions. Add new transactions, as needed.**

New Transaction ▾

| ☑ | Oct 1, 2020 | ➦ Irene Francis | INV-0002 \| INV-029 | | 38.31 USD |
|---|---|---|---|---|---|

**3. The sum of your selected transactions must match the money received. Make adjustments, as needed.**

| Subtotal | | | | | | 38.31 USD | ➕ Adjustments ▾ |
|---|---|---|---|---|---|---|---|

**Include Bank Fees**

| To | Description | | Account | Tax Rate | Location | | Amount **USD** |
|---|---|---|---|---|---|---|---|
| Merchant fee | | | 6040 - Bank Service ▾ | Tax Exempt (0%) ▾ | ▾ | | 1.22 |

**Must match: Money Received** 37.09 USD                    37.09 USD

*Source:* Xero Limited

To match the deposit to the awaiting payment invoice:

1. Navigate to the **Reconciliation** tab and find the deposit in the bank queue.

2. Click the **Find & Match** link in the top right corner of the corresponding tile.

3. Select the awaiting payment invoice.

4. Use the **Adjustments** pull-down and access **Bank Fee** to create a transaction against Sales Revenue for the difference. Even though the adjustment is labeled "Bank Fee," it can be used to create a transaction for any single general ledger account.

**10**

It is not recommended that you use the **Minor Adjustment** option under the Adjustments pull-down, even though this would appear to be the best solution. Using Minor Adjustment will create an entry on the **Rounding** general ledger account, which is a balance sheet account. Using this account will create a liability balance that remains on the balance sheet until it is corrected or zeroed out with a journal entry.

### Recording an Overpayment

An overpayment is an amount received from a customer or paid by the company by mistake. An overpayment is linked to the customer with the intention that the overpayment will be refunded or applied on subsequent invoices. An overpayment can be recorded as a Receive (or Spend) Money transaction from the + menu but is usually created in Find & Match because the mistake is noticed during bank reconciliation.

Assume the company has an invoice for a customer outstanding in the amount of $341.92 but receives and deposits a check for $431.92 for payment of the invoice. Xero will not match the deposit to the awaiting payment invoice because the amounts are different. The company will record the overpayment of $90 and refund the customer. You will first need to manually match the deposit to the invoice, then process a refund for the difference.

To match the deposit to the awaiting payment invoice and create an overpayment:

1. Navigate to the **Reconciliation** tab and find the deposit in the bank queue.
2. Click the **Find & Match** link in the top right corner of the corresponding tile.
3. Select the awaiting payment invoice.
4. Use the **New Transaction** pull-down and access **Receive Money**.
5. Change the **Received as** pull-down to **Overpayment** (Figure 10.26).
6. Enter the contact name in the **From** field so the overpayment will be accurately tracked.

**FIGURE 10.26**

Change the Received as pulldown to Overpayment.

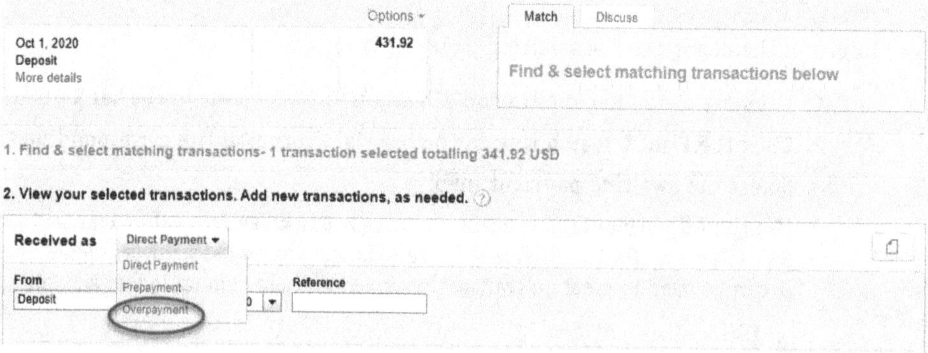

*Source:* Xero Limited

7. Enter a **Reference**, if desired.

8. Enter a **Description**.

9. Xero will populate the amount with the difference between the deposit and the invoice (Figure 10.27).

10. Click **Save Transaction**. This creates a new overpayment transaction.

11. Click **OK** to complete the reconciliation.

To refund the overpayment:

1. Navigate to **Business**, then **Invoices**.

2. Under the **Awaiting Payment** tab, open the **Overpayment**. The overpayment will have a yellow box icon (Figure 10.28).

3. At the bottom of the screen, enter the **Date** and the bank account that the refund will be **Paid From**. To generate a check image, check the **Pay by check** box (Figure 10.29).

4. Click **Add Refund**.

If the customer would prefer that the overpayment be applied to an invoice created later, follow the instructions for applying a credit note found in Chapter 11.

### FIGURE 10.27

Xero will populate the amount with the difference between the deposit and the invoice.

| Received as | Overpayment ▼ | | | | | | |
|---|---|---|---|---|---|---|---|
| **From** | | **Date** | **Reference** | | | | |
| Ricardo Mercado | | Oct 1, 2020 ▼ | Overpayment | | | | |
| | | | | | | | |
| Currency USD United States Dollar ▼ | | | | | | | |
| Description | | Amount | Account | Tax Rate | Location | Amount USD | |
| Overpayment | | 90.00 | 1200 - Accounts Receivable | Tax Exempt (0%) | | 90.00 | |
| | | | | | Subtotal | 90.00 | |
| | | | | | TOTAL | **90.00** | |

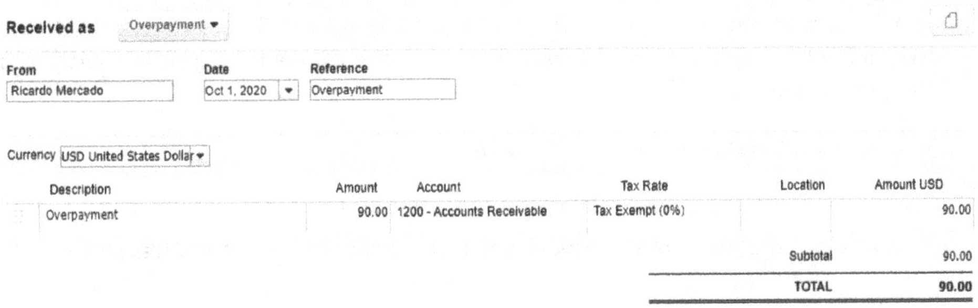

*Source:* Xero Limited

### FIGURE 10.28

Under the Awaiting Payment tab, open the Overpayment. The overpayment will have a yellow box icon.

| | Overpayment | Ricardo Mercado | Oct 1, 2020 | 0.00 | (90.00) |
|---|---|---|---|---|---|

*Source:* Xero Limited

**FIGURE 10.29**

At the bottom of the screen, enter the Date and the bank account that the refund will be Paid From. To generate a check image, check the Pay by check box.

*Source:* Xero Limited

## Recording a Prepayment

A prepayment is an amount received from a customer or paid by the company in advance of future work. A prepayment is linked to the customer with the intention that the prepayment will be applied to subsequently created invoices. A prepayment can be recorded as a Receive Money transaction from the + menu or created in bank reconciliation by using the Add Details link or in Find & Match (even though there is no existing entry to match the prepayment to).

To create a prepayment from **Add Details**:

1. Navigate to the **Reconciliation** tab and find the deposit in the bank queue.
2. Click the **Add Details** link in the lower right corner of the **Create** tab of the corresponding tile.
3. Change the **Received as** pull down to **Prepayment** (Figure 10.30).
4. Complete the prepayment entry screen. The contact name must exactly match the contact used later in creating an invoice so that the prepayment can be applied. Choose a general ledger account for the sales or unearned revenue account that should be recognized at the creation of the prepayment. When the prepayment is later applied, this account posting will be reversed.
5. To apply the prepayment to an invoice later, follow the instructions for applying a credit note found in Chapter 11.

**FIGURE 10.30**

Change the Received as pulldown to Prepayment.

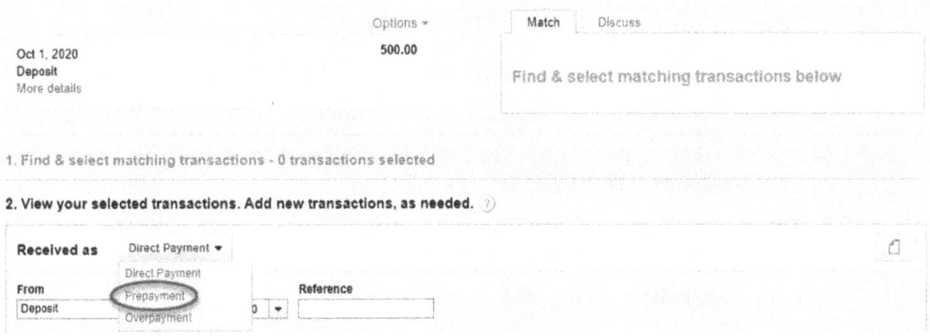

*Source:* Xero Limited

| Quick comparison | |
|---|---|
| **Prepayments** | **Overpayments** |
| Payment in advance of future work | Accidental payment made in excess of amount owed |
| Can include sales tax | Does not include sales tax |
| Shown on Invoices screen as an amount paid, but nothing due | Shown on Invoices screen as a negative amount due and no payments |
| Not included in Accounts Receivable balance | Included (as a negative) in Accounts Receivable balance |
| Upon creation: generally recorded against a revenue account or unearned revenue liability, but can be book against almost any general ledger account | Upon creation: recorded against Accounts Receivable |
| Upon application to an invoice: original general ledger posting is reversed | Upon refund or application to an invoice: Accounts Receivable is reduced |

Note that this chart refers to prepayments and overpayments where money is being received. Although less common, the comparison for prepayments and overpayments where money is being spent is the same.

### Recording a Partial Payment

In some cases a customer will remit payment for only a portion of an outstanding invoice. Because the transaction amount will differ from the outstanding invoice balance, you will have to use **Find & Match** to apply the partial payment to the correct invoice.

10

To match the partial payment to the appropriate invoice, follow these steps:

1. Navigate to the **Reconciliation** tab and find the deposit in the bank queue.
2. Click the **Find & Match** link in the top right corner of the corresponding tile.
3. Select the correct awaiting payment invoice by clicking the box to the left.
4. Notice that a **Split** link appears in the invoice line. Click this link (Figure 10.31).
5. A new screen appears showing the full invoice amount and the deposit amount as a **Part payment**. Click **Split** (Figure 10.32).
6. Xero will split the invoice into two portions—one that is paid and one that is unpaid. This is shown in the listing.
7. Click **Reconcile** to apply the partial payment.

## Recording a Transfer

In Xero, a transfer is the movement of funds between two bank or credit card accounts that are set up as such in the accounting system. This may be the same as a bank transfer, but it may not. For example, a company may move funds from a business bank account to an owner's personal account. On the bank feed, this will appear as a transfer; however, for purposes of Xero, this would not be recorded as a transfer in the system, because the personal bank account would not be in the Xero organization. Conversely, the payment of a business credit card bill from the business bank account using a check would be considered a transfer in Xero because both accounts—the business bank account and the business credit card—would be listed as bank accounts in Xero.

**FIGURE 10.31**

Notice that a Split link appears in the invoice line. Click this link.

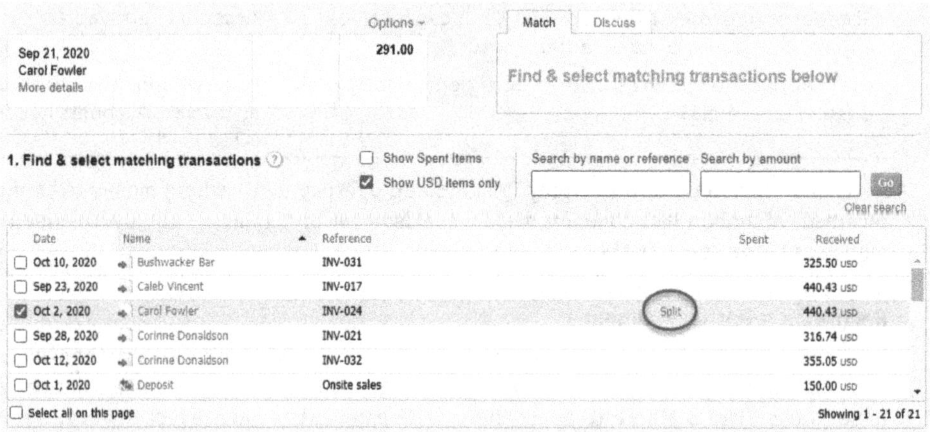

*Source:* Xero Limited

**FIGURE 10.32**

A new screen appears showing the full invoice amount and the deposit amount as a Part payment. Click Split.

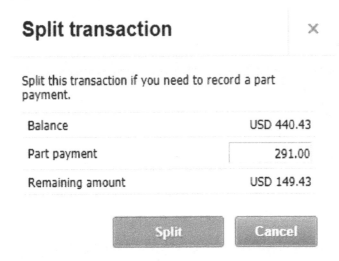

Split transaction

Split this transaction if you need to record a part payment.

| Balance | USD 440.43 |
| Part payment | 291.00 |
| Remaining amount | USD 149.43 |

Split    Cancel

*Source:* Xero Limited

| Transaction in the bank feed | Treatment in Xero |
|---|---|
| Funds are transferred from a business account to an owner's personal account at the same bank. The bank line shows "Transfer" from one account number to another. | Not a transfer. This should be recorded as an owner's draw or distribution. |
| Funds are automatically moved from an interest-bearing business savings account to the operating account to prevent an overdraft. | Transfer from the savings account to the operating account. |
| Funds are automatically swept from an operating account to a payroll account to cover wages paid. | Transfer from operating account to payroll account. |
| A credit card payment is made with funds from the company's operating bank account. The credit card is used for business expenses and is a listed bank account in Xero. | Transfer from operating account to credit card account. |
| A credit card payment is made with funds from the company's operating bank account. The credit card is used primarily for personal expenses, but the payment made is to cover specific business expenses charged. The credit card is not listed as a bank account in Xero. | Not a transfer. Use the **Add details** link to itemize the expenses being reimbursed. |

To record a transfer, use the **Select a bank account** pull-down to choose the compatible bank account. Edit the **Reference** field, if needed. Note that this transfer will appear in the other bank account as an automatch and no transfer details will need to be entered.

10

## Reconciling Subordinate Credit Cards

In Xero, a transfer is the movement of funds between two bank or credit card accounts that are set up as such in the accounting system. However, the transfer does not have to be a representation of a direct transfer of cash. The Transfer functionality in Xero can be used for managing credit cards where there is a primary–subordinate relationship. This is a common structure in business cards where there is a need for multiple employee credit cards with controls.

The most common framework of a primary–subordinate relationship in credit cards would be a primary card, sometimes issued to the owner, that is the designated priority card for the account. The problem is that when bank feeds for the cards are connected to Xero, the payments are shown only in the primary card, where expenses are shown in both the primary and the subordinate employee cards.

| Feed | Payments Applied | Expenses Shown |
|------|------------------|----------------|
| Master level card | Yes | Possibly |
| Subordinate cards | No | Yes |

Some advisors get frustrated and end up with subordinate cards with huge balances due and primary cards with negative balances in Xero because payments are applied only to the primary. They may even disconnect the feeds to the subordinate cards and instead import the subordinate statements into the primary card. This is a more manual process, subject to human error, and does not leverage the automation built into Xero.

A better method is to use the Transfer functionality to transfer from the primary card an amount equal to the subordinate card balances on the statement date. This has the effect of moving the credit balance of the underlying cards to the primary card. This will close the subordinate balances to the primary card, so the primary card balance will then tie to the credit card statement. Because there is no bank line from the feed that will match this transfer, the transfer will need to be forcibly reconciled in Xero.

To reconcile subordinate credit cards in Xero:

1. Create a new bank account for each of the feeds available on the account. Including the last four digits of each card in the name of the account, as suggested in Chapter 5, will make the reconciliation process much easier.

2. Establish bank feeds for each of the subordinate cards.

3. Navigate to the primary card account and use the **Manage Account** pull-down to select **Transfer Money**.

4. Select the subordinate card in the **To Account** pull-down. Use the **Date** of the credit card statement. Enter an **Amount** equal to the charges posted to the subordinate card for the statement period. Add a **Reference** such as "To close balance to primary card" (Figure 10.33). Click **Transfer**.

**FIGURE 10.33**

Select the subordinate card in the To Account pulldown. Use the Date of the credit card statement. Enter an Amount equal to the charges posted to the subordinate card for the statement period. Add a Reference such as "To close balance to primary card." Click Transfer.

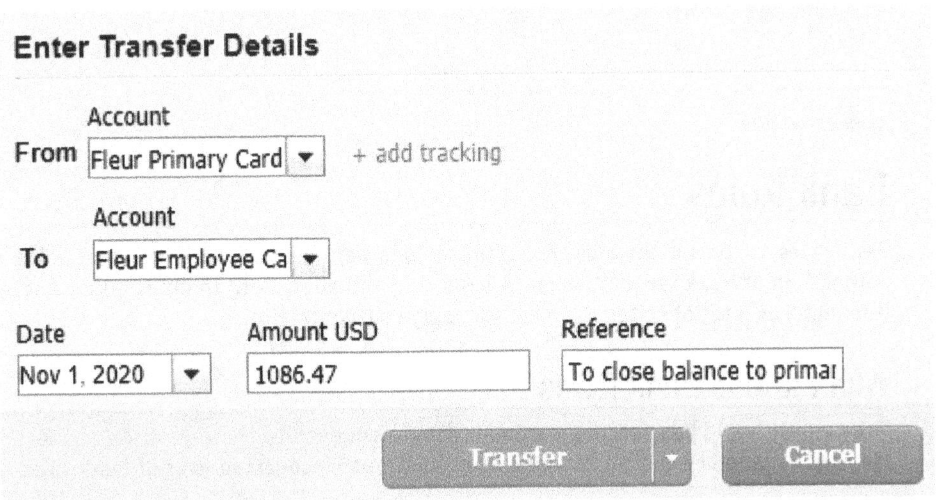

## Enter Transfer Details

Account

From Fleur Primary Card ▼     + add tracking

Account

To    Fleur Employee Ca ▼

Date            Amount USD            Reference

Nov 1, 2020 ▼  1086.47               To close balance to primar

Transfer ▼     Cancel

*Source:* Xero Limited

5. On each credit card account, locate the transfer created in the **Account transactions** tab. Check the box on the left and use the **More** pull-down to select **Mark as Reconciled**. (If the **More** pull-down does not appear on your screen, use the Help menu to **Enable mark as reconciled**.)

6. Run the Bank Reconciliation reports at the statement date for each credit card to confirm that the subordinate cards have $0 balances and the primary card has a balance equal to the statement.

# Discuss Tab

The **Discuss** tab is the fourth tab on the bank reconciliation tile (Figure 10.34). The Discuss tab is not for coding or reconciling, but for entering comments that will remain attached to the transaction. It is generally used to ask another user or client for guidance or explanation on a topic. Enter comments in the blank field, then click **Save**. An asterisk will appear on the Discuss tab, letting users know that a note exists. The comments will be saved in History & Notes at the bottom of the transaction, even after the transaction is reconciled. Any comments will also appear on the Uncoded Statement Lines report.

10

**FIGURE 10.34**

The Discuss tab is the fourth tab on the bank reconciliation tile

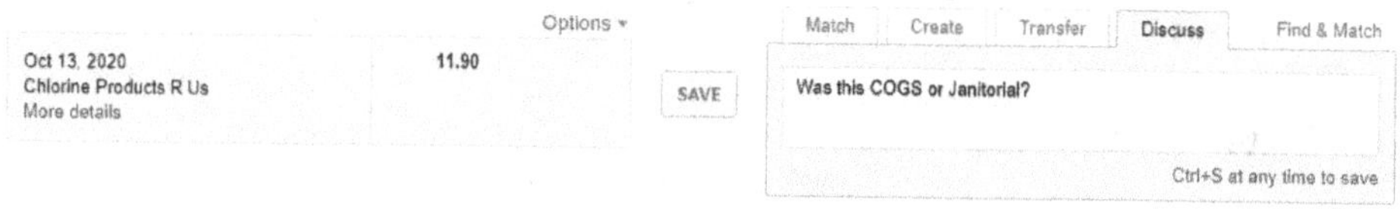

*Source:* Xero Limited

# Bank Rules

Bank rules are one of the most powerful tools in Xero because they allow for bulk automation of bank reconciliation. A bank rule will allow Xero to determine whether a bank line matches a set of criteria, and if so, apply coding details.

## When to Use Bank Rules

Bank rules should be used when there is some frequency to the repetition of the transaction and the coding is always the same. Some suggested uses of bank rules are:

- Transactions that appear in the bank feed frequently, usually once or more per month, like purchases of gas or drafts for utilities
- Interest income deposits
- Transfers between business bank or credit card accounts
- Merchant deposits made to a bank account that are consistently coded to a clearing account as part of a workflow

The first step in identifying which rules should be created in Xero is to consider the bank data. This is especially important when onboarding new companies. When setting up a Xero file for a new client, look for patterns in the bank transactions and create rules for those repeating, yet simple bank lines (Figure 10.35). A little bit of time investment in setting up well-designed bank rules will save hours of reconciling in the future. The easiest way to look at the data in aggregate is to view it in a spreadsheet format. You can either look at a bank export file in a .csv or .xls file or use the Cash Coding tab in Xero. In either case, sort the data by Payee or Reference, whichever field the bank is using for identifying information. Look for repeating vendors or transactions and build bank rules from there.

## Creating Bank Rules

The simplest way to create a new bank rule is to create it directly from an existing bank transaction. To create a new bank rule from a transaction:

1. Navigate to the **Accounting** tab, then **Bank Accounts**.
2. Select the bank account that includes the transaction you wish to create a bank rule from.

**FIGURE 10.35**

The first step in identifying which rules should be created in Xero is to consider the bank data. This is especially important when onboarding new companies. When setting up a Xero file for a new client, look for patterns in the bank transactions and create rules for those repeating, yet simple bank lines.

*Source:* Xero Limited

**FIGURE 10.36**

Select the Options pulldown at the top of the bank transaction tile. Select Create bank rule.

*Source:* Xero Limited

3. Navigate to the **Reconcile** tab.

4. Select the **Options** pull-down at the top of the bank transaction tile. Select **Create bank rule** (Figure 10.36).

5. The bank rule screen will appear, with details from the transaction line prepopulated. Build the rule by modifying or adding conditions and creating the coding specifications.

6. Click **Save**.

Bank rules can also be created from scratch:

1. Navigate to the **Accounting** tab, then **Bank Accounts**.

2. Select the **Bank Rules** button (Figure 10.37).

10

**FIGURE 10.37**

Select the Bank Rules button.

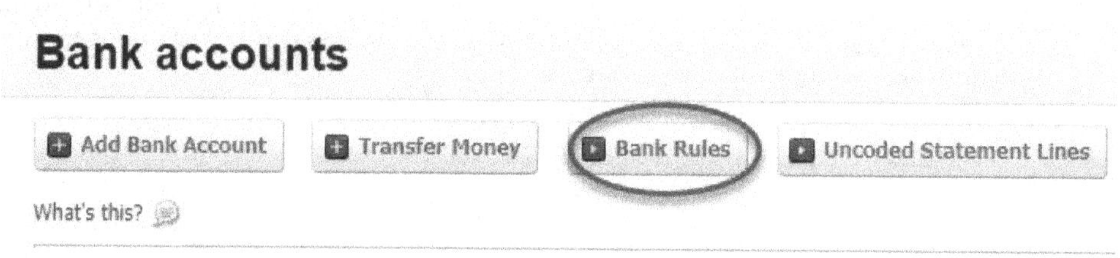

## Bank accounts

➕ Add Bank Account    ➕ Transfer Money    ◉ Bank Rules    ▶ Uncoded Statement Lines

What's this?

*Source:* Xero Limited

3. Notice that there are three tabs at the top of this screen: Spend Money Rules, Receive Money Rules, and Transfer Rules. Select the appropriate tab. Note that bank rules will only apply to bank transactions in the direction of the tab they are set up within. If you wish to create rules with the same conditions, like for a particular payee, you must create it within both tabs.

4. Select the **Create rule** button to open a blank bank rule screen.

5. Build the rule by specifying conditions and creating the coding specifications.

6. Click **Save**.

## Bank Rule Conditions

Each bank rule must have a minimum of one condition, but you can add as many conditions as needed to have Xero correctly query transactions.

The rule conditions are specified in Section 1 of the rule screen. (**When money spent on the bank statement matches the following conditions.**)

When creating conditions, you must decide whether all or any of the conditions must be met to run the rule. Using **All** means that every condition listed must apply, or the rule will not run. Using **Any** means that if even only one of the conditions is met, the rule will continue.

For example, if a company wants to code transactions from a particular vendor under a certain amount to a general line, you would use All. Assume a client's employees use a company credit card to pay for street parking which is maintained by the city. You construct the rule to require that Payee equals City of New Orleans and the amount is less than $10, so that other payments to the city, like sales or property tax, are excluded from the rule (Figure 10.38).

Using **Any** can be useful in constructing rules that run on more than one vendor. For example, Payee could be Shell or BP or Exxon, with coding to Automobile Expenses. This would eliminate the need to create many similar rules.

**FIGURE 10.38**

For example, if a company wants to code transactions from a particular vendor under a certain amount to a general line, you would use All. Assume a client's employees use a company credit card to pay for street parking which is maintained by the city. You construct the rule to require that Payee equals City of New Orleans and the amount is less than $10, so that other payments to the city, like sales or property tax, are excluded from the rule.

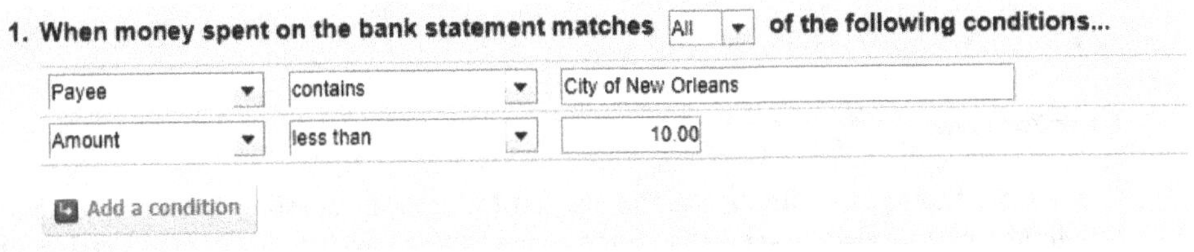

1. **When money spent on the bank statement matches** All ▼ **of the following conditions...**

| Payee ▼ | contains ▼ | City of New Orleans |
| Amount ▼ | less than ▼ | 10.00 |

➕ Add a condition

*Source:* Xero Limited

The conditions also have modifiers. Be careful about using **equals** in conditions because banks will often add extraneous data, like transaction numbers or vendor locations, in the data. Using **includes** will yield more results.

## Bank Rule Coding Specifications

Sections 2 through 6 of the bank rules screen are the instructions to Xero on what to do with the bank transaction once the conditions under Section 1 have been met.

## Section 2: Set the Contact

This establishes the contact for the transaction. This is important because Xero organizes transactional detail by contact within the contact record. The choices are to make the contact:

- An existing or new contact
- The Payee from the bank
- Entered during reconciliation

It is generally preferable to use an existing or new contact for reasons discussed later. Using a specific named contact will ensure consistency among similar transactions.

In practice, banks often include transaction numbers and identification codes along with the vendor in the Reference or Description fields. Bank rules can filter the bank data and override the contact to be an existing vendor. By coding directly in bank reconciliation rather than using bank rules, it would be easy to have dozens, or even hundreds, of transactions to the same vendor appear as separate contacts. Bank rules can force the contact on the record and eliminate many duplicate, junk contacts.

10

**FIGURE 10.39**

Many bank rules will be set to code the entire amount of a transaction to one general ledger account. This is done in Section 4 by allocating the transaction amount to a general ledger account at one hundred percent.

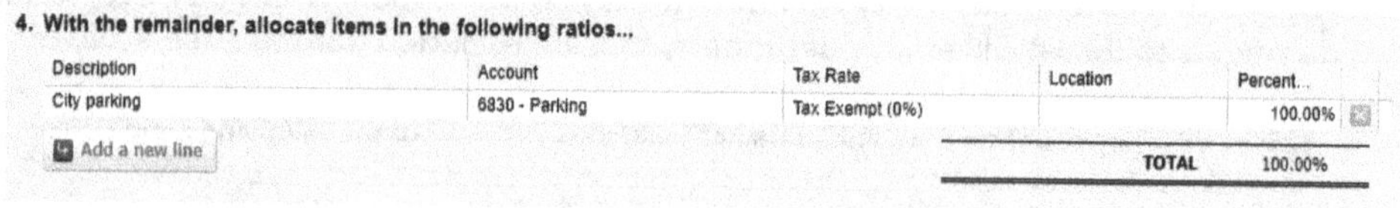

**4. With the remainder, allocate items in the following ratios...**

| Description | Account | Tax Rate | Location | Percent.. |
|---|---|---|---|---|
| City parking | 6830 - Parking | Tax Exempt (0%) | | 100.00% |
| Add a new line | | | TOTAL | 100.00% |

*Source:* Xero Limited

Payee from the bank could be a viable option for contact naming; however, in practice banks do not always send the payee name in the Payee field. Often, a string of transactional data will feed in the Reference or Description fields instead. There is not much standardization. To see how the company's bank is sending its data to Xero, use the Cash Coding screen. The bank data fields will be clear by looking at the columns in Cash Coding. (See below for more information about Cash Coding.)

The last option for specifying Contact is to enter one during reconciliation. This is incredibly inefficient and undermines any efficiency gained in bank rules. The point of bank rules is to automate the coding of data in bulk, so the least desirable option here would be to stop to type in a contact for every line.

### Sections 3 and 4: Allocating Items

These sections specify the coding of the transaction to one or more general ledger accounts. We discuss them together because they work in tandem.

Many bank rules will be set to code the entire amount of a transaction to one general ledger account. This is done in Section 4 by allocating the transaction amount to a general ledger account at 100% (Figure 10.39).

In some cases, you may want to divide the transaction amount between more than one account. An example would be related companies that may split overhead costs equally. In this case, 50% of the value is posted to an expense account and 50% is posted to a liability from the related company (Figure 10.40).

Note that the percentages can actually be negative, which has the effect of reversing the direction of the rule for that portion. One example of the use of negative ratios would be for estimating the merchant fee deducted from a deposit. Several years ago, we had a client who used a bank-issued card reader occasionally at art markets to sell his wares. The bank would make summary deposits, net of the merchant fee. The system did not integrate with Xero and the sales were minimal, so we elected not to make monthly entries to the general ledger to gross up those sales. What we did was create a Receive money bank rule that allocated 103% of the deposit amount to sales revenue and -3% of the deposit to merchant fees.

**FIGURE 10.40**

In some cases, you may want to divide the transaction amount between more than one account. An example would be related companies that may split overhead costs equally. In this case, fifty percent of the value is posted to an expense account and fifty percent is posted to a liability from the related company.

| 4. With the remainder, allocate items in the following ratios... | | | | |
|---|---|---|---|---|
| Description | Account | Tax Rate | Location | Percent... |
| Travel | 6820 - Travel | Tax Exempt (0%) | | 50.00% |
| Due from Related Co | 2260 - Due from Related Company | Tax Exempt (0%) | | 50.00% |
| Add a new line | | | TOTAL | 100.00% |

*Source:* Xero Limited

This very closely approximated the true gross sales revenue and offset the merchant fee. At the end of the year, we would make an adjusting journal entry, but this method was so accurate that the entry was always less than $10 (Figure 10.41).

Section 3 codes a fixed dollar amount from the transaction amount before applying any ratios for the remainder. An example of a use for this feature would be a company who pays for a lunch networking organization, where a portion of the monthly bill is a membership and a portion is for meals consumed. By allocating the base membership fee to Dues & Subscriptions in Section 3, the remainder can be automatically coded to Meals, which has a different tax character (Figure 10.42).

## Section 5: Set the Reference

This creates a reference for the transaction. The choices are to set the reference as the data coming from one of the bank fields or to enter one during reconciliation. Entering a reference during reconciliation will eliminate the efficiency gained by bank rules, so it is preferable to have the reference set automatically.

Depending on the bank, the data that should be used as a reference could be in one of several fields. It is a good idea to use Cash Coding (discussed later in this chapter) to see the data options at a high level.

**FIGURE 10.41**

At the end of the year, we would make an adjusting journal entry, but this method was so accurate that the entry was always less than $10.

| 4. With the remainder, allocate items in the following ratios... | | | | |
|---|---|---|---|---|
| Description | Account | Tax Rate | Location | Percent... |
| Gross Sales | 4020 - Equipment Sales Revenue | Tax Exempt (0%) | | 103.00% |
| Fees | 6040 - Bank Service Charges | Tax Exempt (0%) | | -3.00% |
| Add a new line | | | TOTAL | 100.00% |

*Source:* Xero Limited

10

**FIGURE 10.42**

By allocating the base membership fee to Dues & Subscriptions in Section 3, the remainder can be automatically coded to Meals, which has a different tax character.

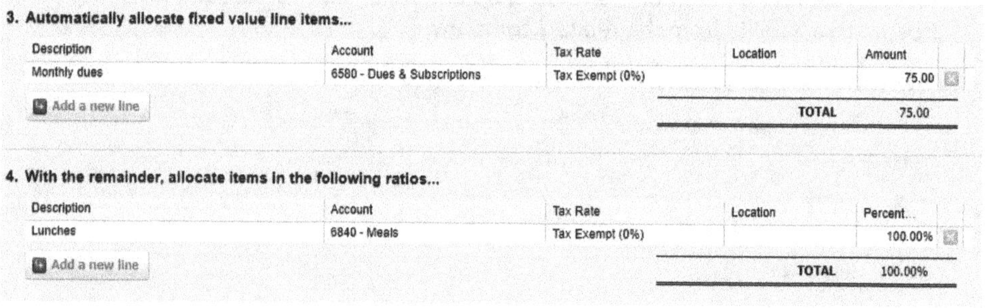

**3. Automatically allocate fixed value line items...**

| Description | Account | Tax Rate | Location | Amount |
|---|---|---|---|---|
| Monthly dues | 6580 - Dues & Subscriptions | Tax Exempt (0%) | | 75.00 |
| Add a new line | | | | TOTAL  75.00 |

**4. With the remainder, allocate items in the following ratios...**

| Description | Account | Tax Rate | Location | Percent... |
|---|---|---|---|---|
| Lunches | 6840 - Meals | Tax Exempt (0%) | | 100.00% |
| Add a new line | | | | TOTAL  100.00% |

*Source:* Xero Limited

**FIGURE 10.43**

By targeting a specific credit card account, and therefore user, in Section 6, the company can automate which department or location the charge is allocated to.

## 6. Target a bank account...

Run this rule on    Fleur Employee Card x8873          ▼

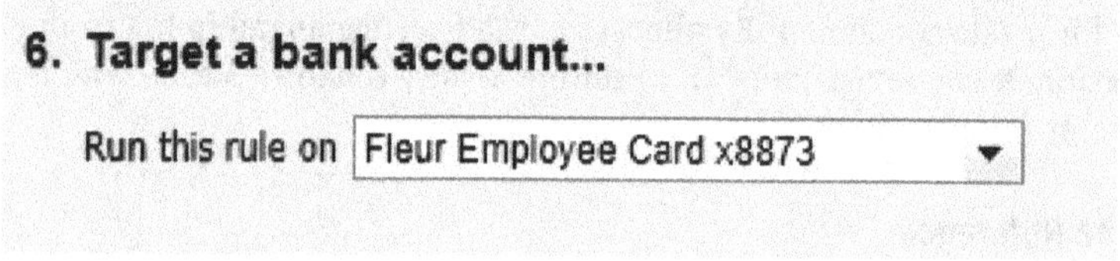

*Source:* Xero Limited

### Section 6: Target a Bank Account

Bank rules can be set to run on one or all bank and credit card accounts. They cannot be set to run on more than one, but not all, accounts. In most cases, targeting all bank and credit card accounts is a good idea. This will keep you from having to recreate rules when the company adds new employee credit cards or changes banks. One example of when targeting specific accounts is helpful would be if the company makes use of tracking categories, such as for department or location, and the tracking category is dependent on the employee. By targeting a specific credit card account, and therefore a specific user, in Section 6, the company can automate which department or location the charge is allocated to (Figure 10.43).

### Section 7: Give the Rule a Title

While the titling of a bank rule does not seem important to the efficiency of the bank reconciliation process, it is. The default title of any bank rule will be the Contact name. This is whether the rule is generated from a bank transaction or created from scratch.

**FIGURE 10.44**

For example, instead of Young Bros., use Young Bros.- Travel so that it is clear from the reconciliation screen how the transaction will be classified.

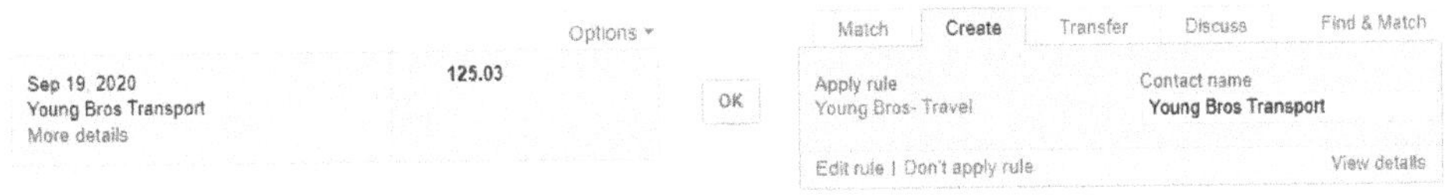

Source: Xero Limited

It is important to understand that when a rule is being suggested in bank reconciliation, Xero identifies it by only the title. While Contact name is helpful, it does not describe much of the rule, particularly the coding. To see the underlying coding action of the rule, you must open the rule. Consider giving the rule a title that includes how the transaction will be coded. For example, instead of **Young Bros.**, use **Young Bros. – Travel** so that it is clear from the reconciliation screen how the transaction will be classified (Figure 10.44).

## Applying Bank Rules

When Xero recognizes that a bank line matches the conditions established in a bank rule, the fields in the **Create** tab will be replaced with the name of the bank rule. To apply the rule, click the **OK** button between the bank tile and the coding tile.

If the bank rule should not be applied, click the **Don't apply rule** link and the tab will revert to allow input. Declining to apply a rule to a transaction will only decline that specific transaction. The bank rule match will still suggest other transactions that also match the conditions.

## Layering Bank Rules

Bank rules can be used on top of each other for the same vendor to filter transactions for coding. Let us take an example of an owner who occasionally uses a business credit card for personal expenses, such as gasoline. Employees of the company also use business cards for gasoline, but in those cases the cost is a business expense. By creating a rule for the owner's transaction where the only targeted bank account is the owner's card, those bank lines can be coded to Owner's Draw. Another bank rule would target all bank and credit card accounts and code those transactions to Automobile Expense. The key is indicating the order in which the rules should run on the bank transaction.

Bank rules are applied in the order in which they appear on the Bank Rules screen. The most restrictive rule, in this case the owner's rule, should be run first. If the conditions apply, it will be suggested in bank reconciliation and can be confirmed. If the conditions do not apply, Xero will move on and the automobile expense rule will be suggested. To reorder bank rules, click and drag the rule lines in the Bank Rules screen (Figure 10.45).

10

**FIGURE 10.45**

To reorder bank rules, click and drag the rule lines in the Bank Rules screen.

| Spend Money Rules (3) | Receive Money Rules (0) | Transfer Rules (0) |
| --- | --- | --- |

| | Delete | No items selected. Drag & drop to re-order. |
| --- | --- | --- |
| | 1 | Conner Grocery- Supplies |
| | 3 | Conner Grocery- Meals |
| | 2 | Young Bros- Travel |

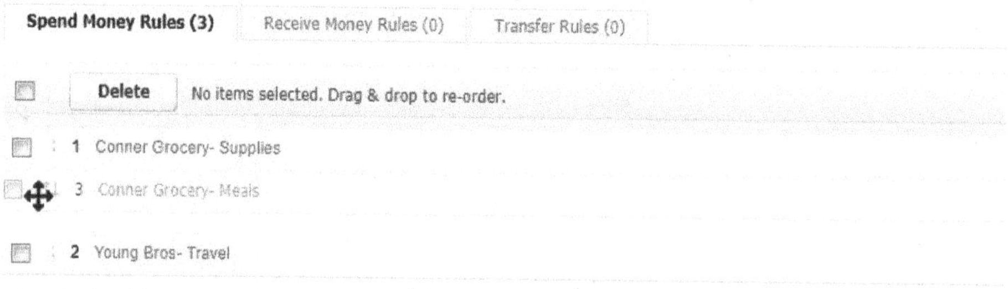

*Source:* Xero Limited

## Managing Bank Rules

Existing bank rules are listed in the bank rules screen. To manage bank rules:

1. Navigate to the Accounting tab, then Bank Accounts.
2. Select the Bank Rules button.

Clicking on the blue bank rule title will open the rule. Edits can be made here and saved. If a bank rule is obsolete and needs to be deleted, select the box to the left of the rule and click **Delete**. Confirm the deletion by clicking **OK**.

## Common Problems with Bank Rules

In most cases, problems with bank rules are with a created bank rule not showing as a suggested match when it is expected. There are several reasons this can happen:

**The conditions are too restrictive.** Review Section 1 to determine whether the match requires **All** conditions to be met rather than **Any**. Also consider whether the condition requires an exact field match by use of **equals.**

**The rule is for a specific bank or credit card account and the company has a new account.** If a rule is built to run only on one bank or credit card account, and the company opens a new account or issues an additional employee card, Xero will not suggest the match. Either modify the current rule or create a new rule that includes the new bank account or credit card.

**The bank changes the format of its data.** Xero bank rules are driven by conditions on data fields. If the bank or credit card issuer reformats its banking interface, data may be presented in different fields than when the rule was created. Use cash coding to examine which columns are now populated with identifying data and edit the bank rule.

**There is a hyphen in the conditions.** Xero does not recognize hyphens in conditions. If a vendor has a hyphen in its name, separate the two parts of the name in two conditions and require **All** to match.

# Cash Coding

From the outset, cash coding has been one of the best tools in Xero for efficient bank reconciliation. Cash coding gathers most of the unreconciled bank items in the reconcile queue and reformats them in a spreadsheet-like layout. This has a few benefits:

- It makes it possible to code and reconcile bank lines in bulk, which is especially useful in catch-up and tax preparation write-up work.
- It allows the user to see the company's data easily at a macro level.
- Bank rules are populated in cash coding, so many line items can be reconciled in just three clicks from logging in.

## Overview of Cash Coding

Cash coding is its own tab in the bank screen.

To access cash coding:

1. Navigate to **Accounting**, then **Bank Accounts**.
2. Select the bank account you wish to work in.
3. Open the second tab labeled **Cash Coding**.

The first thing to note is that cash coding will not include all unreconciled bank lines. Because it is designed for quick coding of bank lines to general ledger accounts, any line items that automatch to existing general ledger accounts will not be shown. If they were, it would be too easy to code these to general ledger accounts, which would effectively duplicate the transaction because it already exists as an unreconciled line.

The bank transactions are shown as horizontal lines in cash coding. Each column represents a field from the bank data. Because banks and third-party bank scraping tools differ in how data is structured, the columns may not match exactly with the description of the field. In practice, many bank feeds do not include a Payee column, but instead show the payee in the Reference field. In this way, cash coding gives the user a high-level view of how bank data is being imported, which is useful in creating meaningful bank rules.

The default number of bank lines shown in cash coding is 200. If there are more than 200 unreconciled bank lines, use the **Show more** button in the top right. Note that the more lines that are shown at a time, the slower the bulk coding will be, but it will still be much more efficient than coding lines individually.

Each column header can be used to sort. Click on a header to sort the data by the field in the column. This allows the user to see very quickly which vendors a company uses often or to locate an unreconciled line by dollar amount.

10

To cash code many transactions at once:

1. Sort by the column that includes the payee information so that transactions are grouped by vendor.

2. Highlight multiple lines for a payee by checking the boxes to the left of each line. Alternatively, check the box to the left of the first line, hold the **Shift** button, and check the box to the left of the last line.

3. When all lines are highlighted, enter an account in the Account column (Figure 10.46).

4. Hit the **Tab** button to apply the account and tax coding to all highlighted transactions.

5. Select **Save & Reconcile Selected** at the bottom of the screen.

6. Xero will confirm the number of coded lines. Click **OK**.

As in regular bank reconciliation from the **Create** tab, using cash coding to code a line is actually creating a Spend or Receive Money transaction on the general ledger, then linking that transaction to a bank statement line.

## Create Bank Rule from Cash Coding

As in reconciliation in the Reconcile tab, a bank rule can be drafted from a transaction line in cash coding. Use the triangle pull-down on the right side of a line in cash coding to access **Create a bank rule**. This will open a bank rule creation screen with the conditions prepopulated from the bank data (Figure 10.47).

## Split from Cash Coding

There are times when one bank line needs to be coded to more than one general ledger account. In some cases, the line may need to be classified to one account, but more than one tracking category. Xero makes it easy to accomplish this directly in cash coding without returning to the main Reconcile tab.

**FIGURE 10.46**

When all lines are highlighted, enter an account in the Account column.

*Source:* Xero Limited

**FIGURE 10.47**

As in reconciliation in the Reconcile tab, a bank rule can be drafted from a transaction line in cash coding. Use the triangle pulldown on the right side of a line in cash coding to access Create a bank rule. This will open a bank rule creation screen with the conditions prepopulated from the bank data.

*Source:* Xero Limited

While on a bank line in cash coding, use the triangle pull-down on the right and access **Split**. Use the table to classify the transaction as needed. Use the **Add a new line** button to add more coding lines.

## Cash Coding Keystroke Shortcuts

When you realize the efficiency that can be gained in using cash coding, you will likely spend a notable amount of time on that screen. The following keystroke shortcuts can help you move around faster without the use of a mouse.

| | |
|---|---|
| Enter | Moves down one cell |
| Shift + Enter | Moves up one cell |
| Tab | Moves right one cell |
| Shift + Tab | Moves left one cell |
| + | Applies coding from row above to current row |
| / | Opens a split screen so row can be coded to more than one account |
| Shift + Down Arrow | Highlights current row and moves down one |
| Alt + Down Arrow | Changes case of payee from all capital letters to capital first and lowercase thereafter |

## Cash Coding with Bank Rules

While cash coding and bank rules each separately creates efficiencies in bank coding, using the two together is powerful. When bank rules are set up in an organization, they will automatically be applied in the cash coding screen. To confirm the coding and reconcile the lines, simply click the **Save & Reconcile All** button at the bottom of the screen. This allows you to code bank lines within three clicks of logging into Xero—one to access the bank account, one to select the **Cash Coding** tab, and one to reconcile.

Note that there is no way to decline a bank rule in cash coding as there is in the Reconcile tab, so you must be sure the bank rule is set up correctly before clicking **Save & Reconcile All**.

# Reconciling a Stripe Feed

If your client uses Stripe for payment collection, it is often time saving to connect the Stripe account as a direct bank feed. Doing so will populate Xero with every transaction on the account, meaning that gross collections will be shown in the received column of bank reconciliation and fees and payout will be shown in the spent column. This will allow for proper matching of invoices or recognition of gross sales, yet easily allow the coding of the merchant fees (Figure 10.48).

The only problem in connecting the direct feed is the risk that the payout into the business checking account will get miscoded as additional income. If you choose to connect the Stripe feed, it is important to ensure that only Stripe transactions are booked to income and that the payouts collected in the bank account are recognized as transfers.

The reconciliation process should be as follows:

1. Reconcile the Stripe deposits first. Code collections as revenue or match them to invoices, if appropriate. If invoices are not used, a bank rule could be set up.
2. Reconcile Stripe merchant fees. Set up a bank rule to automate this.
3. Mark the Stripe payouts as transfers to the receiving checking account.
4. In the receiving bank account, confirm the transfers in by using the OK button.

## FIGURE 10.48

This will allow for proper matching of invoices or recognition of gross sales, yet easily allow the coding of the merchant fees.

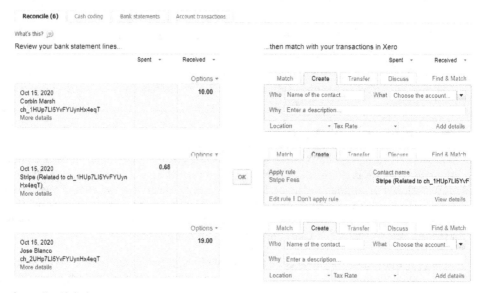

*Source:* Xero Limited

# Optimal Workflow for Bank Reconciliation

With all these options for bank reconciliation, it can be confusing to know which tools should be used in which order for the most efficient workflow. Because any bank transaction could meet the criteria for more than one automation tool, it is important to first understand Xero's own hierarchy in applying.

Beginning in the Reconcile tab, automatch to existing general ledger transactions based on dollar amount will be applied first. This means that even if the matched bank line meets the conditions for a bank rule or autosuggest, those options will not be shown. It also means that these matched bank lines will not appear in cash coding.

The second tool in Xero's bank automation hierarchy is bank rules. Bank rules will be offered for any transactions meeting the criteria specified, rather than showing the autosuggest option.

Autosuggest from previous coding is the last tool in the hierarchy and will only be offered when the bank line matches neither an existing general ledger transaction nor bank rule criteria.

In considering the hierarchy of automation, here is the optimal workflow:

1. Reconcile payment processor feeds, like **Stripe** and **PayPal**, first.

2. Use the **Cash Coding** tab to apply bank rules. In three clicks, any transactions matching bank rule conditions can be coded. Because any automatching lines will be excluded, you can safely code transactions in bulk using this method.

3. Use the **Reconcile** tab to evaluate any automatching bank lines. Take care to choose the correct invoice, bill, payment, spend money, or receive money when more than one match applies.

4. Return to the **Cash Coding** tab to code unmatched lines. This is most appropriate for electronically generated, cash-based transactions, such as those created from the use of a debit or credit card. These transactions will have flush identifying detail in the bank feed. Use the tips mentioned earlier to code lines in bulk by payee. The risk in coding lines here is neglecting to match transactions that should be linked with existing invoices or bills but are not automatching because of the difference in amount.

5. Return to the **Reconcile** tab to code transactions individually. In a company who uses Xero properly (posting check payments and receipts) and makes use of other cloud tools, like bill payment and sales applications, there should not be many lines left. Take care with these remaining lines. Consider source information to determine whether the bank lines might be associated with existing general ledger transactions, like deposits for multiple invoices or minor differences.

10

# Errors in Bank Coding and Matching

Errors in bank or credit card entries occur one of two ways:

1. Incorrect bank data was imported or fed into Xero.
2. Correct bank data was miscoded or mismatched in Xero.

Managing bank lines and correcting errors is covered in Chapter 9. This section covers the occurrence of accurate bank transactions that were imported or fed into Xero, but the coding or matching was wrong.

A coding error is one where a spend money or receive money transaction was created in bank reconciliation or cash coding and the accounts posted against the bank line are incorrect. Coding errors are generally found by a review of the ledger or an account transactions report.

A mismatching error is one in which a bank line is linked to the wrong general ledger already existing in Xero or incorrectly creating a new spend or receive money transaction, when the general ledger transaction already exists. An error in mismatching is more obvious, but also more problematic. This type of error may be identified by review of the bank reconciliation, accounts receivable, or accounts payables reports, because unmatched and uncleared items will be listed.

For either type of error, the resolution begins with finding the transaction in Xero.

1. Navigate to **Accounting**, then **Bank Accounts**.
2. Select the bank or credit card account with the error.
3. Navigate to the **Account Transactions** tab. (Because we are looking for a reconciled line item, the transaction will no longer be visible in the Reconcile or Cash coding tabs.)
4. Click the **Search** button in the upper right corner of the transactions listing. The easiest way to find a specific transaction is to check the Exact Amount option and enter the transaction amount. Click **Search**.
5. When the reconciled line is found, open the transaction by clicking the blue payee (Figure 10.49).

It is important to understand the infrastructure behind banking in Xero in order to understand how errors must be fixed. Click the **View Details** link at the top of a reconciled transaction (Figure 10.50).

As we covered in an earlier chapter, reconciliation in Xero is the connection of a bank statement line to a general ledger line. We can see that relationship visually here. On the left is the bank data, whether from a feed or imported. On the right are the general ledger transactions that the bank line is reconciled with. These can be either spend or receive money transactions created in bank reconciliation, invoices or bill, or payments applied to invoices or bills.

**FIGURE 10.49**

When the reconciled line is found, open the transaction by clicking the blue payee.

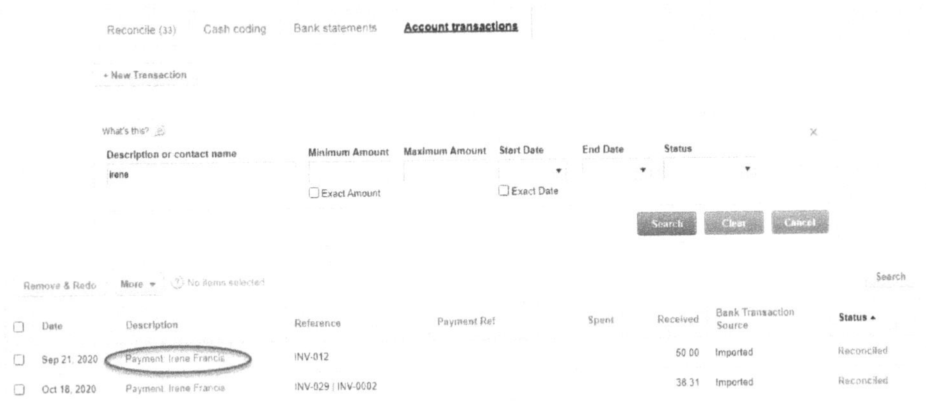

*Source:* Xero Limited

**FIGURE 10.50**

It is important to understand the infrastructure behind banking in Xero in order to understand how errors must be fixed. Click the View Details link at the top of a reconciled transaction.

*Source:* Xero Limited

# Fixing Coding Errors in Bank Transactions

Assume a company codes a bank transaction to Cost of Goods Sold rather than Meals. There are no objective controls that would highlight this mistake. The bank reconciliation report would still be accurate. Book basis net income would be correct. However, the detail within the income statement would be off, and taxable income would be understated.

For a coding error, you would want to either edit the spend money or receive money transaction on the right or delete it entirely and create a new one in bank reconciliation.

For the miscoding example above, where the user incorrectly reconciled a bank line to Cost of Goods Sold rather than Meals, the transaction should be edited. To edit a spend or receive money transaction:

1. Open the transaction from the **Account Transactions** tab. The transaction screen looks similar to input screens throughout Xero.
2. Use the **Options** pull-down to access **Edit Transaction** (Figure 10.51).
3. Change the coding under the Account field and click **Update**.

**FIGURE 10.51**

Use the Options pulldown to access Edit Transaction.

*Source:* Xero Limited

An alternative would be to entirely delete the spend money or receive money transaction that is linked to the bank line:

1. Open the transaction from the **Account Transactions** tab. The transaction screen looks similar to input screens throughout Xero.

2. Use the **Options** pull-down to access **Remove & Redo**. The spend-or-receive money will be deleted, the link between the bank line and the transaction will be removed, and the bank line will reappear in the **Reconcile** tab so that coding can be redone (Figure 10.52).

## Fixing Mismatching Errors in Bank Reconciliation

There are two kinds of mismatching:

1. Matched to wrong GL item.

2. Did not match to any GL items and created a new transaction instead.

For errors where the incorrect existing transaction was matched, such as choosing the wrong invoice when applying a payment, the bank line must be unlinked from the general ledger side without deleting the invoice. This requires the use of **Unreconcile**.

To unreconcile a matched transaction:

1. Open the transaction from the **Account Transactions** tab.

2. Use the **Options** pull-down to select **Unreconcile**.

3. Xero provides a confirmation screen that this action will break the link between the two transactions. Click **OK** (Figure 10.53).

**FIGURE 10.52**

Use the Options pulldown to access Remove & Redo. The spend or receive money will be deleted, the link between the bank line and the transaction will be removed and the bank line will reappear in the Reconcile tab so that coding can be redone.

*Source:* Xero Limited

**FIGURE 10.53**

Xero provides a confirmation screen that this action will break the link between the two transactions. Click OK.

*Source:* Xero Limited

Assume a company does not match a deposit of $1,000 to the appropriate awaiting payment invoice, but instead codes the deposit to revenue. The accounts receivable report would show the invoice as unpaid and the customer would receive invoice reminders, if activated. Revenue would be overstated by $1,000. In this situation, use Remove & Redo to delete the revenue transaction and send the bank line back to the Reconcile tab where it can be properly matched to an invoice.

10

# Sales and Invoicing

X ero has made invoicing and getting paid really simple. Create one-time or repeating invoices manually or even bulk import invoices to be sent to your clients. Add in a payment service and get paid quicker.

*—Jay Kimelman, Founder and CEO of the digital CPA*

One of the biggest struggles for small businesses is cash flow, and the simplest solution is to collect on sales as quickly as possible. Xero makes invoice preparation and collection very efficient. Many Xero clients use the electronic invoicing functionality in Xero, and many of those will connect invoices to an electronic payment platform, which creates a seamless sales cycle.

Advising clients on the best practices for sales management is a great way to add value to the relationship. Clients may need help in streamlining the revenue cycle. As an accountant or bookkeeper, you can advise your client on processes and workflows and help leverage Xero to automate invoicing and collection, shortening the days to paid.

In this chapter, we will cover all the variations of invoicing and sales documents, including group invoices, repeating invoices, credit notes, quotes, and statements.

## Overview of Sales

In Xero, the accounts receivable module is referred to as **Sales**, and documents requesting payment for products or services are called **Invoices**. This is in contrast to accounts payable, which is referred to as Purchases, and payment documents, which are referred to as Bills.

The Sales Overview screen is a dashboard showing accounts receivable and is accessed by navigating to **Business,** then **Sales overview.** This screen shows all sales activity. Note that selecting either Invoices or Quotes from the Business pull-down will bring you directly to those detail screens rather than the summary for all sales activity.

**FIGURE 11.1**

At the top of the screen are a few useful buttons.

**Sales overview**

| + New ▾ | Send Statements | Import | | Search 🔍 |

*Source:* Xero Limited

**FIGURE 11.2**

In Sales, there are four categories of invoices which are represented by a graphic in the top half of the screen:

Invoices  Paid  Repeating  See all

| Draft | Awaiting Approval | Awaiting Payment (21) | Overdue (9) |
|---|---|---|---|
| None | None | 5,235.06 | 2,849.57 |

*Source:* Xero Limited

At the top of the screen are a few useful buttons (Figure 11.1). The **+New** pull-down allows a user to create most of the sales document variations quickly: Invoice, Quote, Repeating invoice, Credit note, or Group invoice. The **Send Statements** button will redirect the user to a screen that shows receivables activity over a period and allow the user to email or print statements. The **Import** button will allow the user to bulk import invoices. The **Search** button opens search fields for finding invoices or quotes. There is detailed information about these features further in this chapter.

In Sales, there are four categories of invoices that are represented by a graphic in the top half of the screen (Figure 11.2):

- **Draft:** Draft invoices are invoices that have been created but are not yet final so they are not included on the general ledger. This category is used to hold invoices that still need to be edited.
- **Awaiting Approval:** Awaiting Approval invoices are similar to Draft invoices in that they are not yet final. In general, these invoices are pending approval by a different user than the user that created the invoice. Awaiting Approval invoices are also not included in the general ledger Accounts Receivable balance.
- **Awaiting Payment:** Awaiting Payment invoices are invoices that are approved, final, sent to the customer, and waiting to be paid. The Awaiting Payment balance equals the Accounts Receivable balance on the general ledger.
- **Overdue:** Overdue invoices are a subset of Awaiting Payment invoices that are past the stated due date.

**FIGURE 11.3**

Below the invoices graphic are two charts. (Figure 11.3) The first is Money coming in.

*Source:* Xero Limited

Clicking into any of these categories will redirect the user to a listing of those invoices that make up the balance.

Below the invoices graphic are two charts (Figure 11.3). The first is **Money coming in**. This is a timeline of expected invoice collections. Invoices are represented on the timeline based on due date, unless an expected date has been entered for the payment. The second is a table or a pie chart that shows **Customers owing the most**. The user can toggle between the formats by using the **List** and **Pie** links above the chart. In both graphics, the user can drill into the underlying invoices by clicking the blue or red (overdue) links.

The next section on the overview screen is **Quotes** (Figure 11.4). Like the invoices graphic, there are four categories for quotes:

- **Draft:** Quotes that have been created but not finalized and sent to the customer.
- **Sent:** Quotes that have been sent or marked as sent to the customer.
- **Accepted:** Quotes that are accepted electronically by the customer or marked as accepted.
- **Expired:** Quotes that were neither accepted nor declined before the expiry date set at creation.

**FIGURE 11.4**

The next section on the overview screen is Quotes. (Figure 11.4) Like the invoices graphic, there are four categories for quotes:

**Quotes**  See all

| Draft | Sent (1) | Accepted | Expired |
|---|---|---|---|
| None | 2,325.00 | None | None |

*Source:* Xero Limited

The final section will be **Billable Expenses**, if any outstanding billable expenses exist. (If there are no outstanding billable expenses, this section will not appear.) Billable expenses are costs to the company that need to be recovered from a customer. There is more information later in this chapter.

# Viewing the Invoice Listing

While the Sales Overview screen shows a high-level perspective of accounts receivable, the Invoices screen is a detailed listing of each invoice. Access the invoice listing by clicking the Awaiting Payment category on the Sales Overview or by navigating to the **Business** tab, then **Invoices**.

The **All** tab shows all invoices created in the system, except for voided or deleted invoices.

The fastest way to locate a specific invoice is to use the Search button at the top right of the listing. Xero can search based on contact name, invoice number, reference, or amount, and the search can be limited to a specific date range. To include void or deleted invoices in the search, check the box next to **Include Deleted & Voided**.

Most of the management of receivables will happen in the **Awaiting Payment** tab, as this represents current outstanding invoices and is the detail of the Accounts Receivable balance (Figure 11.5).

## FIGURE 11.5

Most of the management of receivables will happen in the Awaiting Payment tab, as this represents current outstanding invoices and is the detail of the Accounts Receivable balance.

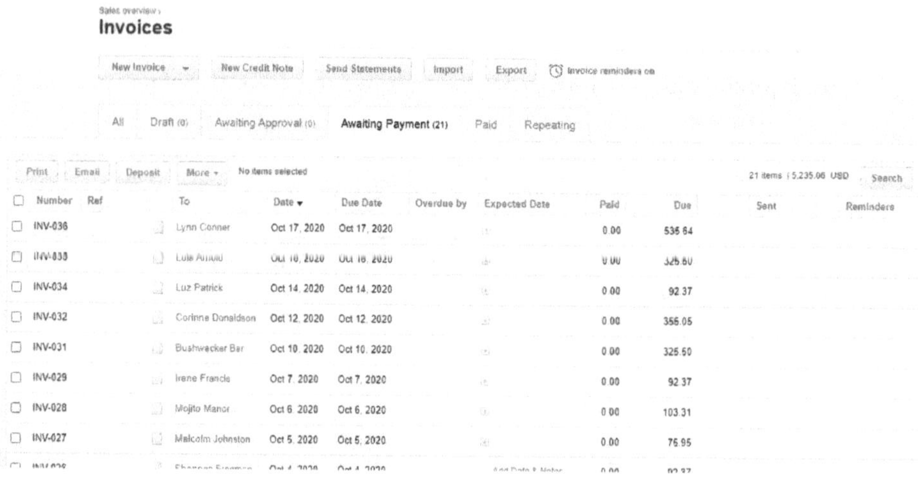

*Source:* Xero Limited

The **Draft** and **Awaiting Approval** tabs list invoices that have not yet been fully finalized and, therefore, are not posted to the general ledger.

The **Paid** tab shows invoices that have been fully paid and have no outstanding balance.

The **Repeating** tab lists repeating invoice templates, not invoices that have been created by a repeating invoice template. Once an invoice is created by a template, the invoice will be listed in the appropriate status tab. Learn more about Repeating templates later in this chapter.

The column headings in the invoice listings can be used to sort the listing. Clicking on the blue header will reorder the list according to the data values in that column. The **Awaiting Payment** tab has these important columns that are helpful in managing receivables:

- **Overdue by:** The Overdue by column calculates the days past the due date on any invoices with an outstanding balance, so that sorting by this column gives the user a clear understanding of the most stale receivables.
- **Expected Date:** The Expected Date column is a functional column, where the user can input an expected collection date for an invoice. If an invoice has an expected date, that date, rather than the due date, will be used in the **Money coming in** graphic in Sales Overview and the **Short-term cash flow** dashboard.
- **Sent:** This column shows which invoices have been sent to customers, but more importantly, it shows which have been viewed by customers using the online link.
- **Reminders:** If you have invoice reminders activated, this column will tell you whether reminders have been sent for the contact. For more details about invoice reminders, see Chapter 6.

# Creating an Invoice

The most simple task in sales is levying a single sales invoice. The creation of an invoice is the transaction in an accrual basis business that recognizes sales revenue and increases the accounts receivable balance on the general ledger. (In a cash-basis business, revenue is not recognized until the invoice is paid.) Invoices are used when there is a timing difference between the company providing goods or services and the customer making a payment.

Xero has two views for invoicing—new and classic. **New invoicing** is consistent with Xero's cleaner interface and is built to incorporate machine learning to suggest account codes based on previous transactions. New invoicing allows credit blocks to be added to prevent invoices from being sent to customers exceeding their credit limit. Invoices in progress will be automatically saved in new invoicing.

While new invoicing is the future of the Xero sales module, there are advisors who prefer to create invoices in Classic invoicing. Additionally, at the time of writing, billable expenses could not be recorded on new invoices. Both are discussed next.

## Creating an Invoice in New Invoicing

To create a new single invoice:

1. Navigate to the **Business** tab, then **Invoices**.

2. Click the **+New Invoice** button.

3. If Classic invoicing appears, use the link below the input tile to **Switch to new invoicing**.

4. Type the customer name in the **To** field. As you type, Xero will filter known contacts. If the customer is not an existing contact, enter the complete name. Xero will add the contact to the Customers group in Contacts.

5. Enter an optional **Reference**.

6. The Invoice number field will show a suggested invoice number, but it can be changed.

7. Enter or accept a date in the **Date** field. The default invoice day will be today, but it can be changed. The invoice date will be the date the sale is recognized on the books.

8. Enter or accept a date in the **Due Date** field. The default due date here is based on Invoice Settings discussed in Chapter 6, but can be changed.

9. Use the **Branding** pull-down to select the appropriate invoice branding theme.

10. On the **Add an item** line, either type a description or use an inventory item code to autopopulate the line. If a general ledger account is associated with an inventory item, that account will be the default for the line. To change, use the overflow menu at the right, and choose another account with the pull-down.

11. Use the **Send** pull-down to choose what happens with the invoice (Figure 11.6).

## Creating an Invoice in Classic Invoicing

To create a new single invoice:

1. Navigate to the **Business** tab, then **Invoices**.

2. Click the **+New Invoice** button.

3. If New invoicing appears, use the link below the input tile to **Switch to classic invoicing**.

4. Type the customer name in the **To** field. As you type, Xero will filter known contacts. If the customer is not an existing contact, enter the complete name. Xero will add the contact to the Customers group in Contacts.

5. Enter or accept a date in the **Date** field. The default invoice day will be today, but it can be changed. The invoice date will be the date the sale is recognized on the books.

**FIGURE 11.6**

Use the Send pulldown to choose what happens with the invoice.

6. Enter or accept a date in the Due Date field. The default due date here is based on Invoice Settings discussed in Chapter 6, but can be changed. See below for some common date entry shortcuts.

7. The **Invoice #** field is also a default based on the numbering system specified in Invoice Settings.

8. The **Reference** field will be visible in Find & Match in bank reconciliation and is a field that will be considered in invoice search queries, so many advisors use a descriptive phrase here.

9. Use the **Branding** pull-down to select the appropriate invoice-branding theme.

10. If you wish to attach files to the invoice, either for internal recordkeeping or to forward with the invoice to the customer, use the .pdf icon button (Figure 11.7).

Most static file types can be uploaded to Xero, including .pdf, .doc, .csv, .jpg, .png, and .xls, but .pdf files generally work best. Files may be attached to an invoice from the File Library or directly uploaded to the invoice. Use **+Add from file library** to select a file that already exists in the library. Note that attaching a file from the file library to a transaction will remove the file from the library. For more information on the Xero file library, see Chapter 4. You can also attach a file directly in the invoice by using the **+Upload files** link.

Once a file or files have been attached to the invoice, they will remain part of the invoice record forever. To make the file available as an attachment to the invoice

**FIGURE 11.7**

If you wish to attach files to the invoice, either for internal recordkeeping or to forward with the invoice to the customer, use the .pdf icon button.

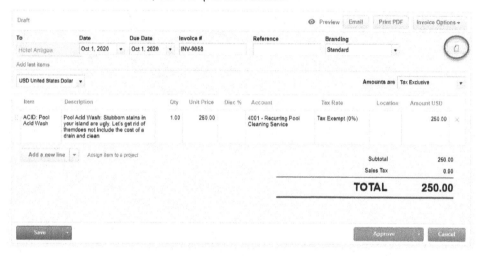

Source: Xero Limited

and viewable by the recipient customer, use the gear icon to the right of the file and select **Include with invoice.**

11. Enter the invoice details in the table shown.

**Item:** If there are inventory items set up in the Xero organization, this field can be used to populate many of the remaining fields. Enter the Inventory Item Code here. The item code will generally not be visible on customer invoices.

**Description:** Enter a description of the item or service sold, if it is not already populated. This field will be visible on emailed and printed invoices, so it should give customers enough information on the sale.

**Qty:** Enter the number of units sold (or hours billed or other measure) in this field. Xero will multiply by the unit price to calculate the total amount of the sale. A value must be entered, so use a "1" if there is no quantity.

**Unit Price:** Enter the cost per unit to the customer.

**Disc %:** If you wish to extend a discount on the sale to the customer, you can enter a percentage here. Note that Xero will only post the net amount to the general ledger account. Many advisors prefer to show the gross amount as sales revenue and add an additional invoice line as a negative value that will post to a contra-revenue discounts account. This method will also make the discount more clear to the customer.

**Account:** Select the general ledger account that the invoice line amount should be posted to. A new account can be created here without leaving this screen and navigating to the chart of accounts. Use the pull-down and select **+Add new account**. Complete the account details and click **Save**. The new account will be created and used for the sales invoice line.

**Tax Rate:** The sales tax rate to be applied will default to the rate associated with the general ledger account. To change, use the pull-down to select the appropriate tax rate. A new tax rate can be created here without leaving the screen and navigating to settings. Use the pull-down and select **+Add new tax rate**. Create the rate and underlying components, and click **Save**. The new rate will be created and used for the sales invoice line.

**Tracking categories:** Each invoice line can be allocated to one or both tracking categories, if they are enabled. For more information on tracking categories, see Chapter 6.

12. Once the invoice details have been entered, you can:

**Save as draft:** Draft invoices can be accessed in the Draft category on the Sales Overview screen or in the Draft tab on the Invoices screen.

**Save (continue editing):** This option saves your work and keeps the invoice screen open.

**Save & submit for approval:** Saving and submitting for approval will move the invoice to the Awaiting Approval category on the Sales Overview screen or in the Awaiting Approval tab on the Invoices screen.

**Save & add another:** This option will save the created invoice as a Draft and open a new, blank invoice screen.

**Approve:** Clicking Approve will save the invoice, add it to the Awaiting Payment category of invoices, and increase the accounts receivable general ledger balance by the amount of the invoice.

**Approve & add another:** This option has the same effect as Approve but redirects the user to a new, blank invoice input screen.

**Approve & print:** This option has the same effect as Approve but creates a .pdf download of the invoice as well.

13. Once the invoice is approved, you can send electronically to the customer or print out for mailing.

# Sending Invoices Electronically

When an invoice has been created and approved, it must be delivered to the customer for payment. The fastest way to send an invoice is to email a link directly from Xero.

**FIGURE 11.8**

Xero will show a preview of the email.

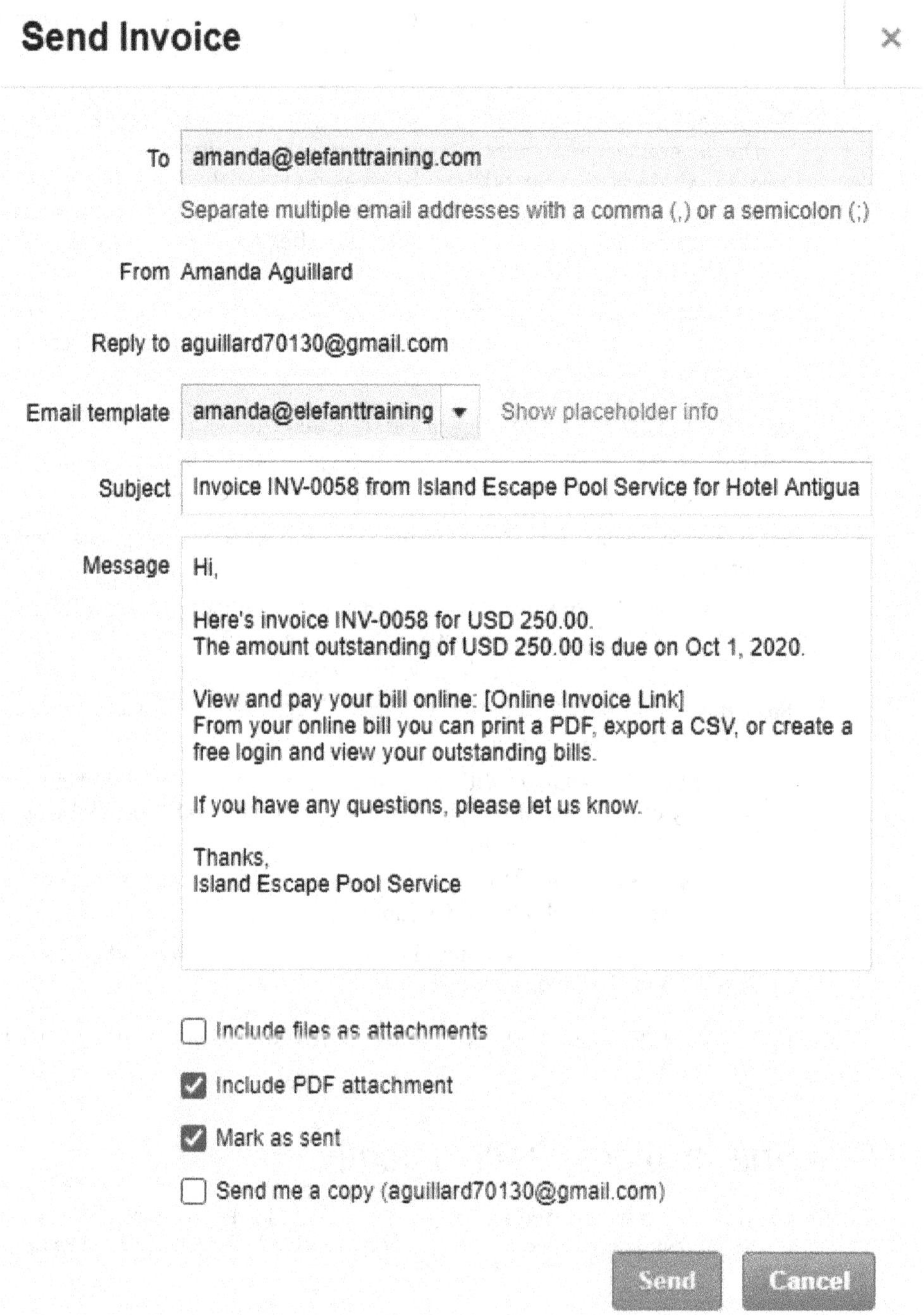

## Send Invoice                                                    ✕

To amanda@elefanttraining.com

Separate multiple email addresses with a comma (,) or a semicolon (;)

From Amanda Aguillard

Reply to aguillard70130@gmail.com

Email template amanda@elefanttraining ▼  Show placeholder info

Subject Invoice INV-0058 from Island Escape Pool Service for Hotel Antigua

Message Hi,

Here's invoice INV-0058 for USD 250.00.
The amount outstanding of USD 250.00 is due on Oct 1, 2020.

View and pay your bill online: [Online Invoice Link]
From your online bill you can print a PDF, export a CSV, or create a
free login and view your outstanding bills.

If you have any questions, please let us know.

Thanks,
Island Escape Pool Service

☐ Include files as attachments

☑ Include PDF attachment

☑ Mark as sent

☐ Send me a copy (aguillard70130@gmail.com)

[ Send ]  [ Cancel ]

*Source:* Xero Limited

To email an invoice:

1. Locate the invoice in the **Awaiting Payment** tab and open it by clicking the blue customer name.
2. Click the **Email** button at the top of the screen.
3. Xero will show a preview of the email (Figure 11.8).

   The recipient defaults to the primary contact for the contact. Additional recipients can be added by separating addresses with a semicolon or comma.

   The outgoing email body is based on the template set in Email settings. You can edit the text here for this particular email, but the template can only be updated in Email settings. For more information, see Chapter 6.

   The option to **Include files as attachments** refers to including files that are attached to the invoice in Xero by the user as described earlier in this chapter.

   The option to **Include PDF attachment** refers to including a .pdf file of the invoice as an attachment to the email. Note that without this selected, the recipient must use the online invoice link in the body of the email to view the invoice. In most cases, it would be preferable to "force" a recipient to use the link because Xero will recognize that the invoice has been viewed and will note that in the status column of the invoice. If a recipient can view the invoice as a .pdf without using the unique link, there will not be a digital trail.

   You can elect to have a copy of the email sent to you by clicking the box next to **Send me a copy**.

4. Click **Send** to send the email.

# Managing Invoices

Once an invoice is created but before it has been paid, it will be found in one of three categories or tabs in Sales: Draft, Awaiting Approval, and Awaiting Payment. You may need to edit the invoice, void it, or use it as a template for another similar invoice.

## Editing an Invoice

There are situations where an invoice that has been approved may need to be edited or corrected. Prior to any payments being applied, the invoice can be fully edited. Once a payment has been applied to an invoice, even if it is a partial payment, only certain fields can be edited: Contact, Due date, Invoice number, Reference, Description, Account, and Tracking category. These are fields that do not affect the invoice total. If other fields need to be changed, the payment must be removed first.

**FIGURE 11.9**

Use the Invoice Options pulldown to access Edit.

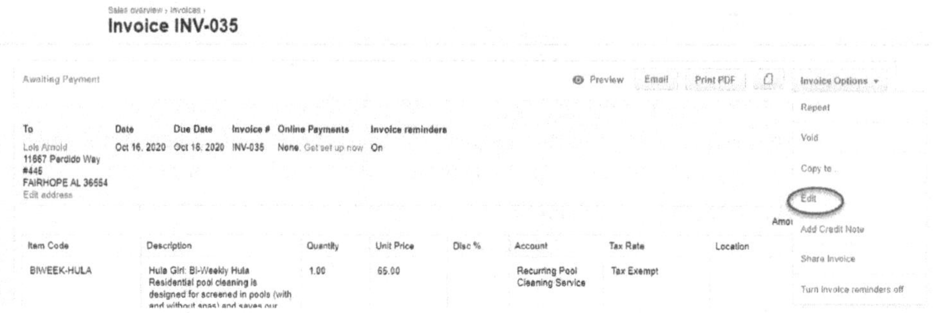

*Source:* Xero Limited

To edit an invoice that has not been paid:

1. Locate the invoice and open it by clicking the blue customer name.
2. Use the **Invoice Options** pull-down to access **Edit** (Figure 11.9).
3. Make needed changes to the invoice.
4. Click **Update**.

## Voiding an Invoice

If an invoice was created and approved in error, the best way to remove it from the accounts receivable balance is to void it. An invoice with payments or credits applied cannot be voided. Any payments or credits must be removed before voiding.

To void an invoice:

1. Locate the invoice and open it by clicking the blue customer name.
2. Use the **Invoice Options** pull-down to access **Void**.
3. Confirm that you wish to void the invoice by clicking **OK**.

## Duplicating an Invoice

If you must create an invoice with similar charges or settings of one that already exists, it may be more efficient to duplicate it than creating a new invoice from scratch.

**FIGURE 11.10**

Select Invoice and type the contact name in the Create it for field.

## Copy to a new...                                                    ✕

○ Invoice

Create it for:

Beach, Tony

○ Quote

○ Purchase Order

○ Bill

Cancel    **Copy**

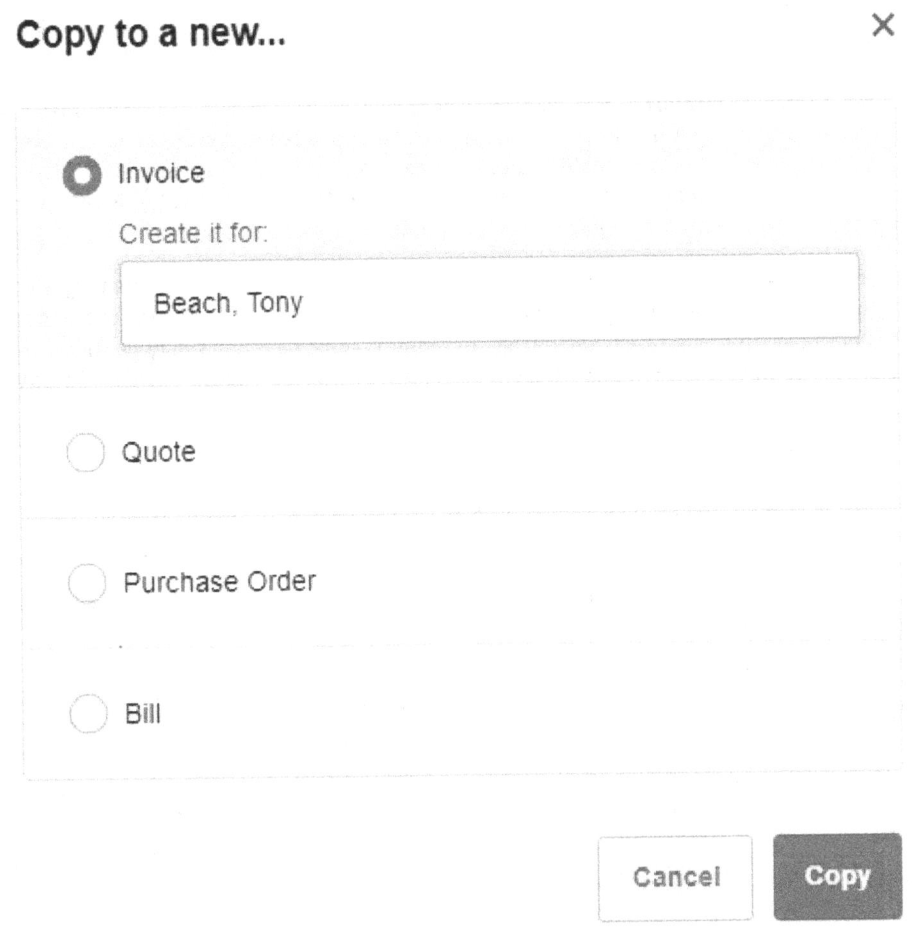

*Source:* Xero Limited

To create a copy of an invoice:

1. Locate the invoice and open it by clicking the blue customer name.
2. Use the **Invoice Options** pull-down to access **Copy to....**
3. Select **Invoice** and type the contact name in the **Create it for** field (Figure 11.10).
4. Click **Copy.**
5. Edit the invoice for any needed changes from the original.
6. Click **Approve.**

# Applying Payments to Invoices

Many companies will wait for a deposit for an invoice payment to appear in bank transactions before applying it to the invoice. Others will want to show the payment as soon as it is received, rather than waiting for it to show in the bank feed.

The payment workflow will depend on the needs of the company. In companies where checks are received in the mail and may not be deposited and reconciled in a timely manner, it would be advisable to note the payment as soon as it is received. This is especially important when invoice reminders are being sent automatically. A customer should not receive a reminder to pay when the invoice has, in fact, been paid.

For companies who collect payments electronically, however, there is usually a very quick turnaround between the payment processing and the acknowledgment of the deposit in the bank feed. In these cases, separately applying invoice payments may be unnecessary. Some payment processors, such as Stripe, will mark the invoice paid as soon as the payment is initiated, as long as Stripe is properly integrated with Xero.

To record a payment to an invoice:

1. Locate the invoice and open it by clicking the blue customer name.
2. Scroll to the **Receive a payment** tile at the bottom of the invoice page.
3. Enter the **Amount Paid**. The default figure will be the invoice balance, but you can change this if only a partial payment was received.
4. Enter the **Date Paid**.
5. Choose the account that the payment will be **Paid To**.

   In general, this will be the bank account that the funds will be deposited in. It is very important that the correct bank account is chosen, because Xero will only match payments recorded to deposits in the same bank account.

   The account chosen does not have to be a bank account, though. This account can be any account that is set up in the chart of accounts with the option to enable payments. (See Chapter 5 for details.) The most common use for applying a payment from a nonbank account would be a clearing or holding account.

6. Enter an optional **Reference**. This can be a check number or other identifying information.
7. Click **Add Payment** (Figure 11.11).

**FIGURE 11.11**

Click Add Payment.

Receive a payment

| Amount Paid | Date Paid | Paid To | Reference | |
|---|---|---|---|---|
| 325.50 | Nov 1, 2020 ▾ | 1010 - Sunny Bank Checl ▾ | Check #445 | Add Payment |

*Source:* Xero Limited

**FIGURE 11.12**

The payment and payment date will be noted under the invoice amount and the invoice will have a zero balance or revised amount due.

| | |
|---|---|
| Subtotal | 303.00 |
| Total Orleans Parish 5% | 11.91 |
| Total No Tax 0% | 0.00 |
| Total Lousiana 4.45% | 10.59 |
| **TOTAL** | **325.50** |
| Less Payment Nov 1, 2020 | 325.50 |
| **AMOUNT DUE** | **0.00** |

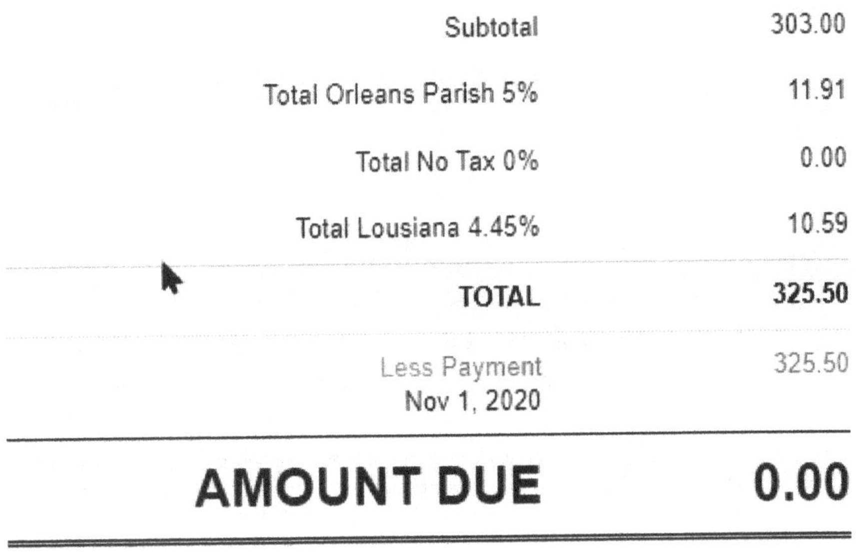

*Source:* Xero Limited

The payment and payment date will be noted under the invoice amount and the invoice will have a zero balance or revised amount due (Figure 11.12).

# Batch Deposits

If a customer has more than one outstanding invoice, it would be expected that they would remit one payment for all the invoices rather than separate payments for each. It is also possible that more than one customer may remit payments that are deposited to the bank account at one time. Because Xero will match bank lines to existing transactions by exact amount, posting a batch deposit will create a payment transaction that will be automatically matched in bank reconciliation.

To record a batch deposit for multiple invoices:

1. In the **Awaiting Payment** tab of Invoices, select the invoices paid in the batch by checking the boxes to the left of each (Figure 11.13).

**FIGURE 11.13**

In the Awaiting Payment tab of Invoices, select the invoices paid in the batch by checking the boxes to the left of each.

*Source:* Xero Limited

2. Click the **Deposit** button at the top of the listing.

3. Enter the **Payment Date**, which would be the date the batch deposit is made.

4. Add a **Reference**. This is a required field but can be something as simple as the date.

5. Choose the **Bank Account** the deposit will be made to. It is very important to choose the correct bank. Choosing the wrong bank will keep the batch from matching to the bank statement line for the deposit.

6. Click **Deposit** (Figure 11.14).

**FIGURE 11.14**

Click Deposit.

Sales › Awaiting Payment ›

**New Batch Deposit**

| Payment Date | Reference | | Bank Account | | | | |
|---|---|---|---|---|---|---|---|
| Nov 1, 2020 | 11/1/20 | | 1010 - Sunny Bank Check x4343 | | | | |

| From | Invoice Number | Due Date | Reference/Check No | Amount Due USD | | Payment USD | |
|---|---|---|---|---|---|---|---|
| Bushwacker Bar | INV-031 | Oct 10, 2020 | | 325.50 | | 325.50 | × |
| Corinne Donaldson | INV-021 | Sep 28, 2020 | | 316.74 | | 316.74 | × |
| Corinne Donaldson | INV-032 | Oct 12, 2020 | | 355.05 | | 355.05 | × |
| Hotel Antigua | INV-0056 | Oct 01, 2020 | | 250.00 | | 250.00 | × |

**Total**    **1,247.29 USD**

Deposit    Cancel

*Source:* Xero Limited

**FIGURE 11.15**

The batch deposit will now be listed in the Account Transactions tab of the bank account as an unreconciled line and will be matched with the deposit of the same amount.

The batch deposit will now be listed in the **Account Transactions** tab of the bank account as an unreconciled line and will be matched with the deposit of the same amount (Figure 11.15).

# Credit Notes

If the amount due from a customer must be reduced, such as in the case of a return or allowance, a **credit note** should be issued. A credit note is created and then applied to an invoice to reduce the amount due. A credit note is so named because it posts a credit to the accounts receivable balance.

There are two main ways to issue and apply credit notes to invoices in Xero:

1. Create a credit note from the invoice that will be adjusted.
2. Create a credit note at the customer level and apply to one or more invoices.

## Create a Credit Note from an Invoice

Creating directly within the invoice that will be adjusted is the fastest way to issue and apply a credit note because both steps are handled at once. This would be the most efficient workflow to adjust a specific invoice.

To create a credit note from an invoice:

1. Locate the invoice and open it by clicking the blue customer name.
2. Use the **Invoice Options** pull-down to access **Add Credit Note**.
3. Xero will reverse the invoice details for the credit note input screen. The background of the screen changes to a pale yellow, which indicates that this is a transaction that is the opposite direction of normal.
4. Edit fields as necessary, remembering that the posting will be the opposite of the invoice. Positive numbers will reduce the sales accounts. You can delete unnecessary lines by using the X on the right.
5. Review the summary at the bottom, which shows the credit note amount and which invoice it will be applied to.
6. Click **Approve** (Figure 11.16).

**FIGURE 11.16**

Click Approve.

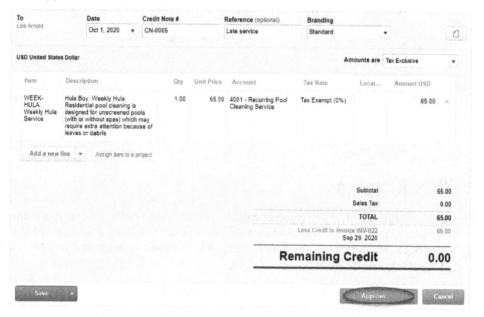

Source: Xero Limited

## Create a Credit Note from the Sales Overview Screen

Sometimes a credit note needs to be applied to more than one invoice. In this case, it is easiest to create the note in the Sales Overview screen and then apply to invoices.

To create a credit note from the Sales Overview screen:

1. Navigate to the **Business** tab, then **Sales Overview**.

2. Use the **+New** pull-down to access **Credit Note** (Figure 11.17).

3. Xero will provide a blank credit note screen similar to the invoice screen, but with a pale yellow background. This is a cue that the direction of this transaction will be the opposite of a normal invoicing transaction.

4. In the **To** field, enter the contact name. Since this is going to be a credit note applied to an existing invoice, the contact should be in the system and populated as you type.

**FIGURE 11.17**

Use the +New pulldown to access Credit Note.

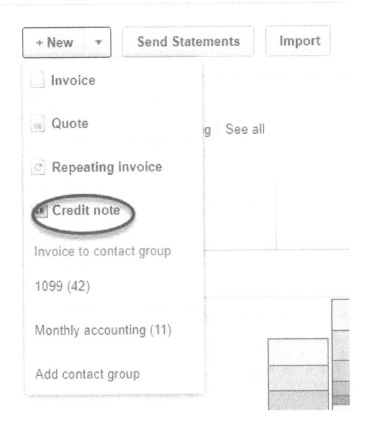

*Source:* Xero Limited

5. Complete the details of the credit note.

6. Click **Approve**.

7. If there are multiple outstanding invoices for the contact, Xero will provide a screen where the credit can be allocated. Enter the amounts of the credit to be applied to each outstanding invoice. Click **Allocate Credit** to save (Figure 11.18).

**FIGURE 11.18**

If there are multiple outstanding invoices for the contact, Xero will provide a screen where the credit can be allocated. Enter the amounts of the credit to be applied to each outstanding invoice. Click Allocate Credit to save.

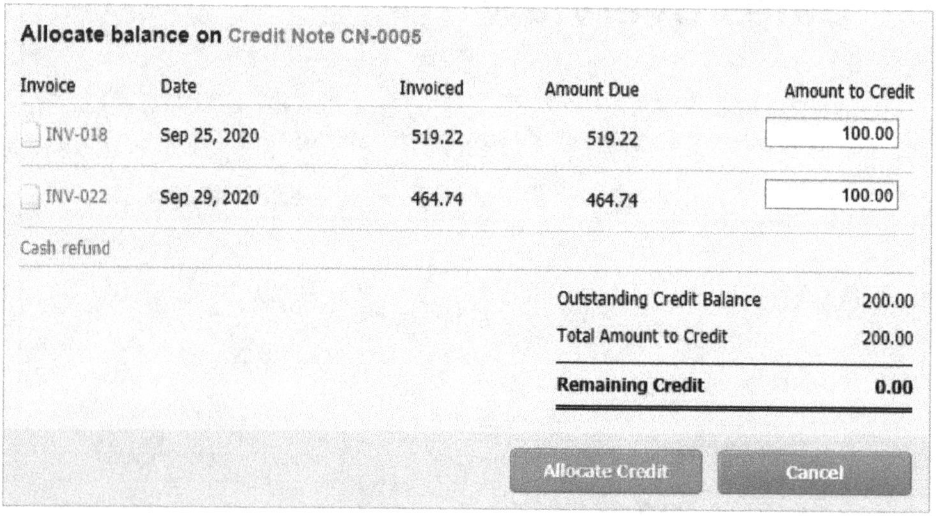

**Allocate balance on** Credit Note CN-0005

| Invoice | Date | Invoiced | Amount Due | Amount to Credit |
|---------|------|----------|------------|------------------|
| INV-018 | Sep 25, 2020 | 519.22 | 519.22 | 100.00 |
| INV-022 | Sep 29, 2020 | 464.74 | 464.74 | 100.00 |
| Cash refund | | | | |

| | |
|---|---|
| Outstanding Credit Balance | 200.00 |
| Total Amount to Credit | 200.00 |
| **Remaining Credit** | **0.00** |

Allocate Credit      Cancel

*Source:* Xero Limited

# Repeating Invoices

## Creating a Repeating Invoice Template

Many companies have the need to invoice a customer the same amount every month or week. A repeating invoice template allows you to create the framework for identical invoices to be created for a specific customer on a given cadence.

Note that you will create the invoice template, rather than the invoices. Xero will automatically generate the invoices on the schedule you assign. This is important because repeating templates are found in the **Repeating** tab of the Invoices screen, whereas the invoices created by Xero using the template are found in the tab appropriate for the current level of the generated invoice, either **Draft** or **Awaiting Payment**.

To create a repeating invoice template:

1. Navigate to the **Business** tab, then **Invoices**.
2. Use the **+New Invoice** pull-down to access **+New Repeating Invoice**.

3. Set the cadence on which invoices will be created by entering the number of weeks or months between invoices.

4. Choose the date of the first invoice to be created. Note that you can set a repeating invoice to start in the past. Invoices will be created for historical dates, but they will not be emailed to customers.

5. Set the due date of the invoices.

6. Add an optional end date. This would be appropriate for a contract or lease that has a term.

7. Choose how you would like Xero to handle the invoice when it is created.

   **Save as Draft:** With this option, Xero will create the invoice and save it in the Draft category of invoices. It must be manually approved before it will be included in the accounts receivable balance and can be sent to the customer.

   **Approve:** This option will save the created invoice in the Awaiting Payment category and add it to the accounts receivable balance but will not email it to the customer. Advisors may use this option to create invoices for customers whose payments are automatically drafted. Those deposits will be able to be matched to an invoice, but not sending the invoice keeps the customer from double paying for an ongoing service.

   **Approve for Sending:** This would be better named "Approve & Send." Xero will create, approve, and send the invoice to the customer email associated with the contact. When the template is saved with this option, a screen will show, confirming the email template that will be sent to the customer with the invoice. Confirm or edit, then click **Done.**

8. Enter the contact name in **Invoice to.**

9. Complete the **Reference** field. Xero allows you to insert placeholders, which are dynamic fields, changing each time an invoice is generated. You can use the Preview placeholders link at the bottom of the screen to see how they will appear.

10. Enter the invoice details.

11. Click **Save.**

12. If you have chosen to **Approve for sending**, Xero will provide a sample of the email that will be used for your confirmation.

| Placeholder | Effect if invoice date is March 15, 2021 |
| --- | --- |
| Week | 11 |
| Month | March |
| Year | 2021 |
| Week Year | 11 2021 |
| Month Year | March 2021 |

**FIGURE 11.19**

To delete a repeating template, select the box to the left of the template and click Delete.

*Source:* Xero Limited

## Managing Repeating Invoice Templates

Active repeating templates will be found in the **Repeating** tab of the Invoices screen. To edit a template, click the blue link for the customer name of the template you wish to open. Make any changes and click **Save.**

To delete a repeating template, select the box to the left of the template and click **Delete** (Figure 11.19). This will cancel the creation of any future invoices, but invoices previously created will still be active, unless you delete them separately.

Note that the invoices created each occurrence can be found under the Draft or Awaiting Payments tabs, depending on the option chosen when the template was created.

## Using Repeating Invoices to Schedule an Invoice

While Xero does not officially have an option to create an invoice to be delivered to the client at a later date, you can achieve this by using the repeating invoice template. By creating a repeating template that generates only one invoice and then ends, you can effectively preschedule electronic invoice delivery.

To use a repeating invoice template to schedule an invoice:

1. Navigate to the **Business** tab, then **Invoices.**
2. Use the **+New Invoice** pull-down to access **+New Repeating Invoice.**
3. Leave the default **Repeat this transaction** every as **1 Month.**
4. Set the invoice date as the date you wish the invoice to be created and delivered to the customer.
5. Select an **End Date** as the day after the invoice date.
6. Select **Approve for Sending** as the action.
7. Complete all other invoice details needed.
8. Click **Save.**

# Group Invoices

Where repeating invoice templates are a means to create the same invoice over and over for one contact, group invoices are creating the same invoice once for many different contacts. An example would be a real estate brokerage that is charging a group of agents for an annual desk rental or a school invoicing students the same amount for a course.

The first step in creating group invoices is to create a contact group that includes all of the recipients of the invoice. See Chapter 7 about contact groups.

Once the group is set up, to create the invoices:

1. Navigate to the **Business** tab, then **Invoices**.
2. Use the **New Invoice** pull-down to choose a group under the subheading **Invoice To** (Figure 11.20).

**FIGURE 11.20**

Use the New Invoice pulldown to choose a group under the subheading Invoice To.

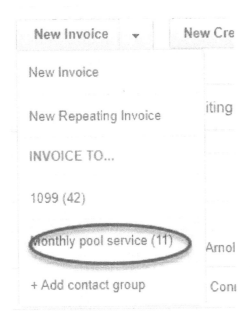

*Source:* Xero Limited

**FIGURE 11.21**

Click Create draft invoices at the bottom left. (Figure 11.21) There is no option to create approved group invoices. Each new invoice will be in draft status.

Source: Xero Limited

3. Xero will show an invoice input screen very similar to the normal invoice input screen, except that the contact is the name of the group.

4. Complete the invoice details.

5. Click **Create draft invoices** at the bottom left (Figure 11.21). There is no option to create approved group invoices. Each new invoice will be in draft status.

6. Xero will redirect you to the Draft tab in the Invoices screen, where you must approve the invoices to finalize. You can approve in bulk by highlighting the invoices by checking the box to the left of each, then clicking Approve at the top of the listing (Figure 11.22).

# Quotes

Depending on the nature of the business, there may be a need to create estimates for sales. In Xero, these estimates are called **Quotes**. Using Xero to prepare quotes will save time because they can be communicated to customers and accepted electronically. Additionally, accepted quotes are easily converted to invoices.

**FIGURE 11.22**

Xero will redirect you to the Draft tab in the Invoices screen, where you must approve the invoices to finalize. You can approve in bulk by highlighting the invoices by checking the box to the left of each, then clicking Approve at the top of the listing.

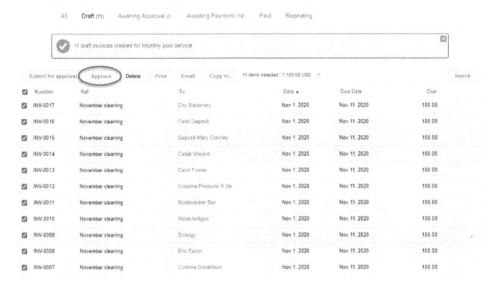

| | Number | Ref | To | Date ▾ | Due Date | Due |
|---|---|---|---|---|---|---|
| ☑ | INV-0017 | November cleaning | City Stationery | Nov 1, 2020 | Nov 11, 2020 | 100.00 |
| ☑ | INV-0016 | November cleaning | Cash Deposit | Nov 1, 2020 | Nov 11, 2020 | 100.00 |
| ☑ | INV-0015 | November cleaning | Deposit Mary Crawley | Nov 1, 2020 | Nov 11, 2020 | 100.00 |
| ☑ | INV-0014 | November cleaning | Caleb Vincent | Nov 1, 2020 | Nov 11, 2020 | 100.00 |
| ☑ | INV-0013 | November cleaning | Carol Fowler | Nov 1, 2020 | Nov 11, 2020 | 100.00 |
| ☑ | INV-0012 | November cleaning | Chlorine Products R Us | Nov 1, 2020 | Nov 11, 2020 | 100.00 |
| ☑ | INV-0011 | November cleaning | Bushwacker Bar | Nov 1, 2020 | Nov 11, 2020 | 100.00 |
| ☑ | INV-0010 | November cleaning | Hotel Antigua | Nov 1, 2020 | Nov 11, 2020 | 100.00 |
| ☑ | INV-0009 | November cleaning | Entergy | Nov 1, 2020 | Nov 11, 2020 | 100.00 |
| ☑ | INV-0008 | November cleaning | Eric Eaton | Nov 1, 2020 | Nov 11, 2020 | 100.00 |
| ☑ | INV-0007 | November cleaning | Corinne Donaldson | Nov 1, 2020 | Nov 11, 2020 | 100.00 |

*Source:* Xero Limited

## Creating Quotes

The quote screen is very similar to the invoice screen, with good reason. A quote is, in a way, a pre-invoice. It tells the customer what a defined scope of work or group of products would cost so that the customer can decide whether to engage in the transaction. The quote should have enough detail to explain the work clearly. Quotes do not have any effect on the general ledger until they are converted into approved invoices.

To create a quote:

1. Navigate to the **Business** tab, then **Quotes**.

2. Click the **+New Quote** button.

3. Enter the quote details. Note that using tracked inventory items on a quote will not decrease the balance of the inventory item. The item balance will only be decreased when an invoice is created.

4. If desired, use the **+Add a Title & Summary** link to add text that will appear above the quote details. This is a good place to give an overview of the scope of work (Figure 11.23).

**FIGURE 11.23**

If desired, use the +Add a Title & Summary link to add text that will appear above the quote details. This is a good place to give an overview of the scope of work.

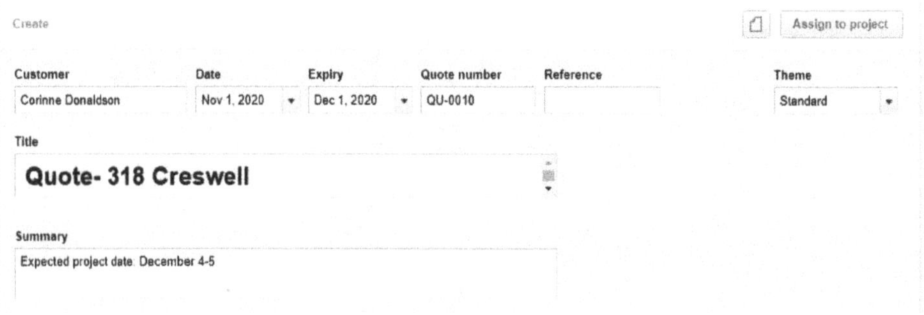

*Source:* Xero Limited

5. Click **Save** to save a draft of the quote or **Send** to approve and email the quote to the customer.

## Accepting or Declining Quotes

The normal workflow for quotes would be for the customer to accept or decline using the online link. However, for those customers who may receive a paper version of the quote rather than electronic, it can be marked as accepted or declined by the Xero user.

When a customer receives an email from the company with a link to an online quote, he or she will see three options at the top of the quote: **Accept**, **Decline**, or **Comment**. If the customer either accepts or declines the quote using the online link, Xero will move the quote from the Sent category to either the Accepted or Declined category at the bottom of the Sales Overview screen.

If the customer uses the Comment button to send notes or questions, the user who created the quote will receive an email with the customer's comments.

Quotes can also be marked as accepted or declined by a Xero user. To manually update the status of a quote:

1. Navigate to the **Business** tab, then **Quotes**.
2. Locate the quote in the Sent tab and open it by clicking the blue customer name.
3. Use the **Options** pull-down to either **Mark as Accepted** or **Mark as Declined** (Figure 11.24). Note that when an invoice is marked as declined, the user must enter a reason.

**FIGURE 11.24**

Use the Options pulldown to either Mark as Accepted or Mark as Declined. Note that when an invoice is marked as declined, the user must enter a reason.

*Source:* Xero Limited

**FIGURE 11.25**

Click the green Create Invoice button at the top of the quote.

*Source:* Xero Limited

## Converting Quotes to Invoices

Once a quote has been accepted, either online or manually, it is very easy to convert the quote to an invoice. To create an invoice from a quote:

1. Navigate to the **Business** tab, then **Quotes**.

2. Locate the quote in the **Accepted** tab and open it by selecting the blue customer name.

3. Click the green **Create Invoice** button at the top of the quote (Figure 11.25).

4. Select the box next to **Mark as Invoiced**. If this box is left unchecked, the quote will remain in the Accepted category, rather than Invoiced. One reason to leave the box unchecked is if only a portion of the quote is converted to an invoice.

5. Xero will populate an invoice input screen with the quote details. If there are no changes, click **Approve**. If there are changes to the invoice, such as a partial delivery of the order, edit the relevant fields before selecting **Approve**. This will create the invoice under the Awaiting Payment category.

# Managing Customer Credit

Small businesses sometimes struggle to manage business risk with customers. Xero makes it easy to view a customer's credit details at a high level. Setting credit limits in Xero will alert users that a customer has reached a limit when a new invoice is created and can even prevent invoices that exceed the credit limit from being sent.

## Setting Customer Credit Limits

Customer credit limits are set in Contacts and are set in the organization's base currency, not in the currency of the customer.

To set a customer's credit limit:

1. Navigate to **Contacts**.

2. Open the contact by clicking the blue contact name.

3. Click the **Edit** button at the top right.

4. Scroll to the Financial Details section and enter an amount in **Credit Limit Amount**.

5. Choose whether to block sending invoices past credit limit in the **Credit Limit Block** field (Figure 11.26).

## View Credit Limit Details

Customer credit limits can be viewed in Contacts on the right side of the contact record, but they will also appear when using new invoicing. When creating an invoice, click the **Contact** name in the **To** field to see an overview of amounts owed and available credit (Figure 11.27).

**FIGURE 11.26**

Choose whether or not to block sending invoices past credit limit in the Credit Limit Block field.

| Credit Limit Amount | 950.00 |
| Credit Limit Block | Do not block sending invoices past credit limit |

**FIGURE 11.27**

Customer credit limits can be viewed in Contacts on the right side of the contact record, but they will also appear when using new invoicing. When creating an invoice, click the Contact name in the To field to see an overview of amounts owed and available credit.

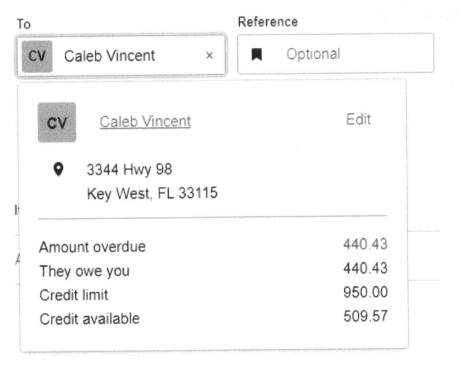

# Sending Customer Statements

In contrast to an invoice, a statement is a summary document of a customer's total balance due to a company. Statements will list invoices, payments, and credit notes on a customer's account.

Xero has two types of statements:

- **Activity** statements show all account activity for a given period of time. The statement begins with a starting balance, then lists in date order all invoices, payments, and credit notes, arriving at a closing balance.
- **Outstanding** statements show only outstanding sales transactions, such as unpaid invoices and unapplied credit notes, yielding a balance at a specific date.

Customer statements can be emailed to customers as a .pdf attachment or printed.

To send a customer statement:

1. Navigate to the **Business** tab, then Sales Overview.
2. Click the **Send Statements** button (Figure 11.28).
3. Use the **Statement Type** pull-down to select either Activity or Outstanding.
4. Use the date pull-downs to choose a date range or ending date for the statement.
5. Use the filter field to search for specific customers, if needed.
6. Check the box next to the customer or customers for which you will generate the statements.
7. Select **Email** to send the statements. You will be able to choose the branding theme and email template and edit the body of the email.
8. Select **Send**.

**FIGURE 11.28**

Click the Send Statements button.

Sales overview

+ New ▼ | Send Statements | Import | Search ⌕

*Source:* Xero Limited

# Sending Customer Receipts

A receipt is a record of a payment received and applied to an invoice. In classic invoicing, a receipt can be generated at the time a payment is applied or at any time by navigating to the paid invoice.

To send a customer receipt at the time a payment is applied, use the **Send Receipt** link that appears when the payment is saved (Figure 11.29). Xero will allow you to choose a branding theme and email template before sending. This is the fastest way to send a receipt, but often a customer will request a receipt of payment long after the payment has been posted.

**FIGURE 11.29**

To send a customer receipt at the time a payment is applied, use the Send Receipt link that appears when the payment is saved.

Payment Received 92.37 - Luz Patrick - Due 14 Oct 2020 - Paid On 1 Nov 2020 - Total 92.37

View Invoice  Send Receipt

*Source:* Xero Limited

**FIGURE 11.30**

Use the Options pulldown and select Send Receipt.

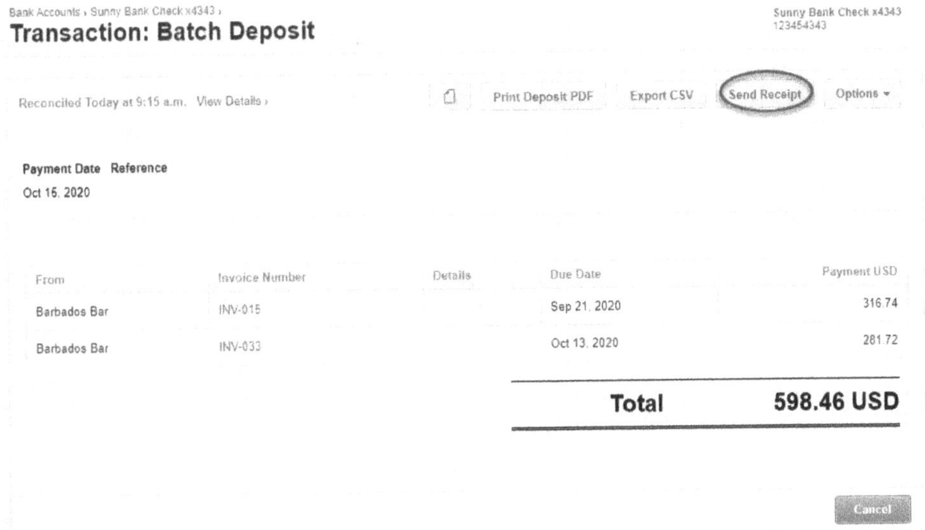

Bank Accounts › Sunny Bank Check x4343 ›

Sunny Bank Check x4343
123454343

## Transaction: Batch Deposit

Reconciled Today at 9:15 a.m.  View Details ›        Print Deposit PDF    Export CSV    Send Receipt    Options ▾

**Payment Date   Reference**
Oct 15, 2020

| From | Invoice Number | Details | Due Date | Payment USD |
|------|---------------|---------|----------|-------------|
| Barbados Bar | INV-015 | | Sep 21, 2020 | 316.74 |
| Barbados Bar | INV-033 | | Oct 13, 2020 | 281.72 |
| | | | **Total** | **598.46 USD** |

Cancel

*Source:* Xero Limited

To send a receipt for a paid invoice:

1. Navigate to the **Business** tab, then **Invoices**.
2. Go to the **Paid** tab and open the invoice by clicking on the blue customer name.
3. Click the blue payment under the invoice total.
4. Use the **Options** pull-down and select **Send Receipt** (Figure 11.30).
5. Confirm or edit the email options and click **Send**.

Note that sending a receipt will only show evidence of the payment that is chosen. To show that an invoice has been paid by the application of a payment, send a statement or the paid invoice instead. Both of those options will show the invoice and payments applied.

# How Sales Tax Is Handled on Invoices

For companies whose invoices include sales tax–eligible sales, Xero will calculate and record a sales tax liability. Each invoice line has a sales tax rate assigned to it. The rate defaults to the sales tax default for the general ledger account for the line, but can be changed. It is important to note that Xero only uses one Sales Tax Payable account for all sales tax rates and underlying components.

In Chapter 6, we covered sales tax settings, including choosing the appropriate tax basis-cash or accrual. It is important to note that the basis used will determine which transactions are included on the Sales Tax Report, which differs from the recording of the sales tax liability on the general ledger. The purpose of the Sales Tax Report is to help calculate sales tax remittances for each of the jurisdictions or governmental entities. The sales tax liability is recorded at the invoice date, regardless of the sales tax basis. If the tax basis is accrual, the tax will be included in the Sales Tax Report for the period that includes the invoice date. If the tax basis is cash, the tax will only be included in the Sales Tax Report for the period the invoice is paid.

Example: Island Escape Pool Service issues an invoice dated September 15 that includes sales tax of $35. The customer pays the entire invoice on October 15.

| Tax Basis | Sales Tax Liability on General Ledger at September 30 | Sales Tax Report for the month ended September 30 | Sales Tax Report for the month ended October 31 |
|---|---|---|---|
| Cash | $35 | $0 | $35 |
| Accrual | $35 | $35 | $0 |

# Viewing Invoice History and Notes

One benefit to using a cloud-based accounting system is that the system keeps a detailed record of activity. The platform not only keeps a log of activity by Xero users but also external parties who access the system, such as invoice recipients. This is very useful in managing invoices.

To view the activity on an invoice, open the invoice by selecting it from the Sales Overview or Invoices screen. At the bottom of the invoice, there is a section called **History & Notes**. To view all the activity on the invoice, select the **Show History** button. This will open the complete log (Figure 11.31).

The log will show important milestones in the life of the invoice, including creation, any changes, and views using the online link. History items will be time- and date-stamped. Each action will be associated with a Xero user or indicated as **System Generated**. System generated means that the action was not performed by a designated user within Xero but was created by an API trigger, either by an external person or an application. An example would be when a customer uses the online link to view an invoice. The customer is not logged into Xero, but the opening of the link will generate an item in History & Notes showing that the invoice was viewed online.

If desired, a custom **Note** can be added at the bottom of the invoice (Figure 11.32). This can be useful to explain changes made to the invoice or to indicate that a customer has been phoned for collection. A note created here will be saved as a history item and cannot be edited or deleted.

### FIGURE 11.31

To view the activity on an invoice, open the invoice by selecting it from the Sales Overview or Invoices screen. At the bottom of the invoice, there is a section called History & Notes. To view all of the activity on the invoice, select the Show History button. This will open the complete log.

History & Notes

Paid by Amanda Aguillard on Oct 1, 2020 at 11:42AM
**Payment received from Lois Arnold on November 1, 2020 for 325.50. This invoice has been fully paid.**

Hide History (3 entries)     Add Note

| Changes | Date | User | Details |
|---|---|---|---|
| Paid | Oct 1, 2020 11:42 AM | Amanda Aguillard | Payment received from Lois Arnold on November 1, 2020 for 325.50. This invoice has been fully paid. |
| Approved | Sep 26, 2020 12:18 PM | Amanda Aguillard | INV-035 to Lois Arnold for 325.50. |
| Created | Sep 26, 2020 12:17 PM | Amanda Aguillard | Imported from Xero file |

*Source:* **Xero Limited**

**FIGURE 11.32**

If desired, a custom Note can be added at the bottom of the invoice.

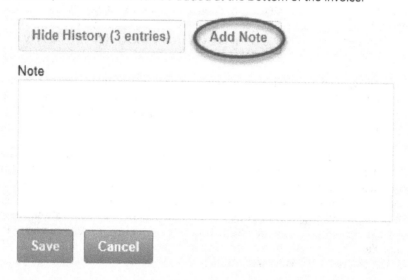

*Source:* Xero Limited

# Bulk Importing Invoices

Xero offers a way to import invoices into the system in bulk. There are several reasons you may want to import invoices as a batch rather than entering one at a time.

- There may be many outstanding invoices at the conversion date when setting up a new Xero file.
- The company may need to issue many invoices at frequent intervals, and it is more efficient to maintain and update an import file that can be imported over and over.
- The company may have a sales system that does not integrate with Xero, so invoices are used as a way to enter sales data.

Invoices are imported using a .csv file type. It is important to understand the structure of the import file.

Each line in the spreadsheet is an invoice line. Just like lines in an invoice created directly in Xero, each line in the spreadsheet needs a Description, Quantity, Unit Amount, Account Code and Tax Type. There are also required columns that are used at the invoice, rather than line, level. Contact Name, Invoice Number, Invoice Date, and Due Date are required fields.

**FIGURE 11.33**

If an invoice contains more than one line, be sure that the invoice number is the same for all of the lines that should be on the invoice. Xero will aggregate invoice lines based on invoice number.

| | A | B | C | D | E | F | G | H |
|---|---|---|---|---|---|---|---|---|
| 1 | *ContactName | EmailAddress | POAddressLine1 | POCity | PORegion | POPostalCode | *InvoiceNumber | Referenc |
| 2 | Jean Lafitte | | 123 Bourbon Street | New Orleans | LA | 70112 | INV-012 | |
| 3 | Jean Lafitte | | 123 Bourbon Street | New Orleans | LA | 70112 | INV-012 | |
| 4 | James Buffett | | 455 Magazine Street | New Orleans | LA | 70111 | INV-013 | |
| 5 | Hotel Antigua | | 3577 Times Square | New York | NY | 21111 | INV-014 | |
| 6 | Hotel Antigua | | 3577 Times Square | New York | NY | 21111 | INV-014 | |
| 7 | Hotel Antigua | | 3577 Times Square | New York | NY | 21111 | INV-014 | |
| 8 | Hotel Antigua | | 3577 Times Square | New York | NY | 21111 | INV-014 | |
| 9 | Hotel Antigua | | 3577 Times Square | New York | NY | 21111 | INV-014 | |
| 10 | Hotel Antigua | | 3577 Times Square | New York | NY | 21111 | INV-014 | |
| 11 | Bayside Resort | | 106 Creswell Street | Lafayette | LA | 70583 | INV-029 | |
| 12 | Barbados, Jill | | 68888 Miami Blvd | Miami | FL | 33177 | INV-015 | |

*Source:* Xero Limited

If an invoice contains more than one line, be sure that the invoice number is the same for all of the lines that should be on the invoice. Xero will aggregate invoice lines based on invoice number (Figure 11.33). The other fields in the import file are optional.

To import invoices in bulk:

1. Navigate to the **Business** tab, then **Sales Overview.**
2. Click the **Import** button.
3. Download the template file, if needed.
4. Prepare the invoice file using the instructions above and save.
5. Click the **Browse** button in Xero and select the saved import file.
6. Indicate whether you would like for Xero to update contacts with information in the import file.
7. Confirm that the **Unit Amount** field is tax exclusive. (This would be the appropriate choice for U.S. transactions. If you are creating transactions outside of the United States, select the correct option.)
8. Click **Import.**
9. You will see a notification screen summarizing the number of invoices that will be drafted. Confirm.
10. You will be redirected to the Draft invoices tab. To approve the invoices, select the box to the left of the invoice and click **Approve.** The invoices can now be found in the Awaiting Payment tab and are included in the Accounts Receivable balance.

You can access a template in the digital resources.

# Invoices from Third-Party Sales Systems

Many companies use some kind of sales platform for engaging with their customers. This could be an online store or ecommerce platform, like Shopify. It could be a cash register point-of-sale system, like Vend. It could even be a legal billing system, like Clio. The one commonality is that the integration with the third-party application sends sales data to Xero via invoices.

Note that different systems will aggregate (or not) sales data in different ways. The best integrations will send a summary invoice for each day's sales. This will be generally easy to reconcile against bulk credit card and cash deposits while still recording sufficiently detailed data in the general ledger. By keeping each day's sales data separate, you can prepare comparative reports such as week-to-week or even comparing a specific day in the year, such as the day after Thanksgiving.

Some sales system integrations will send an invoice for every sales transaction. This becomes incredibly cumbersome quickly, especially in high-volume companies. Reconciling individual sales to bulk deposits is difficult. In these cases, we would recommend introducing an intermediate application that will aggregate individual transactions to a day's summary before recording in Xero, like A2X.

There are many key components to invoices, so it is important to understand how the application is conveying those components to the general ledger. Each has qualities that impact the reconciliation of the sales recording to the related deposits. The type of invoice sent by the system can even determine the level of Xero subscription required.

There are three basic variations of invoices that are sent from sales systems:

1. Unpaid invoices
2. Fully paid invoices
3. $0 invoices

## Unpaid Invoices

An unpaid invoice is an invoice sent by the third-party application that has no payments applied to it. It will be found in the Awaiting Payment section of Sales Invoices, with a balance due that equals the total transaction amount. The invoice will include lines for each item or service sold and will show an accrual for sales tax payable, if applicable, at the bottom. Until reconciled, these invoices will be included in the accounts receivable balance of the company.

## Fully Paid Invoice

A fully paid invoice will have payments applied that resolve the transaction. These invoices have no outstanding balance and are shown in the Paid tab of Sales Invoices. In a way, these invoices completely bypass the accounts receivable process because they are recorded as fully paid. This means that a lower level subscription, like Starter, may be available for use.

Like the unpaid invoice, a fully paid invoice will include lines for the sales of items or services, as well as an accrual for sales tax payable. Below the invoice total, there will also be noted a payment or payments that resolve the invoice, leaving a balance of $0 (Figure 11.34). The payments can be applied from a bank account or any other general ledger account where payments have been enabled. (See Chapter 5 for more information.) In most cases, payments posted to non-bank accounts are sent to a clearing account (Figure 11.35).

**Clearing accounts** are meant to be temporary holding spots for transactions. By using a clearing account, the resolution of an invoice can be recorded and held until the deposit for the payment is recognized in the bank account. Since the deposit may be net of processing fees, using a clearing account for the payment makes the segregation of the fee from the gross payment easier to manage.

In practice, many applications use two different clearing accounts: a cash clearing account and a bank card clearing account. The cash clearing account represents cash and checks received for payment that will be deposited into a bank account at some point. Few

**FIGURE 11.34**

Like the unpaid invoice, a fully paid invoice will include lines for the sales of items or services, as well as an accrual for sales tax payable. Below the invoice total, there will also be noted a payment or payments that resolve the invoice, leaving a balance of $0.

| | | | | | | | | | |
|---|---|---|---|---|---|---|---|---|---|
| Paid | | | | | | Preview | Email | Print PDF | Invoice Options ▾ |

| To | Date | Due Date | Invoice # | Reference | Branding theme | Online Payments | Invoice reminders | | Total |
|---|---|---|---|---|---|---|---|---|---|
| POS | Nov 1, 2020 | Nov 1, 2020 | INV-0020 | 10/31/20 Sales | Standard | None Get set up now | On | | 499.57 |
| No address | | | | | | | | | |
| Add address | | | | | | | | | |

Amounts are Tax Exclusive

| Item Code | Description | Quantity | Unit Price | Disc % | Account | Tax Rate | Location | Amount USD |
|---|---|---|---|---|---|---|---|---|
| | 10/31/20 Sales | 1.00 | 456.44 | | Equipment Sales Revenue | New Orleans | | 456.44 |

| | | |
|---|---|---|
| | Subtotal | 456.44 |
| | Total Orleans Parish 5% | 22.82 |
| | Total Lousiana 4.45% | 20.31 |
| | **TOTAL** | **499.57** |
| | Less Payment Nov 1, 2020 | 499.57 |
| | **AMOUNT DUE** | **0.00** |

*Source:* Xero Limited

**FIGURE 11.35**

In most cases, payments posted to non-bank accounts are sent to a clearing account.

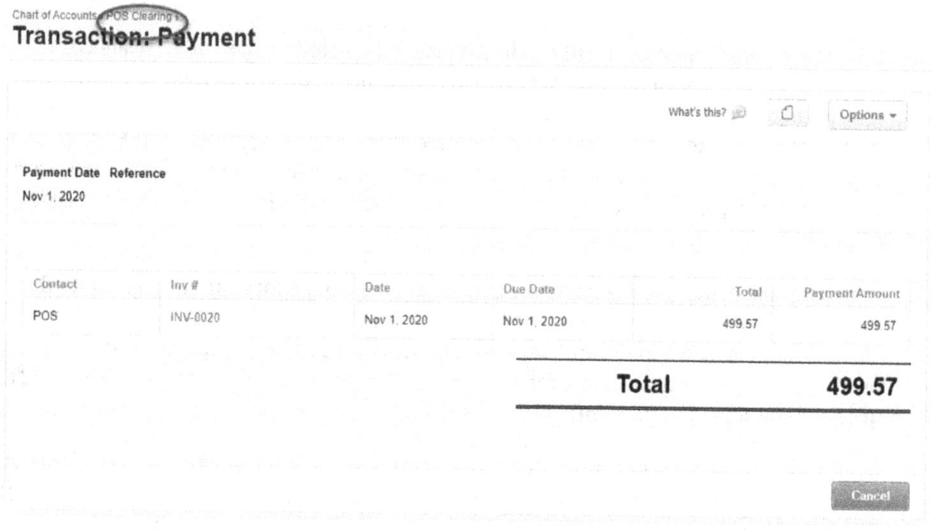

Chart of Accounts POS Clearing
## Transaction: Payment

What's this?    Options ▾

**Payment Date  Reference**
Nov 1, 2020

| Contact | Inv # | Date | Due Date | Total | Payment Amount |
|---|---|---|---|---|---|
| POS | INV-0020 | Nov 1, 2020 | Nov 1, 2020 | 499.57 | 499.57 |

**Total**    **499.57**

Cancel

*Source:* Xero Limited

business owners make daily bank deposits, so this clearing account accumulates until deposits are posted to the bank. The bank card clearing account is the transitional account for any merchant deposits that will be processed. In general, deposits are made to the business bank account within a few days, so this clearing account should only hold two or three days of pending deposits at any time. For even more efficiency, set up bank rules (discussed in Chapter 10) that will code the merchant deposits to the clearing account when received.

## $0 Invoices

A $0 invoice is an invoice that includes invoice lines that offset and leave an invoice total of $0. Like the other invoice types, the sales are recorded on the invoice lines, but in this instance, the resolution of the invoice total is a separate, negative invoice line, usually to a clearing account. The net effect is similar to the fully paid invoice.

# Workarounds for Sales Integrations

With ecommerce becoming a more prevalent sales channel, companies are using a plethora of website management and shopping cart applications, many of which do not have direct integrations with Xero. Using the tools introduced earlier, there are ways to work around this deficiency.

Most ecommerce platforms will have reporting that allows for the export of sales data. By manipulating the reports into a format that will mimic an invoice integration and importing the data using bulk importing, you can easily import sales details into Xero. For efficiency, follow the method for $0 invoices with the invoice balances posted to a clearing account or accounts.

To import sales data from a nonintegrating sales platform to Xero:

1. Examine the reporting options from the sales application. Ideally, there will be a way to filter sales data to a particular period, such as one month, and export that data to a spreadsheet.

2. Determine at what level of detail sales will be recorded in the general ledger: individual sales or a daily, weekly, or monthly summary. Consider how payments will be batched and deposited. If payments are deposited on a daily basis, then recording sales batched by day will make reconciliation easier. Alternatively, if there is a need to access individual transactional data in the general ledger, such as for low-volume, high-value sales, each sale should be recorded separately.

3. Using the import template, create a file from the sales report data where each line of the file is a separate general ledger transaction and lines are aggregated by using the same invoice number. Advisors often use a clear reference for the invoice number such as "SALES 2021.2.28" to indicate a sales summary for February 28, 2021. Make sure that each invoice has a negative posting to one or more clearing accounts for the total of the sales for that invoice.

4. Use the instructions under **Bulk importing invoices** to import the data into Xero.

# Invoicing for Billable Expenses

In Xero, expenses or costs paid by a company can be assigned to a customer or project so that the company can later bill the expense or cost on an invoice. An expense or cost can be identified as a billable expense when the company incurs it in one of two ways: in the creation of a bill or in bank reconciliation. Once an expense is recognized as a billable expense, it can be added to an invoice.

When an invoice is created for a customer to whom a billable expense has been assigned, a link will appear under the contact name that indicates one or more billable expenses can be added (Figure 11.36). To add the expense, click the blue link and use the checkboxes to select the expenses to be added (Figure 11.37). A line will be created on the invoice using the description and amount of the original expense. You must indicate which general ledger account the invoice line should post to. It can be the account used when the expense was originally paid by the company, creating a net zeroing effect, or it can be a separate revenue account, like Reimbursed Expense Revenue. Using a separate revenue account is more commonly used by advisors because it will keep the transactions segregated and make any discrepancies clear.

**FIGURE 11.36**

When an invoice is created for a customer to whom a billable expense has been assigned, a link will appear under the contact name that indicates one or more billable expenses can be added.

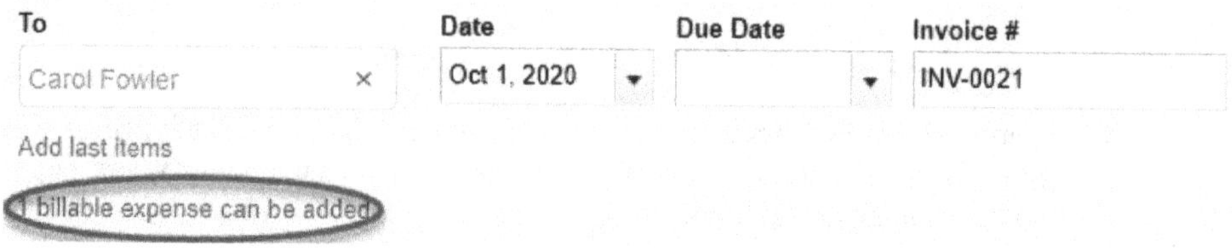

Source: Xero Limited

**FIGURE 11.37**

To add the expense, click the blue link and use the checkboxes to select the expenses to be added.

Source: Xero Limited

When the invoice is saved, the billable expense will be removed from the queue of awaiting assignment costs and the Billable Expenses–Outstanding report.

# Handling Returned or NSF Checks

Occasionally, a company may receive a check as payment on an invoice, then have that deposited check returned for insufficient funds in the customer's account. The payment will need to be removed from the invoice, so that the invoice becomes outstanding again, and the bank lines for both the original deposit and the returned check will need to be reconciled.

To remove the payment applied to the invoice:

1. Open the invoice paid by the returned check by searching the Paid tab of the Invoices screen and selecting it from the listing.

2. Click the payment applied at the bottom to open the payment details screen.

3. Use the **Options** pull-down to select **Remove & Redo**. This will remove the payment from the invoice and send the deposit to the **Reconcile** tab. Note that if the returned check was part of a batch deposit, removing the payment will result in all payments in the batch being unreconciled and returned to the queue for bank reconciliation.

4. Confirm that the invoice is now in the **Awaiting Payment** tab of the Invoices screen. The unpaid invoice can now be edited to add a bounced-check fee, if desired, and resent to the customer.

The bank feed will show two transactions for the returned check–one for the original deposit and one for the adjustment to the bank account reversing the deposit. Both will need to be recorded and classified. The easiest way to handle this is to use a clearing account. To reconcile the bank lines for the original payment and the returned check:

1. Create a liability account in the chart of accounts for "NSF Check Clearing" if one does not already exist. This will be a holding account for the returned check for the few days between the deposit and reversal.

2. Locate the original deposit in the **Reconcile** tab of the bank account.

3. Use the **Create** tab to choose the NSF Clearing account. Be careful not to accept a suggested Xero match to the invoice. Click OK.

4. Locate the reversal by the bank in the **Reconcile** tab of the bank account.

5. Use the **Create** tab to choose the NSF Clearing account. Click **OK**.

6. Confirm that the NSF Clearing account balance is $0.

**11**

# Purchases and Bills

*It is essential for business owners to accurately track additional expenses that will be included as add-on charges to their customers, so I often help our Xero Partners leverage Billable Expenses. It's in-product insurance against losing track of chargeable customer costs.*

*—Corey Green, Partner Consultant at Xero*

Helping clients manage cash flow by having a complete understanding of the company's obligations is a way for accountants and bookkeepers to add value. Additionally, streamlining processes for bill payments either using Xero's native workflow or by adding third-party payment applications can save lots of time.

In this chapter, we will cover all the variations of bills and purchasing documents, including repeating bills, credit notes, and purchase orders, and explain options for bill payment management.

An efficient workflow for accounts payable would look something like this:

1. Receive bill from supplier and input in accounting system
2. Create payment for bill on a scheduled basis, generally weekly or biweekly
3. Gain approvals for bill payment
4. Send payment to supplier
5. Reconcile payment in general ledger

## Overview of Purchases

In Xero, the accounts payable module is referred to as **Purchases,** and documents confirming obligations for products or services are called **Bills.** This is in contrast to accounts receivable, which is referred to as Purchases and collection documents, which are referred to as bills.

The Purchases Overview screen is a dashboard showing accounts payable and is accessed by navigating to **Business,** then **Purchases overview.** This screen shows all purchasing activity. Note that selecting either Bills to pay or Purchase orders from the Business pull-down will bring you directly to those detail screens rather than the summary for all purchasing activity.

At the top of the screen are a few useful buttons. The **+New** pull-down allows a user to create most of the purchases document variations quickly: Bill, Repeating bill, Credit note, or Purchase order. The **Import** button will allow the user to bulk import bills. The **Search** button opens search fields for finding bills or purchase orders. There is detailed information about these features further in this chapter (Figure 12.1).

Just as in Purchases, there are four categories of bills, which are represented by a graphic in the top half of the screen (Figure 12.2):

- **Draft:** Draft bills are bills that have been created but are not yet final so are not included on the general ledger. This category is used to hold bills that still need to be edited.
- **Awaiting Approval:** Awaiting Approval bills are similar to Draft bills in that they are not yet final. In general, these bills are pending approval by a different user than the user that created the bill. Awaiting Approval bills are also not included in the general ledger Accounts Payable balance.
- **Awaiting Payment:** Awaiting Payment bills are bills that are approved, final, and waiting to be paid by the company. The Awaiting Payment balance equals the Accounts Payable balance on the general ledger.
- **Overdue:** Overdue bills are a subset of Awaiting Payment bills that are past the stated due date.

Clicking into any of these categories will redirect the user to a listing of those bills that make up the balance.

**FIGURE 12.1**

There is detailed information about these features further in this chapter.

### Purchases overview

| + New ▾ | Import | | Search 🔍 |
|---------|--------|--|-----------|

*Source:* Xero Limited

**FIGURE 12.2**

Just as In Purchases, there are four categories of bills, which are represented by a graphic in the top half of the screen:

**Bills**  Paid  Repeating  See all

| Draft (1) | Awaiting Approval | Awaiting Payment (2) | Overdue (1) |
|-----------|-------------------|----------------------|-------------|
| 850.00 | None | 711.55 | 54.55 |

*Source:* Xero Limited

**FIGURE 12.3**

Below the bill categories is a chart that shows Upcoming bills. This is a timeline of expected bill payments. Bills are represented on the timeline based on due date, unless a planned date has been entered for the payment. There is a slider below the chart that allows the user to change the time perspective for the chart. Within the chart, the user can drill into the underlying bills by clicking the blue bars.

*Source:* Xero Limited

**FIGURE 12.4**

The next section on the overview screen is Purchase orders.

| Purchase orders See all  Billed | | |
|---|---|---|
| Draft | Awaiting Approval | Approved (1) |
| None | None | 4,350.00 |

*Source:* Xero Limited

Below the bill categories is a chart that shows **Upcoming bills**. This is a timeline of expected bill payments. Bills are represented on the timeline based on due date, unless a planned date has been entered for the payment. There is a slider below the chart that allows the user to change the time perspective for the chart. Within the chart, the user can drill into the underlying bills by clicking the blue bars (Figure 12.3).

The next section on the overview screen is **Purchase orders** (Figure 12.4). Like the bills graphic, there are categories for the level of approval:

- **Draft:** Draft purchase orders are purchase orders created but not finalized.
- **Awaiting Approval:** Purchase orders that need approval from another user before being finalized.
- **Approved:** Purchase orders that are finalized and approved.

# Viewing the Bill Listing

While the Purchases Overview screen shows a high-level perspective of accounts receivable, the bills screen is a detailed listing of each bill. Access the bill listing by clicking the Awaiting Payment category on the Purchases Overview or by navigating to the **Business** tab, then **Bills to pay.**

The **All** tab shows all bills created in the system, except for voided or deleted bills. The fastest way to locate a specific bill is to use the Search button at the top right of the listing. Xero can search based on contact name, bill number, reference, or amount, and the search can be limited to a specific date range. To include void or deleted bills in the search, check the box next to **Include Deleted & Voided**.

Most of the management of payables will happen in the **Awaiting Payment** tab, as this represents current outstanding bills and is the detail of the Accounts Payable balance (Figure 12.5).

The **Draft** and **Awaiting Approval** tabs list bills that have not yet been fully finalized and therefore are not posted to the general ledger.

The **Paid** tab shows bills that have been fully paid and have no outstanding balance.

The **Repeating** tab lists repeating bill templates, not bills that have been created by a repeating bill template. Once a bill is created by a template, the bill will be listed in the appropriate status tab. Learn more about Repeating templates later in this chapter.

The column headings in the bill listings can be used to sort the listing. Clicking on the blue header will reorder the list according to the data values in that column. The Awaiting Payment tab has these important columns that are helpful in managing payables:

- **Due Date:** The Due Date column shows the date a bill is due. It is useful to sort on this column so that bills that are nearing their due dates can be paid in batches.
- **Planned Date:** The Planned Date column is a functional column, where the user can input an expected payment date for a bill. If a bill has a planned date, that date, rather than the due date, will be used in the **Upcoming bills** graphic in Purchases Overview.

**FIGURE 12.5**

Most of the management of payables will happen in the Awaiting Payment tab, as this represents current outstanding bills and is the detail of the Accounts Payable balance.

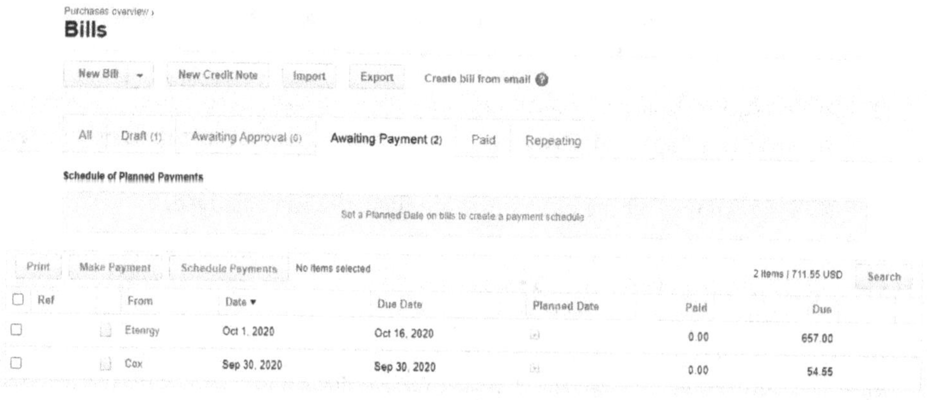

*Source:* Xero Limited

# Creating a Bill

The simplest task in Purchases is levying a single bill. The creation of a bill is the transaction in an accrual basis business that recognizes expenses or costs and increases the accounts payable balance on the general ledger. (In a cash basis business, an expense is not recognized until the bill is paid.) Bills are used when there is a timing difference between the company receiving goods or services and making a payment.

To create a new single bill:

1. Navigate to the **Business** tab, then **Bills to pay**.
2. Click the **+New bill** button.
3. Type the supplier name in the **From** field. As you type, Xero will filter known contacts. If the supplier is not an existing contact, enter the complete name. Xero will add the contact to the Suppliers group in Contacts.
4. Enter or accept a date in the **Date** field. The default bill day will be today, but it can be changed. The bill date will be the date the purchase is recognized on the books.
5. Enter or accept a date in the **Due Date** field. The default due date here is based on Invoice Settings discussed in Chapter 6, but can be changed. The same date entry shortcuts covered in the Sales chapter can be used for bills.
6. The **Reference** field will be visible in Find & Match in bank reconciliation and is a field that will be considered in bill search queries, so most advisors use the invoice number issued by the supplier, such as "Inv. 3678."
7. If you wish to attach files to the bill, either for internal recordkeeping or to forward with the bill to the customer, use the .pdf icon button.

Most static file types can be uploaded to Xero, including .pdf, .doc, .csv, .jpg, .png, and .xls, but .pdf files generally work best. Files may be attached to a bill from the File Library or directly uploaded to the bill. Use **+Add from file library** to select a file that already exists in the library. Note that attaching a file from the file library to a transaction will remove the file from the library. You can also attach a file directly in the bill by using the **+Upload files** link. Once a file or files have been attached to the bill, they will remain part of the bill record forever.

8. Enter the bill details in the table shown.

   **Item:** If there are inventory items set up in the Xero organization, this field can be used to populate many of the remaining fields. Enter the Inventory Item Code here.

   **Description:** Enter a description of the item or service purchase, if it is not already populated. This can be identifying information provided by the vendor invoice.

   **Qty:** Enter the number of units purchased in this field. Xero will multiply by the unit price to calculate the total amount of the sale. A value must be entered, so use a "1" if there is no quantity.

**Unit Price:** Enter the cost per unit.

**Account:** Select the general ledger account that the bill line amount should be posted to. A new account can be created here without leaving this screen and navigating to the chart of accounts. Use the pull-down and select **+Add new account**. Complete the account details and click **Save**. The new account will be created and used for the bill line.

**Tracking categories:** Each bill line can be allocated to one or both tracking categories, if they are enabled. For more information on tracking categories, see Chapter 6.

9. Once the bill details have been entered, you can:

    **Save as draft:** Draft bills can be accessed in the Draft category on the Purchases Overview screen or in the Draft tab on the bills screen.

    **Save (continue editing):** This option saves your work and keeps the bill screen open.

    **Save & submit for approval:** Saving and submitting for approval will move the bill to the Awaiting Approval category on the Purchases Overview screen or in the Awaiting Approval tab on the bills screen.

    **Save & add another:** This option will save the created bill as a Draft and open a new, blank bill screen.

    **Approve:** Clicking Approve will save the bill, add it to the Awaiting Payment category of bills, and increase the accounts payable general ledger balance by the amount of the bill.

    **Approve & add another:** This option has the same effect as Approve but redirects the user to a new, blank bill input screen.

    **Approve & view next:** This option has the same effect as Approve but opens the next bill in the approval chain.

# Billable Expenses

In Xero, expenses or costs paid by a company can be assigned to a customer or project so that the company can later recover the expense or cost on an invoice. In Chapter 11, we discuss how to include a billable expense on an invoice.

To track a transaction as a billable expense when creating a Bill:

1. Create the bill, completing the necessary fields and adding details for each bill line.

2. Click the **Assign expenses to a customer** (or **Assign expenses to a customer or project**, if Xero Projects is enabled) button at the bottom of the invoice.

3. Find the customer or project in the **Search for a customer or project** field.

**FIGURE 12.6**

Enter the bill details in the table below.

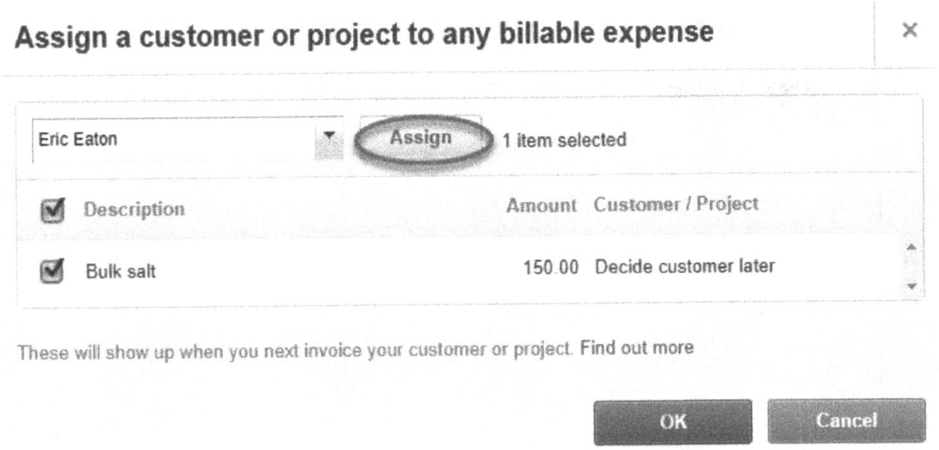

### Assign a customer or project to any billable expense          ×

| Eric Eaton ▾ | Assign | 1 item selected |
|---|---|---|
| ☑ Description | Amount | Customer / Project |
| ☑ Bulk salt | 150.00 | Decide customer later |

These will show up when you next invoice your customer or project. Find out more

OK     Cancel

*Source:* Xero Limited

4. Select the transaction lines to apply to the customer. Note that for split transactions where there is more than one bank line, each line can be assigned to a customer or project separately.

5. Click **Assign** next to the customer or project name (Figure 12.6).

6. Confirm that the correct customer or project is shown to the right of the transaction.

7. Click **OK** to save.

8. The assignment of the expense will be noted in the **Description** field of the bill.

9. **Save** or **Approve** the bill.

# Creating a Bill from a File

As mentioned in the Chapter 4, Xero has a built-in file storage functionality. Many advisors use Files (sometimes informally referred to as the "filebox") to hold documents like W9s and contracts in the organization, but one of the best uses of Files is as an Accounts Payable queue.

Clients can forward bills to be paid to the filebox using the unique email address found in the upper right of the screen. Bills can accumulate here until a payables batch will be run, then each file can be used to easy create a bill with the original attached.

To create a bill from a file:

1. Navigate to the pull-down of the company's name in the top left, then **Files**.

2. Select the bill to be paid by checking the box on the left.

**FIGURE 12.7**

Xero will open side-by-side screens of the bill image and the bill input screen.

*Source:* Xero Limited

3. Use the **Add to new** pull-down to select **Bill**.

4. Xero will open side-by-side screens of the bill image and the bill input screen (Figure 12.7).

5. Complete the fields on the bill input screen and click **Approve**. An approved bill will be created in the Awaiting Payment tab of Bills with the file attached, and the file will be removed from the filebox.

# Managing Bills

Once a bill is created but before it has been paid, it will be found in one of three categories or tabs in Purchases: Draft, Awaiting Approval, and Awaiting Payment. You may need to edit the bill, void it, or use it as a template for another similar bill.

## Editing a Bill

There are situations in which a bill that has been approved may need to be edited or corrected. Prior to any payments being applied, the bill can be fully edited. Once a payment has been made on a bill, even if it is a partial payment, only certain fields can be edited: Contact, Due date, Reference, Account, and Tracking categories. These are fields that do not affect the bill total. If other fields need to be changed, the payment must be removed first.

To edit a bill that has not been paid:

1. Locate the bill and open it by clicking the blue customer name.

2. Use the **Bill Options** pull-down to access **Edit** (Figure 12.8).

**FIGURE 12.8**

Use the Bill Options pulldown to access Edit.

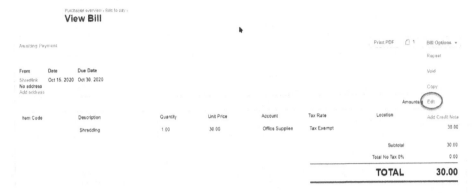

*Source:* Xero Limited

3. Make needed changes to the bill.

4. Click **Update**.

## Voiding a Bill

If a bill was created and approved in error, the best way to remove it from the accounts payable balance is to void it. A bill with payments or credits applied cannot be voided. Any payments or credits must be removed before voiding.

To void a bill:

1. Locate the bill and open it by clicking the blue customer name.

2. Use the **Bill Options** pull-down to access **Void** (Figure 12.9).

3. Confirm that you wish to void the bill by clicking **Yes**.

## Duplicating a Bill

If you must create a bill with similar charges or settings of one that already exists, it may be more efficient to duplicate it than creating a new bill from scratch.

To create a copy of a bill:

1. Locate the bill and open it by clicking the blue customer name.

2. Use the **Bill Options** pull-down to access **Copy** (Figure 12.10).

3. Edit the bill for any needed changes from the original.

4. Click **Approve**.

**FIGURE 12.9**

Use the Bill Options pulldown to access Void.

*Source:* Xero Limited

**FIGURE 12.10**

Navigate to the Business tab, then Purchases Overview.

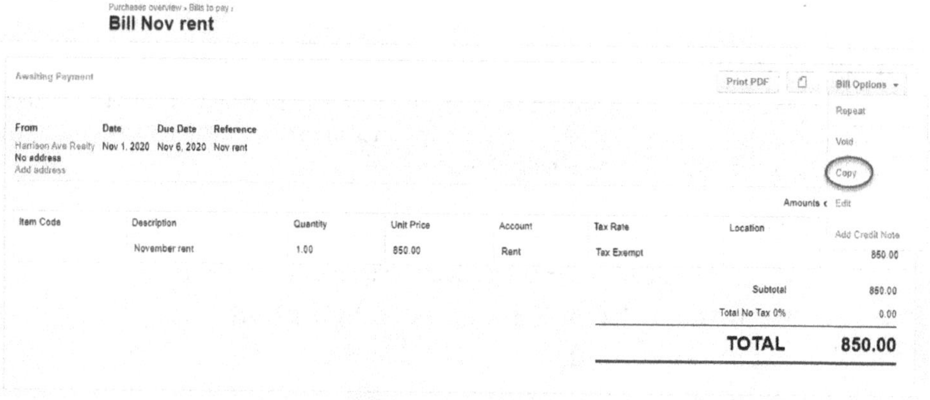

*Source:* Xero Limited

# Credit Notes

If the amount due on a bill must be reduced, such as in the case of a return or allowance, a **credit note** should be created, then applied to a bill to reduce the amount due.

There are two main ways to issue and apply credit notes to bills in Xero:

1. Create a credit note from the bill that will be adjusted.
2. Create a credit note at the supplier level and apply to one or more bills.

## Create a Credit Note from a Bill

Creating directly within the bill that will be adjusted is the fastest way to issue and apply a credit note because both steps are handled at once. This would be the most efficient workflow to adjust a specific bill.

To create a credit note from a bill:

1. Locate the bill and open it by clicking the blue customer name.
2. Use the **Bill Options** pull-down to access **Add Credit Note**.
3. Xero will reverse the bill details for the credit note input screen. The background of the screen changes to a pale yellow, which indicates that this is a transaction that is the opposite direction of normal.
4. Edit fields as necessary, remembering that the posting will be the opposite of the bill. Positive numbers will reduce the general ledger accounts.
5. Review the summary at the bottom which shows the credit note amount and which bill it will be applied to.
6. Click **Approve** (Figure 12.11).

**12**

**FIGURE 12.11**

Use the +New pulldown to access Credit Note.

*Source:* Xero Limited

# Create a Credit Note from the Purchases Overview Screen

Sometimes a credit note needs to be applied to more than one bill. In this case, it is easiest to create the note in the Purchases Overview screen and then apply it to bills.

To create a credit note from the Purchases Overview screen:

1. Navigate to the **Business** tab, then **Purchases Overview.**
2. Use the **+New** pull-down to access **Credit Note.**
3. Xero will provide a blank credit note screen similar to the bill screen, but with a pale yellow background. This is a cue that the direction of this transaction will be the opposite of a normal purchases transaction.
4. In the **From** field, enter the contact name. Since this is going to be a credit note applied to an existing bill, the contact should be in the system and populate as you type.
5. Complete the details of the credit note.
6. Click **Approve.**
7. If there are multiple outstanding bills for the contact, Xero will provide a screen where the credit can be allocated. Enter the amounts of the credit to be applied to each outstanding bill. Click **Allocate Credit** to save (Figure 12.12).

**FIGURE 12.12**

If there are multiple outstanding bills for the contact, Xero will provide a screen where the credit can be allocated. Enter the amounts of the credit to be applied to each outstanding bill. Click Allocate Credit to save.

| Bill | Date | Billed | Amount Due | Amount to Credit |
|------|------|--------|------------|------------------|
| Bill | Sep 30, 2020 | 850.00 | 850.00 | 15.00 |
| Nov rent | Nov 1, 2020 | 850.00 | 850.00 | 15.00 |
| Cash refund | | | | |

Allocate balance on Credit Note Parking credit

| | |
|---|---|
| Outstanding Credit Balance | 30.00 |
| Total Amount to Credit | 30.00 |
| **Remaining Credit** | 0.00 |

Allocate Credit    Cancel

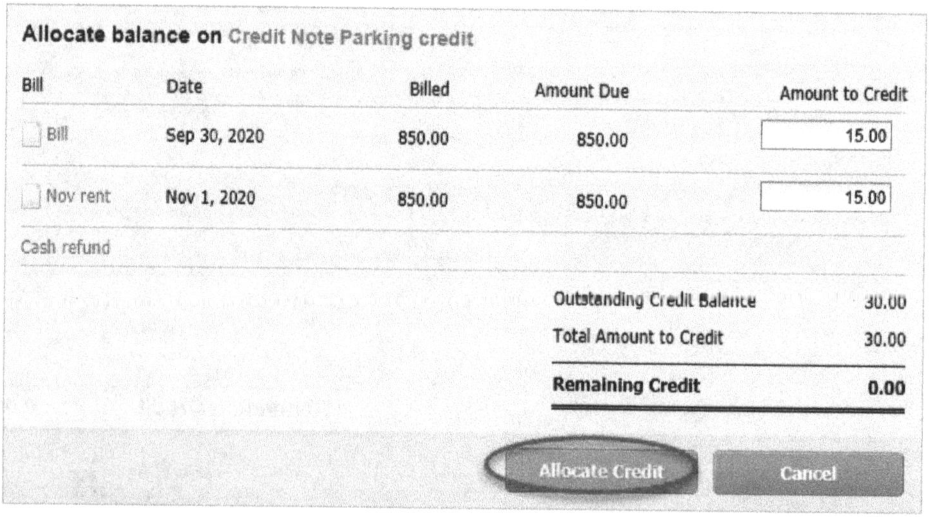

*Source:* Xero Limited

# Repeating Bills

## Creating a Repeating Bill Template

Many companies have bills, like rent, that are the same each month or week. A repeating bill template allows you to create the framework for identical bills to be created for a specific supplier on a given cadence.

Note that you will create the bill template, rather than the bills. Xero will automatically generate the bills on the schedule you assign. This is important because repeating templates are found in the **Repeating** tab of the bills screen, whereas the bills created by Xero using the template are found in the tab appropriate for the current level of the generated bill, either **Draft** or **Awaiting Payment**.

To create a repeating bill template:

1. Navigate to the **Business** tab, then **bills**.
2. Use the **+New bill** pull-down to access **+New Repeating bill**.
3. Set the cadence on which bills will be created by entering the number of weeks or months between bills.
4. Choose the date of the first bill to be created. Note that you can set a repeating bill to start in the past. Bills will be created for historical dates.
5. Set the due date of the bills.
6. Add an optional end date. This would be appropriate for a contract or lease that has a term.
7. Choose how you would like Xero to handle the bill when it is created.

   **Save as Draft:** With this option, Xero will create the bill and save it in the Draft category of bills. It must be manually approved before it will be included in the accounts payable balance and can be paid.

   **Approve:** This option will save the created bill in the Awaiting Payment category and add it to the accounts payable balance. Advisors may use this option to create bills for supplier where payments are automatically drafted. Those payments will be automatched to the bill.

# Managing Repeating Bill Templates

Active repeating templates will be found in the **Repeating** tab of the bills screen. To edit a template, click the blue link for the customer name of the template you wish to open. Make any changes and click **Save**.

To delete a repeating template, select the box to the left of the template and click **Delete**. This will cancel the creation of any future bills, but bills previously created will still be active, unless you delete them separately.

Note that the bills created each occurrence can be found under the Draft or Awaiting Payments tabs, depending on the option chosen when the template was created.

# Purchase Orders

Depending on the controls within the company, there may be requirements for preapprovals for spending. In some cases, vendors will demand evidence of purchase preapprovals to process orders. In Xero, these preapprovals are called **purchase orders**. Using Xero to prepare purchase orders gives companies a way to manage purchase authorizations. Approved purchase orders are easily converted to bills to save time. Purchase orders can even be replicated as invoices when a customer will be charged for the order.

# Creating Purchase Orders

The purchase order screen is very similar to the bill screen. It communicates to a supplier what items or services are authorized. The purchase order will also show the supplier the delivery address and include any specific delivery instructions. Purchase orders do not have any effect on the general ledger until they are converted into approved bills.

To create a purchase order:

1. Navigate to the **Business** tab, then **Purchase orders**.

2. Click the **+New Purchase Order** button.

3. Enter the purchase order details. Note that using tracked inventory items on a purchase order will not increase the balance of the inventory item. The item balance will only be increased when a bill is created.

4. Use the **Delivery Address** pull-down to add a separate delivery address for the supplier. Adding a new address will let you create new multiple delivery addresses. Adding a one-off address will create a delivery address for just one purchase order. Search from contacts is useful if you want to send the order to a contact, such as items to be shipped directly to a customer (Figure 12.13).

5. Use the **Attention, Telephone**, and **Delivery Instructions** fields to specify additional details for the supplier.

6. Click **Save & submit** for approval if the purchase order needs additional levels of oversight. Click **Approve** to finalize the purchase order.

**FIGURE 12.13**

Use the Delivery Address pulldown to add a separate delivery address for the supplier. Adding a new address will let you create new multiple delivery addresses. Adding a one-off address will create a delivery address for just one purchase order. Search from contacts is useful if you want to send the order to a contact, such as items to be shipped directly to a customer.

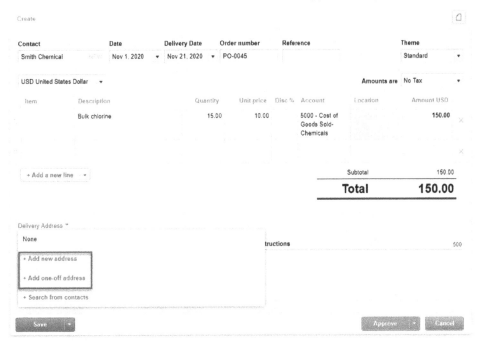

*Source:* Xero Limited

## Creating Bills from Purchase Orders

Once a purchase order has been approved and the supplier has fulfilled the order, it is easy to convert the purchase order to a bill.

To create a bill from a purchase order:

1. Navigate to the **Business** tab, then **Purchase orders**.
2. Locate the purchase order in the **Approved** tab and open it by selecting the blue supplier name.
3. Use the **Options** pull-down to select **Copy to. . .**
4. Select **Bill** and check the box next to **Mark this purchase order as billed.** Checking this box moves the purchase order from the Accepted category, to Billed (Figure 12.14).
5. Click **Create draft.** Xero will create a draft bill with all of the purchase order lines.
6. Edit the bill details and click **Approve.** The bill will be listed in the Awaiting Payment tab and included in the accounts payable balance.

FIGURE 12.14

Select Bill and check the box next to Mark this purchase order as billed. Checking this box moves the purchase order from the Accepted category, to Billed.

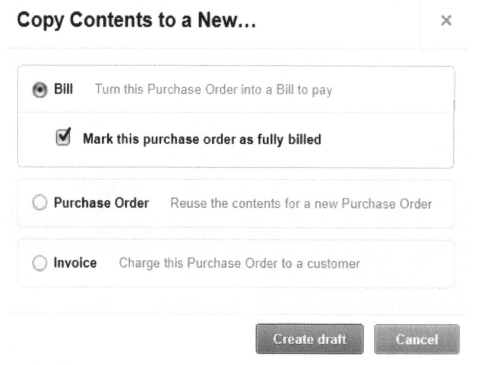

## Copy Contents to a New...   ✕

- ⦿ **Bill**   Turn this Purchase Order into a Bill to pay

  ☑ **Mark this purchase order as fully billed**

- ◯ **Purchase Order**   Reuse the contents for a new Purchase Order

- ◯ **Invoice**   Charge this Purchase Order to a customer

Create draft   Cancel

*Source:* Xero Limited

If a purchase order has been partially fulfilled, a bill can be created for the portion fulfilled, and the original purchase order can be edited to show the remaining unfulfilled order.

To create a bill for a partially fulfilled purchase order:

1. Navigate to the **Business** tab, then **Purchase orders**.
2. Locate the purchase order in the **Approved** tab and open it by selecting the blue supplier name.
3. Use the **Options** pull-down to select **Copy to. . .**
4. Select **Bill**. Uncheck the box next to **Mark this purchase order as billed**. Leaving the box unchecked will keep the original purchase order in the Accepted category, rather than moving it to Billed.
5. Click **Create draft**.
6. Edit the bill details, changing the quantity of items ordered to reflect the portion fulfilled and click **Approve**. The bill will be listed in the Awaiting Payment tab and included in the accounts payable balance (Figure 12.15).

**FIGURE 12.15**

Edit the bill details, changing the quantity of items ordered to reflect the portion fulfilled and click Approve. The bill will be listed in the Awaiting Payment tab and included in the accounts payable balance.

*Source:* Xero Limited

7. Navigate back to the Business tab, then Purchase orders to edit the original purchase order.

8. Find the purchase order in the Approved tab and open it.

9. Use the Options pull-down to select Edit.

10. Change the quantity of items to reflect the portion of the order that remains unfulfilled.

11. Click Update.

## Creating Invoices from Purchase Orders

Some companies place orders on behalf of a customer, then invoice the customer when the order is received. Xero makes it easy to replicate a purchase order as an invoice.

To create an invoice from a purchase order:

1. Navigate to the **Business** tab, then **Purchase orders**.

2. Locate the purchase order in the Approved tab and open it by selecting the blue supplier name.

3. Use the **Options** pull-down to select **Copy to. . .**

4. Select **Invoice** and click **Create draft**. Xero will create a draft invoice with all of the purchase order lines. Note that if inventory items are included, Xero will replace the unit price with the sales price associated with the item (Figure 12.16).

5. Enter the customer name in the To field.

6. Edit the other bill details, and click Approve. The invoice will be listed in the Awaiting Payment tab and included in the accounts receivable balance.

**FIGURE 12.16**

Select Invoice and click Create draft. Xero will create a draft invoice with all of the purchase order lines. Note that if inventory items are included, Xero will replace the unit price with the sales price associated with the item.

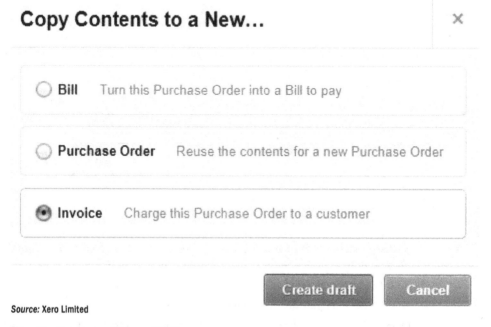

# Copy Contents to a New...                                    ✕

    ◯ **Bill**   Turn this Purchase Order into a Bill to pay

    ◯ **Purchase Order**   Reuse the contents for a new Purchase Order

    ◉ **Invoice**   Charge this Purchase Order to a customer

                               **Create draft**         **Cancel**

*Source:* Xero Limited

# Bulk Importing Bills

Xero offers a way to import bills into the system in bulk. There are several reasons you may want to import bills as a batch rather than entering one at a time.

- There may be many outstanding bills at the conversion date when setting up a new Xero file.
- The company may need to issue many bills at frequent intervals, and it is more efficient to maintain and update an import file that can be imported over and over.

Bills are imported using a *.csv* file type. It is important to understand the structure of the import file.

Each row in the spreadsheet is a bill line. Just like lines in a bill created directly in Xero, each line in the spreadsheet needs a Description, Quantity, Unit Amount, Account Code, and Tax Type. There are also required columns that are used at the bill, rather than line, level. Contact Name, Invoice Number, Invoice Date, and Due Date are required fields. If a bill contains more than one line, be sure that the invoice number is the same for all of the lines that should be on the bill. Xero will aggregate bill lines based on invoice number. The invoice number used in the import will be converted to the bill reference, since bills are not numbered like invoices. The other fields in the import file are optional.

To import bills in bulk:

1. Navigate to the **Business** tab, then **Purchases Overview**.

2. Click the **Import** button.

3. Download the template file, if needed.

4. Prepare the bill file using the instructions above and save.

5. Click the **Browse** button in Xero and select the saved import file.

6. Indicate whether you would like for Xero to update contacts with information in the import file.

7. Confirm that the Unit Amount field is tax exclusive. (This would be the appropriate choice for U.S. transactions. If you are creating transactions outside of the United States, select the correct option.)

8. Click **Import**.

9. You will see a notification screen summarizing the number of bills that will be drafted. Confirm.

10. You will be redirected to the Draft bills tab. To approve the bills, select the box to the left of the bill and click **Approve**. The bills can now be found in the Awaiting Payment tab and are included in the Accounts Payable balance.

# Payments

A company will likely spend money in more than one way. Costs can be paid by:

- A draft from a bank account, initiated by the vendor, such as with an established ACH draw for recurring expenses.
- An electronic payment generated by a credit or debit card charge.
- The payment of an accrued liability through accounts payable.

The first two types of payments are covered in the bank reconciliation chapter. Those costs are recorded when cash leaves the bank account or the credit card is charged. The section that follows will deal with the third option, payments made when the cost is first accrued to accounts payable.

Many companies use bill payment applications to manage the processing of accounts payable payments. However, there are still many companies in the United States that depend on printed paper checks to pay their bills.

## Setting Up Check Styles

The formats of how paper checks are printed from Xero are called **check styles**. A company can have multiple check styles, such as for different office locations or divisions.

Check styles are created and managed in **Organization Settings.** To access check style, use the company name pull-down in the top left to navigate to **Settings.** Click the **Check Styles** link on the right.

Xero changed its original check layout screen several years ago. Most organizations will default to the new check style screen, but in the event that the organization you are working in is still using the old format, you may be prompted to **Upgrade to new check style.**

Every Xero organization will have a Standard check layout when it is created. The Check Styles screen will show a tile for this layout. To add additional styles, use the **+New Style** button at the top. The Standard layout, as well as any additional layouts created, will need to be formatted before checks are printed. To update the formatting of a style, use the **Options** pull-down on the upper right of the tile and choose the **Edit** link. This will open the check layout editor (Figure 12.17).

The check style layout editor has three sections: print settings, the check layout, and the voucher details.

### Print Settings

The top of the check style screen shows the overriding settings for this check style. The name of the style can be changed by updating the **Style name** field.

**FIGURE 12.17**

To update the formatting of a style, use the Options pulldown on the upper right of the tile and choose the Edit link. This will open the check layout editor.

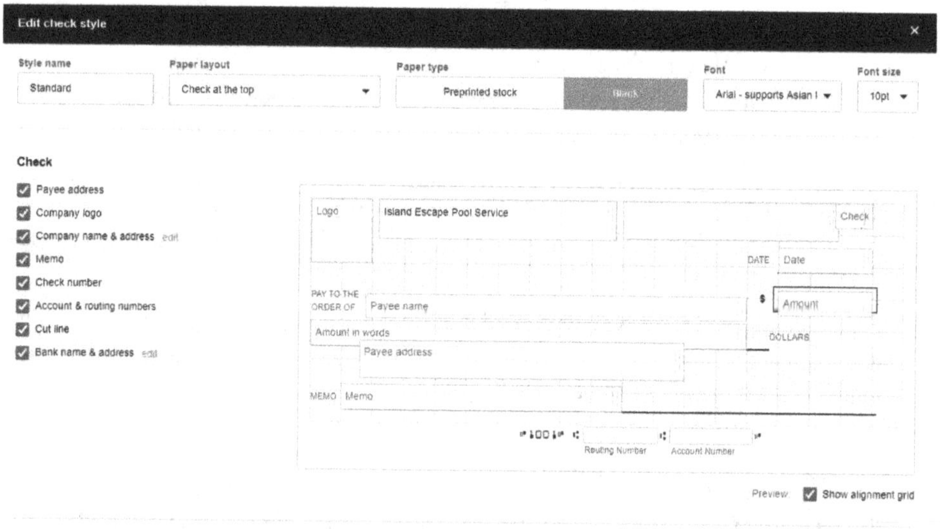

*Source:* Xero Limited

**Paper layout** refers to the format of each page of check stock. Xero supports check stock of either three checks per page or one check and two vouchers per page. On layouts of one check and two vouchers, the arrangement must be selected. The most common format in the United States is the check at the top of the page, with two vouchers below.

**Paper type** refers to whether the check stock is preprinted or blank. In the United States, preprinted stock is more common. Selecting Preprinted stock will keep Xero from printing lines and other details, like routing and account numbers, on the check. (Figure 12.18).

**Font** and **font size** can be selected from limited options using the pull-downs.

### Check Layout

The first thing to notice about the check layout editor is that each field shown on the check image on the right can be moved by dragging and dropping with your mouse. This allows for complete customization of the alignment of each field against preprinted check stock.

When creating a new style or formatting a style for the first time, it is important to review the available print fields on the left side. In many cases, some of these fields will already be included on preprinted stock, so they should be unchecked. Many advisors in the United States will need to uncheck the Company logo, Company name & address, Check number, Cut line, and Bank name & address fields. Removing these fields will leave Date, Payee name, Amount, Amount in words, Payee address, and Memo on the layout grid (Figure 12.19).

It is helpful to print a sample check image on regular paper and hold it in the light over the check stock. Use your mouse to adjust the fields until the layout aligns with the preprinted stock. Once the format is correct, click **Save** at the bottom of the screen.

### Voucher Details

The final section of the Check Styles screen allows users to select what details will be visible on the check vouchers. Vouchers are usually sent with check payments so the recipient can see details for the payment. In general, advisors remove the Bank account and Account numbers fields from the voucher. Beyond that, it is a matter of preference with regard to

**FIGURE 12.18**

Paper type refers to whether the check stock is preprinted or blank. In the United States, preprinted stock is more common. Selecting Preprinted stock will keep Xero from printing lines and other details, like routing and account numbers, on the check.

*Source:* Xero Limited

**FIGURE 12.19**

Many advisors in the United States will need to uncheck the Company logo, Company name & address, Check number, Cut line and Bank name & address fields. Removing these fields will leave Date, Payee name, Amount, Amount in words, Payee address and Memo on the layout grid.

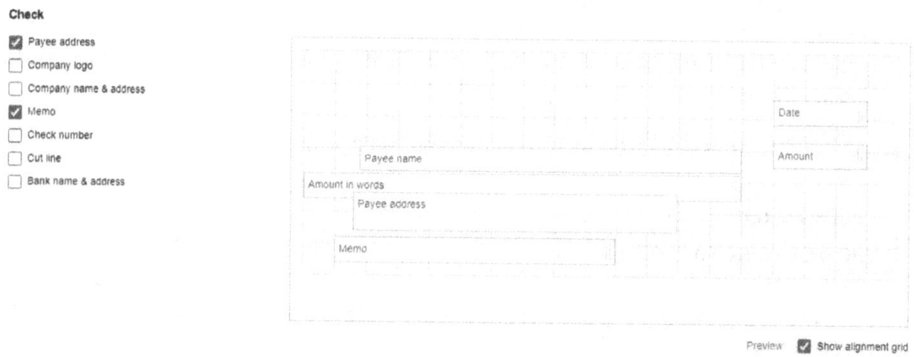

*Source:* Xero Limited

how much detail a company wishes to include. Once the voucher is final, click **Save** at the bottom of the screen to lock the settings within the check style.

## Quick Check

Even if the company uses the accounts payable process to enter bills, then batch payments, there will be instances where a check will be needed to pay an expense immediately. The method for printing a check without creating a bill first, or a **quick check**, is to add a Spend Money transaction and elect to pay by check. This will create a normal spend money transaction, but a check number will be associated with it for matching purposes. It will also create the check image for download and printing.

Using this method for check printing rather than handwriting checks will save vast amounts of time on the reconciliation end. The bank data will likely show only an amount and check number when the check clears. If the check is generated from the system, Xero will recognize the outstanding check as a match against the bank line, requiring just one click to reconcile. If the check is handwritten, there will be no match, the advisor will have to research the bank line, usually by viewing a check image, and confirm the payee and coding.

To create a quick check:

1. From the Dashboard, click the + at the top right, then select **Spend money**.
2. Choose the bank account the check will be written from. Click **Next**.
3. Enter the payee in the **To** field.
4. Select the **Date** for the check.
5. Check the **Pay by check** box (Figure 12.20).

**FIGURE 12.20**

Check the Pay by check box.

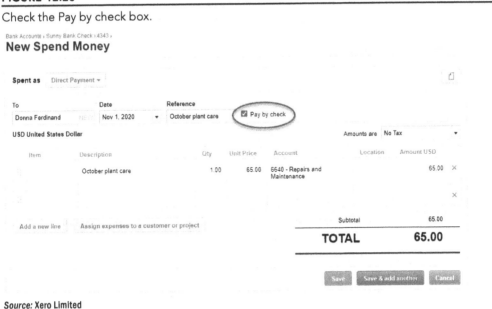

*Source:* Xero Limited

**FIGURE 12.21**

In the next screen, confirm the check number and payee. Add a memo if desired.

*Source:* Xero Limited

6. Complete the other input fields.

7. Click **Save**.

8. In the next screen, confirm the check number and payee. Add a memo if desired (Figure 12.21).

9. Click **Save & Print PDF**.

10. Xero will download a check image file to be printed on check stock.

## Single Bill Payment

In many cases, a company will create checks for accounts payable in batches, often every week or every other week, but there are times when an account payable must be paid off schedule.

To generate a check payment of a single bill:

1. Navigate to the **Business** tab, then **Bills to pay**.

2. Locate the bill and open it by clicking the blue supplier name.

3. Scroll to the **Make a payment** tile at the bottom of the bill page.

4. Enter the **Amount Paid.** The default figure will be the bill balance, but you can change this if only a partial payment will be made.

5. Enter the **Date Paid**.

6. Choose the account that the payment will be **Paid From.** This should be the checking account that the check will be drawn on.

7. Enter an optional **Reference**.

8. Check the box next to **Pay by check**.

9. Click **Add Payment** (Figure 12.22).

**FIGURE 12.22**

Click Add Payment.

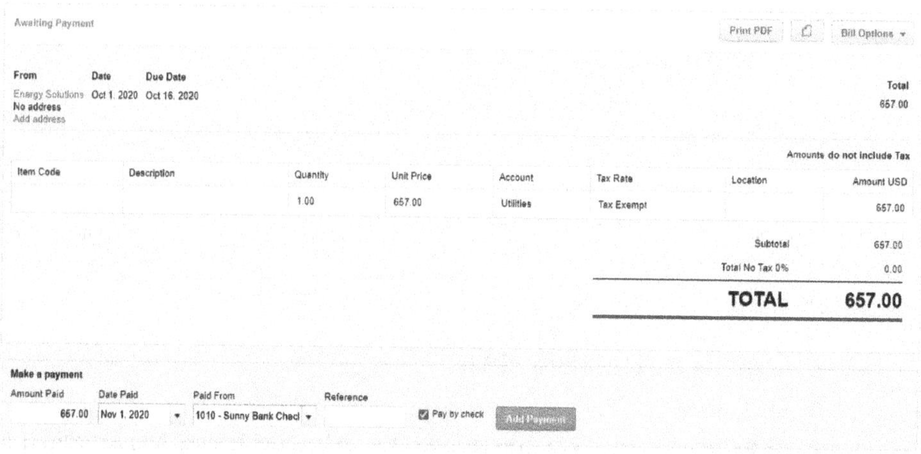

*Source:* Xero Limited

10. A Pay by Check screen will appear. Confirm the check number. (The default **Check # will be the next check available in the chosen account.) Add a **Memo**, if desired. Choose the **Check Style**. Select **Save & Print PDF**.

11. The check image will be downloaded in your browser. Open it and print to check stock.

In this process, the bill is marked as paid on the general ledger. The bill is removed from the Awaiting Payments tab. An unreconciled payment is created against the bank account, which will automatch when the check clears.

## Batch Checks for Bill Payments

It is much more efficient to process a batch of checks for a group of bills, rather than to process each individually. In many companies, the accounts payable cycle runs on a weekly or biweekly basis.

To process a batch of checks for multiple bills:

1. In the **Awaiting Payment** tab of bills, select the bills to be paid by checking the boxes to the left of each. (Many advisors use the Due Date header to sort the bills to determine which will be due in the next process period.)

2. Click the **Make Payment** button at the top of the listing (Figure 12.23).

3. Select **Pay By Check** (Figure 12.24).

4. Choose the **Bank Account** that the checks will be drawn on. It is very important that the correct account is chosen. The unreconciled check payments will only appear in bank reconciliation for the bank account chosen here.

5. Choose the **Check Style** to be used.

6. Notice that Xero shows the number of bills paid by each check in the far left column. To see the details of the underlying bills, click on the number button.

**FIGURE 12.23**

Click the Make Payment button at the top of the listing.

| | Ref | From | Date | Due Date ▲ | Planned Date | Paid | Due | |
|---|---|---|---|---|---|---|---|---|
| ☑ | | Harrison Ave Realty | Sep 30, 2020 | Sep 30, 2020 | | 0.00 | 836.00 | |
| ☑ | | Cox | Sep 30, 2020 | Sep 30, 2020 | | 0.00 | 54.55 | |
| ☑ | | Energy Solutions | Oct 1, 2020 | Oct 16, 2020 | | 0.00 | 657.00 | |
| ☐ | | Shredlink | Oct 15, 2020 | Oct 30, 2020 | | 0.00 | 30.00 | |
| ☐ | Nov rent | Harrison Ave Realty | Nov 1, 2020 | Nov 6, 2020 | | 0.00 | 836.00 | |
| ☐ | PO-0045 | Smith Chemical | Nov 1, 2020 | Nov 15, 2020 | | 0.00 | 150.00 | |

*Source:* Xero Limited

**FIGURE 12.24**

Select Pay By Check.

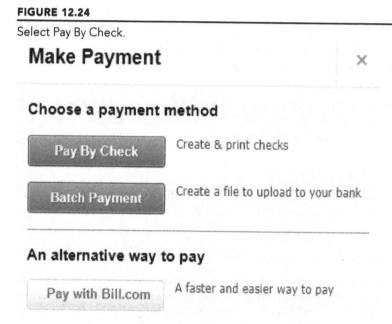

7. Confirm the check numbers by reviewing the Check # column. To make changes, click the Check Numbering button and update the starting check number.

8. If a supplier does not have an address saved in the contact record, Xero will show a red **No address button.** Click the button to add an address. The address will then be saved to the contact record (Figure 12.25).

9. The default date will be today's date, but by clicking in the field, it can be changed.

10. A **Memo** can be added, if desired.

**FIGURE 12.25**

If a supplier does not have an address saved in the contact record, Xero will show a red No address button. Click the button to add an address. The address will then be saved to the contact record.

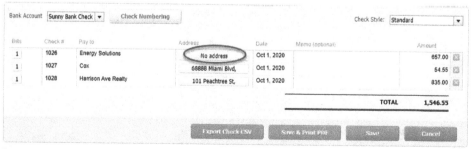

11. The **Amount** field will be for the full amount of the bills chosen to be paid, but can be edited here (Figure 12.26).

12. To remove a check from the batch, use the **X** on the right to cancel that line.

13. Choose **Save & Print PDF** to save the check payments against the bills and download a .pdf file that can be printed to check stock. Because the download is a separate file, the .pdf can even be sent to remote clients so they can print and sign checks.

## Creating a Batch Export File for the Bank

Depending on the company's bank, it may be possible to upload a file to send payments in bulk to vendors directly from the bank. The process is nearly the same as creating checks, except that the end product will be an upload file rather than check images.

To create a batch export file for electronic payment of bills:

1. In the **Awaiting Payment** tab of bills, select the bills to be paid by checking the boxes to the left of each. (Many advisors use the Due Date header to sort the bills to determine which will be due in the next process period.)

2. Click the **Make Payment** button at the top of the listing.

**FIGURE 12.26**

The Amount field will be for the full amount of the bills chosen to be paid, but can be edited here.

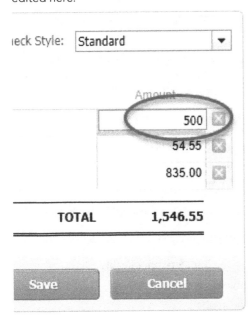

*Source:* Xero Limited

3. Select **Batch Payment**.

4. Enter the **Payment Date** and select the **Bank Account** the payments will be drawn from.

5. Click **Make Payments**.

6. On the next screen, click the **Export Batch File** button to generate a .csv file to be uploaded to the bank.

The unreconciled batch payment can be found in the Account Transactions tab of the bank account. Note that the total amount is shown singularly, and it is this amount that Xero will expect to match to a bank line. If your bank offers to process the batch as a single line or multiple lines, choose the single statement line so that the unreconciled batch transaction in Xero will match to the single bank line in the feed.

## Managing Handwritten Checks

One of the most time-consuming tasks for an accountant or bookkeeper is recording checks that were generated outside of the accounting system, often referred to as **handwritten checks**. An example would be a company that must provide a vendor with a check on the spot when receiving a delivery. Another example would be bringing a paper check to a supplier's location to pay for an order, where the total cannot be determined ahead of time.

When checks are issued outside of the accounting system, the advisor is often left searching for the details as the checks clear the bank. In general, the bank will only transmit the check number and amount through the bank feed to Xero. The advisor must then request details from the company or attempt to retrieve an image of the check from the bank. Even if an image is available from the bank, it oftens requires deciphering of handwriting or additional coding details from the client. This creates tremendous delays in monthly reconciliation.

A better option than handwritten checks is for clients to use the method for creating a quick check described earlier in this chapter. This will ensure that the check coding is accurate and the check is being kept track of even before it clears the bank.

If that is not possible, it is extremely helpful for the client to keep a listing of details for checks issued so they can be entered into Xero by the advisor. If the company issues many handwritten checks each month, the payments can be imported into Xero in bulk by using the method for bulk import of bills. Columns are added to the import file for payment. Each check will be recorded by the creation of a bill, then the immediate application of a check payment to that bill. By recording the payments, the cleared checks will be auto-matched in bank reconciliation, eliminating the need to track down the check details.

Using the bill import feature to record handwritten checks is a three-step process.

1. Prepare the import file, including the handwritten checks.

2. Import file to draft bills and approve.

3. Confirm the check payments to be applied.

### Preparing the Import File

In order to import handwritten checks as bill payments, you must prepare the import file. A sample import file can be found in the digital resources. The import file will show one bill line on each spreadsheet row, which must include the required fields for bill imports. It must also include a check number and payment date for each row. If a handwritten check is a payment for a multi-line bill, use the same number and date for each row that makes up the bill (Figure 12.27).

### Importing Bills

Once the file is prepared, use the same process to import as for importing unpaid bills:

1. Navigate to the **Business** tab, then **Purchases Overview**.
2. Click the **Import** button.
3. Click the **Browse** button in Xero and select the saved import file.
4. Click **Import**.
5. You will see a notification screen summarizing the number of bills that will be drafted (Figure 12.28).
6. Click **Complete Import**. You will be redirected to the Draft bills tab.
7. Approve the bills by selecting the box to the left of the bills and clicking **Approve**.

**12**

### FIGURE 12.27

If a handwritten check is a payment for a multi-line bill, use the same number and date for each row that makes up the bill.

| | *ContactName | EmailAddress | *InvoiceNumber | *InvoiceDate | *DueDate | InventoryItemCo | Description | *Quantity | *UnitAmount | *AccountCode | *TaxType | CheckNumber | PaymentDate |
|---|---|---|---|---|---|---|---|---|---|---|---|---|---|
| 1 | | | | | | | | | | | | | |
| 2 | Creative Dudes | | 1548 | 10/15/2020 | 10/15/2020 | | Website Hosting | 1 | 25 | 6510 | Tax Exempt (0% | 12851 | 10/15/2020 |
| 3 | Creative Dudes | | 1548 | 10/15/2020 | 10/15/2020 | | Website Hosting | 2 | 50 | 6510 | Tax Exempt (0% | 12851 | 10/15/2020 |
| 4 | Jimmy Kirby | NA | | 10/24/2020 | 10/24/2020 | | Retail products | 12 | 12 | 5002 | Tax Exempt (0% | 12852 | 10/24/2020 |
| 5 | Hotel Antigua | | 852 | 10/25/2020 | 10/25/2020 | | Cleaning | 1 | 75 | 6080 | Tax Exempt (0% | 12853 | 10/25/2020 |
| 6 | | | | | | | | | | | | | |

*Source:* Xero Limited

### FIGURE 12.28

You will see a notification screen summarizing the number of bills that will be drafted.

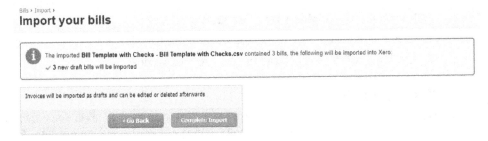

Bills › Import ›

**Import your bills**

The imported **Bill Template with Checks - Bill Template with Checks.csv** contained 3 bills, the following will be imported into Xero:
✓ 3 new draft bills will be imported

Invoices will be imported as drafts and can be edited or deleted afterwards

‹ Go Back   Complete Import

*Source:* Xero Limited

The bills are now in the Awaiting Payment tab and therefore in the accounts payable balance. You must complete the process to apply the payments from the import file.

### Applying Check Payments

At this point, the check payments are in limbo and barely connected to the bills. You must force Xero to acknowledge that the bills have actually been paid by the checks specified in the import file.

1. In the Awaiting Payment tab, select the bills that were imported. You can sort by the **Ref** field, which will show the Invoice Numbers used in the data file.
2. Select the bills by checking the box to the left of the line.
3. Click the **Make Payment** button at the top of the listing.
4. Select **Pay By Check**.
5. You will see the normal batch check payment screen, but the **Check #** field should be populated with the check numbers from the data file.
6. It is very important to choose the correct bank account at the top. Be sure this is the account the checks were cut from.
7. Click **Save**. (Since the checks have already been written, there is no need to generate a check image .pdf.)

The handwritten checks will now automatch in bank reconciliation when they clear the bank.

# Managing Checks

## Using the Check Register

Xero offers a simple listing of all checks created. This **check register** can be accessed under the Business tab. A listing of all checks and their status can be exported as a spreadsheet.

To export a complete check register:

1. Navigate to the **Business** tab, then **Checks**.
2. Click the **Export** button at the top (Figure 12.29).
3. A .csv file will be downloaded in your browser window.

## Reprinting Checks

In some cases a check that has been processed will need to be reprinted, voided, or deleted. To locate a particular check, sort the list by clicking any of the column headers. You can

**FIGURE 12.29**

Click the Export button at the top.

**Checks**

| Spend Money | Export | Edit Check Styles |

| Print PDF | Void | Delete | No items selected | | | | Search |

| | Check # | Pay to | Dated ▾ | Memo | Payment | Status & History | Amount |
|---|---|---|---|---|---|---|---|
| ☐ | 1025 | Donna Ferdinand | Nov 1, 2020 | | Sunny Bank Check x4343 | Uncleared | 65.00 |
| ☐ | 1029 | Hotel Antigua | Oct 25, 2020 | | Sunny Bank Check x4343 | Uncleared | 75.00 |
| ☐ | 1028 | Jimmy Kirby | Oct 24, 2020 | | Sunny Bank Check x4343 | Uncleared | 144.00 |
| ☐ | 1027 | Smith Chemical | Oct 1, 2020 | | Sunny Bank Check x4343 | Uncleared | 150.00 |
| ☐ | 1026 | Harrison Ave Realty | Oct 1, 2020 | | Sunny Bank Check x4343 | Uncleared | 835.00 |

*Source:* Xero Limited

also use the Search button at the top right of the listing to search by check number, contact, or memo. The results can be filtered by bank account, status, date, or amount.

A company may need to reprint a check exactly as it was processed. This could be because the generated check image was accidentally printed on plain paper instead of check stock, or the user is trying to verify image alignment.

To reprint a check without changes:

1. Navigate to the **Business** tab, then **Checks.**
2. Locate the check to be reprinted.
3. Use the checkbox to the left of the line to select the check and click the **Print PDF** button (Figure 12.30).
4. Confirm the check to print by clicking **OK.**
5. A .pdf file will download in your browser.

**FIGURE 12.30**

Use the checkbox to the left of the line to select the check and click the Print PDF button.

**Checks**

| Spend Money | Export | Edit Check Styles |

| Print PDF | Void | Delete | 1 item selected | 65.00 USD | | | | Search |

| | Check # | Pay to | Dated ▾ | Memo | Payment | Status & History | Amount |
|---|---|---|---|---|---|---|---|
| ☑ | 1025 | Donna Ferdinand | Nov 1, 2020 | | Sunny Bank Check x4343 | Uncleared | 65.00 |

*Source:* Xero Limited

# Editing Checks

If the originally processed check has an error, it may be possible to fix the error and reprint the check without voiding the check payment. A few notes on the fields that can be edited:

- Check number: If a check was printed on a wrong-numbered check, you can simply change the check numbers in Xero, rather than voiding and reprinting.
- Pay to: You can change the payee on the check. The original payee name will be shown as a reference.
- Memo: Add or edit the memo field to be printed on the check.
- Address: Changing the address in the check screen will also update the address for the contact.
- Check style: A different check style can be selected if the wrong one was initially used.

To edit and reprint a check:

1. Navigate to the **Business** tab, then **Checks**.
2. Open the check to be edited by clicking the blue **Pay to** name.
3. Edit the fields.
4. Click **Save**.

## Voiding or Deleting Checks

In some cases, you may need to void or delete a check that was processed. Often a check will be lost and the recipient will request a replacement. It could be that the check image was misprinted on check stock and needs to be reprinted.

Both voiding and deleting a check will remove the payment from the bill or spend money. A bill from which a check payment is removed will be returned to Awaiting Payment. A spend money from which a check payment is removed will be deleted.

**Voiding a check** will leave the check on the register and mark it as void. A check can be voided on the day it was created, as if it never happened, or voided on a specific date. In the case of a lost check, you would want to void the check on the date it is found to be lost, then reissue a new check.

**Deleting a check** will remove the check payment as if it never happened. Deleted checks are removed from the check register entirely and check numbers can be reused. You would delete a check when a batch of checks are printed on the wrong numbers, such as when a printer prints in reverse order. Delete the checks, then reassign check numbers.

## Viewing Bill History and Notes

Like in Sales, Xero keeps a detailed record of all activity for Purchases. To view the activity on any bill, open the bill by selecting it from the Purchases Overview or bills screen. At the bottom of the bill, there is a section called **History & Notes**. To view all the activity on the bill, select the **Show History** button. This will open the complete log (Figure 12.31).

The log will show important milestones in the life of the bill, including creation, any changes, and payments applied. History items will be time and date-stamped. Each action will be associated with a Xero user or indicated as **System Generated**. System generated means that the action was not performed by a designated user within Xero, but was created by an API trigger, such as in the use of third-party bill payment applications.

If desired, a custom **Note** can be added at the bottom of the bill. This can be useful to explain changes made to the bill or to indicate that a customer has been phoned for collection. A note created here will be saved as a history item and cannot be edited or deleted.

# Expense Claims

As long as Xero has been in the United States, there has been a function for handling expense reports, or claims, filed by employees. The original feature, referred to as **classic expense claims**, is being phased out in favor of Xero Expenses and at the time of writing is only available to organizations that used it in the six months prior to July 2018. Because there are some U.S. Xero users who still use classic expense claims, it is covered briefly here.

**FIGURE 12.31**

To view all of the activity on the bill, select the Show History button. This will open the complete log.

History & Notes

Paid by Amanda Aguillard on Oct 1, 2020 at 14:55PM
**Payment made to Smith Chemical on October 1, 2020 for 150.00. This bill has been fully paid.**

Hide History (4 entries)     Add Note

| Changes | Date | User | Details |
|---------|------|------|---------|
| Paid | Oct 1, 2020 2:55 PM | Amanda Aguillard | Payment made to Smith Chemical on October 1, 2020 for 150.00. This bill has been fully paid. |
| Approved | Oct 1, 2020 2:15 PM | Amanda Aguillard | PO-0045 from Smith Chemical for 150.00. |
| Copied | Oct 1, 2020 2:15 PM | Amanda Aguillard | Copied from Purchase Order PO-0045 |
| Created | Oct 1, 2020 2:15 PM | Amanda Aguillard | PO-0045 from Smith Chemical for 150.00. |

*Source:* Xero Limited

If the file qualifies, navigating to **Business**, then to **Expense Claims accesses classic expense claims.** An employee must create the claim by adding a receipt with the details necessary for coding. It is important to understand that the claim will be associated with the user who enters the claim, and claims cannot be entered on behalf of others. When all receipts have been added, the user will select the receipts to be reimbursed and **Submit for Approval.** Once an employee has submitted the claim for approval, the receipts must be authorized and set for payment.

When the claim is authorized, it is sent to the Awaiting Payment tab of Expense Claims. At this point, it is included in the Unpaid Expense Claims liability account on the general ledger, not Accounts Payable. To pay the claim, locate it in the Awaiting Payment tab, open it by selecting the employee's name, and note a payment at the bottom of the screen. A check can be created here for the reimbursement.

Xero has not publicly announced a sunset date for classic expense claims, but has encouraged users to migrate to Xero Expenses, discussed in Chapter 19.

# Fixed Assets

*I'm a big fan of recording depreciation monthly so small businesses know their actual profitability at the end of each month. I love Xero Fixed Assets because it makes it so easy to track fixed assets and record the depreciation, even for months at a time, with the click of a button. And if you make a mistake, you can also easily roll back the depreciation. It's quick and slick.*

*—Patti Scharf, Co-Founder and CEO of Catching Clouds*

## Overview of Fixed Assets

Xero's fixed assets module has greatly improved over the last few years. With a clean setup, it will calculate and post depreciation for companies. Some advisors do not use the functionality of the fixed assets module, choosing to use subordinate files (usually spreadsheets) to track assets and making journal entries monthly or annually.

The fixed assets module is best used when the company is keeping track of depreciation on a strictly book basis, with any differences for tax purposes managed strictly as a function of tax preparation and kept off the books. Fixed assets can also be used to calculate depreciation using simple tax depreciation methods; however, tax depreciation methods change almost yearly, such as with bonus depreciation, and there are limitations with using Xero. The fixed assets modules should not be used by companies who wish to track book depreciation throughout the year, then make a year-end adjustment to tie to the tax return. When using the fixed assets module, no journal entries should be made to depreciation. Either use the functionality or book manually calculated journal entries, but not both.

It is important to understand how the general ledger and the fixed assets ledger are related. There is no direct link between the assets subledger and the general ledger. Assets must be entered on the asset subledger, or registered, separately. Xero helps out by suggesting that certain transactions be registered. As bills or spend money transactions are posted to accounts specified as a fixed asset account type in the chart of accounts, Xero will create draft fixed assets. Assets must be confirmed by registering them. Registering an asset means that it has been added to the fixed asset listing and assigned to a set of rules that will determine the calculation of depreciation.

# Accessing the Fixed Asset Module

Fixed asset functionality is found under **Accounting**, then **Advanced**. **Fixed assets settings** (on the right of the Advanced screen) is where the setup is done. **Fixed assets** (on the left side of the Advanced screen) is where depreciation is calculated. Only **Fixed assets** is included in the default favorites menu. View the entire Advanced menu to get to **Fixed assets settings** (Figure 13.1).

# Setting Up the Fixed Assets Module

The first step in using the fixed asset functionality in Xero is to choose a start date for using the fixed asset module. This must be the beginning of a fiscal year. It can be any fiscal year in the past plus the upcoming fiscal year. The only exception is when a fiscal year begins within a month, like August 15. Depreciation will not work correctly with a non-first start date. If this is the case for the company, you must either change the fiscal

## FIGURE 13.1

Only Fixed assets is included in the default favorites menu. View the entire Advanced menu to get to Fixed assets settings.

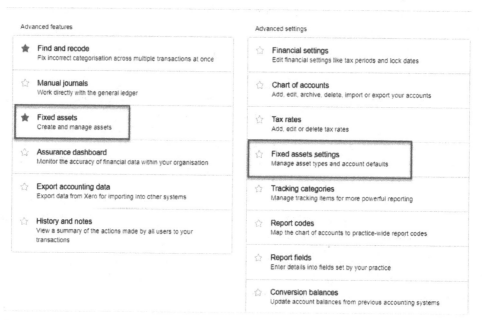

**Advanced accounting**

Advanced features

★ Find and recode
Fix incorrect categorisation across multiple transactions at once

☆ Manual journals
Work directly with the general ledger

★ Fixed assets
Create and manage assets

☆ Assurance dashboard
Monitor the accuracy of financial data within your organisation

☆ Export accounting data
Export data from Xero for importing into other systems

☆ History and notes
View a summary of the actions made by all users to your transactions

Advanced settings

☆ Financial settings
Edit financial settings like tax periods and lock dates

☆ Chart of accounts
Add, edit, archive, delete, import or export your accounts

☆ Tax rates
Add, edit or delete tax rates

☆ Fixed assets settings
Manage asset types and account defaults

☆ Tracking categories
Manage tracking items for more powerful reporting

☆ Report codes
Map the chart of accounts to practice-wide report codes

☆ Report fields
Enter details into fields set by your practice

☆ Conversion balances
Update account balances from previous accounting systems

*Source:* Xero Limited

year to the first of a month or not use the fixed asset functionality and rely on manual calculations and journal entries.

To set the start date for fixed assets:

1. Navigate to the **Accounting** tab, then **Advanced. Select Fixed Asset Settings.**
2. Click the **Set Start Date** or **Change Start Date** button.
3. Use the **Start Date** pull-down to select from the available options (Figure 13.2).
4. Click **Save.**

**FIGURE 13.2**

Use the Start Date pulldown to select from the available options.

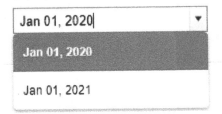

## Change Start Date ✕

### If you click Save, the following will happen:

- All depreciation and disposal journals will be reversed
- Start Date will change from **Jan 01, 2020** to the date you select below
- You will need to re-enter the accumulated depreciation for any assets purchased before the new start date

If you've set a lock date in Financial Settings, some start dates may be unavailable

If your organisation is changing financial year end, make sure you follow these steps in the help guide **before making changes**

**Start Date**

| Jan 01, 2020 | ▼ |

Jan 01, 2020

Jan 01, 2021

Save    Cancel

*Source:* Xero Limited

The next step is to set up **asset types**. These are categories of assets with particular attributes and settings. An asset type will be assigned mappings to general ledger accounts for the asset, accumulated depreciation, and depreciation expense. Every asset assigned to that type will have entries posted to those accounts. Asset types also set the default depreciation method and life for the assets assigned to it.

Asset types can be more specific than the general ledger asset account it is associated with. For example, under the general ledger account Heavy Equipment, a company could have asset types for bulldozers, forklifts, and such. However, most of the Xero reports do not use asset type as a field, so that kind of detail would be mostly meaningless. Most advisors create one asset type per fixed asset account in the trial balance. This keeps reconciliation simple.

To add an asset type:

1. Confirm that the general ledger accounts to be used for the asset, accumulated depreciation, and depreciation expense for the asset type already exist.
2. Navigate to the **Accounting** tab, then **Advanced**. Select **Fixed Asset Settings**.
3. Click the **+Asset Type** button.
4. Enter a name in the **Asset Type** field.
5. Map the **Asset Account**, **Accumulated Depreciation Account**, and **Depreciation Expense Account** to accounts in the general ledger using the pull-downs.
6. Set the **Book Depreciation Default** fields. These are the variables used in calculating depreciation (Figure 13.3).

**FIGURE 13.3**

Set the Book Depreciation Default fields. These are the variables used in calculating depreciation.

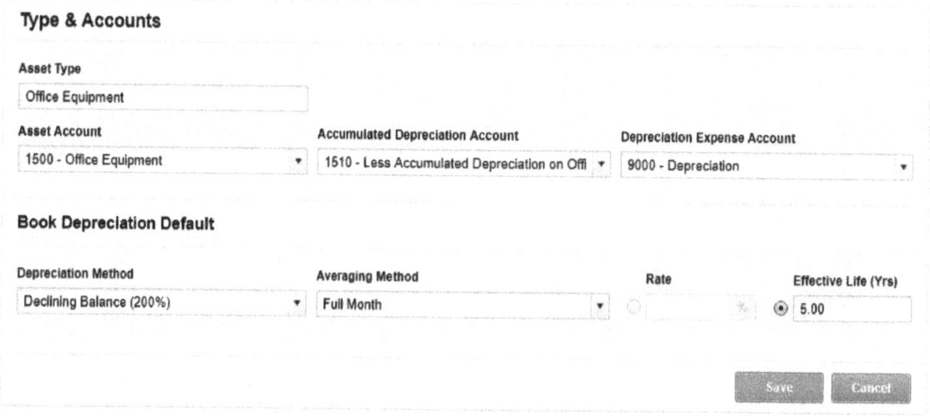

*Source:* Xero Limited

The next step in setting up fixed assets for use is to set the accounts to be used in disposing of assets.

To set disposal default accounts:

1. Confirm that the general ledger accounts to be used for capital gain on disposal, gain on disposal, and loss on disposal already exist. In practice, this may be one single account called "Gain or Loss on Disposal of Assets."
2. Navigate to the **Accounting** tab, then **Advanced**. Select **Fixed Asset Settings**.
3. Navigate to the **Accounts** tab.
4. Map each of the gain or loss types to the general ledger accounts to be used (Figure 13.4).
5. Click **Save**.

These settings can also be reached by using the **Settings** button in Fixed Assets.

The final step in setting up fixed assets for use is to enter opening balances on the general ledger and adding assets that total those balances to the asset register. You will use the conversion balances screen to enter the balances of fixed asset accounts at the date of conversion. Then you will use the fixed assets solution to create the underlying asset register.

To enter balances for the fixed asset ledger accounts:

1. Select **Accounting** from the top menu, then **Advanced**.
2. Select **Conversion balances**.
3. Enter the balance at the conversion date for each of the asset accounts. If the asset account is not shown on the screen, use the **Add a new line** button to add it.
4. Add or import assets to the fixed asset register using the directions below.

**FIGURE 13.4**

Map each of the gain or loss types to the general ledger accounts to be used.

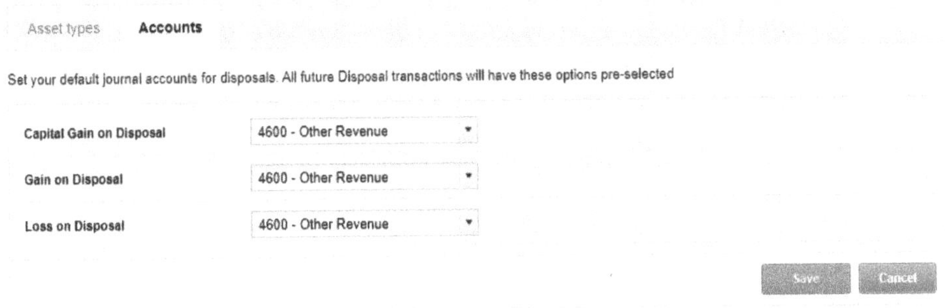

*Source:* Xero Limited

# Adding Fixed Assets

Xero does not automatically add assets to the fixed asset ledgers. A user must add assets to the ledger in one of two ways:

1. Created manually in fixed assets: This is used mainly when assets need to be added to subledger during a conversion.
2. Confirmed from the Draft tab in Fixed assets: When a transaction is coded to a fixed asset account type, Xero creates a draft of an asset that must be confirmed.

## Adding a New Asset

As mentioned earlier, assets will need to be created manually for the fixed asset subledger when there is no transaction that initiates a draft asset. During conversion, only the general ledger totals are added. The details of the underlying assets must be added manually.

To manually add a new asset:

1. Navigate to the **Accounting** tab, then **Advanced**. Select **Fixed Assets**.
2. Click the **+New Asset** button at the top of the screen.
3. Enter an **Asset Name**.
4. If desired, change the **Asset Number** by using the pull-down and editing the **Prefix** or **New Number**.
5. Enter the **Purchase Date** and **Purchase Price**.
6. If desired, add a **Warranty Expiry** date and **Serial Number**.
7. Choose the **Asset Type**.
8. Enter a **Tracking Category**, if desired.
9. Enter a **Description**.
10. Review the depreciation defaults set in the **Book Value** section by the Asset Type selected. Make any adjustments using the **Depreciation Method** and **Averaging Method** fields and entering a **Rate** or **Effective Life**. Use a Depreciation Method of **No Depreciation** for assets such as land.
11. Use the **+Show more options** link to add a Cost Limit or Residual Value to the asset. A **Cost Limit** is the portion of the purchase price that will be used for the depreciation calculation. A **Residual Value** is the book value at which Xero will stop depreciating the asset.
12. Click **Register** (Figure 13.5).

This is also useful when existing transactions are recoded to fixed asset accounts. Once a transaction is coded, recoding or editing to a fixed asset account will not initiate the draft of an asset.

**FIGURE 13.5**

Click Register.

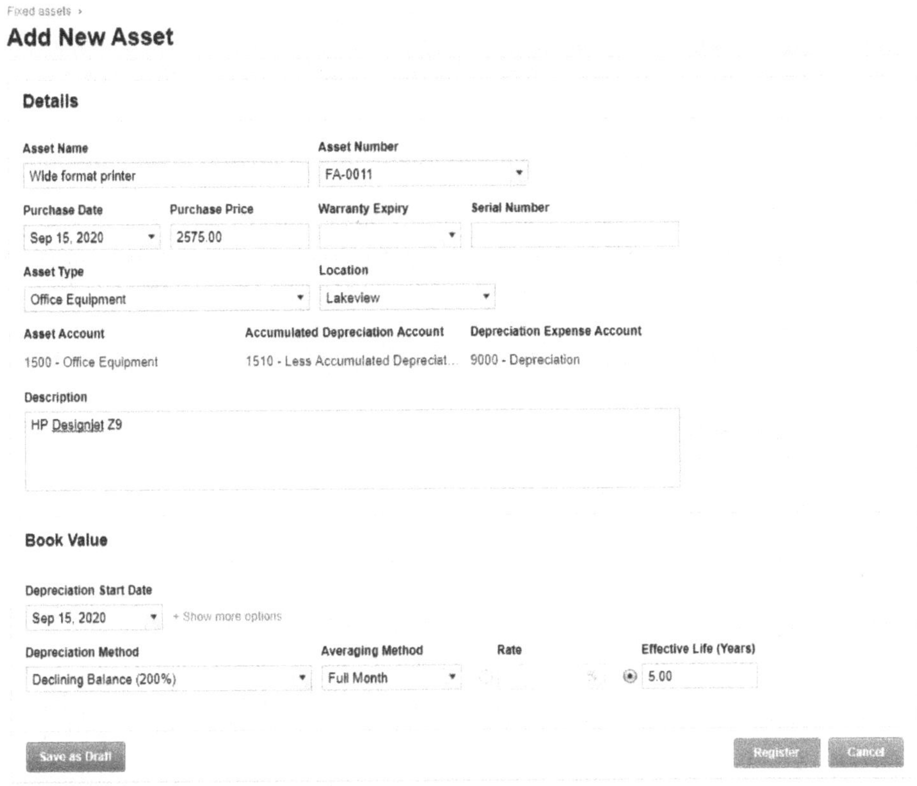

Fixed assets >

## Add New Asset

### Details

**Asset Name**
Wide format printer

**Asset Number**
FA-0011

**Purchase Date**
Sep 15, 2020

**Purchase Price**
2575.00

**Warranty Expiry**

**Serial Number**

**Asset Type**
Office Equipment

**Location**
Lakeview

**Asset Account**
1500 - Office Equipment

**Accumulated Depreciation Account**
1510 - Less Accumulated Depreciat...

**Depreciation Expense Account**
9000 - Depreciation

**Description**
HP Designjet Z9

### Book Value

**Depreciation Start Date**
Sep 15, 2020    + Show more options

**Depreciation Method**
Declining Balance (200%)

**Averaging Method**
Full Month

**Rate**

**Effective Life (Years)**
5.00

Save as Draft                                    Register    Cancel

*Source:* Xero Limited

# Adding Accumulated Depreciation to a New Asset

If an asset added to the register has prior depreciation, the depreciation can be added in the register.

To add a new asset with depreciation:

1. Follow the preceding instructions for manually adding a new asset.

2. In the Book Value section of the screen, enter the **Depreciation Start Date** as the date depreciation was begun outside of Xero. When recognizes a date prior to the Fixed Assets Start Date established in Fixed Asset Settings, a field will appear for entering Accumulated Depreciation as of the start date. Enter the accumulated depreciation.

3. Click **Register**.

## Registering from the Fixed Asset Queue

When a bill, expense claim, or spend money transaction is posted to a general ledger account with a Fixed Asset type, Xero will add a draft asset in the fixed assets module. Since the assets subledger is not directly tied to the general ledger, Xero only suggests the addition, and you must register this draft asset in order to begin depreciating it.

To register an asset drafted from a transaction:

1. Navigate to the **Accounting** tab, then **Advanced**. Select **Fixed Assets**.
2. Open the **Draft** tab and locate the asset created from the transaction. Note that the Description from the transaction will be the asset name. Select the asset by clicking the **Asset Number** in blue.
3. Enter the asset details, including **Asset Type**, and make any updates to the depreciation details at the bottom.
4. Click **Register** (Figure 13.6).

## Copying Fixed Assets

The most efficient way to add an asset with similar details as one that already exists is to make a copy.

To copy an asset:

1. Navigate to the **Accounting** tab, then **Advanced**. Select **Fixed Assets**.
2. Open the **Registered** tab and locate the asset to be duplicated. Select the asset by clicking the **Asset Number** in blue.
3. Use the **Options** pull-down at the top right to select **Copy** (Figure 13.7).
4. Make any changes to the asset details.
5. Click **Register**.

## Importing Assets

When many assets need to be added to Xero, such as during a conversion, the easiest way is to import the assets with details in bulk. Assets are imported using a .csv file type. It is important to understand the structure of the file.

Each row in the spreadsheet is an asset. The only required fields in order for the import file to work are Asset Name and Asset Number; however, only including these fields will result in a lot of additional requirements in Xero in order to finalize the registration of the assets. It is recommended that as much detail be included on the import file as possible. While Asset Type is not a required field, it will make the import faster by applying the default

## FIGURE 13.6

Click Register.

Fixed assets ›

### Add New Asset

**Details**

| Asset Name | | Asset Number | |
|---|---|---|---|
| 2014 Ford Transit Van | | FA-0009 | ▼ |

| Purchase Date | Purchase Price | Warranty Expiry | Serial Number |
|---|---|---|---|
| Dec 01, 2019 ▼ | 18775.00 | ▼ | |

| Asset Type | | Location | |
|---|---|---|---|
| Trucks | ▼ | Midcity | ▼ |

| Asset Account | Accumulated Depreciation Account | Depreciation Expense Account |
|---|---|---|
| 1750 - Trucks | 1760 - Less Accumulated Depreciat... | 9000 - Depreciation |

Description

1D4GP24R44B515773

**Book Value**

Depreciation Start Date

| Dec 01, 2019 ▼ | + Show more options |
|---|---|

| Depreciation Method | Averaging Method | Rate | Effective Life (Years) |
|---|---|---|---|
| Declining Balance (200%) ▼ | Full Month ▼ | | ⦿ 5.00 |

The Depreciation Start Date for this asset is before the Fixed Assets Start Date: Jan 1, 2020

| Accumulated Depreciation as at Dec 31, 2019 | Book Value as at Dec 31, 2019 |
|---|---|
| 626.00 | 18149.00 |

Save as Draft          Register    Cancel

Source: Xero Limited

## FIGURE 13.7

Use the Options pulldown at the top right to select Copy.

Fixed assets › Registered ›

### FA-0011 Wide format printer

**Summary**    Value

Options ▾

Edit

Copy

Dispose

Delete

**Details**

| Asset Name | | Asset Number | |
|---|---|---|---|
| Wide format printer | | FA-0011 | |

| Purchase Date | Purchase Price | Warranty Expiry | Serial Number |
|---|---|---|---|
| Sep 15, 2020 | 2575.00 | | |

Source: Xero Limited

depreciation details; however, you must have set up Asset Types before starting the import. Asset Types were discussed earlier in this chapter.

| Field | Data |
|---|---|
| AssetName | The name of the asset. This name will be used in reports, so it should be something descriptive. |
| AssetNumber | Can be any text, but must be unique. |
| PurchaseDate | The date the asset was purchased in date format. |
| PurchasePrice | The price paid for the asset in number format. This should tie to the cost in the fixed asset account on the general ledger. This will be the depreciable basis, unless there is a cost limit or residual value. |
| AssetType | The exact name of the asset type in Xero that the system will default to for depreciation calculations. |
| Description | A description of the asset. Be detailed here so that assets can be managed correctly. |
| TrackingCategory1 | The category name for tracking (i.e. Region) in exact text. |
| TrackingOption1 | The option name for tracking (i.e. EastSide) in exact text. |
| TrackingCategory2 | The category name for tracking (i.e. Region) in exact text. |
| TrackingOption2 | The option name for tracking (i.e. EastSide) in exact text. |
| SerialNumber | The serial number of the asset in any text. |
| WarrantyExpiry | The expiration date of the asset's warranty in date format. |
| Book_DepreciationStartDate | The date to start depreciation calculations. |
| Book_CostLimit | The portion of the purchase price that will be depreciated in number format. |
| Book_ResidualValue | The value below which the asset will not be depreciated in number format. |
| Book_DepreciationMethod | A method to override the defaults set by Asset Type. Must be exactly this text:<br><br>No Depreciation<br>Straight Line<br>Declining Balance<br>Declining Balance (150%)<br>Declining Balance (200%)<br>Full Depreciation at Purchase |
| Book_AveragingMethod | A method to override the defaults set by Asset Type. Must be exactly this text:<br><br>Actual Days<br>Full Month |

| Field | Data |
|---|---|
| Book_Rate | The percentage in whole numbers to be depreciated each period. If this column is used, do not use the Book_EffectiveLife column. |
| Book_EffectiveLife | The years in whole numbers asset will be depreciated over. If this column is used, do not use the Book_Rate column. |
| Book_OpeningBook AccumulatedDepreciation | The accumulated depreciation associated with the asset up to the Fixed Asset Start Date. Do not use if asset was acquired after Fixed Asset Start Date. |

To import fixed assets in bulk:

1. Navigate to the **Accounting** tab, then **Advanced**. Select **Fixed Assets**.
2. Click the **Import** button (Figure 13.8).
3. Select **Download template** or use the template in the digital resources for this book.
4. Open the import file and enter the asset details. Save the file where it can be easily located.
5. In the Import screen verify Asset Types by using the **Asset Type list** link.
6. Select the date format for the import file. In the United States the format is mm/dd/yyyy.
7. Use the **Browse** button to select the file to import.
8. Click the **Continue** button.
9. Click the **Import** button.

The imported assets will now be visible on the Draft tab of the Fixed Assets screen. They can be registered by opening each asset and using the Register button as covered above, or they can be registered in bulk.

**FIGURE 13.8**

Click the Import button.

## Fixed assets

| + New Asset | Run Depreciation | Import | Export | Settings | Last depreciation: Sep 30, 2020 |

*Source:* Xero Limited

**FIGURE 13.9**

Click the Register button at the top of the listing.

**Fixed assets**

Show Help

| + New Asset | Run Depreciation | Import | Export | Settings | Last depreciation: Sep 30, 2020 |

**Draft (4)**   Registered (3)   Sold & Disposed (0)

| Delete | Register | items selected | | | 4 Items | Asset Name, Number, Type or Description 🔍 |

| | Asset Name | Asset Number | Asset Type | Purchase Date ▾ | Purchase Price |
|---|---|---|---|---|---|
| ☑ | iPad Pro | FA-0004 | | Oct 1, 2019 | 1,350.00 |
| ☑ | Laptop 2 | FA-0002 | | Jul 15, 2019 | 1,875.00 |
| ☑ | Desktop Main Office | FA-0003 | | Jul 15, 2019 | 2,350.00 |
| ☑ | Laptop 1 | FA-0001 | | Jun 30, 2019 | 1,800.00 |

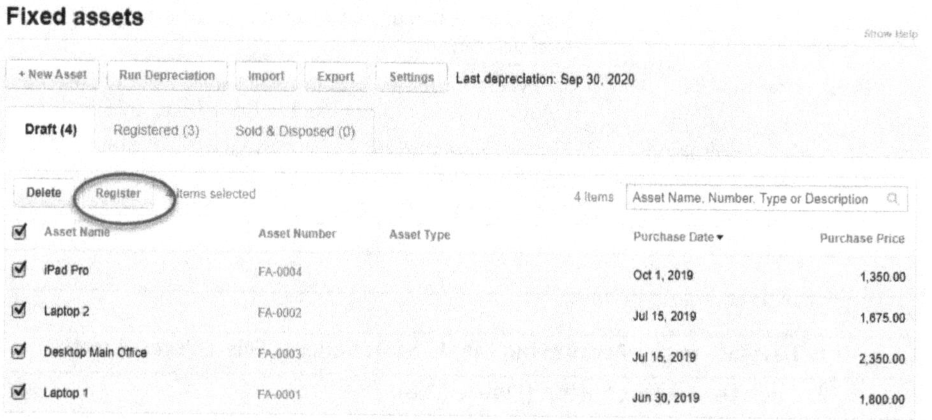

*Source:* Xero Limited

To register more than one asset:

1. Navigate to the **Draft** tab in the Fixed Assets module.
2. Select the assets to be registered by checking the boxes to the left.
3. Click the **Register** button at the top of the listing (Figure 13.9).
4. Xero will offer a summary of the action. Click **Register Assets** to complete.

# Depreciation

In Xero, "running" depreciation means that Xero will calculate the depreciation for the period and post an entry. "Rolling back" depreciation is the undoing of those actions. When depreciation is run, only registered assets are included, not draft or disposed of or sold assets.

## Running Depreciation

To run depreciation:

1. Navigate to the **Accounting** tab, then **Advanced**. Select **Fixed Assets**.
2. Click the **Run Depreciation** button.

**FIGURE 13.10**

Click Confirm at the bottom of the screen.

**Depreciate**

| From | To |
|------|-----|
| Jan 01, 2020 | Sep 30, 2020 ▼ |

| Asset Type | Accumulated Depreciation Account | Depreciation Expense Account | Book Amount |
|------------|----------------------------------|------------------------------|-------------|
| Office Equipment | 1510 - Less Accumulated Depreciation on Office... | 9000 - Depreciation | 2,238.33 |
| Trucks | 1760 - Less Accumulated Depreciation on Trucks | 9000 - Depreciation | 8,229.70 |

Confirm    Cancel

*Source:* Xero Limited

3. Choose the period for which to run depreciation. If the date range is more than one month, entries will be posted for each month separately.

4. Xero will show a summary of the depreciation for each asset account.

5. Click **Confirm** at the bottom of the screen (Figure 13.10).

## Understanding How Depreciation Is Calculated

After years of only offering straight-line depreciation, Xero now allows advisors to choose between many depreciation methods:

- Straight Line
- Declining Balance
- Declining Balance (150%)
- Declining Balance (200%)
- Full Depreciation at Purchase

Additionally, you can choose whether the same amount of depreciation is calculated for each month of the year or if the depreciation will be calculated at a daily rate.

- **Full Month** depreciation: the annual depreciation is divided by 12 and each month has equal deprecation expense.
- **Actual Days** depreciation: the annual depreciation is divided by 365 and each month has depreciation calculated depending on the number of days in the month.

## Rolling Back Depreciation

If an error is made in depreciation, it is simple to correct. Rolling back depreciation in Xero reverses the depreciation entries over the period specified. Depreciation can then be corrected and rerun.

To roll back depreciation:

1. Navigate to the **Accounting** tab, then **Advanced**. Select **Fixed Assets**.
2. Click the **Run Depreciation** button.
3. Click the Rollback Depreciation button at the top right.
4. Choose a date to **Rollback to** (Figure 13.11).
5. Click **Save**.

**FIGURE 13.11**

Choose a date to Rollback to.

# Rollback Depreciation ✕

**Rollback to**

Jan 01, 2020 ▼

## If you click Save, the following will happen

- All depreciation in the Rollback period will be reversed
- Any registered assets will remain registered
- Any disposed assets will remain disposed
- Any deleted assets will remain deleted

Save    Cancel

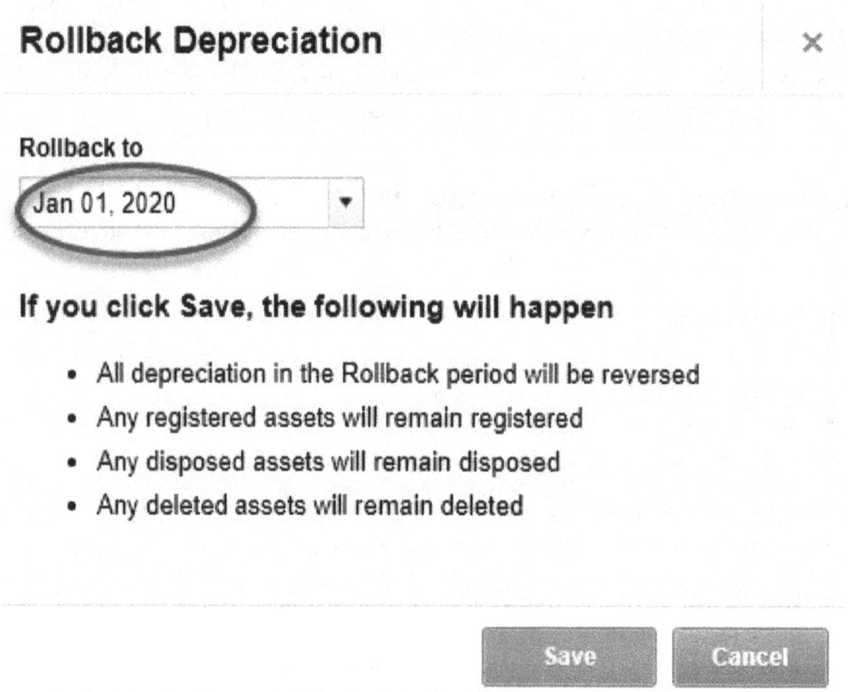

*Source:* Xero Limited

# Disposing Fixed Assets

When assets are sold, donated, or retired, they need to be removed from the fixed asset listing. This is called disposal. A disposal of an asset retains the activity of the asset including the purchase and depreciation, then creates an entry for the disposal. In contrast, deleting an asset removes it and any related depreciation from the system.

To dispose of an asset:

1. Navigate to the **Accounting** tab, then **Advanced**. Select **Fixed Assets**.
2. Open the asset record by clicking the blue asset number.
3. Use the **Options** pull-down to select **Dispose** (Figure 13.12).
4. Enter **Date Disposed**. This will be the date of the journal entry for the disposal.
5. Enter **Sale Proceeds**. For a donation or retirement, enter $0.
6. Enter **Sale Proceeds Account**.
7. Choose whether depreciation should be calculated for the year of disposal. If depreciation will be calculated, you must also include the date through which it will be recorded.
8. Use the **Show Summary** button to see the entries that will be posted.
9. If the summary is correct, click **Review Journals** (Figure 13.13).
10. If there is a gain or loss on the disposal, select the account where it should be posted.
11. Click **Post**.

**FIGURE 13.12**

Use the Options pulldown to select Dispose.

Fixed assets › Registered ›

**FA-0002 Laptop 2**

| Summary | Value |
| --- | --- |

**Details**

| Asset Name | | Asset Number | |
| --- | --- | --- | --- |
| Laptop 2 | | FA-0002 | |

| Purchase Date | Purchase Price | Warranty Expiry | Serial Number |
| --- | --- | --- | --- |
| Jul 15, 2019 | 1675.00 | | |

Options ▾
Edit
Copy
Dispose
Delete

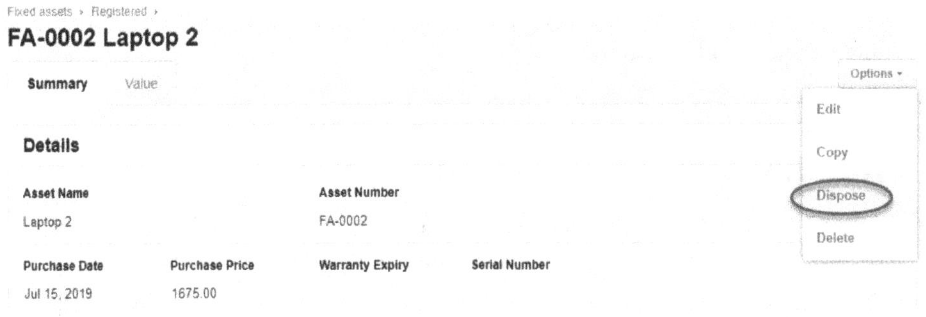

*Source:* Xero Limited

FIGURE 13.13

If the summary is correct, click Review Journals.

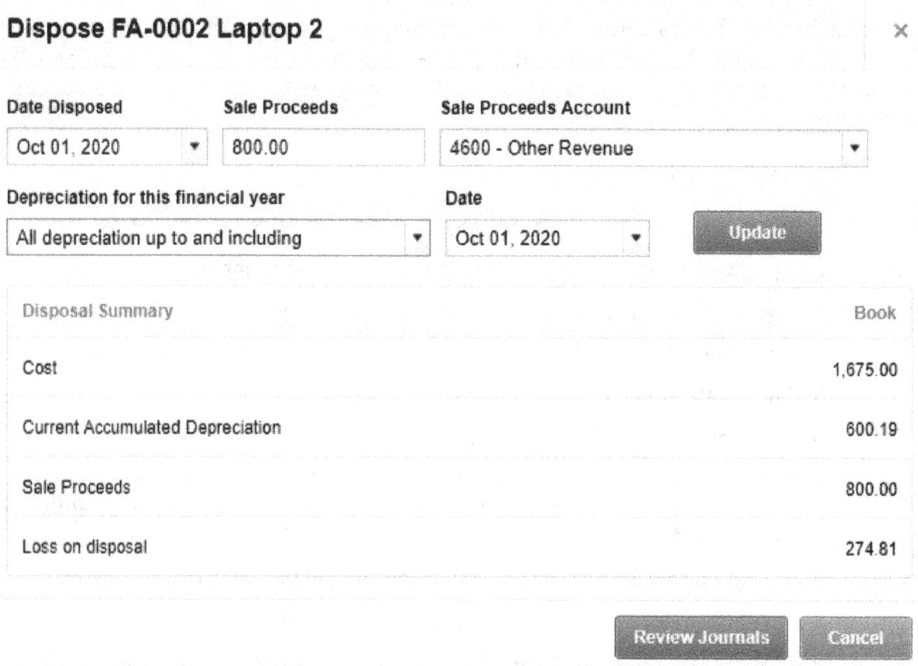

## Dispose FA-0002 Laptop 2 ✕

| Date Disposed | Sale Proceeds | Sale Proceeds Account |
|---|---|---|
| Oct 01, 2020 ▾ | 800.00 | 4600 - Other Revenue ▾ |

| Depreciation for this financial year | Date | |
|---|---|---|
| All depreciation up to and including ▾ | Oct 01, 2020 ▾ | Update |

| Disposal Summary | Book |
|---|---|
| Cost | 1,675.00 |
| Current Accumulated Depreciation | 600.19 |
| Sale Proceeds | 800.00 |
| Loss on disposal | 274.81 |

Review Journals    Cancel

*Source:* Xero Limited

## Deleting Assets

If an asset was added in error, it should be deleted rather than disposed. To delete an asset, use the **Options** pull-down to select **Delete**. Confirm the deletion. Deleting an asset will remove the asset and all depreciation from the fixed asset ledger. The original transaction line will not be affected.

# Reconciling the Asset Subledger

Because the fixed asset subledger is not connected to the general ledger, you must review the reconciliation report regularly to be sure all assets are recorded.

The Fixed Asset Reconciliation report shows the total fixed assets on the general ledger by account compared to the assets that are registered in the system. Any differences will need to be corrected. Generally, differences are attributable to postings made to the fixed assets accounts without registering assets (Figure 13.14).

**FIGURE 13.14**

Any differences will need to be corrected. Generally differences are attributable to postings made to the fixed assets accounts without registering assets.

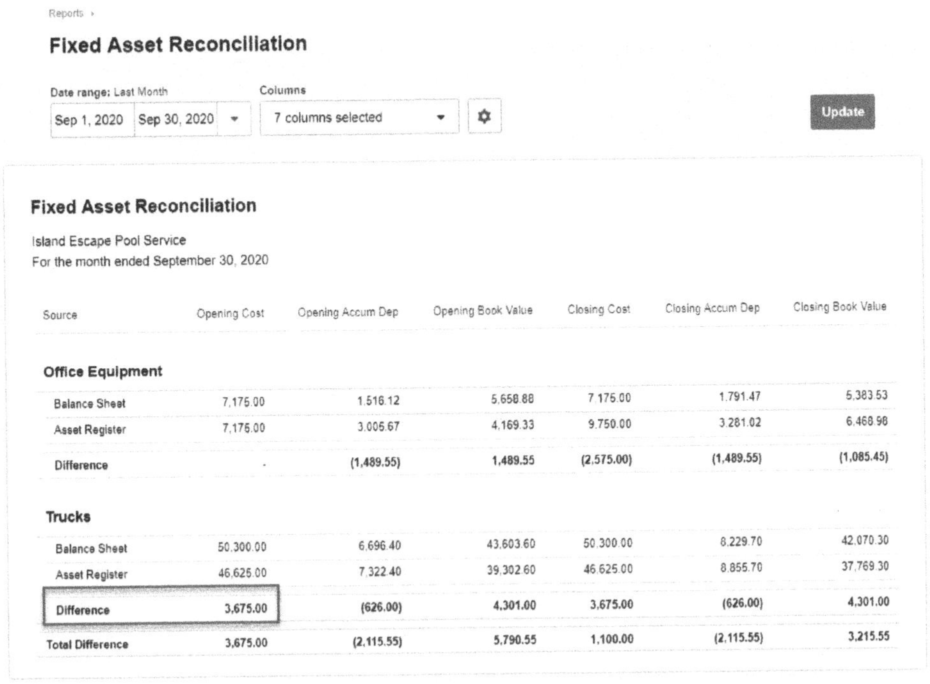

Reports ›

**Fixed Asset Reconciliation**

Date range: Last Month      Columns

| Sep 1, 2020 | Sep 30, 2020 ▾ | 7 columns selected ▾ | ⚙ |

Update

**Fixed Asset Reconciliation**

Island Escape Pool Service
For the month ended September 30, 2020

| Source | Opening Cost | Opening Accum Dep | Opening Book Value | Closing Cost | Closing Accum Dep | Closing Book Value |
|--------|--------------|-------------------|--------------------|--------------|-------------------|--------------------|
| **Office Equipment** | | | | | | |
| Balance Sheet | 7,175.00 | 1,516.12 | 5,658.88 | 7,175.00 | 1,791.47 | 5,383.53 |
| Asset Register | 7,175.00 | 3,005.67 | 4,169.33 | 9,750.00 | 3,281.02 | 6,468.98 |
| Difference | - | (1,489.55) | 1,489.55 | (2,575.00) | (1,489.55) | (1,085.45) |
| | | | | | | |
| **Trucks** | | | | | | |
| Balance Sheet | 50,300.00 | 6,696.40 | 43,603.60 | 50,300.00 | 8,229.70 | 42,070.30 |
| Asset Register | 46,625.00 | 7,322.40 | 39,302.60 | 46,625.00 | 8,855.70 | 37,769.30 |
| Difference | 3,675.00 | (626.00) | 4,301.00 | 3,675.00 | (626.00) | 4,301.00 |
| Total Difference | 3,675.00 | (2,115.55) | 5,790.55 | 1,100.00 | (2,115.55) | 3,215.55 |

*Source:* Xero Limited

To run a Fixed Asset Reconciliation:

1. Navigate to **Accounting**, then **Reports**.
2. Select **Fixed Asset Reconciliation** from the Fixed Asset section.
3. Choose the **Date range** and click **Update**.

# Depreciation Reports

To view the details of depreciation expense posted to the system, use the Depreciation Schedule (Figure 13.15).

To run a Depreciation Schedule:

1. Navigate to **Accounting**, then **Reports**.
2. Select Depreciation Schedule from the Fixed Asset section.
3. Choose the **Date range** and click **Update**.

**FIGURE 13.15**

To view the details of depreciation expense posted to the system, use the Depreciation Schedule.

## Depreciation Schedule

Island Escape Pool Service
For the month ended September 30, 2020

| Name | Cost | Opening Value | Purchases | Disposals | Depreciation | Closing Value |
|---|---|---|---|---|---|---|
| **Office Equipment** | | | | | | |
| Desktop Main Office | 2,350.00 | 1,723.33 | - | - | 78.33 | 1,645.00 |
| iPad Pro | 1,350.00 | - | - | - | - | - |
| Laptop 1 | 1,800.00 | 1,320.00 | - | - | 60.00 | 1,260.00 |
| Laptop 2 | 1,675.00 | 1,126.00 | - | - | 51.19 | 1,074.81 |
| Wide format printer | 2,575.00 | - | 2,575.00 | - | 85.83 | 2,489.17 |
| **Total Office Equipment** | **9,750.00** | **4,169.33** | **2,575.00** | **-** | **275.35** | **6,468.98** |
| **Trucks** | | | | | | |
| 2014 Ford Transit Van | 18,775.00 | 13,309.27 | - | - | 604.97 | 12,704.30 |
| 2018 Ford F150 | 27,850.00 | 25,993.33 | - | - | 928.33 | 25,065.00 |
| **Total Trucks** | **46,625.00** | **39,302.60** | **-** | **-** | **1,533.30** | **37,769.30** |
| **Total** | **56,375.00** | **43,471.93** | **2,575.00** | **-** | **1,808.65** | **44,238.28** |

*Source:* Xero Limited

# Multicurrency

*Xero Partners love when we show them how Xero's multicurrency automates the calculation of exchange rate gains and losses using the industry standard rate aggregator,* XE.com. *This functionality simplifies their reconciliation process and streamlines period-end reporting, saving them countless hours of manual work.*

—*Daniel Gallagher, Partner Consultant Manager at Xero*

One of the biggest benefits of Xero is the availability of multicurrency accounting. Multicurrency accounting is included in the Established Xero subscription.

## About Multicurrency

Multicurrency will allow companies to send invoices and receive bills in more than 160 currencies. Xero uses XE.com to calculate exchange rates hourly.

When a Xero organization is created, a base currency must be chosen. This currency cannot be changed once the organization has been added. Before you create any transactions involving other currencies, you must first add the currencies in Settings. See Chapter 6 for more details.

## Creating a Foreign Currency Transaction

When creating an invoice or bill, the default currency will be your base currency unless you copy an existing transaction, like an invoice or bill, created in another currency. In those cases the currency of the original transaction will be used.

To create a foreign currency transaction:

1. Go to the create screen of a transaction such as an invoice or bill.
2. Complete the fields for the transaction.

3. Before approving the transaction, use the currency pull-down to select the currency to be used (Figure 14.1).

4. Click **Approve**.

The exchange rate at the time the transaction will be shown on the transaction screen. Any unrealized gains or losses will also be shown at the bottom of the screen (Figure 14.2).

## FIGURE 14.1

Before approving the transaction, use the currency pulldown to select the currency to be used.

*Source:* Xero Limited

## FIGURE 14.2

The exchange rate at the time the transaction will be shown on the transaction screen. Any unrealized gains or losses will also be shown at the bottom of the screen.

*Source:* Xero Limited

# Advanced Tools

*In our practice, we use Find and Recode often because it saves so much time when having to adjust multiple transactions. With twelve search conditions to choose from, we can find and recode almost any data point in Xero.*

—Brian Clare, CEO of Blueprint Accounting

Xero has a few tools that are made specifically for accountant or bookkeeper use. These tools can dramatically change financial data and should only be used by people with accounting or bookkeeping experience or knowledge.

## Manual Journal Entries

In Xero, journal entries, as they are known in the United States, are called manual journals. For the most part, Xero is built to minimize the need for manual journal entries. The framework of Xero is to require users to use the tools embedded in the program, rather than to override them with journal entries. This keeps the integrity of important account data. To that point, there are some general ledger accounts that cannot be included in a journal entry, including:

- Bank accounts
- Credit card accounts
- Accounts Payable
- Accounts Receivable

This does not mean that adjustments to these accounts cannot be made. Bank and credit card accounts can be adjusted by using Spend or Receive Money transactions. By adjusting the underlying specific customer invoice or supplier bill, accounts payable and accounts receivable balances are modified. Although not recommended, to make a general adjustment to these accounts, create a Contact with a name such as "Unassigned" and create the appropriate transaction.

Methods for adjusting these accounts are covered in Chapter 10 for bank and credit cards and Chapters 11 and 12 for accounts receivable and accounts payable.

Additionally, there are tools like Find and Recode, discussed later in this chapter, that make reclassification, which would normally be handled with journal entries, more efficient. Even though Xero is built to handle most financial data without using journal entries, there are times when they are necessary. Some examples include:

- Posting depreciation expense for companies not using the fixed asset modules
- Recording payroll expense when the payroll processor used does not integrate with Xero
- Recording year-end accruals for income
- Posting business expenses paid from an owner's personal account
- Accruing interest on loans
- Grossing sales for merchant fees at year-end

## Overview of the Manual Journals Screen

The manual journals (or journal entries) screen is where entries are created and managed. To access manual journals, use the **Accounting** tab to navigate to **Advanced**, then **Manual journals**. At the top are two quick add buttons: **New Journal** and **New Repeating Journal**. There is also a bulk **Import** button. These are discussed below.

There are a series of tabs for different categories of journal entries (Figure 15.1).

- **All** contains all Draft, Posted, Voided, and Archived entries. It does not include Repeating entry templates, but it does include entries that were created by a repeating template and previously posted.
- **Draft** contains entries saved as Drafts and not yet posted.
- **Posted** contains entries that have been posted to the general ledger.
- **Voided** contains entries that have been voided in the system.

**FIGURE 15.1**

There are a series of tabs for different categories of journal entries.

**Source: Xero Limited**

- **Repeating** shows templates for repeating entries.
- **Archive** shows entries that have been archived. Note that archived entries are still posted in the general ledger, and this tab is used to help organize entries, not delete them.

Within each tab are bulk action buttons. For example, in Draft several entries can be selected and posted at once.

## Creating a Journal Entry

A journal entry can be created and posted, or created and saved as a draft for later review. By default, journal entries are recognized in accrual basis reports. To also have a journal entry appear in cash basis reports, that election must be made when the entry is posted.

To create a journal entry:

1. Navigate to the **Accounting** tab, then **Advanced**.
2. Select **Manual journals**.
3. Click **+New Journal**.
4. Enter details in the **Narration** field. This is a description of the purpose of the journal entry. If the **Default narration to journal line description** box is checked, the narration field will also be in the **Description** of each of the postings in the general ledger.
5. If you would like the entry to be included in cash basis reports, check the box **Show journal on cash basis reports**.
6. Add the date that the entry will be posted in the Date field.
7. If you would like the entry to be reversed, enter a date for the reversal in the **Auto Reversing Date** field.
8. In the **Amounts are** field, indicate whether tax should be added or included in the journal lines. The default is **No Tax**.
9. If desired, enter an optional **Description** for each line of the entry.
10. Select a general ledger **Account** for each line of the entry along with the **Tax Rate** for that account.
11. If tracking categories are used, enter categories for the journal lines.
12. Enter a value in the debit or credit column. As you enter new lines, the amount to balance the entry will appear in one of the columns. To change, type over the amounts.
13. If more lines are needed, use the **Add new line button**.
14. Select **Save as draft** to save the entry for further review or **Post** to post the entry (Figure 15.2). Note that debits must equal credits in order to post the entry; however, unbalanced entries can be saved as drafts.

15

**FIGURE 15.2**

Select Save as draft to save the entry for further review or Post to post the entry.

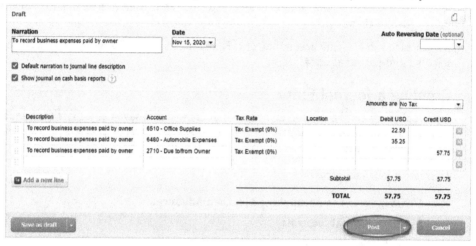

*Source:* Xero Limited

## Deleting or Voiding a Journal Entry

Journal entries made by mistake can be deleted or voided. A draft entry can be deleted, which will remove it entirely from the system. A deleted entry cannot be recovered.

To delete a draft journal entry:

1. Navigate to the **Accounting** tab, then **Advanced**.
2. Select **Manual journals**.
3. Navigate to the **Draft** tab and check the box to the left of the entry.
4. Click the **Delete** button at the top of the listing (Figure 15.3).
5. Confirm the deletion by selecting **OK**.

Posted journal entries can only be voided to remove them from the general ledger. They cannot be deleted.

**FIGURE 15.3**

Click the Delete button at the top of the listing.

*Source:* Xero Limited

To void a draft journal entry:

1. Navigate to the **Accounting** tab, then **Advanced**.
2. Select **Manual journals**.
3. Navigate to the **Posted** tab and check the box to the left of the entry (Figure 15.4).
4. Click the **Void** button at the top of the listing.
5. Confirm the deletion by selecting **OK**.

The voided entry will now be listed in the Voided tab (Figure 15.5). It cannot be recovered, but it can be copied to a new entry by using the **Journal Options** pull-down and **Copy**.

## Archiving a Journal Entry

Some companies will require hundreds of entries. To help organize those entries, Xero allows you to archive posted entries. Archiving an entry will not remove the posting from the general ledger, but acts as a way to store entries in a different tab.

To archive a posted journal entry:

1. Navigate to the **Accounting** tab, then **Advanced**.
2. Select **Manual journals**.

### FIGURE 15.4

Navigate to the Posted tab and check the box to the left of the entry.

*Source:* Xero Limited

### FIGURE 15.5

The voided entry will now be listed in the Voided tab.

*Source:* Xero Limited

15

3. Navigate to the **Posted** tab and check the box to the left of the entry.

4. Click the **Archive** button at the top of the listing.

5. Confirm the deletion by selecting **OK**.

The archived entry will now be listed in the Voided tab. It cannot be recovered, but it can be copied to a new entry by using the **Journal Options** pull-down and **Copy**.

## Editing a Journal Entry

Occasionally, you may need to edit a posted entry.

To edit a posted journal entry:

1. Navigate to the **Accounting** tab, then **Advanced**.

2. Select **Manual journals**.

3. Navigate to the **Posted** tab and open the entry by clicking the blue narration.

4. Use the Journal Options pull-down to select **Edit** (Figure 15.6).

5. Make the needed changes.

6. Click **Post**.

## Copying a Journal Entry

Many companies post similar journal entries every year, such as adjusting depreciation to the tax return deduction or accruing owner paid expenses. Copying a previously posted entry will save time and create consistency from year to year.

**FIGURE 15.6**

Use the Journal Options pulldown to select Edit.

| Posted | | | | | Print PDF | | Journal Options ▲ |
|---|---|---|---|---|---|---|---|
| **Narration** | **Date** | | | | | | Repeat |
| To record business expenses paid by owner | Nov 15, 2020 | | | | | | Reverse |
| | | | | | | | Void |
| Accrual and cash basis | | | | | | Amou | Copy |
| **Description** | | **Account** | **Tax Rate** | **Location** | | Debit US | Edit |
| To record business expenses paid by owner | | 6510 - Office Supplies | Tax Exempt | | | 22.50 | |
| To record business expenses paid by owner | | 6480 - Automobile Expenses | Tax Exempt | | | 35.25 | |
| To record business expenses paid by owner | | 2710 - Due to/from Owner | Tax Exempt | | | | 57.75 |
| | | | | | Subtotal | 57.75 | 57.75 |
| | | | | | **TOTAL** | **57.75** | **57.75** |

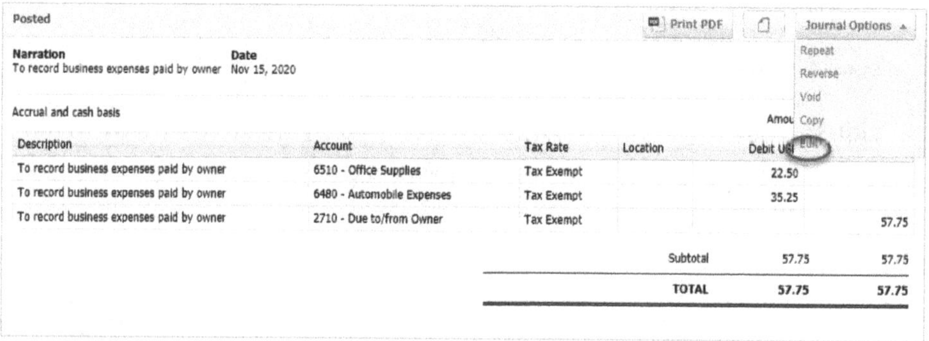

*Source:* Xero Limited

To copy a posted journal entry:

1. Navigate to the **Accounting** tab, then **Advanced**.
2. Select **Manual journals**.
3. Navigate to the **Posted** tab and open the entry by clicking the blue narration.
4. Use the Journal Options pull-down to select **Copy**.
5. Add the posting date and reversing date, if necessary.
6. Update the line amounts.
7. Click **Post**.

## Creating a Repeating Journal Entry

For instances where the same journal entry needs to be made over many periods, such as a monthly depreciation accrual, you can create a repeating journal that can either be created as a draft or posted at a specified cadence. Note that creating a repeating entry is actually crafting a template for generating entries, much like repeating invoice templates. Journal entries are created from the template and then can be found in the appropriate tab of the Manual Journals screen.

To create a repeating journal template:

1. Navigate to the **Accounting** tab, then **Advanced**.
2. Select **Manual journals**.
3. Click the **+New Repeating Journal** button at the top of the screen (Figure 15.7).
4. In **First Journal Date**, choose the date that the first entry should be posted. Note that you can select a date in the past and Xero will create all prior entries, but only to the first day of the previous financial year.

**FIGURE 15.7**

Click the +New Repeating Journal button at the top of the screen.

*Source:* Xero Limited

5. In the **Repeat the journal every** fields, indicate the cadence that the entry should be posted. This can be a number of months or weeks.

6. Add an optional **End Date.**

7. Select whether the entry should be saved as a draft or posted automatically.

8. Enter details in the **Narration** field. This is a description of the purpose of the journal entry. If the **Default narration to journal line description** box is checked, the narration field will also be in the Description of each of the postings in the general ledger. In repeating entries, an **Insert Placeholder** button will appear. This allows the Narration field to include dynamic data that will update for each generated entry. An example of this use would be for a depreciation accrual, where the narration would include the specific month for which the accrual is made. For more details about the fields available for placeholders, see Chapter 11.

9. If you would like the entry to be included in cash basis reports, check the box **Show journal on cash basis reports.**

10. Add the date that the entry will be posted in the Date field.

11. If you would like the entry to be reversed, enter a date for the reversal in the **Auto Reversing Date** field.

12. In the **Amounts are** field, indicate whether tax should be added or included in the journal lines. The default is **No Tax.**

13. If desired, enter an optional **Description** for each line of the entry. Dynamic placeholders can also be added here by using the **Insert Placeholder** pull-down that appears.

14. Select a general ledger **Account** for each line of the entry along with the **Tax Rate** for that account.

15. If tracking categories are used, enter categories for the journal lines.

16. Enter a value in the debit or credit column. As you enter new lines, the amount to balance the entry will appear in one of the columns. To change the amount, type over the amount.

17. If more lines are needed, use the **Add new line button.**

18. Note that you can view samples of any placeholders added in the Narration or Description fields by clicking the **Preview placeholders** link.

19. Click **Save** (Figure 15.8).

## Posting a Cash-Only Journal Entry

Journal entries are automatically included in accrual basis financials. There are times when a company may need to record a cash-only journal entry, but unfortunately, Xero has no option for this. You can make such an entry, however, with a workaround. You will post the entry needed for cash basis reporting as a normal journal entry, electing to show the entry on cash basis reports, then make an offsetting entry to only accrual basis books.

**FIGURE 15.8**

Click Save.

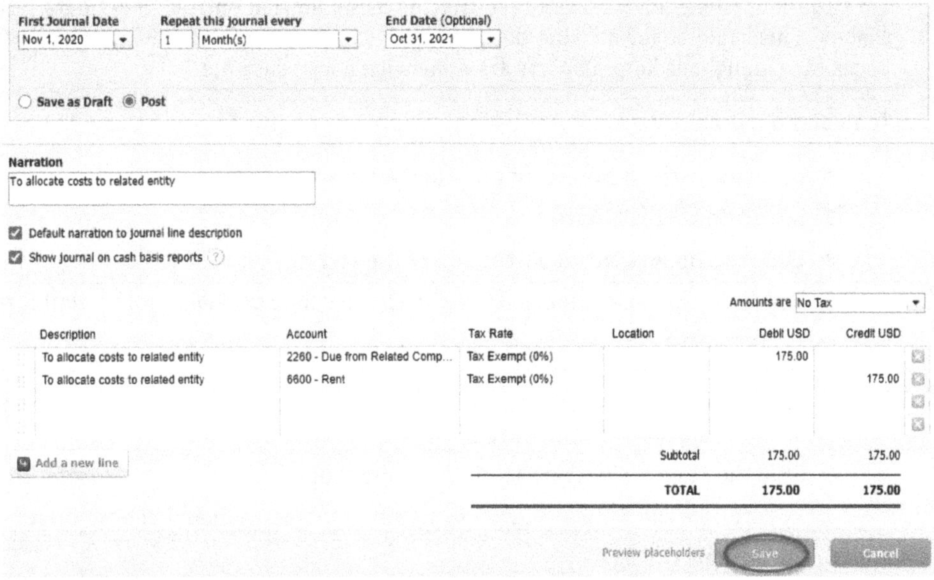

*Source:* Xero Limited

To post a cash-only entry:

1. Navigate to the **Accounting** tab, then **Advanced**.
2. Select **Manual journals**.
3. Click the **+New Journal** button at the top of the screen.
4. Enter the information for the cash basis entry to be posted.
5. Be sure that **Show journal on cash basis reports** is checked.
6. Click **Post**.
7. Find the posted entry in the **Posted** tab of the Manual journals screen and open it.
8. Use the **Journal Options** pull-down to select **Copy**.
9. Enter a date the same as the posted entry.
10. Uncheck the **Show journal on cash basis reports** box.
11. Enter reversing amounts for all of the lines in the entry. Where there is debit value, enter the same amount as credit and vice versa.
12. Click **Post**.

15

## Importing Journal Entries

Although Xero is built to reduce the need for journal entries as much as possible, there are situations where advisors can save time by using journal entries to get data into the system. This could be for booking detailed sales data or entering monthly comparative balances. As throughout Xero, imports are done with a .csv data file.

To import a journal entry:

1. Navigate to the **Accounting** tab, then **Advanced**.
2. Select **Manual journals**.
3. Click the **Import** button at the top of the screen.
4. Download the import template or use the template provided in the digital resources for this book.
5. Complete the data import file, entering a narration, date, account code, tax rate, and amount for each line. In the Amount column, positive values are treated as debits and negative values are treated as credits.
6. Save the import file where it can be easily found.
7. In Xero, use the **Browse** button to locate the import file and choose **Open**.
8. Click **Import**.
9. Xero will show an alert summarizing that a draft journal will be imported. Select **Complete Import**.
10. The new entry can be found in the **Draft** tab of the manual journals screen. To post the entry, select the box to the left of the entry line and select **Post** at the top of the listing.

Importing manual journal entries can be used as a workaround for unavailable or low-quality integrations, but be aware that you may not be able to import entries with more than about 1,000 lines.

Multiple entries can be uploaded in the same file. Populate the **Narration** and **Date** fields for the first line of each entry. Xero will assume lines with blank fields to be the same as the row above. There is an example in the digital resources.

# Find and Recode

If Cash Coding is bulk coding, then Find and Recode is bulk recoding, but it is also much more. Find and Recode is a query and action tool, but many advisors find the query piece singularly valuable. It provides the most customizable search tool in Xero, regardless of the recoding half of the feature. However, used with recoding, it is an invaluable tool in modifying financial data in the system. Many advisors find this tool one of the most powerful in small business accounting for efficient monthly bookkeeping.

## Overview of the Find and Recode Screen

To access Find and Recode, use the **Accounting** tab to navigate to **Advanced**, then **Find and recode**. Upon its first use, the Find and Recode screen does not appear to have much to it. There is a **Find and recode** button that launches the actions, and there is a **History of Recoded Transactions** listing.

To fully understand Find and Recode, it is important to break it into its component parts. The first section is the query. The second part is the bulk editing of data.

## Find and Recode Queries

The query section is where qualifiers are set. Use the **Find and recode** button to enter the search criteria. Conditions for a search can be set to meet **Any** or **All** of the conditions. The condition options are nearly limitless.

| Condition | Qualifier | Explanation |
|---|---|---|
| Type | IS or IS NOT | A specific type of transaction in the system, including sales documents, purchases documents, spend and receive moneys, expense claims, and journal entries. More than one type can be selected. |
| Status | IS or IS NOT | Transactions that are Draft, Awaiting Approval, Awaiting Payment, or Paid. In general, this status is for invoices and bills; however, selecting Awaiting Payment will also include spend and receive money transactions. More than one status can be selected. |
| Account | IS or IS NOT | A specific general ledger account but not bank accounts and other system accounts. More than one account can be selected. |
| Bank account | IS or IS NOT | A bank or credit card account. More than one account can be selected. |
| Date | IS BETWEEN, IS, IS BEFORE, or IS AFTER | Search for transaction dates within a range, on a specific date, before a specific date, or after a specific date. Transactions prior to a lock date for all users cannot be searched. |
| Reconciled between | A specific date range | Transactions that were reconciled between two dates. |
| Transaction total | IS EQUAL TO, IS LESS THAN, or IS MORE THAN | Transactions in which the total meets parameters. Note that individual lines, such as invoice or bill lines, that meet the criteria will not be shown unless the total transaction total does. |

15

| Condition | Qualifier | Explanation |
|---|---|---|
| Tax Rate | IS or IS NOT | An active or archived tax rate. More than one rate can be selected. |
| Enter By | IS or IS NOT | The user who created the transaction. More than one user can be selected. |
| Contact | IS or IS NOT | The contact for the transaction, but limited to active and not archived contacts. More than one contact can be selected. |
| Invoice Number/Reference | IS or CONTAINS | A specific value found in an invoice number or the reference of an invoice or bill. |
| Tracking Category | IS or IS NOT | A category option. More than one option can be selected. |

The results of a search will be shown on the screen in a table. Each row is a transaction that meets the criteria set in the search. The icon on the left of the transaction represents the type of transaction.

| [SM] | Spend Money |
|---|---|
| [RM] | Receive Money |
| [AR] | Accounts Receivable/Invoice |
| [AP] | Accounts Payable/Bill |
| [CR] | Credit Note |
| [MJ] | Manual Journal |
| [EC] | Expense Claim |

The columns represent general journal details rather than bank details. When a bank line is matched to a general ledger entry, the ledger side details will be shown. For example, the Contact/Narration field will display the contact used in reconciliation or in creating an invoice or bill, not the bank's payee field. The same applies with the Reference and Description fields. The columns can be sorted by clicking on the blue column header.

When searching using the Bank Account criteria, Xero will show all transactions for that bank account, including the offsetting coding line (Figure 15.9). This search can provide a substitute for reports in other accounting packages that list a register or split for the bank account transactions, which is not a report available in Xero. In this way, the query portion of Find and recode should not be underestimated as a sophisticated, stand-alone search tool. In fact, the results display can sometimes give more information than reports.

**FIGURE 15.9**

When searching using the Bank Account criteria, Xero will show all transactions for that bank account, including the offsetting coding line.

*Source:* Xero Limited

## Recoding Transactions

Once transactions are searched, they can be edited in bulk. While Xero calls this "recoding" more transaction details than just the general ledger coding can be edited, this is a powerful tool to fine-tuning data in the system. Transactions can be recoded in one of two ways: the source data can be changed or an offsetting journal entry can be made.

Many times a recoding will be necessary to correct a transaction or add detail that was not available at the time of reconciliation, such as tracking categories. In these cases, recoding the original transaction would be the appropriate method. Recoding the source transaction will not change the original date of the transaction.

To recode a source transaction:

1. Navigate to the **Accounting** tab, then **Advanced**.
2. Select **Find and recode**.
3. Click the **Find and recode** button and search for transactions using conditions (Figure 15.10).
4. Locate the transaction or transactions to recode. Sorting by column header can be helpful. Select the transactions by clicking the box to the left of the line.
5. Use the **Recode** pull-down to access **Recode source transactions** (Figure 15.11).
6. On the next screen complete any fields that should be updated. To add or update a tracking category, use the +**Add** link.
7. Click the **Review** button. Xero will warn you that the recode process can take several minutes and cannot be undone. Click **Confirm** to continue.

15

**FIGURE 15.10**

Click the Find and recode button and search for transactions using conditions.

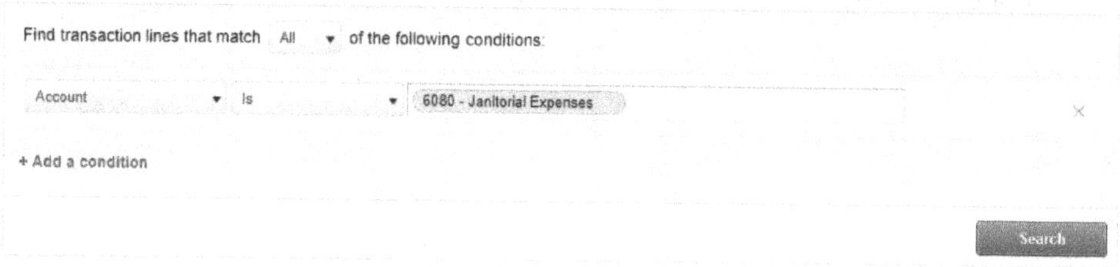

Find transaction lines that match   All   ▼   of the following conditions:

Account   ▼   Is   ▼   [ 6080 - Janitorial Expenses ]   ×

+ Add a condition

Search

*Source:* Xero Limited

**FIGURE 15.11**

Use the Recode pulldown to access Recode source transactions.

| Recode ▼ | 1 item selected | Select all 1 items | | | | | | | | | |
|---|---|---|---|---|---|---|---|---|---|---|---|
| Recode source transactions | | Narration | Inv#/Ref | Inv Ref | Bank Acct | Transaction Total | Description | Account | Tax Rate | Location | Line Total |
| Recode with a manual journal | | tgue | 652 | | | 75.00 | Cleaning | 6080 - Janitorial Expenses | Tax Exempt | | 75.00 |

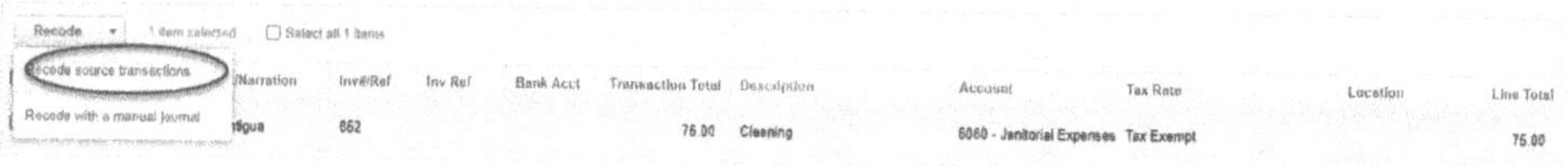

*Source:* Xero Limited

If adjustments need to be made on a date different than the original transaction date or there needs to be an audit trail of changes, use the option to recode with a manual journal. This will not change the underlying source transactions but will instead use those transactions to draft an offsetting journal entry. The date will be adjustable.

To recode a transaction with a manual journal:

1. Navigate to the **Accounting** tab, then **Advanced**.
2. Select **Find and recode**.
3. Click the **Find and recode** button and search for transactions using the query.
4. Locate the transaction or transactions to recode. Sorting by column header can be helpful. Select the transactions by clicking the box to the left of the line.
5. Use the **Recode** pull-down to access **Recode with a manual journal**.
6. On the next screen complete any fields that should be updated. To add or update a tracking category, use the **+Add** link.
7. Xero will create a draft offsetting journal entry, using a default date of today that can be changed (Figure 15.12).
8. Click **Post**.

## Viewing the History of Recoded Transactions

The easiest way to view all recoded transactions included in Find and Recode is the History of Recoded Transactions listing. Every instance of recoding transactions will be

**FIGURE 15.12**

Xero will create a draft offsetting journal entry, using a default date of today that can be changed.

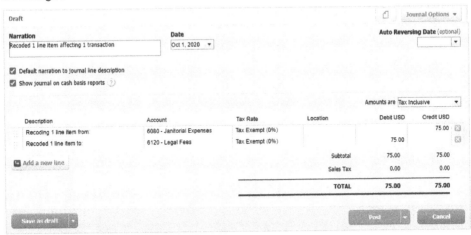

*Source:* Xero Limited

recorded here. To see the details of the transactions, click the **Summary** link within the listing.

The **Recode Summary** includes the date of the recode, the user who completed the recode, a link to the original search query, listing of items that were recoded, the status of the recode, how many transactions were affected, and the date range.

Data about recoded transactions is also included in **History and Notes**, which is covered later in this chapter.

# Assurance Dashboard

The Assurance Dashboard was built to help advisors keep control over the integrity of the accounting data. It allows accountants and bookkeepers to see, at a glance, any anomalies or inconsistencies. To access the Assurance Dashboard, use the **Accounting** tab to navigate to **Advanced**, then **Assurance Dashboard**. There are four tabs: **User Activity**, **Bank Accounts**, **Contacts**, and **Invoices & Bills**.

## User Activity

The user activity tab shows a tile for each user with a heat map of that user's activity in Xero (Figure 15.13). Each day is represented by a square on the tile, with days of no activity shown in gray and days of activity shown in increasingly darker shades of blue. By hovering over any square, you can see the time of day the user was active and how many transactions were affected in major categories.

15

**FIGURE 15.13**

The user activity tab shows a tile for each user with a heatmap of that user's activity in Xero.

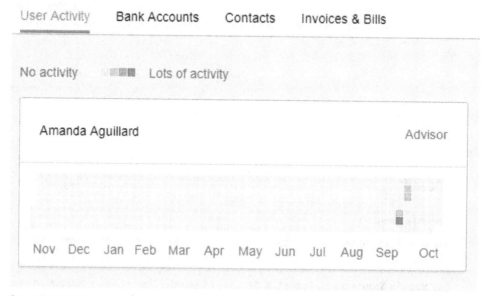

*Source:* Xero Limited

**FIGURE 15.14**

Each line in the listing will show the transaction details, but also the user who modified the data and the date of the modification.

*Source:* Xero Limited

## Bank Accounts

The bank accounts tab shows history of two types of actions that are unusual and can cause reconciliation problems: deleted statement lines and manually reconciled transactions. As discussed previously, these are methods used to correct errors in bank data transfer, but if used erroneously can create bank reconciliation issues. Each line in the listing will show the transaction details, but also the user who modified the data and the date of the modification (Figure 15.14).

## Contacts

As discussed in Chapter 7, you can save bank account details in a contact record for the purpose of creating batch payment files to transmit to the company's bank. Clearly, bank account details are sensitive and any manipulation should be reviewed. The contacts tab shows any changes made to a contact's bank account details or if there is more than one contact with the same account details. Contacts listed can be clicked to redirect to the contact record for further review.

## Invoices and Bills

The invoices and bills tab shows instances of backdating invoices or bills. Backdating of these documents could indicate unethical behavior, but at a minimum distorts the accuracy of financial statements. Use the **by more than number of days** pull-down to filter for transactions. Although there could be valid reasons for backdating, you should be aware of these occurrences.

# History and Notes

As discussed in previous chapters, Xero will post a time and date stamped detail of changes at the bottom of nearly every detail screen, such as noting creation, edits, and payments of invoices. To see a complete detail of activity for the entire organization, rather than a specific transaction, Xero provides the History and Notes screen. In some other software, this is referred to as an audit log. To access History and Notes, use the **Accounting** tab to navigate to **Advanced**, then **History and notes**.

The default view shows changes to the records in Xero in chronological order, with the most recent changes at the top of the list. The Item field shows the transactions or change type in blue, which allows you to open the transaction from this screen.

The date range can be changed by using the pull-down, to select **Today**, **Last week**, **Last month**, **Last year**, or a Custom range. Last week, last month, and last year include today and backward.

The **Items** pull-down allows you to filter the history by changed item or transaction type. Only one item can be selected at a time.

The **User** pull-down allows you to filter by the user who initiated the change or transaction. Only one user can be selected at a time (Figure 15.15).

Xero also provides a blank **Filter results** field that can be used to search for specific text in the system, such as a particular word or note.

It should be pointed out that History and Notes is focused on alterations to the financial data and does not show changes to settings, reporting, printing, or exporting.

15

**FIGURE 15.15**

The User pulldown allows you to filter by the user who initiated the change or transaction. Only one user can be selected at a time.

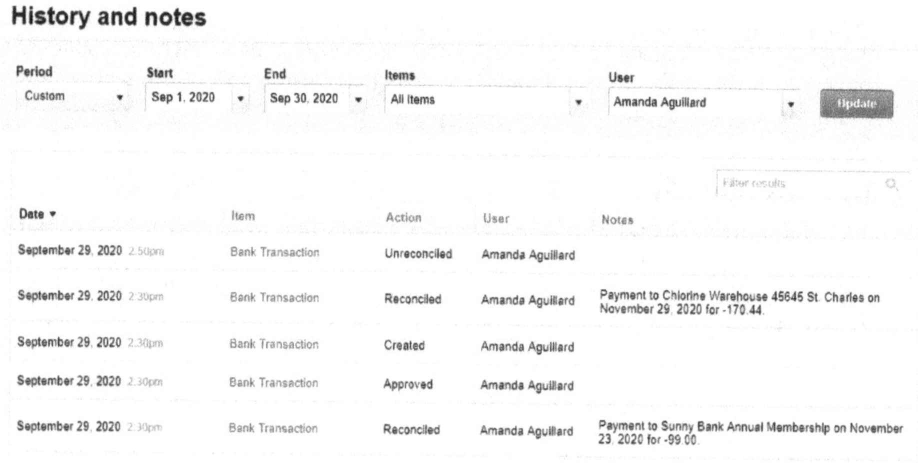

### History and notes

| Period | Start | End | Items | User | |
|---|---|---|---|---|---|
| Custom ▾ | Sep 1, 2020 ▾ | Sep 30, 2020 ▾ | All Items ▾ | Amanda Aguillard ▾ | Update |

Filter results 🔍

| Date ▾ | Item | Action | User | Notes |
|---|---|---|---|---|
| September 29, 2020 2:50pm | Bank Transaction | Unreconciled | Amanda Aguillard | |
| September 29, 2020 2:30pm | Bank Transaction | Reconciled | Amanda Aguillard | Payment to Chlorine Warehouse 45645 St. Charles on November 29, 2020 for -170.44. |
| September 29, 2020 2:30pm | Bank Transaction | Created | Amanda Aguillard | |
| September 29, 2020 2:30pm | Bank Transaction | Approved | Amanda Aguillard | |
| September 29, 2020 2:30pm | Bank Transaction | Reconciled | Amanda Aguillard | Payment to Sunny Bank Annual Membership on November 23, 2020 for -99.00. |

*Source:* Xero Limited

# Exporting Accounting Data

Xero does not have a feature to allow for full backup of an accounting file. For advisors who want to save accounting data outside of the platform, the best practice is to export certain portions of the data. Nearly all reports can be exported, as well as the databases of functions.

Data that can be exported from Xero include:

- Detailed general ledger
- Chart of accounts
- Contacts
- Invoices
- Bills
- Fixed assets
- Inventory items

In general, the export function is found in the module of Xero that holds the data. For reports, run the report desired and use the **Export** button at the bottom of the screen.

In addition to downloading parts of the accounting data, there are also preformatted export templates for certain products, including Crosslink, ProSeries, and TaxACT.

To export data preformatted for another software:

1. Navigate to **Accounting**, then **Advanced**.
2. Select **Export accounting data**.
3. Use the **Select product** pull-down to choose the software format.
4. Select the date or date range and choose **Cash basis** if the data should be on a cash basis.
5. Click the **Download** link.

15

# Reporting

*As an outsourced Controller and CFO, the depth of Xero's reporting functionality through their multiple Tracking Categories provides the detailed information I need to advise my clients effectively.*

*—Dan Schmidt, Founder of EBCFO*

Over the last few years, Xero has improved the interface of many of the reports in the system. These reports look different from the reports in the original product and are generally referred to as "New" reports. For reports where both new and original versions exist, this chapter will cover the new report unless there is a reason to mention the original version.

There are a few dashboards and tools that are included in the Reports list that are covered in Chapter 18 instead, including Budget Manager, Business Snapshot, and Business Performance.

## Overview of Reporting

The Reports screen can be accessed by navigating to **Accounting**, then **Reports**. Note that the default view under **Accounting** shows some favorited reports under the heading "Accounting reports," but this is only a very small sample (Figure 16.1).

To include or remove a report from the selection under Accounting reports, toggle the star next to the report. If the star is blue, it will be shown as a favorited report in the **Accounting** tab (Figure 16.2).

The Reports screen has six headers at the top, each representing a category or status that will be covered in this chapter:

- **Summary:** all reports that can be run in Xero
- **Custom:** versions of reports that have been customized for this organization
- **Advisor:** access to practice level report templates (covered in Chapter 3)
- **Drafts:** reports that have been run, but not finalized

**FIGURE 16.1**

The Reports screen can be accessed by navigating to Accounting, then Reports. Note that the default view under Accounting shows some favorited reports under the heading "Accounting reports," but this is only a very small sample.

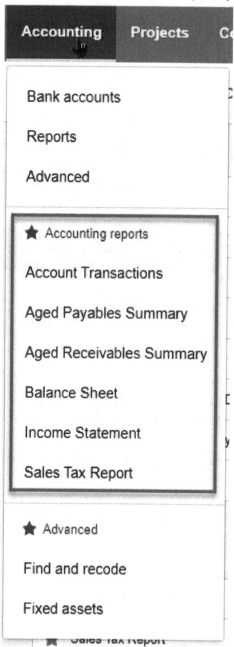

*Source:* Xero Limited

**FIGURE 16.2**

To include or remove a report from the selection under Accounting reports, toggle the star next to the report. If the star is blue, it will be shown as a favorited report in the Accounting tab.

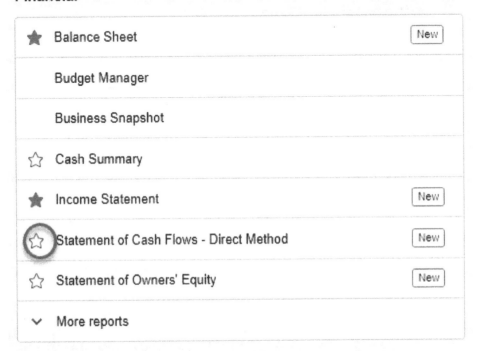

## Financial

Source: Xero Limited

- **Published:** reports that have been run and saved
- **Archived:** reports that were published, but are no longer needed.

The Summary tab shows every report in Xero, including new and classic versions. The screen is divided into eight sections, representing different functions in Xero. It is important to note that the sections are truncated, and you should click the **More reports** pull-down at the bottom of each tile to see the complete list of reports.

The Reports screen also has a **Search** bar for easy location of a desired report.

# Generating Reports

Within new reports, there are two different interfaces for report creation. Each will be explained below.

There are reports that are formula-based and are generally used by businesses. These are the standard financial reports and have fully editable layouts. These are:

- Balance Sheet
- Income Statement
- Statement of Cash Flows—Direct Method
- Statement of Owners' Equity
- Blank Report

Other new reports are transactional or data listing reports and have limited customization. These include Account Transaction reports and Accounts Receivable and Payable reports.

A few things to mention about the default layout of reports found in the Reports section of Xero:

- The order of the accounts on the report is first based on the account types associated with the general ledger accounts.
- Once the accounts are grouped by account type, they are presented in alphabetical order.

In contrast, report templates found in Xero HQ are laid out by report codes.

To run a new report:

1. Navigate to **Accounting**, then **Reports**.
2. Select the desired report from the menu by clicking the title.
3. At the top of the report, the date (or date range) can be changed by using the **Date** pull-down (Figure 16.3). Xero offers common statement dates or periods, such as End of Last Month, End of Last Quarter, and End of Last Financial Year. To enter a custom date or range, type directly in the date field.
4. To add comparative periods to the report as columns, use the **Comparison period(s)** pull-down (Figure 16.4). Select the numbers of prior periods to include on the report.
5. The **Filter** button allows you to filter the report data for only specific tracking categories (Figure 16.5). The report will be created to include only data for the category options selected. You may wish to show one or more categories as columns within a report. That will be covered later in this chapter.
6. The gear icon allows further customization of the report (Figure 16.6). Use it to select either **Accrual** or **Cash** basis, as well as whether to **Show decimals**. On the Income Statement there is also a **Show percentage of Income** option, which adds a column to the report.
7. Once all options have been selected, click the **Update** button to generate the report.

**FIGURE 16.3**

At the top of the report, the date (or date range) can be changed by using the Date pull-down. (Figure 16.3) Xero offers common statement dates or periods, such as End of Last Month, End of Last Quarter and End of Last Financial Year.

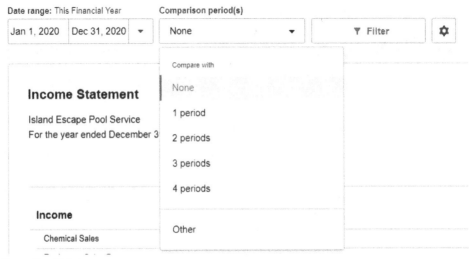

Reports ›

**Income Statement**

Date range: This Financial Year    Comparison period(s)

| Jan 1, 2020 | Dec 31, 2020 | ▾ | None | ▾ | ▼ Filter | ✿ | | Update |

| This Month | Oct 2020 |
| This Quarter | Oct 1 - Dec 31 2020 |
| This Financial Year | Jan 1 - Dec 31 2020 |
| Last Month | Sep 2020 |
| Last Quarter | Jul 1 - Sep 30 2020 |
| Last Financial Year | Jan 1 - Dec 31 2019 |
| Month to Date | Oct 1, 2020 |
| Quarter to Date | Oct 1, 2020 |
| Year to Date | Jan 1 - Oct 1 2020 |

**Income Statement**

Island Escape Pool Servi
For the year ended Dece

2020

**Income**

| Chemical Sales | 64.88 |
| Equipment Sales Revenu | 7,858.43 |
| Interest Income | (105.00) |
| Recurring Pool Cleaning | 2,183.93 |
| **Total Income** | **10,002.24** |

*Source:* Xero Limited

**FIGURE 16.4**

To add comparative periods to the report as columns, use the Comparison period(s) pull-down. (Figure 16.4) Select the numbers of prior periods to include on the report.

**Income Statement**

Date range: This Financial Year    Comparison period(s)

| Jan 1, 2020 | Dec 31, 2020 | ▾ | None | ▾ | ▼ Filter | ✿ |

Compare with

None
1 period
2 periods
3 periods
4 periods

Other

**Income Statement**

Island Escape Pool Service
For the year ended December 3

**Income**

Chemical Sales

*Source:* Xero Limited

The Filter button allows you to filter the report data for only specific tracking categories.

**Location**  ✕

☐ All

☐ Lakeview

☐ Midcity

☐ Unassigned

Cancel  Apply

*Source:* Xero Limited

Some reports have a slightly older interface. Instead of a gear icon, there will be a **Report Settings** link. Open this link to access options like accrual or cash basis, show decimals, and filter for tracking categories.

# Editing Report Layouts

The report layout editor in Xero allows you to completely customize the most used financial reports. The layout editor is accessed by opening a report and clicking the **Edit layout** button in the bottom right corner (Figure 16.7).

## Overview of the Report Layout Editor

At the top of the screen are icons to add or modify sections of the report (Figure 16.8). They include:

- Adding a text block
- Adding a schedule
- Adding a footer

**FIGURE 16.6**

The gear icon allows further customization of the report.

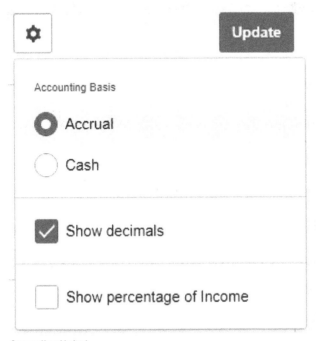

*Source:* Xero Limited

**FIGURE 16.7**

The report layout editor in Xero allows you to completely customize the most used financial reports. The layout editor is accessed by opening a report and clicking the Edit layout button in the bottom right corner.

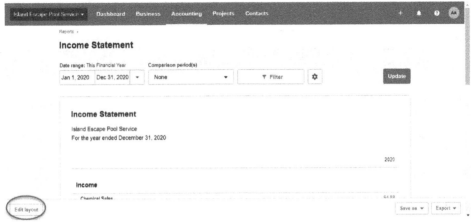

*Source:* Xero Limited

**FIGURE 16.8**

At the top of the screen are icons to add or modify sections of the report.

*Source:* Xero Limited

- Inserting rows
- Inserting columns
- Inserting a page break
- Move a section up
- Move a section down
- Delete a section

Another thing to note on this screen is that each component of the report, such as column header, group titles, and general ledger lines, can be selected by clicking on the component. When selected, a settings screen will appear on the right (Figure 16.9).

## Rearranging Report Rows and Columns

It is not obvious in the report layout editor, but columns and rows can be rearranged within the report easily (Figure 16.10). Select the column or row title and drag to reposition. Click **Done** to save and exit.

## Adding a Text Block

**Text blocks** can be added to reports for narratives or lists. The default placement for the text block is at the bottom of the report, but it can be moved using the up or down arrows at the top of the screen. A text block can include normal text, a table, bullets, or a numbered list (Figure 16.11). It can also have an optional heading or a series of numbered headings.

**FIGURE 16.9**

Another thing to note on this screen is that each component of the report, such as column header, group titles and general ledger lines, can be selected by clicking on the component. When selected, a settings screen will appear on the right.

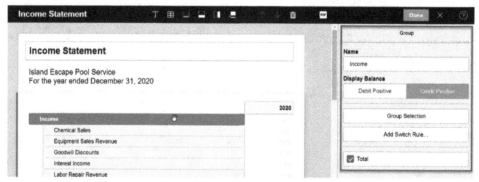

*Source:* Xero Limited

**FIGURE 16.10**

It is not obvious in the report layout editor, but columns and rows can be rearranged within the report easily.

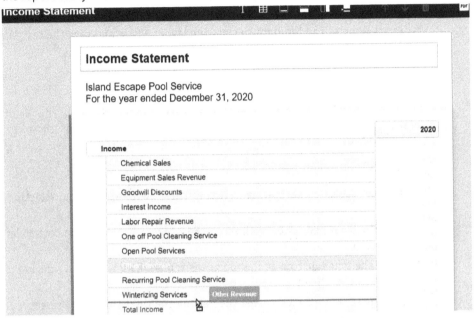

*Source:* Xero Limited

**FIGURE 16.11**

Text blocks can be added to reports for narratives or lists. The default placement for the text block is at the bottom of the report, but it can be moved using the up or down arrows at the top of the screen. A text block can include normal text, a table, bullets or a numbered list.

*Source:* Xero Limited

To add a text block on a report:

1. Open the report by navigating to **Accounting**, then **Reports**, and selecting the report.

2. Open the layout editor by clicking the **Edit layout** button at the bottom left of the screen.

3. Select the text icon at the top of the screen. Xero will add a text block at the bottom of the screen.

4. Choose whether the **Heading** should be Numbered, Standard (without a number), or None by making a selection on the right.

5. Type the copy to be included in the text block. Use the **Formatting** options on the right.

6. Select **Done** in the top right to close the layout editor and save the text block.

To delete a text block, select the block and use the trash icon on the top.

## Adding a Schedule

A **schedule** is a listing of accounts, presumably other than ones listed in the report itself, and their balances. Some advisors use schedules on income statements to show key balance sheet account balances, like cash or receivables.

To add a schedule on a report:

1. Open the report by navigating to **Accounting**, then **Reports**, and selecting the report.

2. Open the layout editor by clicking the **Edit layout** button at the bottom left of the screen.

3. Select the schedule icon at the top of the screen. Xero will add a schedule at the bottom of the screen.

4. Give the schedule a name using the field on the right side of the screen.

5. Choose whether you want the balances to display debits or credits as positive amounts.

6. Click the **Add Accounts** button to choose which accounts to include on the schedule (Figure 16.12). Choose the accounts by checking the box on the left and click **Update.**

7. Choose whether to show a **Total** of accounts and a **Numbered Heading** for the schedule by using the checkboxes on the right.

8. Select **Done** in the top right to close the layout editor and save the schedule.

To delete a schedule, select the schedule and use the trash icon on the top.

## Adding a Footer

Footers can be added to the bottom of each page of a report. Advisors will commonly use footers for notes or disclaimers.

To add a footer to a report:

1. Open the report by navigating to **Accounting**, then **Reports**, and selecting the report.

2. Open the layout editor by clicking the **Edit layout** button at the bottom left of the screen.

**FIGURE 16.12**

Click the Add Accounts button to choose which accounts to include on the schedule.

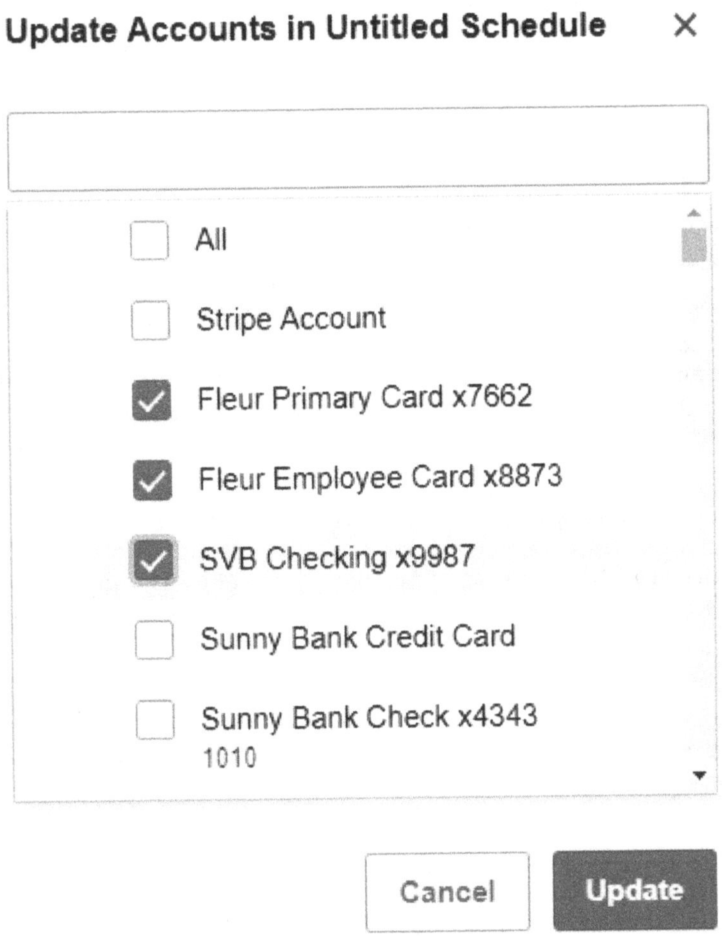

Source: Xero Limited

3. Select the footer icon at the top of the screen. Xero will add a footer at the bottom of the screen. Note that even though the footer is shown once, it will appear on each page of multipage reports.

4. Type the footer copy in the space provided (Figure 16.13). Use the **Formatting** tools on the right to format or highlight the text.

5. Select **Done** in the top right to close the layout editor and save the schedule.

To delete a footer, select the footer and use the trash icon on the top.

**FIGURE 16.13**

Type the footer copy in the space provided.

Report Footer Text...

*Source:* Xero Limited

## Adding Rows

Rows can be added to financial reports, either for grouping general ledger accounts or to embed a formula.

Grouping of accounts by creating **groups rows** is commonly used by advisors to simplify the layout of complex financial statements. In other accounting packages, subaccounts are often used for this purpose. Since Xero does not have subaccounts, account groups are used. A group of accounts can be shown in a financial statement as a detail of lines with its own sum or the details of the group can be hidden so that the sum is presented as its own line.

To add a group row to a financial report:

1. Open the report by navigating to **Accounting**, then **Reports**, and selecting the report.
2. Open the layout editor by clicking the **Edit layout** button at the bottom left of the screen.
3. Highlight any row in the report so that the row icon appears. Select the row icon at the top of the statement, and then select **Group**. Xero will add an Untitled Group to the top of the statement.
4. Drag the Untitled Group to the desired location within the report.
5. Name the group by using the **Name** field on the right side. Note that the name will appear as either the heading of the group when accounts in the group are shown or the identifier on the line when accounts are hidden.
6. Select whether the **Display Balance** should be debit or credit positive.
7. The **Group Selection** button on the right will add a subordinate group to the group created, so that you can embed groups within others.
8. The **Add Switch Rule** button will have Xero move negative balances to another part of the financial statement.
9. Add accounts to the group by dragging the accounts and dropping under the group name (Figure 16.14).

**FIGURE 16.14**

Add accounts to the group by dragging the accounts and dropping under the group name.

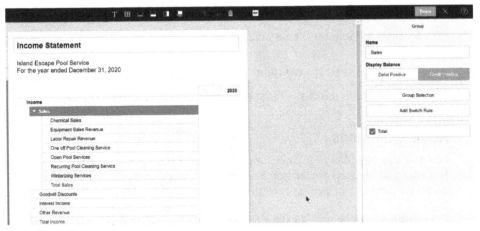

*Source:* Xero Limited

10. Note that if the group is open, indicated by the triangle next to the group name pointing down, each account will be shown in the report. If the group is closed, indicated by the triangle pointing to the right and the underlying accounts being hidden, the report will only show the group name and the sum of the underlying accounts.

11. Select **Done** in the top right to close the layout editor and save the group.

To delete a group, select the group and use the trash icon on the top. Deleting a group will not remove the underlying accounts from the report. It will only delete the group and return the individual accounts to the statement.

**Formula rows** are often added to financials to show calculations within the statement. Formulas can be built on preset account groups (such as Income or Cost of Goods Sold), custom account groups, or formula lines above the new formula row.

To add a formula row to a financial report:

1. Open the report by navigating to **Accounting**, then **Reports**, and selecting the report.

2. Open the layout editor by clicking the **Edit layout** button at the bottom left of the screen.

3. Highlight a row in the statement where you wish to add a formula. Select the row icon at the top of the statement, and then select **Formula**. Xero will add an Untitled formula line.

4. In the **Formula** field, use the **Insert** pull-down to select available groups for the calculation. Select mathematical operators from the panel or use your keyboard to complete the formula. Use the **If** operator to create a conditional formula. Like Excel, If formulas are three parts: condition, true value, false value.

5. Enter a **Name** for the formula, which will be the text shown on the formula line in the report.

6. Select **Done** in the top right to close the layout editor and save the formula.

To delete a formula, select the formula and use the trash icon on the top.

## Adding Columns

Columns can be added to financial reports, for comparing specific time periods, adding formulas and percentages, adding footnote references, comparing to a budget, or showing only data filtered by tracking category.

**Date columns** can be used to show financial data for a time period that differs from the range specified when the report is created. A column can even be created for a specific date or week, which makes it useful in companies who need to view granular financials, such as restaurants.

To add a date column:

1. Open the report by navigating to **Accounting**, then **Reports**, and selecting the report.

2. Open the layout editor by clicking the **Edit layout** button at the bottom left of the screen.

3. Highlight any column in the report so that the column icon appears. Select the column icon at the top of the statement, then select **Date**. Xero will add a date column to the statement.

4. With the column selected, use the **Date Range** pull-down to select the period length for the column. You can also select **Custom** dates here (Figure 16.15).

5. Use the date arrows to select the date range for the column, or for custom dates, use the calendar to highlight the date range.

6. Enter a name for the column in the **Name** field.

7. Select **Done** in the top right to close the layout editor and save the column.

**Budget columns** are useful in comparing actual data to expected data. To use a budget column, you must have created a budget in Xero using the Budget Manager. For details about budgets, see Chapter 18. The budget column will show the saved budget data in a column where it can be compared to actual figures. Because budgets are built on revenues and expenses, they are only available in the income statement.

**FIGURE 16.15**

With the column selected, use the Date Range pulldown to select the period length for the column. You can also select Custom dates here.

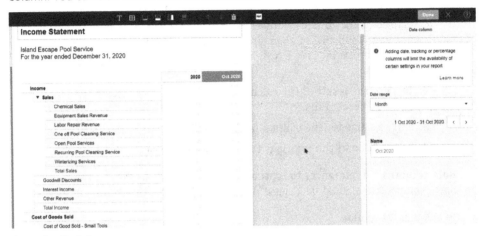

*Source:* Xero Limited

To add a budget column:

1. Open the report by navigating to **Accounting**, then **Reports**, and selecting the report.

2. Open the layout editor by clicking the **Edit layout** button at the bottom left of the screen.

3. Highlight any column in the report so that the column icon appears. Select the column icon at the top of the statement, and then select **Budget**. Xero will add a budget column to the statement.

4. With the column selected, use the **Budget** pull-down to select which budget to use for the column.

5. Use the **Date Range** pull-down to select the period length for the column.

6. Enter a name for the column in the **Name** field.

7. Select **Done** in the top right to close the layout editor, and save the budget column.

**Formula columns** can be used to automate calculations in financial statements and are especially helpful in comparing periods. Formulas can be created using values in columns on the same line.

To add a formula column:

1. Open the report by navigating to **Accounting**, then **Reports,** and select the report.

2. Open the layout editor by clicking the **Edit layout** button at the bottom left of the screen.

3. Highlight any column in the report so that the column icon appears. Select the column icon at the top of the statement, then select **Formula.** Xero will add a formula column to the statement.

4. With the column selected, use the **Insert** pull-down on the right to select available columns for the calculation. Select mathematical operators from the panel or use your keyboard to complete the formula. Use the **If** operator to create a conditional formula. Like Excel, **If** formulas are three parts: condition, true value, false value.

5. To show the result of the calculation as a percentage, check the box to the left of **Show as percentage.**

6. Enter a name for the column in the **Name** field.

7. Select **Done** in the top right to close the layout editor and save the formula.

**Note columns** are references to footnotes or schedules embedded in the report. To use the Notes column, there must be at least one schedule or text block added to the report.

To add a notes column:

1. Open the report by navigating to **Accounting**, then **Reports,** and select the report.

2. Open the layout editor by clicking the **Edit layout** button at the bottom left of the screen.

3. Highlight any column in the report so that the column icon appears. Select the column icon at the top of the statement, and then select **Notes.** Xero will add a notes column to the statement.

4. On the right, use the **Select Link Target** pull-down to select the schedule or text block to reference. Xero will add a number in the column that corresponds to the correct schedule or block.

5. Select **Done** in the top right to close the layout editor and save the notes column.

**Percentage columns** are calculations of the line as a percentage of a formula or group row.

To add a percentage column:

1. Open the report by navigating to **Accounting**, then **Reports,** and selecting the report.

2. Open the layout editor by clicking the **Edit layout** button at the bottom left of the screen.

3. Highlight any column in the report so that the column icon appears. Select the column icon at the top of the statement, and then select **Percentage.** Xero will add a percentage column to the statement.

4. On the right, use the **Show** pull-down to select the column that will be the numerator in the percentage calculation.

5. In the **As a percentage of** pull-down, select the formula or group row that will be the denominator in the calculation.

6. Enter a name for the column in the **Name** field.

7. Select **Done** in the top right to close the layout editor, and save the percentage column.

**Tracking category columns** are columns that show only data associated with one or more chosen tracking category options. While you can filter an entire report for one or more tracking category options by using the **Filter** button as described earlier, using columns allows you to compare multiple options on the same report.

To add a tracking category column:

1. Open the report by navigating to **Accounting**, then **Reports,** and select the report.

2. Open the layout editor by clicking the **Edit layout** button at the bottom left of the screen.

3. Highlight any column in the report so that the column icon appears. Select the column icon at the top of the statement, and then select the name of the tracking category that will be added. Xero will add a column to the report.

4. On the right, use the pull-down to select which category options should be included in the column. If more than one option is selected, the resulting data will be consolidated into that column (Figure 16.16).

**FIGURE 16.16**

On the right, use the pulldown to select which category options should be included in the column. If more than one option is selected, the resulting data will be consolidated into that column.

*Source:* Xero Limited

5. In the **Date range** column, choose the period that this column will include and use the arrows below to select the date range.

6. Enter a name for the column in the **Name** field.

7. Select **Done** in the top right to close the layout editor and save the column.

To delete a column, highlight the column header and use the trash icon on the top.

## Inserting a Page Break

Some reports will exceed one page, and where the break naturally occurs might be in a place that makes reading the report cumbersome. Xero allows you to insert a page break to separate the body from the accompanying schedules and footnotes.

To insert a page break:

1. Open the report by navigating to **Accounting**, then **Reports**, and select the report.

2. Open the layout editor by clicking the **Edit layout** button at the bottom left of the screen.

3. Select the page break icon at the top of the screen. Xero will add a page break at the bottom of the report.

4. To move the page break, select it and use the up or down arrows at the top of the page.

5. When the break is in the correct place, select **Done** to close the layout editor.

## Previewing a .pdf

Xero allows you to export a .pdf of a report directly from the layout editor. This makes review and revision of reports efficient. From the layout editor, use the PDF icon at the top right to download the report.

# Editing Transactional Reports

The process for editing transactional reports is slightly different from the fully editable financial statements discussed above. Reports with limited layout capabilities will have an **Insert content** pull-down in the lower left corner, rather than the **Edit layout** button (Figure 16.17). The Insert content pull-down will allow you to add text blocks, which can include copy, lists and tables, and footnotes. Some customization can also be done using the Report Settings link at the top of the report.

**FIGURE 16.17**

The process for editing transactional reports is slightly different from the fully editable financial statements discussed above. Reports with limited layout capabilities will have an Insert content pulldown in the lower left corner, rather than the Edit layout button.

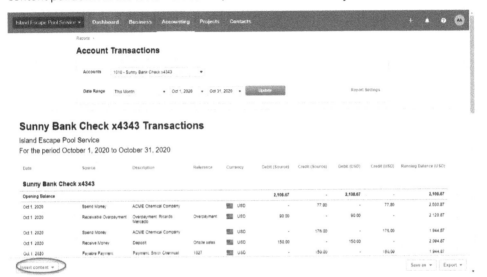

*Source:* Xero Limited

# Saving Custom Report Layouts

When you have refined a report layout for a company, you can save the layout to be used again. Saving a custom report layout is specific to the organization in which it is created. Saved custom reports cannot be transferred between Xero organizations. To create custom reports that can be applied to more than one company, see Report Templates in Chapter 3.

To save a custom report layout:

1. Open the report by navigating to **Accounting**, then **Reports**, and select the report.
2. Modify the report as desired and click **Done**.
3. Use the **Save As** pull-down to select **Custom** (Figure 16.18).
4. Enter a name for the report in the Name field. It is helpful to use a descriptive title, especially if there will be several custom reports built off of the same financial statement.
5. Decide whether this format should be the default layout for this report in this organization. Making a customized report the default means that those changes will be

**FIGURE 16.18**

Use the Save As pulldown to select Custom.

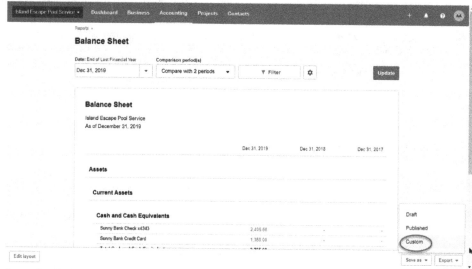

*Source: Xero Limited*

saved under the original report title in the Summary tab in Reports. If you wish for the customized report to replace the standard version, check the box next to **Make custom report the default** (Figure 16.19).

Custom report layouts will be found under the **Custom** tab in Reports.

To run a new report using a previously created custom layout:

1. Navigate to **Accounting**, then **Reports,** and select the **Custom** tab.
2. Open the custom layout desired by clicking the name.
3. Make any updates to the report, such as date or date range.
4. Click **Update**.

If you make a customized report the default, you can remove the default election to restore the original format for the report.

To remove a custom layout that is set as the default for that report:

1. Navigate to **Accounting**, then **Reports**, and select the **Custom** tab.
2. Use the overflow menu at the right of the custom report to select **Remove Default** (Figure 16.20). The custom layout will remain the **Custom** tab, but the original layout in the **Summary** tab will be restored.

**FIGURE 16.19**

If you wish for the customized report to replace the standard version, check the box next to Make custom report the default.

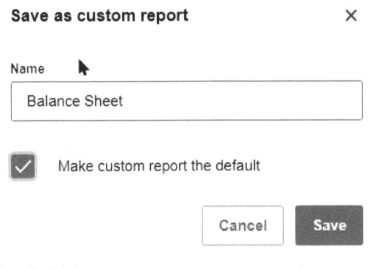

Source: Xero Limited

**FIGURE 16.20**

Use the overflow menu at the right of the custom report to select Remove Default.

Source: Xero Limited

# Publishing Reports

Publishing a report in Xero is akin to creating a digital printout. The data will remain constant, even if the underlying transactions are changed, and the links will stay active. Many advisors publish monthly financial statements and bank reconciliation reports as part of their month-end process.

To publish a report:

1. Generate and customize the report as desired.
2. Use the **Save As** pull-down at the bottom of the screen to select **Published** (Figure 16.21).
3. Enter a title in the space provided (Figure 16.22). The Published reports listing will show the title and date range of each report. It is helpful to edit the report title to best describe the report to reflect any customization or filters before publishing.

Note that in older formatted reports, there is a **Publish** button directly at the bottom of the screen.

Published reports will be found in the **Published** tab of Reports.

Examples of titles for published reports.

**FIGURE 16.21**

Use the Save As pulldown at the bottom of the screen to select Published.

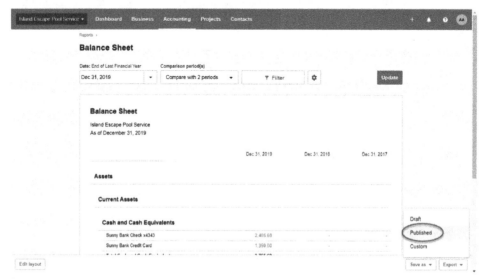

*Source:* Xero Limited

**FIGURE 16.22**

Enter a title in the space provided.

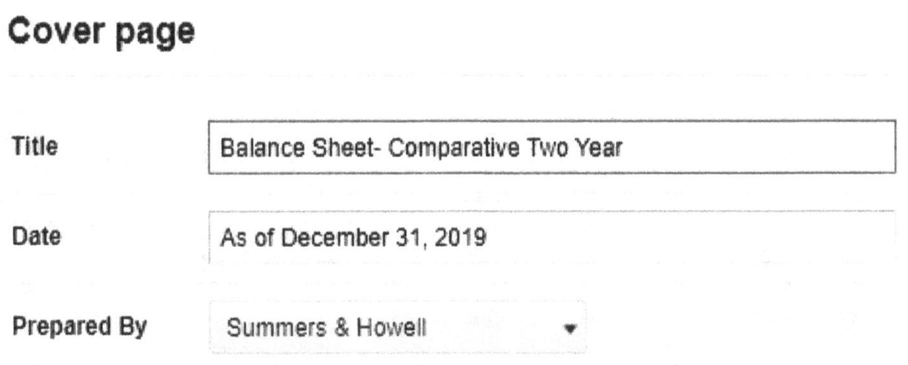

## Cover page

| | |
|---|---|
| Title | Balance Sheet- Comparative Two Year |
| Date | As of December 31, 2019 |
| Prepared By | Summers & Howell ▼ |

*Source:* Xero Limited

**FIGURE 16.23**

To archive or delete a report, navigate to the Published tabs in Reports. Use the overflow menu on the right to select either Archive or Delete.

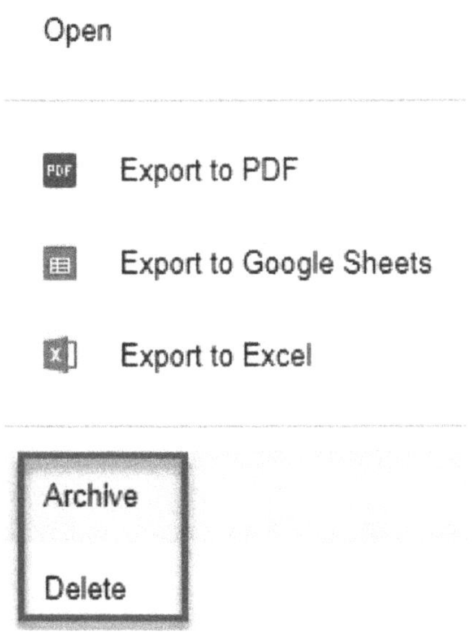

Open

[PDF] Export to PDF

[icon] Export to Google Sheets

[X] Export to Excel

Archive

Delete

*Source:* Xero Limited

| Instead of... | Try... |
|---|---|
| Bank Reconciliation | Bank Rec – Name of Bank Checking x3434 |
| Income Statement | Income Statement – This Tracking Category Only |
| Account Transactions | Cost of Goods Sold Transactions |
| Balance Sheet | Balance Sheet (Cash Basis for Tax Prep) |

Many advisors use the **Published** tab as a report library, keeping reports indefinitely. After years of using Xero, the tab may become cluttered. To clear out old reports, Xero allows published reports to be archived or deleted. Archiving a report will move the report from the Published tab to the Archived tab. It will remain there. Deleting a report permanently removes it from the system. In general, a report should only be deleted if it is no longer accurate because of transactional changes.

To archive or delete a report, navigate to the **Published** tabs in Reports. Use the overflow menu on the right to select either **Archive** or **Delete** (Figure 16.23).

## Exporting Reports

In addition to saving a report as published within Xero, final reports can be exported in several formats.

The Export pull-down at the bottom of a report offers three choices (Figure 16.24):

**FIGURE 16.24**

The Export pulldown at the bottom of a report offers three choices:

*Source:* Xero Limited

- Export as PDF: Xero will create a print-ready download in the browser.
- Excel: New report versions will be exported as .xlsx format. Older versions will be exported as .xls.
- Google Sheets: The user downloading must have a Google account and connect that account with Xero.

PDFs are generally preferred for communicating with company stakeholders and advisors. Excel or Google Sheets formats are useful when additional manipulation is required.

# Leveraging Key Reports

There are reports in Xero that nearly all advisors prepare on a regular basis. What follows are some keys in generating the most-used statements. All reports discussed next are accessed by navigating to **Accounting**, then **Reports**, and selecting the desired report.

## Balance Sheet

The balance sheet is a position report at a specific date. Choose the statement date from the Date pull-down. The preset choices are Today, End of Last Month, End of Last Quarter, and End of Last Year.

You can also select a specific date by clicking in the **Date** field and using the calendar to choose a day.

Use the **Comparison periods** pull-down to select how many prior periods will be shown as columns in the report. The period length is dependent on the date selected.

| Date selected for report | Comparative period length |
| --- | --- |
| Today | One day |
| End of Last Month | One month |
| End of Last Quarter | Three months |
| End of Last Year | One year |
| Custom Date | One year |

For more detailed or custom comparative periods, use the layout editor and add Date columns.

The **Filter** button will filter the entire report for one or more tracking category options. When multiple categories are chosen, all data will be compiled in a single column. To show balances by tracking category option in separate columns or to compare options to the entire company, use the layout editor to add tracking category columns.

The gear icon is used to choose between cash and accrual basis and to toggle decimal display. Many advisors prepare a cash basis balance sheet at the end of the year for tax preparation purposes.

# Income Statement

The income statement is an activity report over a period. Choose a preset date range using the **Date range** pull-down or select a specific date range by clicking and using the calendar to choose dates.

Use the **Comparison periods** pull-down to select how many prior periods will be shown as columns in the report. The period length is dependent on the date range selected.

| Date range selected for report | Comparative period length |
| --- | --- |
| This Month, Last Month | One month |
| This Quarter, Last Quarter | Three months |
| This Financial Year, Last Financial Year | One year |
| Month to Date | The same dates of the month for prior months |
| Quarter to Date | The same dates of the quarter for the prior quarters |
| Year to Date | The same dates of the year for the prior year |
| Custom | The same length as the date range consecutively prior |

For more detailed or custom comparative periods, use the layout editor and add **Date** columns.

The **Filter** button will filter the entire report for one or more tracking category options. When multiple categories are chosen, all data will be compiled in a single column. To show balances by tracking category option in separate columns or to compare options to the entire company, use the layout editor to add tracking category columns.

The gear icon is used to choose between cash and accrual basis, and to toggle decimal display. Many advisors prepare a cash basis balance sheet at the end of the year for tax preparation purposes.

# General Ledger Detail

The General Ledger report is an old-styled report in Xero, but a useful one. Select the date range for the report using the **From** and **To** pull-downs. Many advisors also find it helpful to sort the ledger by **Account Code**, rather than **Account Name**, which generates a listing of accounts in alphabetical order.

The report defaults to a summary view, similar to a trial balance. To access the general ledger details, use the **Export detailed General Ledger to Excel** button at the bottom of the report. This will generate an .xls download in the browser.

# Account Transactions Report

The Account Transactions report is useful for reviewing coding at year-end or verifying with clients. It shows the ledger activity of specified accounts without downloading the entire general ledger and offers more customization than the general ledger detail.

Filter the accounts to be included in the report by using the **Accounts** pull-down and checking the box to the left of the account names. Use the Report Settings link to specify which fields should be included on the report. Advisors often include tracking categories as columns, so those allocations can be reviewed.

## Trial Balance

The Trial Balance is another accounting report that is often used at year-end for tax preparation. You can include comparative balances for prior periods. It should be noted that the balances for the selected period will be shown in debit and credit columns, while comparative periods will be shown in a single column with debits as positive amounts and credits as negative amounts.

## Aged Receivables Detail/Aged Payables Detail

Accounts Receivable and Accounts Payable details are two of the most used internal reports in many companies. They are often generated as of the current day for purposes of sending communications to customers or for paying outstanding bills.

The Report Settings link has several useful options for this report. One is that the aging groupings can be modified. The default is to show invoices and bills in categories of Current, 1–30 Days, 31–60 Days, 61–90 Days and Older, but these can be changed.

Another important note is that additional useful columns can be added to the report. Possibly the most important column to include is the **Total** column. Many advisors add the **Total** column to the report and save the modification as the default layout. It can also be helpful to include contact information like Phone, Mobile, and Primary Person, so that collection calls can easily be made.

## Billable Expenses—Outstanding

As discussed in Chapter 12, billable expenses are handled as a queue of items to resolve, not a specific general ledger account, so it is easy to lose track of them. If a company is posting any transactions to billable expenses in Xero, it is very important to prepare this report each month.

## Blank Report

It may not overwhelm initially, but the Blank Report in Xero is a powerful addition to the reporting toolbox. By giving users a completely empty report, Xero offers the flexibility to create a report from scratch. The report layout editor is the same as other reports, so text boxes and schedules can be added to create a custom report.

# Month-End Reconciliation

*Everything we do as advisors depends on sound bookkeeping and as a fractional CFO, I often find anomalies or errors at month-end that require additional research. Xero's Account Transaction Report lets me drill down based on conditions, allowing me to find the needle in the haystack in just a few minutes as opposed to hours. Xero truly makes business beautiful.*

—Cat Fogarty-Nyman, CEO and Founder of eCatalyst

One of the most important processes in accounting or bookkeeping is the reconciliation of accounts at month-end. Reconciliation is the comparison of a general ledger balance to another set of data, and the scheduling of any differences. It is extremely important to reconcile all bank accounts monthly.

A typical bank reconciliation compares the general ledger balance to the bank's stated balance at the end of the month. Rarely will these two balances be identical on the last day of the month. There are many reasons for differences, but they generally fall into two categories:

1. Timing differences
2. Errors

Timing differences are balance differences attributable to the disparity in time between the recognition on the books and at the bank. In general, these are transactions that have been recorded on the general ledger but have not been posted by the bank. Examples are uncleared checks and deposits in transit. In the time of bank feeds and near instantaneous transmission of bank data, it is unusual to have a timing difference for a transaction that occurs on the bank balance but lags in recording to the general ledger.

Errors can occur on either the bank or general ledger side. Bank errors are increasingly rare because of modern data controls, but they do happen. Errors in the general ledger are much more common, although leveraging the bank data to create general ledger transactions reduces these tremendously. However, especially in the case of third-party bank feeds, general ledger errors occur when duplicate transactions are sent to Xero, when a feed "breaks" and omits transactions, or when transactions are sent to Xero in the opposite direction (debits as credits, refunds as charges).

Bank reconciliation will not identify errors in coding.

# Reconciliation Report

The first step in finding errors and discrepancies is to run a **Reconciliation Report**. This report drafts a reconciliation between the general ledger balance in Xero and a statement balance. The report's bottom line, the statement balance, is a calculated balance based on the general ledger balance at the reconciliation date and taking into account any timing discrepancies. The calculated statement balance on the reconciliation report must match the statement balance from the bank. Any differences must be corrected. Any timing discrepancies that are shown on the report must also be confirmed. If both the statement balance at the bottom and the outstanding lines on the report are correct, then the bank account is fully reconciled. A copy of the report should be saved in the company's records. (See Chapter 16 about publishing reports.)

To generate a Bank Reconciliation Summary report:

1. Navigate to the **Accounting** tab, then **Bank accounts**. Select the bank account to generate the report.

2. Use the **Manage Account** pull-down to select **Reconciliation Report**. The report can also be accessed from the Dashboard by using the overflow menu (three dots) next to the name of the bank account.

3. In the **Date** field, choose the date that represents the statement date for the bank account.

4. Click **Update** (Figure 17.1).

**FIGURE 17.1**

Click Update.

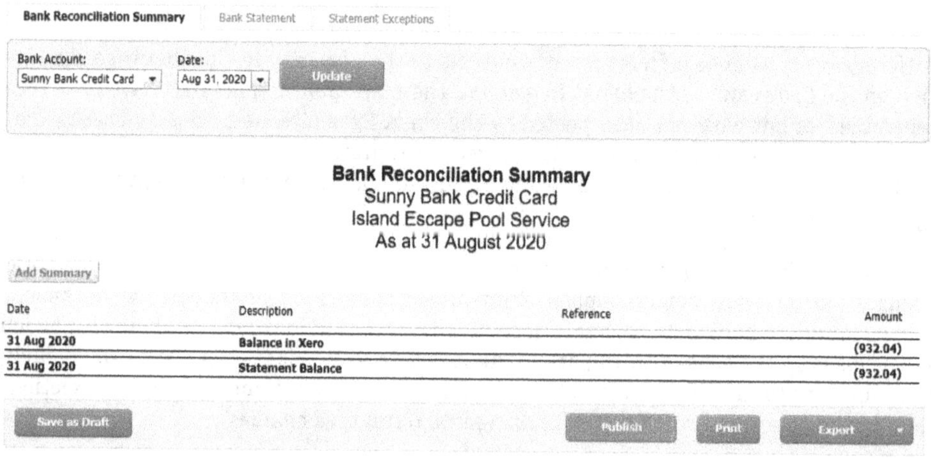

**Bank Reconciliation Summary**
Sunny Bank Credit Card
Island Escape Pool Service
As at 31 August 2020

| Date | Description | Reference | Amount |
|------|-------------|-----------|--------|
| 31 Aug 2020 | Balance in Xero | | (932.04) |
| 31 Aug 2020 | Statement Balance | | (932.04) |

*Source:* Xero Limited

# Understanding the Reconciliation Report

The Bank Reconciliation Report has three tabs. We will examine each.

## Bank Reconciliation Summary Tab

This report is generally considered the report to use to prove that the bank account is reconciled at month-end. These are the sections that do or can appear in this report.

The **Balance in Xero** line (Figure 17.2). This is the general ledger balance as of the report date and the starting point for this report. As discussed in Chapter 9, the general ledger balance of bank accounts does not include any unreconciled bank transactions, but does include any transactions posted to the general ledger that have yet to be matched with a bank line, such as spend moneys, receive moneys, and payments on bills and invoices.

**Plus Outstanding Payments** (Figure 17.3). These are uncleared checks, Spend Moneys, or other payments on bills that have been posted in the bank account but not matched to

**FIGURE 17.2**

The Balance in Xero line.

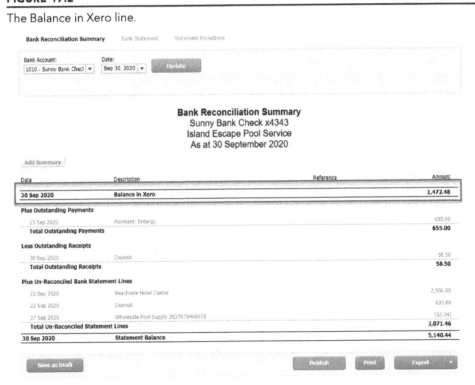

*Source:* Xero Limited

**FIGURE 17.3**

Plus Outstanding Payments.

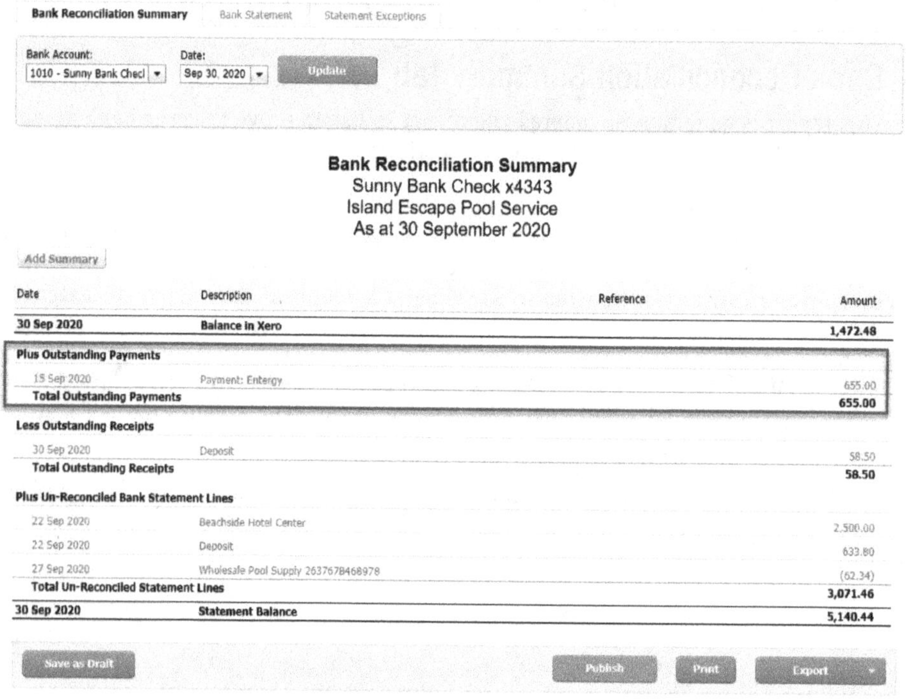


**Bank Reconciliation Summary**
Sunny Bank Check x4343
Island Escape Pool Service
As at 30 September 2020

| Date | Description | Reference | Amount |
|---|---|---|---|
| **30 Sep 2020** | **Balance in Xero** | | **1,472.48** |
| **Plus Outstanding Payments** | | | |
| 15 Sep 2020 | Payment: Entergy | | 655.00 |
| **Total Outstanding Payments** | | | **655.00** |
| **Less Outstanding Receipts** | | | |
| 30 Sep 2020 | Deposit | | 58.50 |
| **Total Outstanding Receipts** | | | **58.50** |
| **Plus Un-Reconciled Bank Statement Lines** | | | |
| 22 Sep 2020 | Beachside Hotel Center | | 2,500.00 |
| 22 Sep 2020 | Deposit | | 633.80 |
| 27 Sep 2020 | Wholesale Pool Supply 2637678468978 | | (62.34) |
| **Total Un-Reconciled Statement Lines** | | | **3,071.46** |
| **30 Sep 2020** | **Statement Balance** | | **5,140.44** |

***Source:*** **Xero Limited**

a bank line. They are added back the Xero balance because even though Xero recognizes them, the bank has not yet.

**Less Outstanding Receipts** (Figure 17.4). These are deposits in transit, Receive Moneys, or other payments on invoices that have been posted in the bank account but not matched to a bank line. This can also include point-of-sale merchant settlements in transit, depending on the integration with the application. They are deducted from the Xero balance because even though Xero recognizes them, the bank has not yet.

**Plus UnReconciled Bank Statement Lines** (Figure 17.5). These are any bank lines that have not been reconciled by creating a transaction or matching to existing general ledger lines. Any transaction that is listed on the Reconcile tab would be shown here. Deposits or credits (from the bank's perspective) on the bank account will be shown as positive amounts. Draws or debits (from the bank's perspective) on the bank account will be shown as negative amounts.

**FIGURE 17.4**

Less Outstanding Receipts.

Source: Xero Limited

**Statement Balance** (Figure 17.6). This is a balance calculated from the above lines. It would also be equal to the starting balance plus or minus all known bank lines. *This line must equal the bank's provided balance at the report date.* If not, you must find and correct the error.

**Imported Statement Balance.** This is a statement balance from the bank at the date of the report and will only show if a running balance is imported or fed from the bank. If the Imported Statement Balance differs from the calculated Statement Balance, the difference will be noted below with a **Balance Out By** line. Note that the Statement Balance line is the value that needs to match the bank statement. The Imported Statement Balance is for information only.

**FIGURE 17.5**

Plus Un-Reconciled Bank Statement Lines.

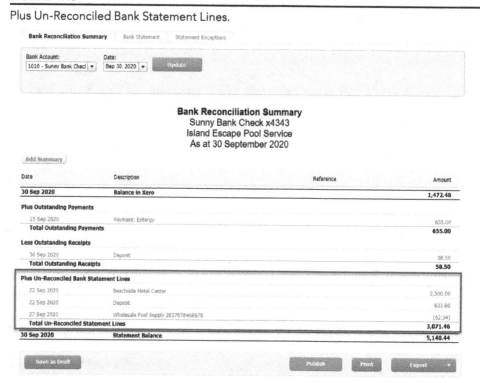

*Source:* Xero Limited

## Bank Statement Tab

The Bank Statement tab is Xero's replication of the statement issued by the bank (Figure 17.7). Choose the opening and closing dates of the bank statement. If the account being reconciled is a credit card with a statement opening date during the middle of the month, be sure the dates on this tab match the statement. The opening balance on the report is the prior month's calculated bank statement balance. Every bank transaction imported or downloaded is listed below in date order and used to calculate a closing balance.

## Statement Exceptions Tab

The Statement Exceptions tab shows any anomalies or outliers in the bank data (Figure 17.8). It includes items such as:

- Bank lines that are manually marked as reconciled
- Statement lines that have been deleted
- Some duplicates

**FIGURE 17.6**

Statement Balance.

*Source:* Xero Limited

The Statement Exceptions tab is a good place to start if there are problems with the Statement Balance on the Summary tab.

# Reconciling Credit Card Accounts

Credit cards rarely close on the last day of the month. The reconciliation report should be run for the date of the credit card statement to verify that there are no discrepancies. Depending on the closing date and how close it is to the end of the month, other reconciliation methods may be used in addition to the reconciliation report.

If the credit card closes early in the month, many advisors will wait until that date to issue month-end financials so the credit card balance can be verified using this process. If the credit card closes late in the month, advisors may do a manual reconciliation on a spreadsheet to verify that all credit card transactions have been recorded. In some cases, however, if there are no systemic problems with the credit card feed, an advisor may only rely on the Xero bank reconciliation that ends mid-month, except for at year-end when a true reconciliation must be done.

## FIGURE 17.7

The Bank Statement tab is Xero's replication of the statement issued by the bank.

Reports ›

# Bank Reconciliation

| Bank Reconciliation Summary | **Bank Statement** | Statement Exceptions |
|---|---|---|

Wide view ⏎

**Bank Account:** 1010 - Sunny Bank Checi ▾  **From:** Sep 1, 2020 ▾  **To:** Sep 30, 2020 ▾  [ Update ]

☐ Reconciled Only

### Bank Statement
Sunny Bank Check x4343
Island Escape Pool Service
From 1 September 2020 to 30 September 2020

[ Add Summary ]

| Date | Description | Date imported into Xero | Reference | Reconciled | Source | Amount | Balance |
|---|---|---|---|---|---|---|---|
| **1 Sep 2020** | **Opening Balance** | | | | | | **1,519.21** |
| 2 Sep 2020 | Key West Marine Supplies Part Payment | 25 Sep 2020 | | Yes | Imported | (250.00) | 1,269.21 |
| 7 Sep 2020 | Cash Deposit | 25 Sep 2020 | | Yes | Imported | 9.50 | 1,278.71 |
| 16 Sep 2020 | Interest earned | 25 Sep 2020 | | Yes | Imported | 34.88 | 1,313.59 |
| 19 Sep 2020 | ACME Chemical Company | 25 Sep 2020 | | Yes | Imported | (16.50) | 1,297.09 |
| 19 Sep 2020 | Deposit | 25 Sep 2020 | | Yes | Imported | 500.00 | 1,797.09 |
| 19 Sep 2020 | Young Bros Transport | 25 Sep 2020 | | Yes | Imported | (125.03) | 1,672.06 |
| 21 Sep 2020 | ACME Chemical Company | 25 Sep 2020 | | Yes | Imported | (45.60) | 1,626.46 |
| 21 Sep 2020 | City Stationery | 25 Sep 2020 | | Yes | Imported | (230.08) | 1,396.38 |
| 21 Sep 2020 | Carol Fowler | 25 Sep 2020 | | Yes | Imported | 291.00 | 1,687.38 |
| 21 Sep 2020 | Carol Fowler | 25 Sep 2020 | | Yes | Imported | 291.00 | 1,978.38 |
| 21 Sep 2020 | Irene Francis | 25 Sep 2020 | | Yes | Imported | 50.00 | 2,028.38 |
| 21 Sep 2020 | Ricardo Mercado Deposit | 25 Sep 2020 | | Yes | Imported | 328.00 | 2,356.38 |
| 22 Sep 2020 | Beachside Hotel Center | 25 Sep 2020 | | No | Imported | 2,500.00 | 4,856.38 |
| 22 Sep 2020 | Deposit | 25 Sep 2020 | | No | Imported | 633.80 | 5,490.18 |
| 22 Sep 2020 | Gavin Rutherford part payment | 25 Sep 2020 | | Yes | Imported | 60.00 | 5,550.18 |
| 22 Sep 2020 | Hotel Antigua | 25 Sep 2020 | | Yes | Imported | 941.55 | 6,491.73 |
| 23 Sep 2020 | Chlorine Products R Us | 25 Sep 2020 | | Yes | Imported | (123.00) | 6,368.73 |
| 24 Sep 2020 | Chlorine Products R Us | 25 Sep 2020 | | Yes | Imported | (98.00) | 6,270.73 |
| 27 Sep 2020 | Wholesale Pool Supply 2637678466978 | 25 Sep 2020 | | No | Imported | (62.34) | 6,208.39 |
| 28 Sep 2020 | ACME Chemical Company | 25 Sep 2020 | | Yes | Imported | (87.65) | 6,120.74 |
| 29 Sep 2020 | Chlorine Products R Us | 25 Sep 2020 | | Yes | Imported | (10.98) | 6,109.76 |
| 30 Sep 2020 | Best Buy Electronics | 25 Sep 2020 | | Yes | Imported | (896.99) | 5,212.77 |
| 30 Sep 2020 | Chlorine Products R Us | 25 Sep 2020 | | Yes | Imported | (12.33) | 5,200.44 |
| 30 Sep 2020 | Tannon Photocopiers | 25 Sep 2020 | | Yes | Imported | (60.00) | 5,140.44 |
| | **Closing Balance** | | | | | | **5,140.44** |

*Source:* Xero Limited

**FIGURE 17.8**

The Statement Exceptions tab shows any anomalies or outliers in the bank data.

*Source:* Xero Limited

# Identifying Errors in the Reconciliation Report

For bank accounts in which there is a direct or high-fidelity third-party feed, errors in the bank reconciliation report are rare, but possible. Where the reconciliation report statement balance does not tie to the bank's statement balance, one or more errors exist. The first step in identifying errors is to confirm that the beginning bank balance in Xero for the period is correct. This can be done by using the Bank Statement tab, or by rolling back the Bank Reconciliation Summary tab date one month. If the beginning bank balance is incorrect, you must continue to go back each month until the bank balance ties. The error or errors will begin in the following month.

One of the quickest ways to find errors is to export the Bank Statement tab in the Reconciliation Report.

To export the Bank Statement data:

1. Navigate to the **Accounting** tab, then **Bank accounts**. Select the bank account to generate the report.

2. Use the **Manage Account** pull-down to select **Reconciliation Report.** The report can also be accessed from the Dashboard by using the overflow menu (three dots) next to the name of the bank account.

3. Choose the **Bank Statement** tab at the top.

4. Verify the bank account and choose a date range that matches with the published bank or credit card statement.

5. Click **Update.**

6. Use pull-down at the bottom to choose a file export type. It is generally best to use either Excel or Google Sheets, so the data can be sorted or filtered (Figure 17.9).

7. Open the export file. Note that Excel and Google Sheets files will have three tabs: one for each of the reports. Navigate to the Bank Statement tab.

8. You will want to compare each line to each line on the published bank statement. It often helps to sort the transactions by amount and subtotal deposits compared to draws. Many banks list those subtotals at the top of the bank statement and, at a quick glance, you may be able to tell which direction the error exists.

9. Note the errors so they can be fixed.

There are three types of errors:

1. **Duplicate bank transactions:** A bank line was imported or downloaded more than once and must be deleted.

2. **Missing bank transactions:** A bank line that is listed on the published bank statement is not in Xero on the general ledger and must be added.

3. **Reversed bank transactions:** A bank line was imported or downloaded as a transaction in the opposite direction, such as a deposit on the bank statement that is recorded as a draw in Xero or a draw on the bank statement that is recorded as a deposit in Xero. The line in Xero must be deleted and a new, correct transaction line added.

**FIGURE 17.9**

Use pulldown at the bottom to choose a file export type. It is generally best to use either Excel or Google Sheets, so the data can be sorted or filtered.

*Source:* Xero Limited

# Deleting Duplicate Bank Transactions

To delete a duplicate transaction in Xero, the line must be located, then deleted. First, determine whether the duplicate transaction has already been reconciled in Xero. The Bank Statement tab of the Reconciliation Report will indicate this in the Reconciled column.

If the duplicate line has not been reconciled:

1. Find the transaction in the Reconcile or Cash Coding tabs of the bank account.
2. In the Reconcile tab, use the **Options** pull-down in the top right of the transaction tile, and select **Delete Statement Line** (Figure 17.10).
3. In the Cash Coding tab, use the arrow pull-down on the right of the line to select **Delete**.
4. Confirm the deletion by selecting **Yes**.

If the duplicate line has been reconciled, it must first be unreconciled before it can be deleted:

1. Find the transaction in the **Account Transactions** tab of the bank account.
2. Open the transaction by clicking the blue payee name or description.
3. Use the **Options** tab to select either **Unreconcile** or **Remove & Redo** (Figure 17.11). These are two different actions, so it is important to choose the correct one.

## FIGURE 17.10

In the Reconcile tab, use the Options pulldown in the top right of the transaction tile, select Delete Statement Line.

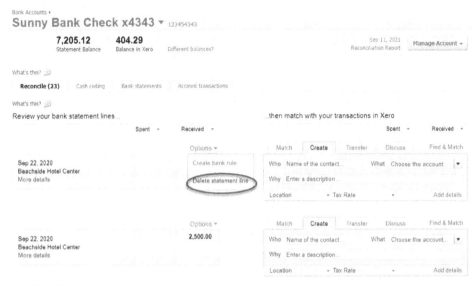

*Source:* Xero Limited

**FIGURE 17.11**

Use the Options tab to select either Unreconcile or Remove & Redo.

Source: Xero Limited

**Unreconcile** will break the link between the bank transaction and the general ledger transaction but not delete the general ledger side. If the duplicated bank line was matched with an existing ledger transaction, such as an invoice payment or outstanding check, you would select **Unreconcile** so the existing ledger transaction would not be deleted.

**Remove & Redo** will break the link between the bank transaction and the general ledger transaction and will delete the general ledger transaction. The general ledger line is removed and the bank line is sent back to the Reconcile tab to redo. If the duplicated bank line was reconciled by creating a new Spend or Receive Money in the Reconcile tab, you would select **Remove & Redo**. Selecting Unreconcile would only undo the matching of the lines and would leave an unreconciled Spend or Receive Money on the ledger, which is incorrect.

Once the reconciled line has been unreconciled, follow the earlier instructions to delete an unreconciled statement line. Deleted bank statement lines can still be found on the Bank statements tab of the bank account screen. The Status of the line will be deleted.

## Adding Missing Bank Transactions

If a transaction appears on the published bank statement but does not appear in Xero, it must be added. This could happen because a bank feed stopped working for a period of time or a statement import was incomplete.

There are two steps to adding missing bank statement lines:

1. Create a spend money or receive money transaction.
2. Force Xero to create a bank line for the spend or receive money transaction and link the two.

To create a spend or receive money transaction:

1. Use the **+** icon at the top right of the screen and select either **Spend money** or **Receive money.**
2. Select the bank account the entry will be posted to. Click **Next.**
3. Enter the transaction details, using the data from the published bank statement.
4. Click **Save.**

Creating a spend or receive money transaction adds a line to the general ledger. In a normal reconciliation process, a bank statement line would match with the spend or receive money and be reconciled. When a statement line is missing, however, there is no bank line to match with. You must force Xero to create the matching bank line using **Mark as Reconciled.**

Mark as Reconciled is a functionality in Xero that must be enabled before use. The default for every user in any organization is that it is disabled. Once it is enabled, it will be available to the user in that organization indefinitely.

To enable mark as reconciled:

1. Navigate to any bank account screen, either from the **Dashboard** or under **Accounting.**
2. Click the **?** icon in the top right of the screen.
3. Select **Enable Mark as Reconciled** (Figure 17.12).

To disable mark as reconciled:

1. Navigate to any bank account screen, either from the **Dashboard** or under **Accounting.**
2. Click the **?** icon in the top right of the screen.
3. Select **Disable Mark as Reconciled.**

**FIGURE 17.12**

Select Enable Mark as Reconciled.

*Source:* Xero Limited

359

**FIGURE 17.13**

Use the More pulldown above the transactions listing to select Mark as Reconciled.

| | Reconcile (21) | Cash coding | Bank statements | **Account transactions** | | | | | |
|---|---|---|---|---|---|---|---|---|---|

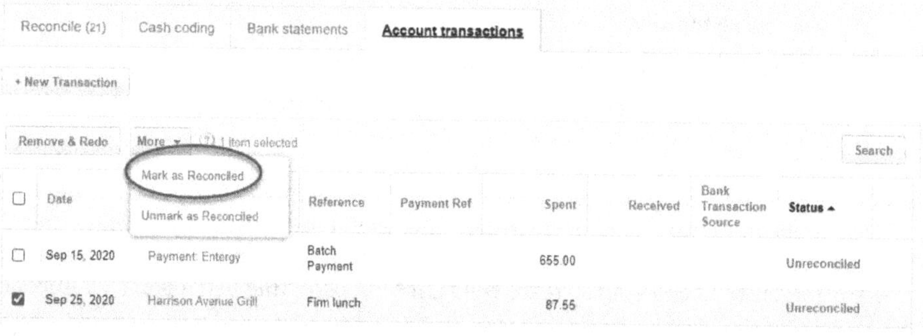

*Source:* Xero Limited

Once Mark as Reconciled is enabled, you can use it to create a bank line from the Spend or Receive Money transaction by forcing a reconciliation of the transaction.

To force a reconciliation of a Spend or Receive Money transaction and create a linked bank line:

1. Navigate to the bank account in which the transaction was created.

2. Locate the unreconciled Spend or Receive Money transaction in the **Account transactions** tab of the bank account.

3. Check the box to the left of the line.

4. Use the **More** pull-down above the transactions listing to select **Mark as Reconciled** (Figure 17.13).

5. If you receive a warning from Xero about only using Mark as Reconciled where original bank transactions cannot be imported, click **Mark as Reconciled** to confirm.

To confirm the line has been created and reconciled, navigate to the **Bank statements** tab and locate the transaction. Statement lines created by using Mark as Reconciled will be identified in the **Bank statements** tab by noting the **Source** as **User**. The Spend or Receive Money will be listed on the **Account transactions** tab with a label under **Bank Transaction Source** as **User**.

In a way, the process for adding missing bank statement lines is the opposite of traditional reconciliation where a Spend or Receive Money is created from a bank line. Here, a bank line is created from a Spend or Receive Money.

If a statement period is missing many bank transactions, the more efficient method would be to use a precoded statement import instead. For instructions, refer to Chapter 9.

## Correcting Reversed Bank Transactions

Occasionally a bank statement line enters Xero in the opposite direction of what it should. These tend to be specific cases, for example, when the return of a debit card purchase is imported into Xero as an additional charge. To correct these reversed transactions, you must first delete the reversed transaction, then add a correct line. See above for instructions on both.

# Verifying Timing Difference Lines

In bank reconciliation, a timing difference is when a transaction has been entered on the general ledger, but a matching bank statement line has not been reconciled with it. These are some examples of typical timing difference items:

- A payment for an invoice is received on the 30th of the month, is noted in Xero, but is not deposited until after the 1st of the following month.
- The company processes a check payment for a bill on the 26th of the month, mails it, but it does not clear the bank until after the 1st of the following month.
- A merchant settlement is recorded in Xero by the point-of-sale system on the last day of the month, but the deposit does not reach the bank until the first business day of the month.
- The company charges an expense on the last day of the month and records a spend money transaction so the expense is reflected on that month's financial statements. The payment is not settled with the credit card company until the first business day of the following month.

These are all legitimate situations that will lead to outstanding lines on the bank reconciliation, but if there are outstanding lines that linger for more than a month, that could be a clue of a mistake. It is critical to review the outstanding items on the bank reconciliation each month. If a user has matched a bank line to the wrong general ledger line, or worse, coded a bank line directly to a general ledger account when it should be matched to one existing, this is the place where those will be obvious.

See Chapter 10 for correcting mismatched and miscoded items.

# Reviewing the Month's Coding

The previously discussed, processes will verify bank and credit card balances but will not identify any errors in coding. It is a good idea to review the coding of transactions each month in the Account Transactions report, which is a general ledger listing for certain accounts.

To run an Account Transactions report:

1. Navigate to **Accounting**, then **Reports**.
2. Open the **Account Transactions** report under Accounting.
3. Choose accounts to include in the report. In general, all accounts except the bank and credit cards (which have already been verified) should be included.
4. Select dates for this month.
5. Use Report Settings to select **Layout Group By Account Code**. This will put accounts in code order, rather than alphabetical order (Figure 17.14).
6. Click **Update**.

Use the report to check each line for the correct coding. If a line needs to be corrected, find the line in the Account Transactions tab. Use the **Options** pull-down to select **Edit Transaction** and recode the line (Figure 17.15). If there are many lines to recode, use Find and Recode, explained in Chapter 15.

### FIGURE 17.14

Use Report Settings to select Layout Group By Account Code. This will put accounts in code order, rather than alphabetical order.

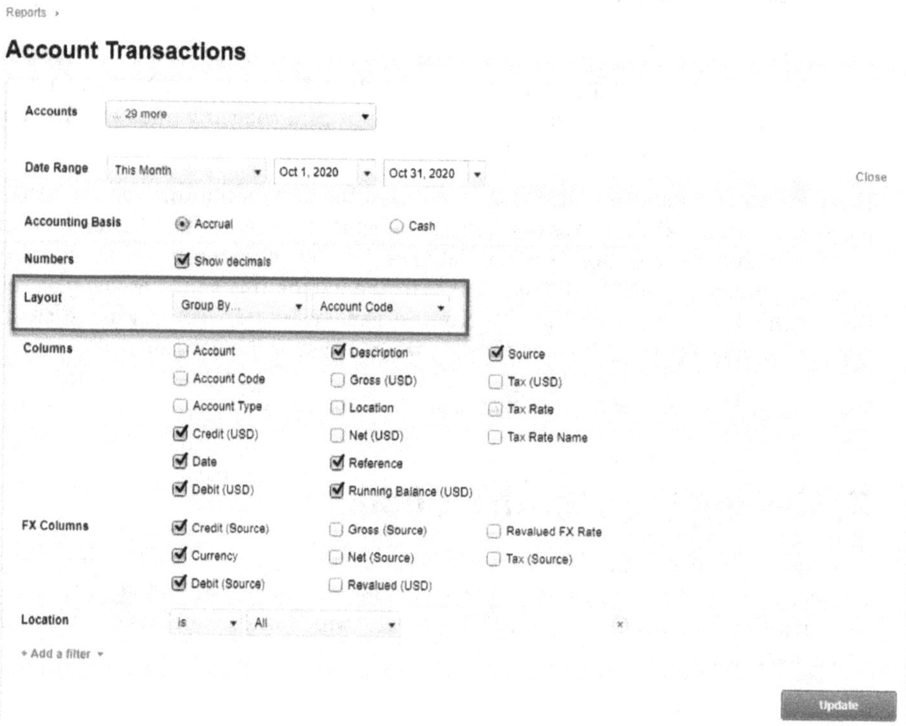

*Source:* Xero Limited

**FIGURE 17.15**

Use the report to check each line for the correct coding. If a line needs to be corrected, find the line in the Account Transactions tab. Use the Options pulldown to select Edit Transaction and recode the line.

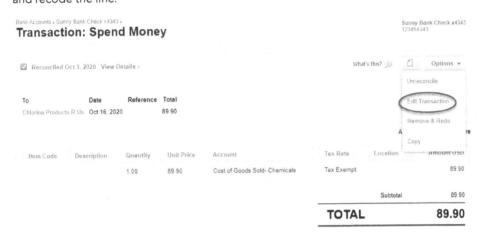

Bank Accounts › Sunny Bank Check x4343 ›

**Transaction: Spend Money**

Sunny Bank Check x4343
123454343

☑ Reconciled Oct 1, 2020  View Details ›

What's this? 💭

Options ▼

Unreconcile

Edit Transaction

Remove & Redo

Copy

| To | Date | Reference | Total |
|----|------|-----------|-------|
| Chlorine Products R Us | Oct 16, 2020 | | 89.90 |

| Item Code | Description | Quantity | Unit Price | Account | Tax Rate | Location | Amount USD |
|-----------|-------------|----------|------------|---------|----------|----------|------------|
| | | 1.00 | 89.90 | Cost of Goods Sold- Chemicals | Tax Exempt | | 89.90 |

Subtotal  89.90

**TOTAL**  **89.90**

*Source:* Xero Limited

# Locking Dates

After the month's financial data is verified, the system should be locked to prevent transactions from inadvertently being changed or added. Locking dates is covered in Chapter 6.

# Month-End Reconciliation Process

1. Reconcile all lines in the bank account.
2. Run the reconciliation report and verify the statement balance. Correct any errors.
3. Examine the unreconciled lines on the report to make sure they should not be matched with existing transactions.
4. Review the coding of the month's transactions from the Account Transactions report.
5. Publish the verified bank reconciliation reports.
6. Lock dates.

# Advisory Tools

*The fact that Xero's Budget Manager is exposed to the API gives us flexibility with our client engagements to either create budgets solely for use in Xero or to integrate with third-party reporting and forecasting applications.*

*—Tate Henshaw, Co-Founder of ARC Management*

In the last few years, Xero has invested in developing tools that assist advisors, as well as business owners, in understanding, not just tracking, financial data. The features discussed in this chapter are not necessarily restricted to Advisor level access, but, rather, create advisory type insights for the company. Although these are not complex forecasting or analysis tools, they are substantial for a small business accounting package at Xero's price point. These tools are included in Business Edition subscriptions.

## Short-Term Cash Flow

The **Short-term cash flow** dashboard (Figure 18.1) projects cash flow over a chosen time frame. The projections are based on the current balances of bank accounts with adjustments for outstanding bills and invoices. For the best results, the bank accounts should be fully reconciled with no outstanding items in the Reconcile tab, and accounts receivable and payable should be as accurate as possible.

To access Short-term cash flow, navigate to **Business**, then **Short-term cash flow**.

The first time **Short-term cash flow** is opened, Xero will ask which bank accounts to include in the cash balance and how far in the future to project the balance, either 7 or 30 days.
The prepared dashboard will then allow the accounts and timeline to be managed from pull-down menus at the top right.

The focus of the dashboard is the projected balance on the desired date shown in bold.
The calculation of the projected balance is the general ledger balance of the selected bank accounts, plus invoices expected to be collected during the time frame, less bills that are expected

**FIGURE 18.1**

The Short-term cash flow dashboard (Figure 18.1) projects cash flow over a chosen time frame.

*Source:* Xero Limited

to be paid during the time frame. Invoice and bills will be included in the projection if the due date falls within the date range. This means that overdue invoices and bills will not be automatically included because the due date is prior to today and therefore outside the projection range. Expected dates (for invoices) or planned dates (for bills) will override the due date on both current and overdue items.

To the right of the projected balance is a graphic showing the daily projected cash balance. Hovering the cursor over each dot will show the details of invoices and bills on each day.

Below the balance calculation and graph are tiles related to invoices and bills. The invoice and bill tiles include details for each item within the range. The lists can be grouped by date or contact by using the pull-down. Within each group, each invoice is shown and can be viewed using the link.

The **Suggested actions** tile shows overdue invoices and bills and recommends adding expected and planned dates, since without them, they are excluded from the projection. The Sales and Purchases screens can be accessed quickly using the buttons in the tile.

Expected and planned dates are easily entered in the Awaiting Payment screens for Invoices and Bills. For each item, use the + button in the line to enter a date. An optional Note can also be added. For overdue bills and invoices, this will allow them to be included in the projection if the entered date falls within the projection range. For other bills and invoices, the planned or expected date will override the due date for inclusion in the projection.

# Business Snapshot

The **Business snapshot** dashboard (Figure 18.2) shows business owners and advisors basic metrics about the company using graphics. Because most of the metrics are comparative, the company must have at least two months of data. For the best results, the bank accounts should be fully reconciled with no outstanding items in the Reconcile tab, and accounts receivable and payable should be as accurate as possible.

To access **Business snapshot**, navigate to **Accounting**, then **Business snapshot**. It can also be found in the **Financial** section of reports.

The time period is selected by using the pull-down at the top right. Unlike in many Xero reports, there is no custom date option. The choices are Last Month, Last Quarter, Last Financial Year, and Year to Date. Because there is currently little flexibility in date range, you must access this quickly after the close of the period you wish to examine. In the tiles where data is compared, the comparative period will be the prior period. For example when Last Month is chosen as a date range, the comparative period will be the month before. When Year to Date is chosen, the comparative period will be the same dates for the year prior.

The tiles in the dashboard are fixed, and at the time of writing cannot be customized. A listing and explanation of each follows.

## Profitability

The **Profitability** section of the Business Snapshot dashboard dissects net income for the company. The **Profit or loss** tile shows the excess (or shortage) of revenues over expenses on an accrual basis. The **Income** figure is the sum of all transactions, on an accrual basis, coded to Revenue type general ledger accounts. The **Expenses** figure shows the sum of accrual basis transactions coded to Direct Cost, Expense, Overhead, or Depreciation account types. The **Cost of goods sold** amount is the subset of Expenses coded to Direct Cost account types. Operating expenses represents the remaining expenses or those coded to Expense, Overhead, and Depreciation account types.

## Efficiency

The **Efficiency** section of the Business Snapshot dashboard examines margin on earnings and highlights operating expenses. The **Gross profit margin** tile shows the percentage by which revenue exceeds cost of goods sold. The **Largest operating expense** listing shows the largest five non-cost of goods sold expenses by dollar amount.

## FIGURE 18.2

The Business snapshot dashboard (Figure 18.2) shows business owners and advisors basic metrics about the company using graphics.

Source: Xero Limited

## Financial Position and Cash

The **Financial position and cash** section of the Business Snapshot dashboard shows specific account positions on the last day of the period selected. The **Balance sheet** tile is a tremendously simplified summary of a balance sheet, showing only total assets, liabilities, and owners' equity. The **Overall cash balance** listing shows a summary of any general ledger accounts with the type Bank.

On the right are tiles that show the pace of collecting receivables and paying payables. The **Average time to get paid** calculation is basically a Days Sales Outstanding (DSO) metric. Xero uses the average accounts receivable over sales times the number of days in the period to get a number of days to paid. The calculation for **Average time to pay suppliers** is similar with accounts payable over cost of goods sold time the number of days. In both calculations, the average accounts balance is the balance on the first day of the period plus balance on the last day of the period, divided by two.

# Business Performance

**Business Performance** graphs (Figure 18.3) in Xero show many of the common financial key performance indicators (KPIs). Where **Business snapshot** is a set view of tiles that can be generated for a few preset date ranges, a custom selection of Business Performance graphs can be added to the main Xero Dashboard. Business Performance graphs show the ratios calculated for the last 12 months and are calculated using account types.

To access graphs available, navigate to **Accounting**, then **Reports**. In the **Financial** section of **Reports**, use the **More reports** pull-down to access **Business Performance**. This screen will show all available ratios with a highlighted calculation for the last 12 months cumulatively in the upper right corner of the tile and a graph showing a column for each of the last 12 months. To see the ratio for any specific month, hover over the column.

The title of each ratio in blue is a redirect link that will open a page for the ratio. It will include an explanation of the ratio and will show the underlying calculations for the prior year and each of the prior 12 months.

A graph can be added to the Business performance tile on the main Xero Dashboard by clicking the star to the left of the name. The graphs that can be added to the dashboard are:

| Ratio | Numerator | Denominator |
|---|---|---|
| Current Liabilities to Net Worth | Closing balance of Current Liabilities | Closing balances of Revenue + Sales + Other Income – Direct Costs – Expense – Depreciation – Overhead + Equity |
| Current Ratio | Closing balances of Current Assets + Bank Accounts | Closing balance of Current Liabilities |

## FIGURE 18.3

Business performance graphs (Figure 18.3) in Xero show many of the common financial key performance indicators (KPIs.)

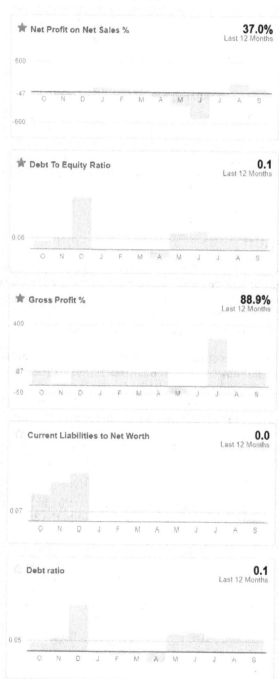

 *Source:* Xero Limited

| Ratio | Numerator | Denominator |
|---|---|---|
| Debt Ratio | Closing balances of Current Liabilities + Liabilities + Non-Current Liabilities | Closing balances of Current Assets + Fixed Assets + Non-Current Assets + Bank Accounts |
| Debt to Equity Ratio | Closing balances of Current Liabilities + Liabilities + Non-Current Liabilities | Closing balances of Revenue + Sales + Other Income – Direct Costs – Expense – Depreciation – Overhead + Equity |
| Gross Profit % | Movement of Revenues + Sales – Direct Costs | Movement of Revenues + Sales |
| Net Profit on Net Sales % | Movement of Revenue + Sales + Other Income – Direct Costs – Expense – Depreciation – Overhead | Movement of Revenues + Sales |
| Working Capital to Total Assets % | Closing balances of Current Assets + Bank Accounts – Current Liabilities | Closing balances of Current Assets + Fixed Assets + Non-Current Assets + Bank Accounts |

From the Dashboard, each graph can be selected to open the screen for that ratio.

# Budget Manager

Xero has a very basic budgeting tool called **Budget Manager**. It is essentially a spreadsheet template that can be completed and used in reports for comparative analysis. It is important to understand that the Budget Manager does not automate assumptions or handle dynamic data. For these purposes, advisors look to third-party applications; however, for simple budget needs, budget manager is a solid option included with the subscription.

It is important to understand that budgets are strictly named data sets. Budgets are not related to each other in Xero. For example, you may create a series of budgets for different tracking categories, but the Overall Budget will not be created automatically. You must manually create a set of data for a summary budget.

## Creating Budgets

There are two kinds of budgets in Xero: an Overall Budget and any others that you add. The Overall Budget is the budget for the entire company. You can create additional budgets for any other segregation, such as by tracking category or different scenarios.

To access Budget Manager:

1. Navigate to **Accounting**, then **Reports**.
2. In the **Financial** section of **Reports**, select **Budget Manager**.

At the top of the screen are the settings for the creation of a budget. The default budget is Overall Budget. An organization can only have one Overall Budget (Figure 18.4).

Select the first month of the budget period by using the pull-down in the **Start** field. Use the **Actuals** pull-down to show actual data from prior months. This will add columns on the left as a reference. The **Period** pull-down refers to how many months the budget will be created for. Budgets can only be created by month.

The budget template includes all income statement general ledger accounts. They are shown on the left by name with the account code in parentheses. To create a budget, enter the budgeted amount in the appropriate cell for the month and general ledger account. You will notice that a green arrow appears to the right of the cell selected. This arrow is a shortcut that will allow Xero to enter figures for the remainder of the budget period in one of three ways (Figure 18.5):

1. **Apply fixed amount to each month**—fills each month with the same dollar amount as the month in the selected cell.
2. **Adjust by amount each month**—fills each month with the dollar amount as the month selected, plus or minus a consistent value.
3. **Adjust by percentage each month**—fills each month with the dollar amount as the previous, plus or minus a percentage change.

**FIGURE 18.4**

At the top of the screen are the settings for the creation of a budget. The default budget is Overall Budget. An organization can only have one Overall Budget.

### Budget Manager

| Select Budget | | Start | | Actuals | | Period | | |
|---|---|---|---|---|---|---|---|---|
| Overall Budget | ▼ | Oct 2020 | ▼ | 3 months | ▼ | 12 months | ▼ | Update |

### Overall Budget

Wide view ▦

| | Jul-20 | Aug-20 | Sep-20 | Oct-20 ⇨ | Nov-20 | Dec-2 |
|---|---|---|---|---|---|---|
| **Income** | | | | | | |
| Chemical Sales (4025) | 0 | 0 | (23) | 5,450 ⇨ | 0 | |
| Equipment Sales Revenue (4020) | 0 | 0 | 4,751 | 0 | 0 | |
| Goodwill Discounts (4999) | 0 | 0 | 0 | 0 | 0 | |
| Interest Income (4700) | 0 | 0 | 0 | 0 | 0 | |
| Labor Repair Revenue (4015) | 0 | 0 | 0 | 0 | 0 | |
| One off Pool Cleaning Service (4005) | 0 | 0 | 0 | 0 | 0 | |
| Open Pool Services (4006) | 0 | 0 | 0 | 0 | 0 | |
| Other Revenue (4600) | 0 | 0 | 0 | 0 | 0 | |
| Recurring Pool Cleaning Service (4001) | 0 | 0 | 870 | 0 | 0 | |
| Winterizing Services (4010) | 0 | 0 | 0 | 0 | 0 | |
| **Total Income** | 0 | 0 | 5,598 | 5,450 | 0 | |
| **Less Cost of Sales** | | | | | | |

*Source:* Xero Limited

**FIGURE 18.5**

This arrow is shortcut that will allow Xero to enter figures for the remainder of the budget period in one of three ways:

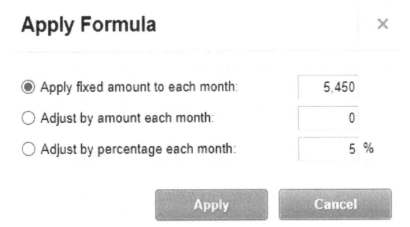

*Source:* Xero Limited

To create budgets in addition to the Overall Budget, use the **Select Budget** pull-down to choose **Add a new budget**. Enter a Name, and if desired, select a tracking category. The purpose of the tracking category is to filter actual data to only certain category options. It has no effect on the creation of the budget data set.

## Importing a Budget

Creating a budget using the Budget Manager within Xero can be time consuming for organizations with many income statement lines. A better option is to build the budget using a spreadsheet tool, then importing the data to Xero. This is especially useful when the company wishes to run multiple scenarios or modify assumptions in a spreadsheet before importing a final budget to Xero.

To import a budget:

1. Navigate to **Accounting**, then **Reports**.
2. Select **Budget Manager** under the Financial section.
3. Click the **Import** button at the bottom of the screen.
4. Use the **Download template** pull-down to select either .csv or .xls format. Xero will download a template file in your browser (Figure 18.6).
5. Add your data to the template and save where it can be easily located.
6. Use the **Browse** button to select the updated file.
7. Click the **Import** button to import the data into the Budget Manager.
8. Click **Save**.

**FIGURE 18.6**

Use the Download template pulldown to select either .csv or .xls format. Xero will download a template file in your browser.

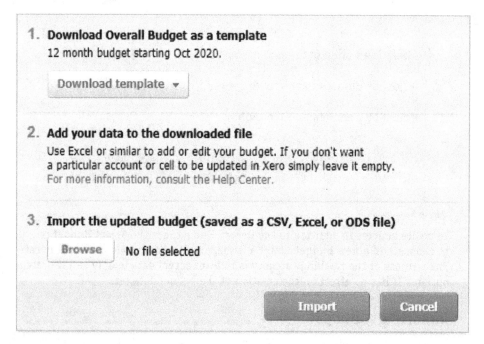

## Overall Budget

1. **Download Overall Budget as a template**
   12 month budget starting Oct 2020.

   Download template ▾

2. **Add your data to the downloaded file**
   Use Excel or similar to add or edit your budget. If you don't want a particular account or cell to be updated in Xero simply leave it empty.
   For more information, consult the Help Center.

3. **Import the updated budget (saved as a CSV, Excel, or ODS file)**

   Browse   No file selected

   Import   Cancel

*Source:* Xero Limited

## Budget Summary Report

Xero's Budget Manager is not the ideal layout for reviewing budgets. To review a budget in the system, use the Budget Summary report:

1. Navigate to **Accounting**, then **Reports**.
2. Select **Budget Summary** under the Financial section.
3. Use the **Budget** pull-down to select the budget.
4. Use the **From** pull-down to select the starting month to view.
5. Select a **Period**, generally one month.
6. Select the **Number of periods to show**.
7. Click **Update**.

This report can be exported as a .pdf or spreadsheet for easy review or sharing.

# Xero Expenses

*Xero Expenses makes reimbursing employees and managing company receipts super easy! Employees simply upload their receipts to the Expenses mobile or web app and it shows up on my dashboard in Xero. I can review the receipt and reimburse it, using our fully integrated business bank, Relay. I can also use Expenses to easily track money spent on our company card. I've tried all sorts of other expense apps, but I think Xero Expenses is the best for small businesses who want a simple tool without having to leave the Xero platform.*

—*Nikole Mackenzie, Founder of Momentum Accounting*

Launched in 2018, Xero Expenses is a notable improvement over the classic expense claim functionality covered in Chapter 12. It has the feel of a stand-alone product rather than an adjunct to a browser-based software platform. Xero Expenses solves what was one of the biggest problems with classic expense claims, advisor controls, by making it much more flexible.

Xero Expenses is included in the Established subscription level and functions, to some extent, like a third-party expensing app.

The approval process is dependent on user permissions, and claim submitters can easily see where their expenses are in the process under the **Your Expenses** tab.

When claims are approved, they are moved to the **To pay** tab, and from there, a reimbursement check can be generated in just five clicks. Clicking the **Pay All** button from Expenses creates a Bill payable to the submitter for each of the submissions. They can then easily be reimbursed in aggregate in Xero's Purchases module.

## Setting Up Xero Expenses

Before the company uses Xero Expenses for the first time, you will need to set up the functionality. To access Xero Expenses, navigate to **Business**, then **Expense Claims**.

When you arrive on this screen, you may be directed to a set-up wizard that will steer you through the steps in setting up. If not, you may be offered a tile with a button **Go to settings**, or you can use the gear in the top right corner to access settings.

## Receipt Analysis

The first step in establishing expense claim settings is to choose whether you wish Xero to extract financial data from the receipt image. Xero uses machine learning to interpret the receipt details over time. Enabling receipt analysis will yield efficiency as the tools are used (Figure 19.1). If you prefer to add the receipt details manually to the expense claim, choose **Skip for now** or uncheck the **Enable receipt analysis** box.

## Expense Claim Accounts

The next step is to select the general ledger accounts that should be offered to users in classifying expenditures. In the Expense claims screen, use the **Edit** button to open the chart of accounts. Use the checkboxes on the left to indicate that the account may be used in coding expense claims (Figure 19.2). The default view includes on Expense type general ledger accounts, but you can select from other account types by using the headers at the top of the listing. Click **Done** to close the account selection screen.

**FIGURE 19.1**

The first step in establishing expense claim settings is to choose whether you wish Xero to extract financial data from the receipt image. Xero uses machine learning to interpret the receipt details over time. Enabling receipt analysis will yield efficiency as the tools are used.

*Source:* Xero Limited

**FIGURE 19.2**

The next step is to select the general ledger accounts that should be offered to users in classifying expenditures. In the Expense claims screen, use the Edit button to open the chart of accounts. Use the checkboxes on the left to indicate that the account may be used in coding expense claims.

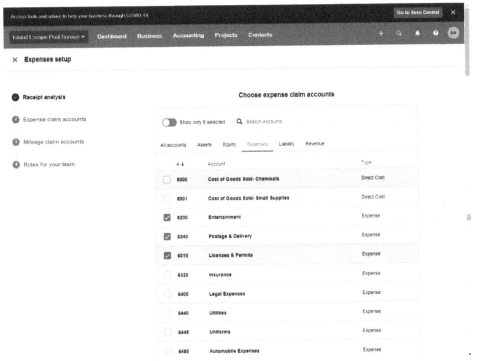

*Source:* Xero Limited

## Mileage Claim Accounts

Just as with expense claims, you must elect which general ledger accounts can be used for mileage claims. Use the **Edit** button to open the chart of accounts and select one or more accounts to be used. Click **Done** to close the selection screen.

## Adding Users

This screen lists the logged in user (you), as well as others in the organization. If you are the only user who needs Expenses access, select the **Just me for now** button at the bottom of the screen. To give other users access to Expenses, check the box to the left of their name and select one of the three user roles:

- Submitter: can capture, submit, and view their own expenses
- Approver: can capture, submit, edit, approve, and decline their own expenses or on behalf of others
- Admin: has same access as Approver, plus management of all expenses settings

**FIGURE 19.3**

Select any bank or credit cards that this user will have access to by checking the box to the left of the account.

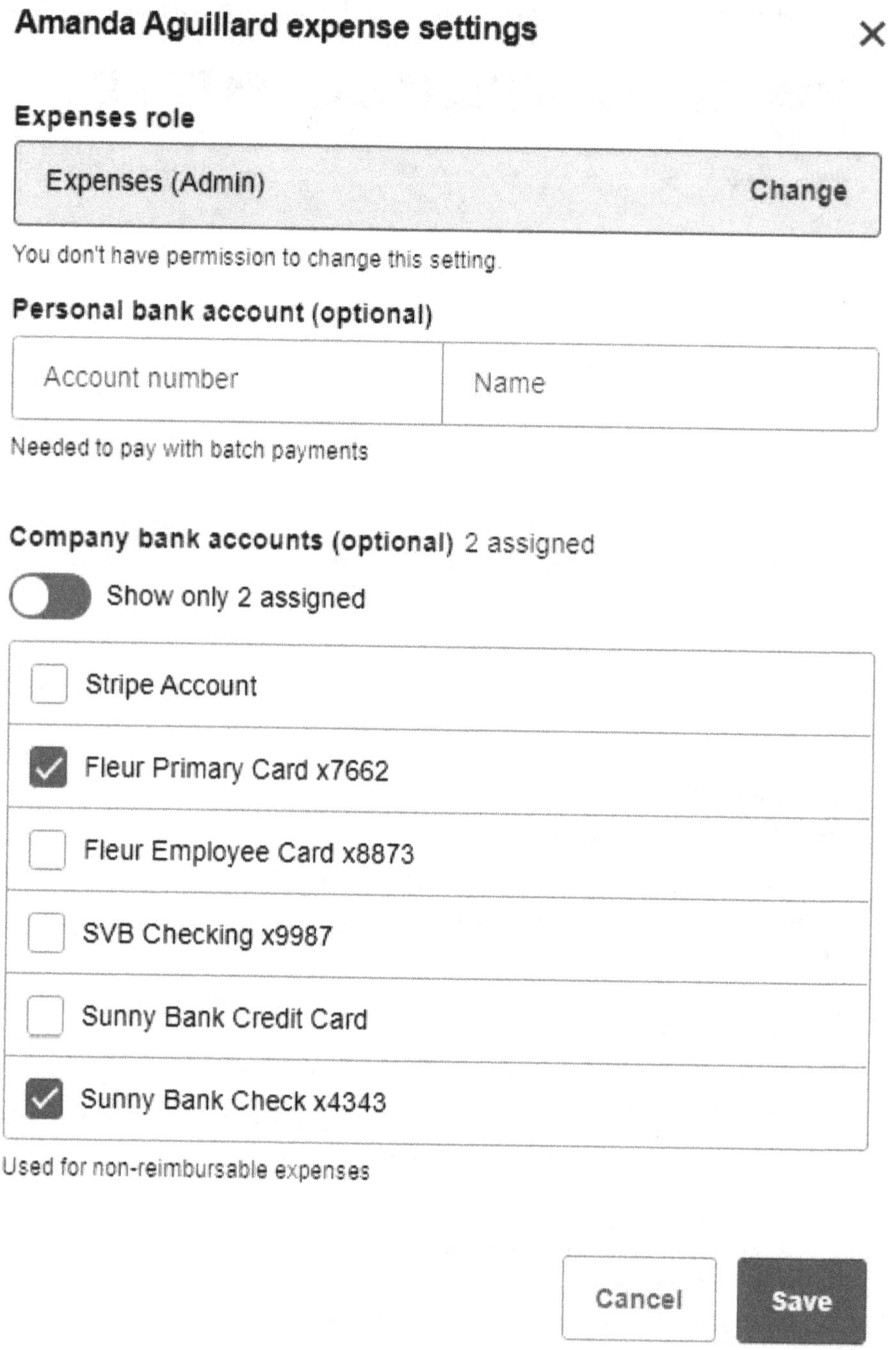

## Amanda Aguillard expense settings ✕

**Expenses role**

| Expenses (Admin) | Change |
|---|---|

You don't have permission to change this setting.

**Personal bank account (optional)**

| Account number | Name |
|---|---|

Needed to pay with batch payments

**Company bank accounts (optional)** 2 assigned

⬤ Show only 2 assigned

| | |
|---|---|
| ☐ | Stripe Account |
| ☑ | Fleur Primary Card x7662 |
| ☐ | Fleur Employee Card x8873 |
| ☐ | SVB Checking x9987 |
| ☐ | Sunny Bank Credit Card |
| ☑ | Sunny Bank Check x4343 |

Used for non-reimbursable expenses

| Cancel | Save |
|---|---|

*Source:* Xero Limited

**FIGURE 19.4**

Give labels names related to trips or projects to help keep claims organized.

Expenses › **Expense settings**

| For the organization | | Labels 2 | | New label |
|---|---|---|---|---|
| Expense claims | | Name | | Last updated ↓ |
| Mileage claims | | Accounting Salon May 2021 | | Oct 4, 2020 ⋮ |
| Users | 1 | Xerocon 2020 | | Oct 4, 2020 ⋮ |
| Just for you | | | | |
| Labels | 2 | | | |

*Source:* Xero Limited

You also have the option to assign **Company bank accounts**. This is important for users with company debit or credit cards because it will allow a non-reimbursable claim to be created in order to match with a bank statement line. Select any bank or credit cards that this user will have access to by checking the box to the left of the account (Figure 19.3).

While employee users are encouraged to download the Xero Expenses application (available for Android and iOS) for a simplified interface, it is not required. The entire Expenses function can be experienced through the browser version of Xero.

## Using Labels

Xero Expenses allows users to create labels to help organize claims. Labels can be created by any Expenses user and are specific to the user. Users cannot view labels of other users. Give labels names related to trips or projects to help keep claims organized (Figure 19.4).

# Reimbursable versus Nonreimbursable Claims

It is important to understand the difference between reimbursable and nonreimbursable claims in Xero Expenses and how each is handled. Reimbursable claims are those where the employee or user pays for a purchase using his or her own funds and needs to be reimbursed by the company. Nonreimbursable claims are a way to submit substantiating documentation for the use of company funds. Both types of claims are submitted through Xero Expenses in the same way.

**Reimbursable claims** by an employee will create Awaiting Payment bills in the Purchases module of Xero where the user is the supplier. The company can then reimburse the user by check payment, processing a batch ACH (automated clearing house) file for the bank, a payroll service, or using a bill payment application.

19

**Nonreimbursable claims** by a user will generate an unreconciled Spend Money transaction in the bank account selected when the claim is created. The Spend Money will match with the bank line when it appears in the Reconcile tab.

# Submitting Expense Claims

Expense claims are generally created by the submitting employee and can be created in either the browser or the mobile app. Both platforms sync automatically, so a claim can be created in one platform and viewed or approved in another seamlessly.

## Creating a Claim in the Browser

To create a Xero Expenses claim from the browser, navigate to **Business**, then **Expense claims**. At the top of the screen, use the green **New expense** pull-down to select **Expense claim**.

Complete the expense claim submission using these steps:

1. Upload or drag and drop a receipt image into the space provided on the left.
2. Enter the **Purchase amount.** The default currency is the currency of the company, but you can change it by using the pull-down to the left of the input field. If you choose a different currency, the exchange rate and restated total will appear at the bottom of the screen.
3. To split the charge between more than one account, use the **Itemize** link above the Purchase amount field.
4. Enter a **Description.**
5. Select whether the expense was paid with **Company money** or **Personal money.** It is very important that this selection is correct, since Xero handles each differently. If Company money is selected, choose the **Company bank account** (or credit card) that was used for the purchase.
6. Enter the vendor name in the **Spent at** field.
7. Select the transaction date in the **Spent on** field.
8. Choose the general ledger **Account** that should be used.
9. Complete the optional details, if desired. These allow you to associate the claim with a tracking category, assign the charge to a project or expense, or add a label to the expense.
10. In the upper right, choose **Save draft** to finalize later, **Submit** to send the expense claim to an approver, or **Approve** to process the claim (Figure 19.5).

## Creating a Claim in the Mobile App

The mobile app for Xero Expenses can be downloaded for either iOS or Android. The detailed instructions below are specific to the iOS application. For directions on submitting using the Android version, visit Xero Central.

**FIGURE 19.5**

In the upper right, choose Save draft to finalize later, Submit to send the expense claim to an approver, or Approve to process the claim.

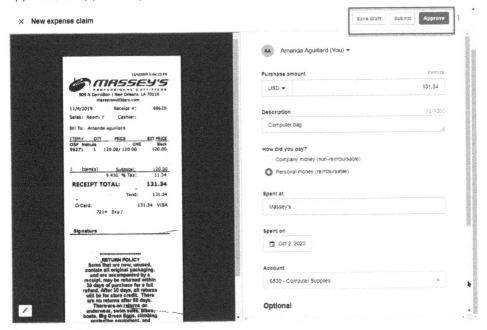

*Source:* Xero Limited

To create a Xero Expenses claim from an iOS device:

1. Use the + icon at the bottom of the screen, then select **Expense claim** (Figure 19.6).

2. Take a photo of the receipt. Putting the receipt on a contrasting background may help the app find the borders of the receipt for cropping. If there is no receipt for the expense claim, select **No receipt** in the top right.

3. Choose either **Save for later** or **Add details now**. If you choose **Save for later**, Xero will analyze the receipt information and auto-populate the claim after a short delay. Choose **Add details now** to enter the claim information manually (Figure 19.7).

4. Complete the fields with the correct data.

5. Tap **Save**.

## Editing Expense Claims

Expense claims can be edited by approver-level users until paid or by submitters until approved.

**FIGURE 19.6**

Use the + icon at the bottom of the screen, then select Expense claim.

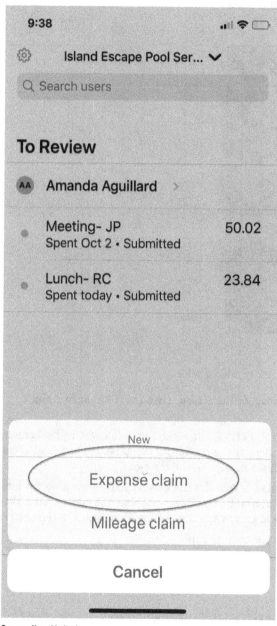

*Source:* Xero Limited

**FIGURE 19.7**

Choose either Save for later or Add details now. If you choose Save for later, Xero will analyze the receipt information and auto populate the claim after a short delay. Choose Add details now to enter the claim information manually.

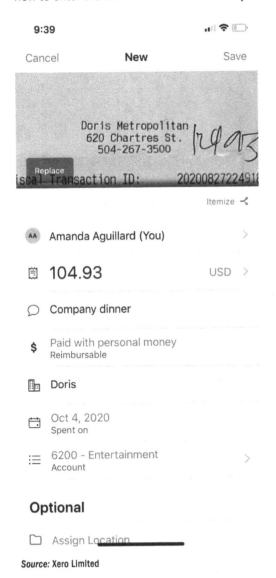

*Source:* Xero Limited

**FIGURE 19.8**

Find the expense claim to be edited and use the overflow menu at the right to select Edit.

*Source:* Xero Limited

To edit an expense claim:

1. Navigate to Xero Expenses by going to the **Business** tab, then **Expense claims**.
2. Find the expense claim to be edited and use the overflow menu at the right to select **Edit** (Figure 19.8).
3. Make any needed changes to the claim.
4. Select **Save**.

# Submitting Mileage Claims

Employees submit mileage claims to be reimbursed for business use of a personal vehicle. They can be submitted in either a browser or from the mobile app.

## Creating a Mileage Claim in the Browser

To create a mileage claim from the browser, navigate to **Business**, then **Expense claims**. At the top of the screen, use the green **New expense** pull-down to select **Mileage claim**.

Complete the expense claim submission using these steps:

1. Enter the **Mileage to claim** and the **Rate** per mile.
2. Enter a **Description**.
3. Select the travel date in the **Traveled on** field.
4. Choose the general ledger **Account** that should be used.
5. Complete the optional details, if desired. These allow you to associate the mileage with a tracking category, assign the charge to a project or expense, or add a label to the expense.
6. Xero will calculate the reimbursement in the company's base currency. In the upper right, choose **Save draft** to finalize later, **Submit** to send the expense claim to an approver, or **Approve** to process the claim (Figure 19.9).

## Creating a Mileage Claim in the Mobile App

The detailed instructions below are specific for creating a mileage claim in the iOS mobile application. For directions on submitting using the Android version, visit Xero Central.

To create a mileage claim from an iOS device:

1. Use the + icon at the bottom of the screen, then select **Mileage claim** (Figure 19.10).
2. Manually enter the distance or click the **Use map** link to calculate the travel between two points (Figure 19.11).
3. Enter the rate per mile.

**FIGURE 19.9**

Xero will calculate the reimbursement in the company's base currency. In the upper right, choose Save draft to finalize later, Submit to send the expense claim to an approver, or Approve to process the claim.

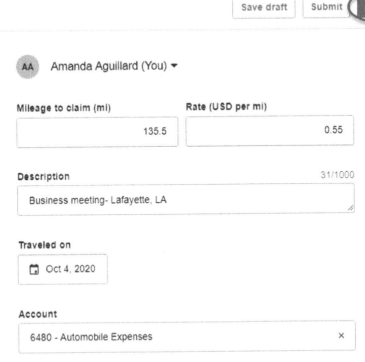

*Source:* Xero Limited

**FIGURE 19.10**

Use the + icon at the bottom of the screen, then select Mileage claim.

*Source:* Xero Limited

**FIGURE 19.11**

Manually enter the distance or click the Use map link to calculate the travel between two points.

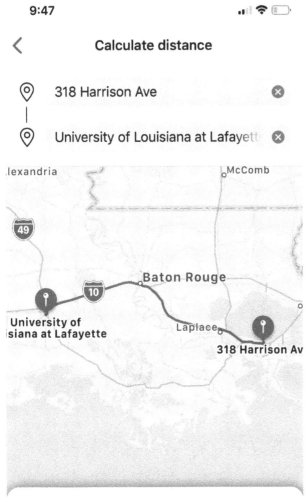

*Source:* Xero Limited

4. Enter a description of the travel in the **What was it for?** field.

5. Enter the date of travel.

6. Choose the general ledger account that should be used.

7. Complete any optional fields.

8. Tap **Save** (Figure 19.12).

**FIGURE 19.12**

Tap Save.

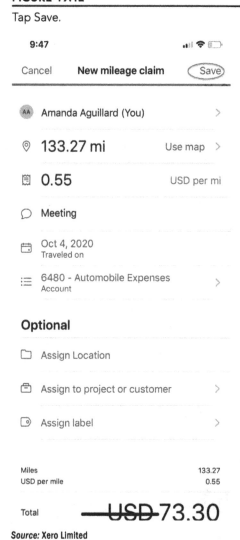

*Source:* Xero Limited

# Approving Expense and Mileage Claims

When expense and mileage claims are submitted by a user for approval, the approver will see the claims in the **To review** tab. You can open the claim for review by clicking on the line. From this screen the claim can be edited, declined, or approved by using the buttons in the top right (Figure 19.13).

When a claim is approved, it will be moved from the **To review** tab to the **To pay** tab, if it is a reimbursable claim. A bill will also be created for the reimbursement in the **Awaiting Payment** tab of Purchases (Figure 19.14). If the claim is nonreimbursable, because it is a use of company money, the claim will be removed from the **To review** tab and converted into an unreconciled spend money transaction associated with the indicated bank account.

# Paying Expense and Mileage Claims

Expense claims awaiting reimbursement are shown in two places: in the **To pay** tab of Expenses and in Bills **Awaiting Payment**. From the Expenses screen, clicking the Pay All button at the top right will redirect you to the Awaiting Payment tab in Bills. From here, employees or other users may have their expenses reimbursed in a number of ways. The company may print a check. It may submit a batch ACH payment to the bank for processing. It may add the reimbursement amount to the employee's paycheck in the payroll software.

**FIGURE 19.13**

When expense and mileage claims are submitted by a user for approval, the approver will see the claims in the To review tab. The claim can be opened for review by clicking on the line. From this screen the claim can be edited, declined or approved by using the buttons in the top right.

*Source:* Xero Limited

**FIGURE 19.14**

When a claim is approved, it will be moved from the To review tab to the To pay tab, if it is a reimbursable claim. A bill will also be created for the reimbursement in the Awaiting Payment tab of Purchases.

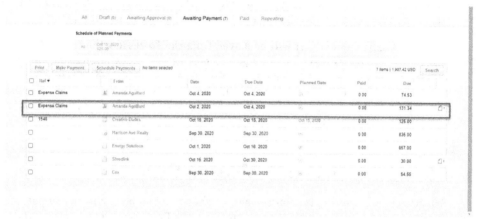

*Source:* Xero Limited

## Paying Claims by Check

Paying claims by check is identical to paying other bills by check. Check the box to the left of the claim or claims. Select **Make Payment**, then **Pay By Check**. Use the **Save & Print PDF** button to generate a file that can be printed on check stock. See Chapter 12 for more details on printing and formatting checks.

## Paying Claims by Batch ACH

If the company uses a batch file to upload to its bank for ACH payments, reimbursements can be handled the same way. Check the box to the left of the claim or claims. Select **Make Payment**, then **Batch Payment**. Enter the payment details, then click **Make Payments**.

In order to generate a usable file, the employee's bank details must be entered in Expenses settings. From the Expenses screen, navigate to the gear icon. Select Users on the left, then to the Edit button to the right of the user name. Enter the **Personal bank account** information.

For more information about making batch ACH payments, see Chapter 12.

## Paying Claims within the Payroll System

Many payroll processors have the ability to add a reimbursement to an employee's paycheck. The reimbursement amount is not included in any wage amounts or tax calculations, but is simply an additional amount of cash remitted to the employee. Because every payroll application is slightly different, you will need to review any integrations between the payroll processor and Xero. What is important to remember is that Xero will be recording the expense on the general ledger as the claim is approved and processed. The payroll software should not be additionally recording an expense for the reimbursement. If the payroll software sends an additional bill to Xero for the reimbursement, this will need to be deleted.

## Reconciling the Bank Statement Line to the Claim

The bank statement line should automatically match with the claim payment, whether paid by check or ACH. For non-reimbursable expense claims, there is no processing of a payment because the company funds have been spent prior to the submission of the claim. A spend money line is posted to the bank account and will be marked Unreconciled until the bank line clears (Figure 19.15). When the bank statement line is imported, the spend money transaction will match automatically.

# Understanding the Company's Expense Claims

When a company is using Xero Expenses, it will want to understand claims pending as well as easily see analytics around claims paid.

## Viewing the Company's Expense Claims

At the top of the Expenses screen are tabs for each status associated with claims. There is also an **All** tab that when selected will show every claim in Xero. In the **All** tab, there are

**FIGURE 19.15**

A spend money line is posted to the bank account and will be marked Unreconciled until the bank line clears.

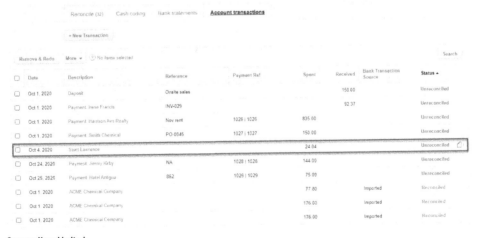

*Source: Xero Limited*

two pull-down menus for filtering. The **Everyone** pull-down will allow the user to filter for submitter. The **Any status** pull-down will filter the listing for the status selected only.

It should be noted that approved and unpaid claims will also be shown in the **Awaiting Payment** tab of Bills, with a reference of "Expense Claims" making them easily identifiable.

## Expense Analytics in Explorer

Xero allows users to see expense claim history graphically by either general ledger account or user. To access, navigate to **Business**, then **Expense Claims**. At the top of the screen select **Explorer**, then use the pull-down on the right to toggle between **by Account** and **by Employee** (Figure 19.16).

### FIGURE 19.16

Xero allows users to see expense claim history graphically by either general ledger account or user. To access, navigate to Business, then Expense Claims. At the top of the screen select Explorer, then use the pulldown on the right to toggle between by Account and by Employee.

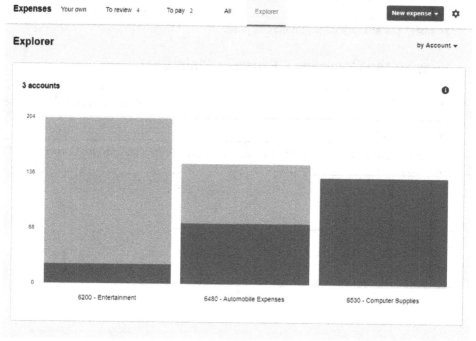

*Source: Xero Limited*

# Xero Projects

*All our clients are agencies and live and die by their ability to drive project level profitability. Xero Projects is how we bring this insight to life.*

*—Ryan Watson, Co-Founder and Principal of Upsourced Accounting*

A long-standing criticism of Xero had been that it did not have a function comparable to other accounting platforms' job costing systems, but that is no longer true. Xero Projects, included in the Established subscription, provides project-based estimates, billing, and reporting.

By using Projects to manage chunks of work, advisors can help company owners understand profitability at a more granular level. It also makes generating estimates and getting paid easier.

## Setting Up Xero Projects

Before the company uses Xero Projects for the first time, you will need to set up the functionality. To access Xero Projects, navigate to **Projects** in the header menu. (If Projects does not appear to be available, you may need to upgrade the subscription.) Access the **All projects** selection from the main Projects menu.

### Adding Users

The first step in employing Xero Projects is to add users. Since projects are based on time attached to users, users must be created first. Like Xero Expenses users, Xero Projects users can be added for project management only, without having access to the business and accounting software.

To add a new user to Projects:

1. Use the Company name pull-down to access **Settings**, then choose **Users**.
2. Click the **Invite a user** button at the top right of the screen.
3. Enter the user's details. The user will log in with their email address.

4. Check **Projects**.

5. Choose the level of access needed (Figure 20.1).

6. Add an optional personal message.

7. Click **Send invite**.

**FIGURE 20.1**

Choose the level of access needed.

Enter their details

First name

Diana

Last name

Taylor

Email

dtaylor@elefanttraining.com

Give them access to:

☑ Projects

**How much access do they need?**

| Limited | Standard | Admin |

ⓘ This limited role is read only but their own time entries can be added and edited. It excludes all financial information. Understand user role details

Enable 'Business and accounting' to use Projects with other Xero business-related features such as invoicing.

☐ **Business and accounting**

Allow this user to access any or all of invoicing and bills, bank accounts, reports, settings, manage users

| Cancel | Add a personal message | Send invite |

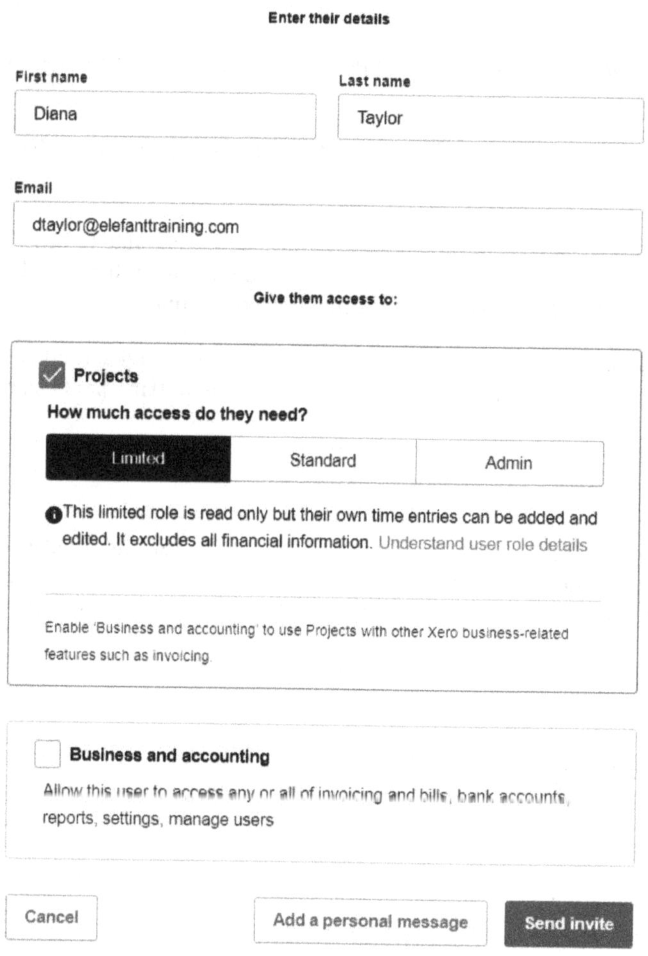

*Source:* Xero Limited

| Permission level in Projects | Access |
|---|---|
| Limited | Can view projects and tasks. Can view, add, or change own time entries. Cannot access reports or create invoices or quotes. |
| Standard | Can create, view, and edit projects, tasks, and expenses. Can create, view, and edit time entries for themselves and others. Can view project estimates and invoices. Can view some reports. |
| Admin | Can create, view, and edit projects, tasks, and expenses. Can create, view, and edit time entries for themselves and others. Can view project estimates and invoices. Can view and edit all costs and staff rates. Can view and export all reports, including the Profitability dashboard. |

To change a current Xero's user permissions with regards to Projects, make the changes on the user's screen and click **Update permissions.**

## Set Up Staff Rates

In order to fully understand the profitability of each project, the underlying expenses must be accurately recorded, including staff costs. Without staff costs established and maintained for updates, project expenses will be incorrect. The Staff cost rates screen lists all staff and their cost per hour (Figure 20.2).

There are several methods for determining staff cost rates. Examples include:

- Hourly pay rate, plus employer taxes and benefits, for each specific employee
- Hourly pay rate, plus employer taxes and benefits, for each specific employee, plus an allocation for other overhead costs
- A blended rate for each staff position, determined by averaging the actual costs of each employee with that position
- A charge out rate that includes the cost of the employee, plus a percentage for profit expected on each project. This is commonly used when projects are compared to a break-even point.

**FIGURE 20.2**

The Staff cost rates screen lists all staff and their cost per hour.

*Source:* Xero Limited

## FIGURE 20.3

Use the overflow menu in the top right to access Projects settings.

*Source:* Xero Limited

To assign staff cost rates to users:

1. Navigate to **Projects**, then **All projects**.
2. Use the overflow menu in the top right to access **Projects settings** (Figure 20.3).
3. Any users with access to Xero Projects will be listed. Click the **Edit** button to the right of the staff member's name.
4. Enter a **Cost rate / hr.**
5. Click **Save**.

# Overview of the Projects Dashboard

The Projects screen shows a listing of projects by status: Draft, In progress, or Closed. **Draft** projects have not yet begun and may not be fully set up. **In progress** projects are actively under way. **Closed** projects are complete or will not be continued past the current point. Navigate between projects by using the tabs at the top of the screen (Figure 20.4).

On the top right of the screen is a redirect button to the **Project Summary Report**, as well as a button for creating a project and an overflow menu that leads to Project settings.

## FIGURE 20.4

Navigate between projects by using the tabs at the top of the screen.

*Source:* Xero Limited

# Creating a Project

Projects are made of time and expenses. Time is associated with tasks within the project. Creating a project includes listing the tasks for the project, estimating time for each, and projecting hard costs, or expenses, for the project.

## Creating a Draft Project

When planning a project, it is a good idea to create a draft with the estimated time and expenses as it is developed, then move to **In progress** once the project is fully outlined and is ready to be started. Projects are associated with a contact, given a project name, and can be opened with a deadline and estimate in dollars.

To create a draft project:

1. Navigate to **Projects**, then **All projects**.
2. Use the **New project** pull-down in the top right to access **Draft**.
3. Enter the customer in the **Contact** field. Xero will filter existing contacts as you type. If the contact does not exist, use the **+Add new contact** link to create it in Xero.
4. Enter the **Project name**.
5. Choose a **Deadline**.
6. Either enter a fixed dollar amount in the **Estimate** field or select **Calculate from tasks & estimated expenses**.
7. Click **Create** (Figure 20.5).

## Adding Tasks

Tasks are used to separate the entire project into segments of work. Setting tasks at the beginning of a project will help in planning the project and its costs. Some examples of tasks on a pool installation project may be:

- Layout and design pool
- Site preparation
- Framing
- Plumbing and electrical
- Pour concrete and finish
- Landscaping and decking

Tasks should be specific enough to be able to identify a portion of the work but not so narrow in scope that they become cumbersome. In general, between three and seven tasks is a good guideline.

20

FIGURE 20.5

Click Create.

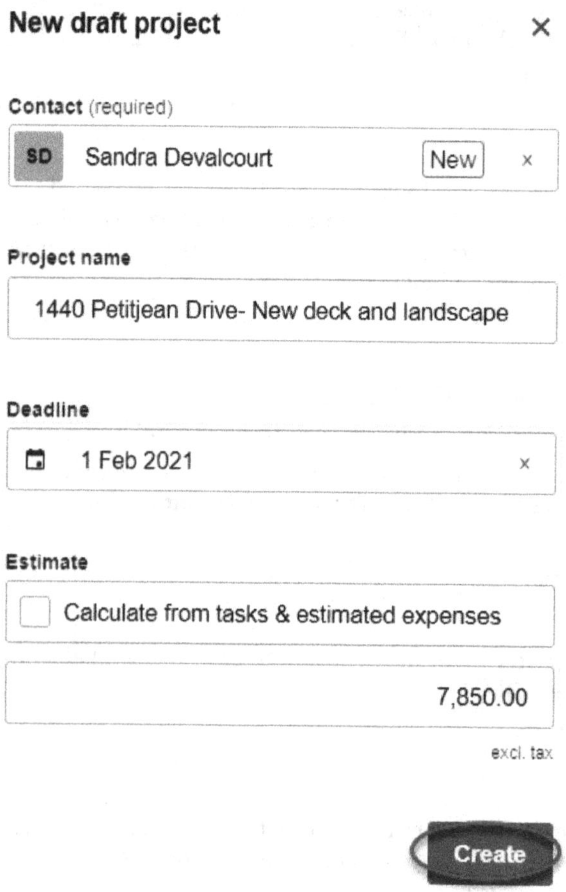

## New draft project ✕

**Contact** (required)

| SD | Sandra Devalcourt | [New] | ✕ |

**Project name**

1440 Petitjean Drive- New deck and landscape

**Deadline**

📅   1 Feb 2021                                          ✕

**Estimate**

☐  Calculate from tasks & estimated expenses

7,850.00

excl. tax

**Create**

*Source:* Xero Limited

To add a task to a project:

1. Navigate to **Projects**, then **All projects**.

2. Open the project by clicking the project name.

3. Use the **Add** pull-down at the top right to select **Task** (Figure 20.6).

4. Enter a name for the task or search for an inventory item to use as the task name.

5. If desired, enter an estimated number of hours for this task. Adding a time estimate for the task will allow Xero to show a graphic of completion on the task line.

6. Choose how to charge for the task, either an amount per hour, a fixed price for the task, or not chargeable.

7. Click **Save** to save and close the new task, or **Save & add another** to save and get another task input screen (Figure 20.7).

**FIGURE 20.6**

Use the Add pulldown at the top right to select Task.

*Source:* Xero Limited

**FIGURE 20.7**

Click Save to save and close the new task, or Save & add another to save and get another task input screen.

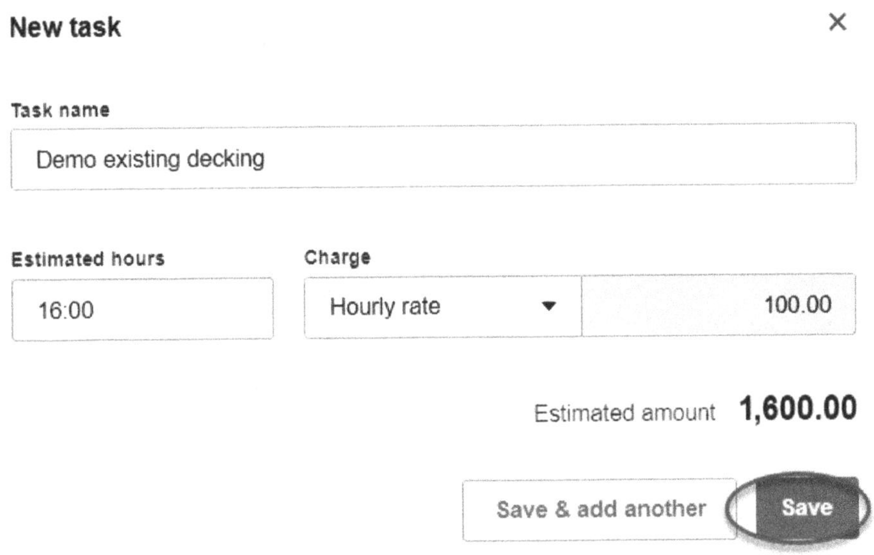

**New task**                                                                    ✕

Task name

Demo existing decking

Estimated hours          Charge

16:00                    Hourly rate          ▼          100.00

Estimated amount **1,600.00**

Save & add another          **Save**

*Source:* Xero Limited

## Estimating Expenses

To fully understand the scope of a project in draft, you will need to add any hard or direct costs of the project as estimated expenses. Expenses are associated with the project but not tied to a specific task within the project.

To add an estimated expense to a project:

1. Navigate to **Projects**, then **All projects.**
2. Open the project by clicking the project name.

20

**FIGURE 20.8**

Click Save.

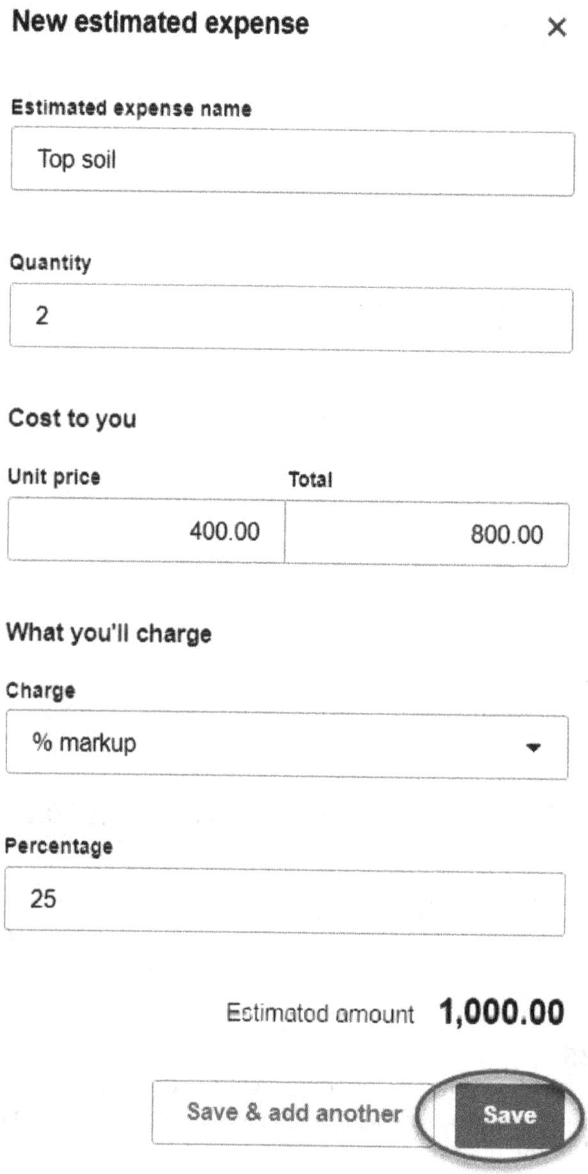

## New estimated expense  ✕

Estimated expense name

Top soil

Quantity

2

## Cost to you

| Unit price | Total |
|---|---|
| 400.00 | 800.00 |

## What you'll charge

Charge

% markup  ▼

Percentage

25

Estimated amount  **1,000.00**

| Save & add another | Save |

*Source:* Xero Limited

3. Use the **Add** pull-down at the top right to select **Estimated expense**.

4. Type the name of the expense in Estimated expense name or have Xero filter for an inventory item.

5. Enter the quantity and unit price. The total will calculate automatically.

6. Determine how the expense will be collected from the customer.

7. Click **Save** (Figure 20.8).

| Charge type | Action |
| --- | --- |
| Nonchargeable | Will not be added to the invoice but will be included in profitability reports |
| % markup | The cost plus an additional percentage will be included on the invoice |
| Pass cost on | The direct cost with no markup will be included on the invoice |
| Custom price | The price entered by the user will be included on the invoice |

### Converting a Draft Project to In Progress

When the project is planned and work is ready to begin, the project should be converted to an active project by moving it from **Draft** status to **In progress**. Use the overflow menu to the right to select **In progress**. The project will now be shown in the **In progress** tab on the Projects dashboard.

# Duplicating a Project

At the time of writing, there is no native templating function yet in Projects. However, an easy workaround would be to duplicate an existing draft project. Create a project with common tasks and save as a draft, giving it an easily identifiable name like New Pool (TEMPLATE). When a new project needs to be created using the template, navigate to the Draft tab and use the overflow menu to the right to **Duplicate project**. Update the details and **Create**.

# Creating a Quote for a Project

When using Xero Projects, quotes should be drafted from Projects, rather than the Sales module of Xero. This keeps all of the data relevant to a project, including revenues and expenses, together. A quote can be issued for the total cost, or a project estimate with tasks and expenses can be converted to a quote.

To create a project amount quote:

1. Navigate to **Projects**, then **All projects**.

2. Open the project by clicking the project name.

20

3. Use the **Quote** pull-down to select **Project amount** (Figure 20.9).

4. Select whether the quote should be for the amount estimated when the project was created or a custom amount. If a custom amount is chosen, enter the **Amount**.

5. Check whether the project name should be the **Quote title**.

6. Click **Open draft quote** to be redirected to a draft in the Quotes screen in Sales.

7. Review and make any changes in this screen. When the quote is ready to be delivered to the customer, click the **Send** button (Figure 20.10).

To create a quote for tasks and expenses:

1. Navigate to **Projects**, then **All projects**.

2. Open the project by clicking the project name.

3. Use the **Quote** pull-down to select **Tasks & estimated expenses**.

4. Use the checkboxes to select which **Tasks and Estimated Expenses** will be included on the quote (Figure 20.11).

5. The default layout for this quote is to show each individual task and expense as a separate line. To change, use the Individual items pull-down to make another selection: **Combined item**, **Combined tasks & combined expenses**, **Combined tasks & individual expenses**, or **Individual tasks & combined expenses**.

6. Check whether the project name should be the **Quote title**.

**FIGURE 20.9**

Use the Quote pulldown to select Project amount.

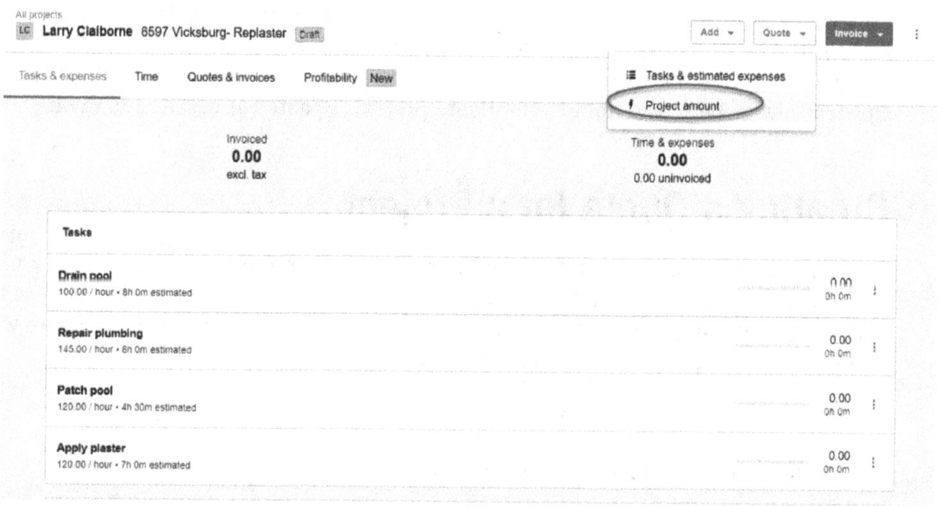

*Source: Xero Limited*

**FIGURE 20.10**

Review and make any changes in this screen. When the quote is ready to be delivered to the customer, click the Send button.

Sales overview › Quotes ›

**Quote QU-0001**

Draft      Send   Print   ☐   Options ▾

| Customer | Date | Expiry | Quote number | Reference |
|---|---|---|---|---|
| Larry Claiborne | Oct 4, 2020 ▾ |   ▾ | QU-0001 | |

Project
6597 Vicksburg- Replaster

Title

## 6597 Vicksburg- Replaster

Summary

USD United States Dollar ▾      Amounts are   Tax Exclusive ▾

| Item | Description | Quantity | Unit price | Disc % | Account | Tax rate | Amount USD |
|---|---|---|---|---|---|---|---|
| | 6597 Vicksburg- Replaster | 1.00 | 9,250.00 | | | | 9,250.00 |

+ Add a new line ▾

| | Subtotal | 9,250.00 |
|---|---|---|
| | **Total** | **9,250.00** |

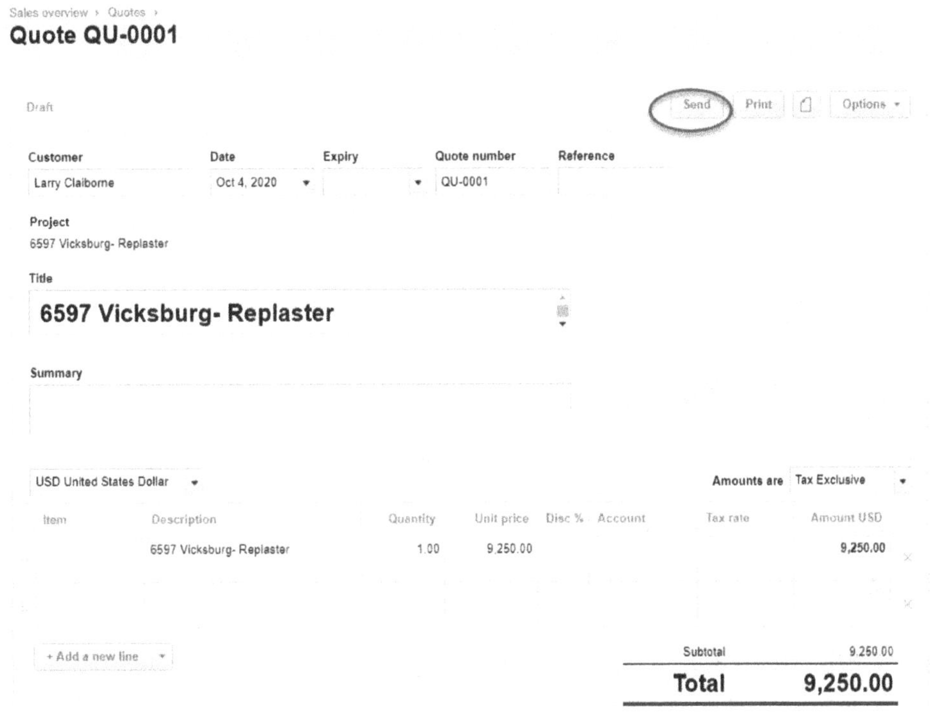

*Source:* Xero Limited

7. Click **Save and open draft quote**.

8. Review and make any changes in this screen. When the quote is ready to be delivered to the customer, click the **Send** button.

For more information about how quotes are accepted or managed, see Chapter 11.

# Adding Time to Project

Time on a project must be associated with a task. This ensures that time is properly recorded and attributable to a specific piece of the project.

20

**FIGURE 20.11**

Use the checkboxes to select which Tasks and Estimated Expenses will be included on the quote.

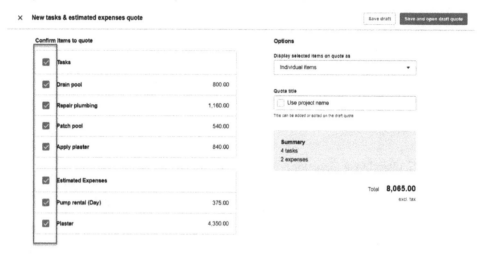

*Source:* Xero Limited

## In the Browser

To add time from a web browser:

1. Navigate to **Projects**, then **All projects**.
2. Open the project by clicking the project name.
3. Use the **Add** pull-down to select **Time entry**.
4. Select a **Task** from the pull-down.
5. Add an optional **Description**.
6. Choose to **Enter time** as either **Duration** or **Start & end** and enter time.
7. Confirm **Date**.
8. Click **Save** (Figure 20.12).

## In the Mobile App

The mobile app for Xero Projects can be downloaded for either iOS or Android. The detailed instructions below are specific to the iOS application. For directions on submitting using the Android version, visit Xero Central.

**FIGURE 20.12**

Click Save.

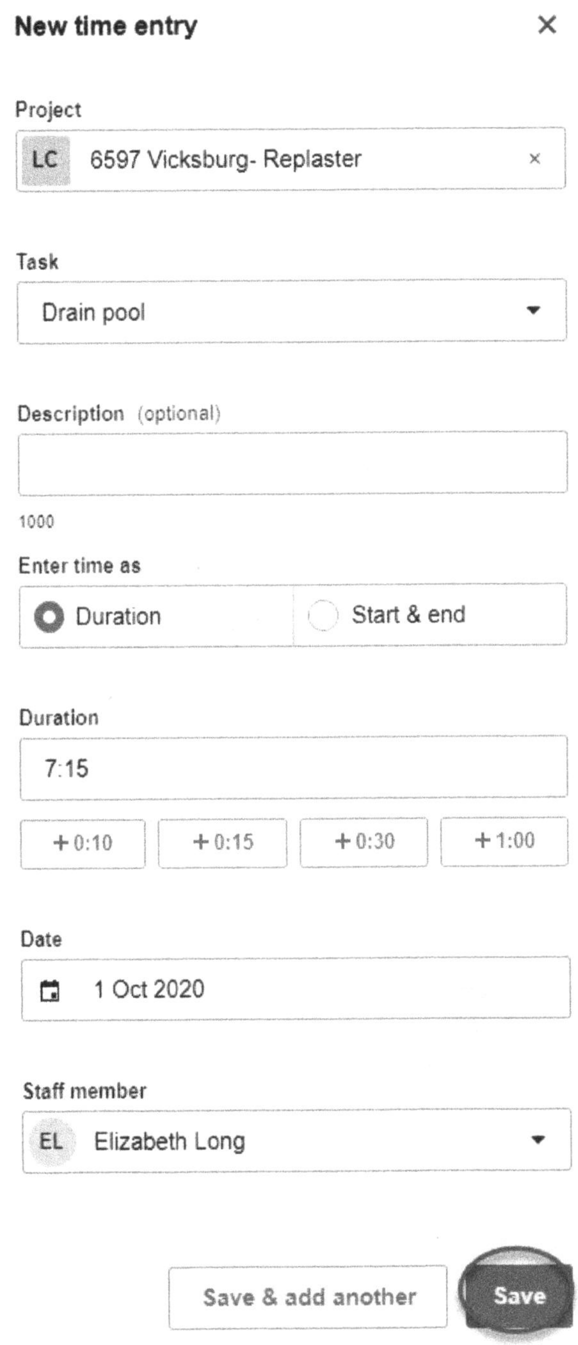

**New time entry**                                        ✕

Project

| LC | 6597 Vicksburg- Replaster | ✕ |

Task

| Drain pool | ▼ |

Description  (optional)

1000

Enter time as

| ⦿ Duration | ◯ Start & end |

Duration

| 7:15 |

| + 0:10 | + 0:15 | + 0:30 | + 1:00 |

Date

| 📅  1 Oct 2020 |

Staff member

| EL | Elizabeth Long | ▼ |

Save & add another        **Save**

*Source:* Xero Limited

Xero allows users to easily add time from the mobile app. To add a time entry:

1. Select the **Time entries** icon at the bottom of the screen (Figure 20.13).
2. Select **Add time**.
3. Choose a project.
4. Choose a task.
5. Enter a total **Duration** or use **Start & end** to have Xero calculate the amount of time assigned (Figure 20.14).
6. Select **Save**.

**FIGURE 20.13**

Select the Time entries icon at the bottom of the screen.

No time entries

Add time

*Source:* Xero Limited

**FIGURE 20.14**

Enter a total Duration or use Start & end to have Xero calculate the amount of time assigned.

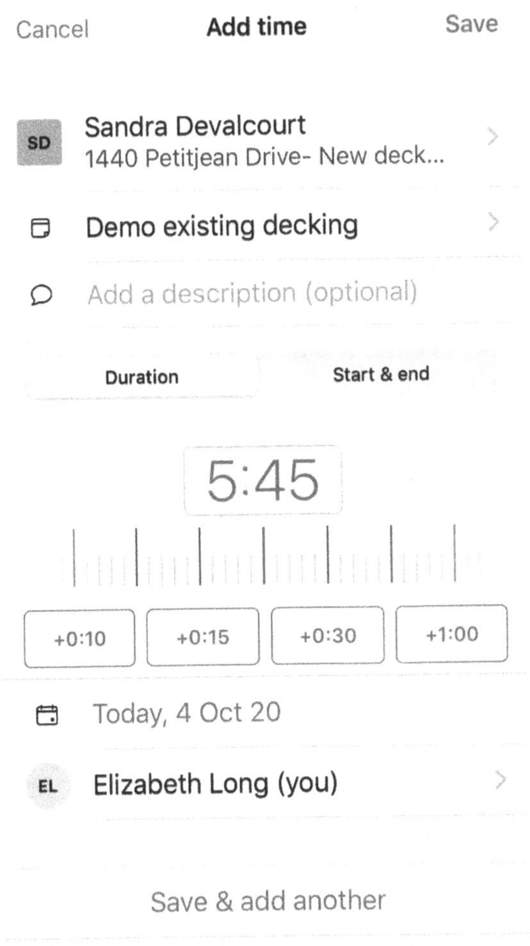

Cancel      **Add time**      Save

| SD | **Sandra Devalcourt** | > |
| | 1440 Petitjean Drive- New deck... | |

🗄    **Demo existing decking**      >

💬    Add a description (optional)

| Duration | Start & end |

$$5:45$$

| +0:10 | +0:15 | +0:30 | +1:00 |

📅    Today, 4 Oct 20

EL    **Elizabeth Long (you)**      >

Save & add another

*Source:* Xero Limited

Users can also use the timer in the app to track time. To enter time using the timer:

1. Select the **Timer** icon at the bottom of the screen.
2. Press the play icon to start the timer and the pause icon to stop.
3. Click **Done**.
4. Choose a project, then a task.
5. Click **Save**.

20

# Adding Expenses to a Project

Expenses or costs can be associated with projects. There are two ways to tie a cost to a project. The first is to note an expense directly in Xero Projects, either using the web browser or in the mobile app. The second way to associate an expense with a project is to assign it from a bank statement line or a bill.

## Adding a New Expense

To add an expense from the web browser:

1. Navigate to **Projects**, then **All projects**.
2. Open the project by clicking the project name.
3. Use the **Add** pull-down to select **Expense** (Figure 20.15).
4. Enter the expense details.
5. Click **Save**.

Note that adding expenses this way will not post any details to the general ledger. It is preferable to assign costs during the reconciliation process so that costs are traceable through the project.

**FIGURE 20.15**

Use the Add pulldown to select Expense.

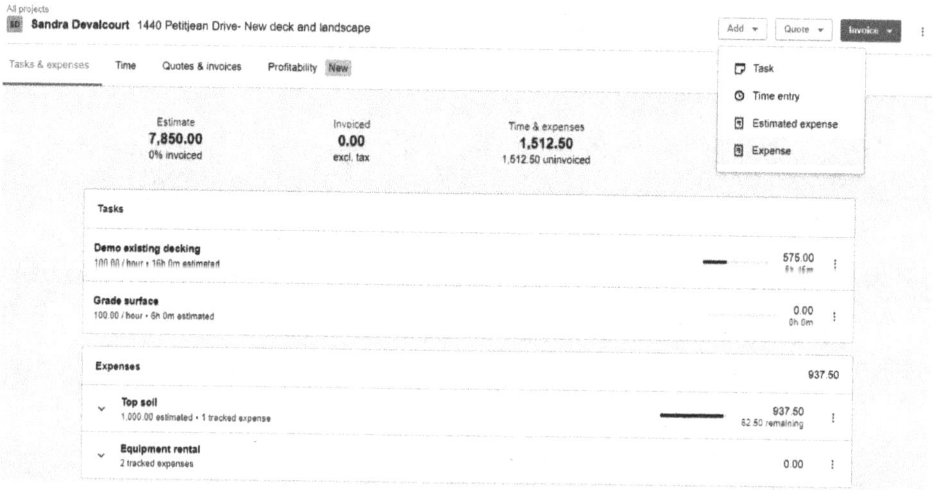

*Source:* Xero Limited

Xero also allows users to easily add expenses from the mobile app. To add an expense entry:

1. Select the Projects icon from the bottom of the screen.
2. Choose the project.
3. Use the + icon at the top to **Add expense** (Figure 20.16).
4. Choose **Actual expense**.
5. Enter the expense details and click **Save** (Figure 20.17).

## Assigning an Expense from Bank Reconciliation

Costs can be assigned to a project directly from a bank statement line in bank reconciliation.

**FIGURE 20.16**

Use the + icon at the top to Add expense.

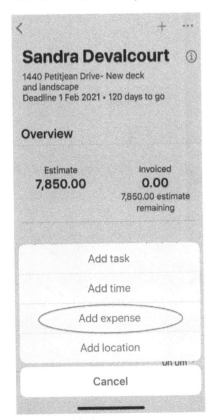

*Source:* Xero Limited

**FIGURE 20.17**

Enter the expense details and click Save.

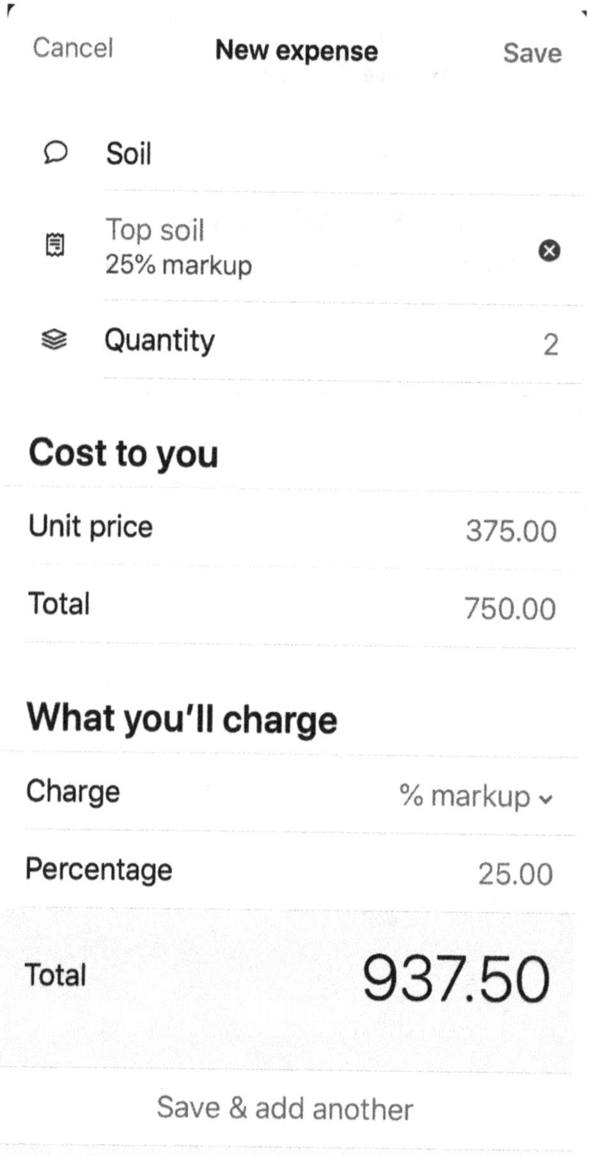

Cancel  **New expense**  Save

Soil

Top soil
25% markup    ✕

Quantity    2

## Cost to you

Unit price    375.00

Total    750.00

## What you'll charge

Charge    % markup ⌄

Percentage    25.00

Total    **937.50**

Save & add another

*Source:* Xero Limited

To assign an expense from a bank line:

1. In the **Reconcile** tab of bank reconciliation, use the **Add details** link in the tile next to the cost.
2. Enter the information for the reconciliation, and click the **Assign expenses to a customer or project** button.
3. Assign the expense to the project using the **Search for a customer or project** field (Figure 20.18).
4. Confirm that the expense is assigned in the **Description** field (Figure 20.19).
5. Click **Save Transaction**.
6. Click **OK** to reconcile the transaction to the bank line.

## Assigning an Expense from a Bill

Costs can also be assigned to a project when creating a new bill.

To assign an expense to a project when creating a bill:

1. Create the bill, completing the necessary fields and adding details for each bill line.
2. Click the **Assign expenses to a customer or project** button at the bottom of the invoice.
3. Find the customer or project in the **Search for a customer or project** field.
4. Select the transaction lines to apply to the customer.

**FIGURE 20.18**

Assign the expense to the project using the Search for a customer or project field.

Assign a customer or project to any billable expense    ✕

Search for a customer or project ▼    Assign    1 item assigned

| | Description | Amount | Customer / Project |
|---|---|---|---|
| ☑ | Delivery fee soil | 125.03 | 1440 Petitjean Drive- New deck ... |

These will show up when you next invoice your customer or project. Find out more

OK    Cancel

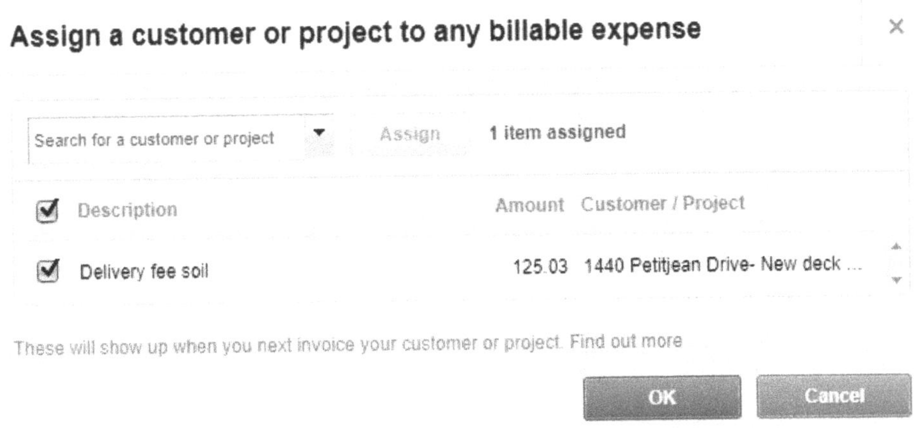

*Source:* Xero Limited

20

**FIGURE 20.19**

Confirm that the expense is assigned in the Description field.

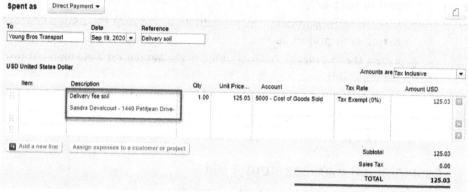

Source: Xero Limited

5. Click **Assign** next to the customer or project name.

6. Confirm that the correct customer or project is shown to the right of the transaction.

7. Click **OK** to save.

8. The assignment of the expense will be noted in the **Description** field of the bill.

9. **Save** or **Approve** the bill (Figure 20.20).

# Invoicing Projects

Invoicing in Projects offers more flexibility than in the Sales screen in Xero. One of the biggest criticisms of Xero in recent years has been that partial or deposit invoices cannot be sent to customers. Xero Projects has this functionality.

In addition to fixed amount invoices and invoices created from quotes, invoices can also be generated from tasks and expenses in a project. This allows for excellent tracking of actual costs that are then passed on to the client.

There are four variations of invoices in Projects:

1. From a quote

2. Deposit invoice

3. Project amount

4. Tasks and expenses

**FIGURE 20.20**

Save or Approve the bill.

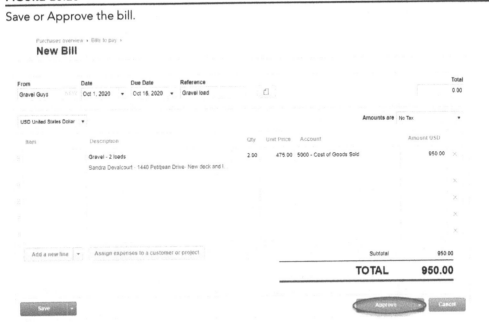

Source: Xero Limited

## Invoices from a Quote

If a quote has been issued on a project, it is easy to use the quote to generate an invoice. To create an invoice from a quote:

1. Navigate to **Projects**, then **All projects**.
2. Open the project by clicking the project name.
3. Use the **Invoice** pull-down to select **Quote** (Figure 20.21).
4. Confirm the quote that should be used for the invoice. Choose if all items should be marked as invoiced and if the project should be closed.
5. Click **Open draft invoice.**
6. A draft invoice will appear in the Invoices screen of Xero. Complete any missing details.
7. Click **Approve.**

20

**FIGURE 20.21**

Use the Invoice pulldown to select Quote.

*Source:* Xero Limited

## Deposit Invoices

A deposit invoice is generally sent to customers as a condition to start work. To create a deposit invoice:

1. Navigate to **Projects**, then **All projects**.
2. Open the project by clicking the project name.
3. Use the **Invoice** pull-down to select **Deposit**.
4. Choose whether to invoice a percentage of the estimated project cost or a specific dollar amount (Figure 20.22).
5. Click **Open draft invoice**.
6. A draft invoice appears in the Invoices screen of Xero. Complete any missing details. It is a good idea to use a liability or holding account for the unearned work (Figure 20.23).
7. Click **Approve**.

Payments received should be noted by matching to a bank line or marked at the bottom of the deposit invoice. When a new invoice is generated on the project, Xero will apply the deposit as a line in the new invoice.

## Project Amount Invoices

A project amount invoice is a fixed fee for the total project. To create a project amount invoice:

1. Navigate to **Projects**, then **All projects**.
2. Open the project by clicking the project name.
3. Use the Invoice pull-down to select **Project amount**.
4. Enter an Amount and choose whether all items should be marked as invoiced and if the project should be closed.

**FIGURE 20.22**

Choose whether to invoice a percentage of the estimated project cost or a specific dollar amount.

New deposit invoice ✕

Estimate
# 7,850.00

Invoice based on

○ Estimate  ● Custom amount

Amount

2,500.00

Total **2,500.00**
excl. tax

**Open draft invoice**

*Source:* Xero Limited

5. Click **Open draft invoice.**

6. A draft invoice will appear in the Invoices screen of Xero. Complete any missing details.

7. Click **Approve.**

## Tasks and Expenses Invoices

A tasks and expenses invoice is an itemized invoice for the time and expenses spent on the project, usually with a markup. To create a tasks and expenses invoice:

20

**FIGURE 20.23**

A draft invoice appears in the Invoices screen of Xero. Complete any missing details. It is a good idea to use a liability or holding account for the unearned work.

*Source:* Xero Limited

1. **Navigate to Projects**, then **All projects**.
2. Open the project by clicking the project name.
3. Use the Invoice pull-down to select Tasks & expenses.
4. Choose whether time on the project should be invoiced as a total for the task or as each separate time entry. If Time entries is selected, choose which details should be shown on the invoice (Figure 20.24).
5. Use the checkboxes on the left to select the tasks to be invoiced.
6. Choose whether expenses should be invoiced in groups according to expense estimates or as individual expenses.
7. Use the checkboxes on the left to select the expenses to be invoiced.
8. Click Save and open draft invoice in the top right corner.
9. A draft invoice will appear in the Invoices screen of Xero. Complete any missing details.
10. Click Approve.

# Viewing Reports

There are three reports for Projects management. All are found in the Projects section of Reports.

## Detailed Time

The Detailed Time report shows the time staff over a given period. You can use the Report Settings to change the view to either group by staff or by project.

**FIGURE 20.24**

Choose whether time on the project should be invoiced as a total for the task or as each separate time entry. If Time entries is selected, choose which details should be shown on the invoice.

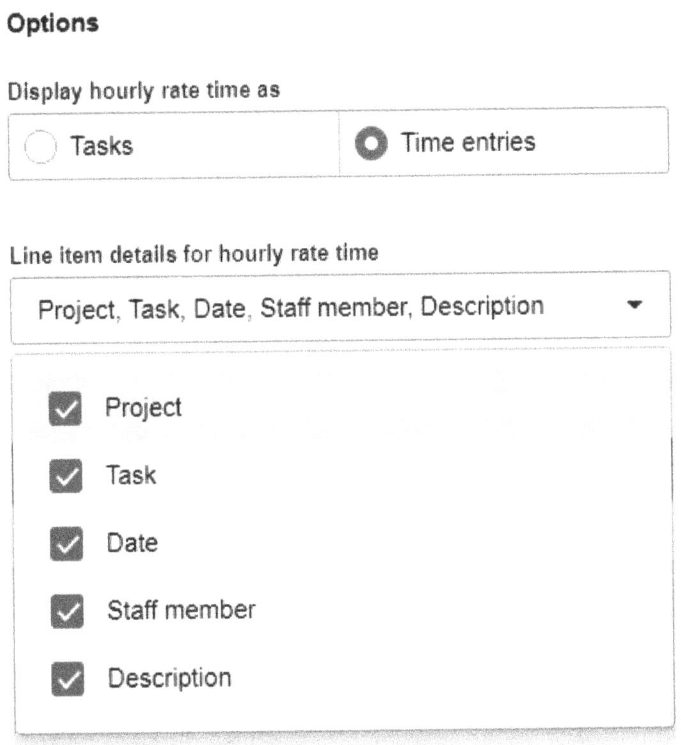

**Options**

Display hourly rate time as

| ◯ Tasks | ◉ Time entries |
|---|---|

Line item details for hourly rate time

| Project, Task, Date, Staff member, Description | ▼ |
|---|---|

- ☑ Project
- ☑ Task
- ☑ Date
- ☑ Staff member
- ☑ Description

*Source:* Xero Limited

# Project Details

The Project Details report shows all activity on projects, filtered by state—Draft, In Progress, or Closed. Projects without any activity will not be shown.

# Project Summary

The Project Summary report gives a higher-level overview of projects with activity. It can also be filtered by status.

# Profitability Dashboard

A newer feature in Xero, the Profitability dashboard gives a visual overview of any project. It includes graphical representations of profit, amount invoiced and remaining to be invoiced, and costs.

To access the profitability dashboard:

1. Navigate to Projects, then All projects.
2. Open the project by clicking the project name.
3. Select the Profitability tab at the top of the screen (Figure 20.25).

**FIGURE 20.25**

Select the Profitability tab at the top of the screen.

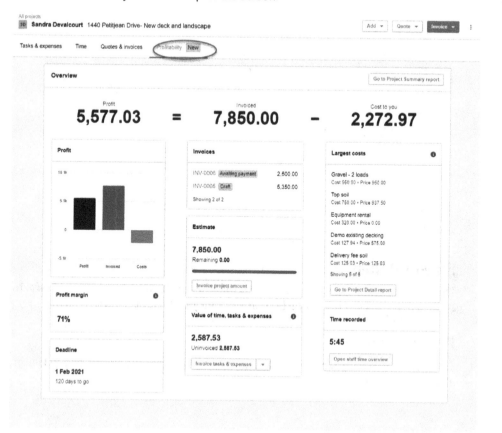

*Source:* Xero Limited

# About the Website

The website www.wiley.com\go\aguillard\xero (password: payroll) provides downloadable supplementary files referred to in this book. The files found on the website are:

- **Chart of accounts with columns for report codes and balances.** Referred to in Chapter 5, this file is helpful in creating Xero organizations with the report codes needed to leverage firm-level report templates. Balances can also be included in the import file, rather than manually entering in the Conversion Balances screen.
- **Inventory items import.** Mentioned in Chapter 8, the inventory item import file allows you to upload inventory items without manual entry. This file is useful in creating new organizations with many inventory items or when an existing company adds many new stock items.
- **Precoded bank statement import.** This import file, referred to in Chapter 9, allows for importing bank transactions along with the proper account coding and allows you to bypass the coding process within Xero.
- **Invoice import.** The invoice import template is useful for not only actual invoices, but also the bulk addition of sales data. This is particularly helpful when the company is using a sales system that does not integrate with Xero. This file is discussed in Chapter 11.
- **Custom invoice template.** This document is a mockup of a custom invoice including common dynamic fields. It can be modified for company use as described in Chapter 11.
- **Bills paid with checks import.** Explained in Chapter 12, this import file is similar to the Bills import file provided by Xero, with the addition of columns for payments. It is used to enter handwritten checks created by the client outside of Xero.
- **Fixed assets import.** The fixed assets import is used to add assets in bulk, rather than individually. It is referred to in Chapter 13.
- **Multiple manual journal entry import.** This template demonstrates how to import multiple journal entries at once and is covered in Chapter 15.

# Index

Note: Figures are identified by *f* following the page number.

# Index

# Index